T0207229

Communications
in Computer and Information Science   1815

Rationale

The CCIS series is devoted to the publication of proceedings of computer science conferences. Its aim is to efficiently disseminate original research results in informatics in printed and electronic form. While the focus is on publication of peer-reviewed full papers presenting mature work, inclusion of reviewed short papers reporting on work in progress is welcome, too. Besides globally relevant meetings with internationally representative program committees guaranteeing a strict peer-reviewing and paper selection process, conferences run by societies or of high regional or national relevance are also considered for publication.

Topics

The topical scope of CCIS spans the entire spectrum of informatics ranging from foundational topics in the theory of computing to information and communications science and technology and a broad variety of interdisciplinary application fields.

Information for Volume Editors and Authors

Publication in CCIS is free of charge. No royalties are paid, however, we offer registered conference participants temporary free access to the online version of the conference proceedings on SpringerLink (http://link.springer.com) by means of an http referrer from the conference website and/or a number of complimentary printed copies, as specified in the official acceptance email of the event.

CCIS proceedings can be published in time for distribution at conferences or as post-proceedings, and delivered in the form of printed books and/or electronically as USBs and/or e-content licenses for accessing proceedings at SpringerLink. Furthermore, CCIS proceedings are included in the CCIS electronic book series hosted in the SpringerLink digital library at http://link.springer.com/bookseries/7899. Conferences publishing in CCIS are allowed to use Online Conference Service (OCS) for managing the whole proceedings lifecycle (from submission and reviewing to preparing for publication) free of charge.

Publication process

The language of publication is exclusively English. Authors publishing in CCIS have to sign the Springer CCIS copyright transfer form, however, they are free to use their material published in CCIS for substantially changed, more elaborate subsequent publications elsewhere. For the preparation of the camera-ready papers/files, authors have to strictly adhere to the Springer CCIS Authors' Instructions and are strongly encouraged to use the CCIS LaTeX style files or templates.

Abstracting/Indexing

CCIS is abstracted/indexed in DBLP, Google Scholar, EI-Compendex, Mathematical Reviews, SCImago, Scopus. CCIS volumes are also submitted for the inclusion in ISI Proceedings.

How to start

To start the evaluation of your proposal for inclusion in the CCIS series, please send an e-mail to ccis@springer.com.

A. Augusto de Sousa · Kurt Debattista ·
Alexis Paljic · Mounia Ziat · Christophe Hurter ·
Helen Purchase · Giovanni Maria Farinella ·
Petia Radeva · Kadi Bouatouch
Editors

Computer Vision, Imaging and Computer Graphics Theory and Applications

17th International Joint Conference, VISIGRAPP 2022
Virtual Event, February 6–8, 2022
Revised Selected Papers

Springer

Editors
A. Augusto de Sousa
University of Porto
Porto, Portugal

Kurt Debattista
University of Warwick
Coventry, UK

Alexis Paljic
Mines ParisTech
Paris, France

Mounia Ziat
Bentley University
Waltham, MA, USA

Christophe Hurter
French Civil Aviation University (ENAC)
Toulouse, France

Helen Purchase
Monash University
Melbourne, VIC, Australia

Giovanni Maria Farinella
Department of Mathematics
University of Catania
Catania, Italy

Petia Radeva
Computer Vision Center
University of Barcelona
Barcelona, Spain

Kadi Bouatouch
IRISA, University of Rennes 1
Rennes, France

ISSN 1865-0929   ISSN 1865-0937 (electronic)
Communications in Computer and Information Science
ISBN 978-3-031-45724-1   ISBN 978-3-031-45725-8 (eBook)
https://doi.org/10.1007/978-3-031-45725-8

This Springer imprint is published by the registered company Springer Nature Switzerland AG
The registered company address is: Gewerbestrasse 11, 6330 Cham, Switzerland

Paper in this product is recyclable.

Preface

The present book includes extended and revised versions of a set of selected papers from the 17th International Joint Conference on Computer Vision, Imaging and Computer Graphics Theory and Applications (VISIGRAPP 2022), which was exceptionally held as an online event, due to COVID-19, from 6–8 February, 2022.

The purpose of VISIGRAPP is to bring together researchers and practitioners interested in both theoretical advances and applications of computer vision, computer graphics and information visualization. VISIGRAPP is composed of four co-located conferences, each specialized in at least one of the aforementioned main knowledge areas.

VISIGRAPP 2022 received 392 paper submissions from 50 countries, of which 4% were included in this book.

The papers were selected by the event chairs and their selection is based on a number of criteria that include the classifications and comments provided by the program committee members, the session chairs' assessment and also the program chairs' global view of all papers included in the technical program. The authors of selected papers were then invited to submit a revised and extended version of their papers having at least 30% innovative material.

The papers selected to be included in this book contribute to the understanding of relevant trends of current research on Computer Vision, Imaging and Computer Graphics Theory and Applications, including: Deep Learning for Visual Understanding, Categorization and Scene Understanding, 3D Deep Learning, Event and Human Activity Recognition, Image Enhancement and Restoration, Machine Learning Technologies for Vision, Segmentation and Grouping, Usability and User Experience, Video Surveillance and Event Detection, and Geographic Information Visualisation.

We would like to thank all the authors for their contributions and also the reviewers who have helped to ensure the quality of this publication.

February 2022

A. Augusto de Sousa
Kurt Debattista
Alexis Paljic
Mounia Ziat
Christophe Hurter
Helen Purchase
Giovanni Maria Farinella
Petia Radeva
Kadi Bouatouch

Organization

Conference Chair

Kadi Bouatouch   IRISA, University of Rennes 1, France

Program Co-chairs

GRAPP

A. Augusto Sousa   FEUP/INESC TEC, Portugal
Kurt Debattista   University of Warwick, UK

HUCAPP

Alexis Paljic   Mines Paristech, France
Mounia Ziat   Bentley University, USA

IVAPP

Christophe Hurter   French Civil Aviation University (ENAC), France
Helen Purchase   Monash University, Australia and University of
                                  Glasgow, UK

VISAPP

Giovanni Maria Farinella   Università di Catania, Italy
Petia Radeva   Universitat de Barcelona, Spain

GRAPP Program Committee

Francisco Abad   Universidad Politécnica de Valencia, Spain
Marco Agus   Hamad Bin Khalifa University, Qatar
Dimitri Bulatov   Fraunhofer IOSB, Ettlingen, Germany
Maria Beatriz Carmo   Universidade de Lisboa, Portugal

Ozan Cetinaslan	Instituto de Telecomunicações & University of Porto, Portugal
Gianmarco Cherchi	University of Cagliari, Italy
Antonio Chica	Universitat Politècnica de Catalunya, Spain
Teodor Cioaca	SimCorp GmbH, Germany
Ana Paula Cláudio	Universidade de Lisboa, Portugal
António Coelho	Universidade do Porto, Portugal
Remi Cozot	University of the Littoral Opal Coast, France
Paulo Dias	Universidade de Aveiro, Portugal
Elmar Eisemann	Delft University of Technology, The Netherlands
Marius Erdt	Fraunhofer IDM@NTU, Singapore
Pierre-Alain Fayolle	University of Aizu, Japan
Shervan Fekri-Ershad	Islamic Azad University, Najafabad Branch, Iran
Jie Feng	Peking University, China
António Fernandes	Universidade do Minho, Portugal
Ioannis Fudos	University of Ioannina, Greece
Davide Gadia	Università Degli Studi di Milano, Italy
Fabio Ganovelli	CNR, Italy
Ignacio García-Fernández	Universidad de Valencia, Spain
Guillaume Gilet	Université de Sherbrooke, Canada
Enrico Gobbetti	CRS4, Italy
Stephane Gobron	HES-SO/Arc, Switzerland
Abel Gomes	Universidade da Beira Interior, Portugal
Alexandrino Gonçalves	Polytechnic Institute of Leiria, Portugal
Daniel Gonçalves	INESC-ID, Instituto Superior Técnico, Portugal
Damiand Guillaume	CNRS/LIRIS, France
Marcelo Guimarães	Federal University of São Paulo/UNIFACCAMP, Brazil
James Hahn	George Washington University, USA
Ludovic Hamon	Le Mans Université, France
Sébastien Horna	University of Poitiers, France
Samuel Hornus	Inria, France
Andres Iglesias	University of Cantabria, Spain
Alberto Jaspe-Villanueva	King Abdullah University of Science and Technology (KAUST), Saudi Arabia
Jean-Pierre Jessel	IRIT, Paul Sabatier University, France
Juan José Jiménez-Delgado	Universidad de Jaén, Spain
Cláudio Jung	Universidade Federal do Rio Grande do Sul, Brazil
Josef Kohout	University of West Bohemia, Czech Republic
Maciej Kot	Dfinity, Japan
Helio Lopes	PUC-Rio, Brazil

GRAPP Additional Reviewers

Cristina Rebollo   Universitat Jaume I, Spain

HUCAPP Program Committee

Andrea Abate	University of Salerno, Italy
Farshad Badie	Aalborg University, Denmark
Mathieu Chollet	University of Glasgow, UK
Yang-Wai Chow	University of Wollongong, Australia
Cesar Collazos	Universidad del Cauca, Colombia
Damon Daylamani-Zad	Brunel University London, UK
Juan Enrique Garrido Navarro	University of Lleida, Spain
Michael Hobbs	Deakin University, Australia
Francisco Iniesto	Open University, UK · Centre for Research in Education and Educational Technology, UK
Alvaro Joffre Uribe Quevedo	Ontario Tech University, Canada
Ahmed Kamel	Concordia College, USA
Suzanne Kieffer	Université catholique de Louvain, Belgium
Chien-Sing Lee	Sunway University, Malaysia
Flamina Luccio	Università Ca' Foscari Venezia, Italy
José Macías Iglesias	Universidad Autónoma De Madrid, Spain
Guido Maiello	University of Southampton, UK
Malik Mallem	Université Paris Saclay, France
Troy McDaniel	Arizona State University, USA
Vincenzo Moscato	Università degli Studi di Napoli Federico II, Italy
Evangelos Papadopoulos	NTUA, Greece
Florian Pecune	Glasgow University, UK
Otniel Portillo-Rodriguez	Universidad Autonóma del Estado de México, Mexico
Juha Röning	University of Oulu, Finland
Andrea Sanna	Politecnico di Torino, Italy
Alessandra Sciutti	Istituto Italiano di Tecnologia, Italy
Fabio Solari	University of Genoa, Italy
Daniel Thalmann	École Polytechnique Federale de Lausanne, Switzerland
Gouranton Valérie	Univ. Rennes, INSA Rennes, Inria, CNRS, IRISA, France
Gualtiero Volpe	Università degli Studi di Genova, Italy

HUCAPP Additional Reviewers

Silas Alves	Universidade de São Paulo, Brazil
Mehdi Ammi	University of Paris 8, France
Quentin Avril	Interdigital, France
Dario Pasquali	Istituto Italiano di Tecnologia, Italy

IVAPP Program Committee

Ayan Biswas	Los Alamos National Laboratory, USA
David Borland	University of North Carolina at Chapel Hill, USA
Alexander Bornik	Ludwig Boltzmann Institute for Archaeological Prospection and Virtual Archaeology, Austria
Romain Bourqui	University of Bordeaux, France
Michael Burch	University of Applied Sciences, Switzerland
Maria Beatriz Carmo	Universidade de Lisboa, Portugal
Guoning Chen	University of Houston, USA
Yongwan Chun	University of Texas at Dallas, USA
António Coelho	Universidade do Porto, Portugal
Danilo B. Coimbra	Federal University of Bahia, Brazil
Celmar da Silva	University of Campinas, Brazil
Georgios Dounias	University of the Aegean, Greece
Danilo Eler	São Paulo State University, Brazil
Sara Irina Fabrikant	University of Zurich, Switzerland
Maria Cristina Ferreira de Oliveira	University of São Paulo, Brazil
Johannes Fuchs	University of Konstanz, Germany
Enrico Gobbetti	CRS4, Italy
Martin Graham	Edinburgh Napier University, UK
Christian Heine	Leipzig University, Germany
Seokhee Hong	University of Sydney, Australia
Torsten Hopp	Karlsruhe Institute of Technology, Germany
Jie Hua	University of Technology Sydney, Australia
Jimmy Johansson	Linköping University, Sweden
Mark Jones	Swansea University, UK
Daniel Jönsson	Linköping University, Sweden
Ilir Jusufi	Blekinge Institute of Technology, Sweden
Steffen Koch	Universität Stuttgart, Germany
Haim Levkowitz	University of Massachusetts, Lowell, USA
Brescia Massimo	INAF, Italy
Eva Mayr	Danube University Krems, Austria
Kenneth Moreland	Oak Ridge National Laboratory, USA

Benoît Otjacques	Luxembourg Institute of Science and Technology, Luxembourg
Jinah Park	KAIST, South Korea
Fernando Paulovich	Eindhoven University of Technology, The Netherlands
Renata Raidou	University of Groningen, The Netherlands
Philip Rhodes	University of Mississippi, USA
Maria Riveiro	University of Skövde, Sweden
Filip Sadlo	Heidelberg University, Germany
Beatriz Santos	University of Aveiro, Portugal
Angel Sappa	ESPOL Polytechnic University, Ecuador and Computer Vision Center, Spain
Falk Schreiber	University of Konstanz, Germany
Juergen Symanzik	Utah State University, USA
Roberto Theron	Universidad de Salamanca, Spain
Gilles Venturini	University of Tours, France
Marcel Worring	University of Amsterdam, The Netherlands
Yalong Yang	Virginia Tech, USA
Jianping Zeng	Microsoft, USA
Yue Zhang	Oregon State University, USA

IVAPP Additional Reviewers

Tiago Araújo	Federal University of Pará, Brazil
Jan-Henrik Haunert	University of Bonn, Germany
Stefan Jänicke	University of Southern Denmark, Denmark
Carlos Gustavo Resque dos Santos	Universidade Federal do Pará, Brazil

VISAPP Program Committee

Amr Abdel-Dayem	Laurentian University, Canada
Vicente Alarcon-Aquino	Universidad de las Americas Puebla, Mexico
Hugo Alvarez	Vicomtech, Spain
Danilo Avola	Sapienza University, Italy
Ariel Bayá	CONICET, Argentina
Anna Belardinelli	Honda Research Institute Europe GmbH, Germany
Fabio Bellavia	Università degli Studi di Firenze, Italy
Robert Benavente	Universitat Autònoma de Barcelona, Spain
Stefano Berretti	University of Florence, Italy

Mitsuharu Matsumoto	University of Electro-Communications, Japan
Rafael Medina-Carnicer	University of Cordoba, Spain
Leonid Mestetskiy	Lomonosov Moscow State University, Russian Federation
Cyrille Migniot	Université de Bourgogne, France
Steven Mills	University of Otago, New Zealand
Pradit Mittrapiyanuruk	Autodesk, Singapore
Birgit Moeller	Martin Luther University Halle-Wittenberg, Germany
Bartolomeo Montrucchio	Politecnico di Torino, Italy
Samuel Morillas	Universidad Politécnica de Valencia, Spain
Kostantinos Moustakas	University of Patras, Greece
Bharti Munjal	OSRAM GmbH, Technical University of Munich, Germany
Dmitry Murashov	Federal Research Center "Computer Science and Control" of Russian Academy of Sciences, Russian Federation
Yuta Nakashima	Osaka University, Japan
Mikael Nilsson	Lund University, Sweden
Félix Paulano-Godino	University of Jaén, Spain
Helio Pedrini	University of Campinas, Brazil
Roland Perko	Joanneum Research, Austria
Stephen Pollard	HP Labs, UK
Vijayakumar Ponnusamy	SRM IST, Kattankulathur Campus, India
Giovanni Puglisi	University of Cagliari, Italy
Sivaramakrishnan Rajaraman	National Library of Medicine, USA
V. Rajinikanth	St. Joseph's College of Engineering, India
Giuliana Ramella	CNR - Istituto per le Applicazioni del Calcolo "M. Picone", Italy
Joao Rodrigues	University of the Algarve, Portugal
Peter Rogelj	University of Primorska, Slovenia
Juha Röning	University of Oulu, Finland
Pedro Rosa	Universidade Lusófona de Humanidades e Tecnologias de Lisboa, Portugal
Peter Roth	Technical University of Munich, Germany
Silvio Sabatini	University of Genoa, Italy
Mohammed A.-M. Salem	German University in Cairo, Egypt
Ovidio Salvetti	National Research Council of Italy - CNR, Italy
Andreja Samcovic	University of Belgrade, Serbia
Alessio Sampieri	Sapienza University, Italy
Yann Savoye	Liverpool John Moores University, UK
Marco Seeland	Ilmenau University of Technology, Germany
Siniša Šegvic	University of Zagreb, Croatia

Oleg Seredin	Tula State University, Russian Federation
Désiré Sidibé	Université d'Evry - Paris Saclay, France
Luciano Silva	Universidade Federal do Parana, Brazil
Seppo Sirkemaa	University of Turku, Finland
Robert Sitnik	Warsaw University of Technology, Poland
Kenneth Sloan	University of Alabama at Birmingham, USA
Ömer Soysal	Southeastern Louisiana University, USA
Amelia Carolina Sparavigna	Polytechnic University of Turin, Italy
Mu-Chun Su	National Central University, Taiwan, Republic of China
Ryszard Tadeusiewicz	AGH University of Science and Technology, Poland
Norio Tagawa	Tokyo Metropolitan University, Japan
Bruno Travençolo	Federal University of Uberlândia, Brazil
Carlos Travieso-González	Universidad de Las Palmas de Gran Canaria, Spain
Du-Ming Tsai	Yuan-Ze University, Taiwan, Republic of China
Muhammad Rameez Ur Rahman	Sapienza University of Rome, Italy
Nicole Vincent	Université de Paris, France
Panayiotis Vlamos	Ionian University, Greece
Frank Wallhoff	Jade University of Applied Science, Germany
Tao Wang	BAE Systems, USA
Laurent Wendling	Paris Descartes University, France
Christian Wöhler	TU Dortmund University, Germany
Yan Wu	Georgia Southern University, USA
Pengcheng Xi	National Research Council Canada, Canada
Alper Yilmaz	Ohio State University, USA
Jang-Hee Yoo	ETRI, South Korea
Sebastian Zambanini	TU Wien, Austria
Ghada Zamzmi	National Institutes of Health (NIH), USA
Pietro Zanuttigh	University of Padova, Italy
Jie Zhang	Newcastle University, UK
Zhigang Zhu	City College of New York, USA
Ju Zou	University of Western Sydney, Australia

VISAPP Additional Reviewers

Dario Allegra	University of Catania, Italy
Gerasimos Arvanitis	University of Patras, Greece
George Azzopardi	University of Groningen, The Netherlands and University of Malta, Malta

Gianluigi Ciocca · University of Milano-Bicocca, Italy
Mariella Dimiccoli · Institut de Robòtica i Informàtica Industrial (CSIC-UPC), Spain
Vítor Filipe · University of Tras-os-Montes e Alto Douro, Portugal
Vlasios Fotis · University of Patras, Greece
Antonino Furnari · University of Catania, Italy
Siyuan He · National Research Council Canada, Canada
Andreas Kloukiniotis · University of Patras, Greece
Riccardo La Grassa · University of Insubria, Italy
Nicola Landro · University of Insubria, Italy
Dimitri Ognibene · Università degli studi Milano-Bicocca, Italy and University of Essex, UK
Nuria Ortigosa · Universitat Politècnica de València, Spain
Humberto Razente · Universidade Federal de Uberlândia, Brazil
Ioannis Romanelis · University of Patras, Greece

Invited Speakers

Roope Raisamo · Tampere University, Finland
Fotis Liarokapis · CYENS - Centre of Excellence and Cyprus University of Technology, Cyprus
Sara Irina Fabrikant · University of Zurich, Switzerland
Andreas Geiger · University of Tübingen, Germany

Contents

Automatic Threshold RanSaC Algorithms for Pose Estimation Tasks

Clément Riu[✉][iD], Vincent Nozick[iD], and Pascal Monasse[iD]

Université Paris-Est, LIGM (UMR CNRS 8049), UGE, ENPC, 77455 Marne-la-Vallée, France
{clement.riu,pascal.monasse}@enpc.fr,
vincent.nozick@univ-eiffel.fr

Abstract. When faced with data corrupted by both noise and outliers robust estimation algorithms like RanSaC are used, especially in the field of Multi-View Stereo (MVS) or Structure-from-Motion (SfM). To find the best model fitting the data, from numerous minimal samples it evaluates models and rates them according to their number of inliers. The classification as inlier depends on a user-set threshold that should be tailored to the noise level of the data. This requires the knowledge of this level, which is rarely available. The few existing adaptive threshold algorithms solve this problem by estimating the value of the threshold while computing the best model. However, it is hard to obtain ground-truth for MVS and SfM tasks and usually test datasets are based on the output on some state of the art algorithm, which prevents the objective evaluation of new algorithms. We propose a new method to generate artificial datasets based on true data to get realistic and measurable results. We use this method to benchmark different automatic RanSaC algorithms and find out how they compare to each other and identify each algorithm's strengths and weaknesses. This study reveals uses cases for each method and the possible tradeoffs between performance and execution time.

Keywords: Perspective from n Points · Multi-view stereo ·
Structure-from-motion · RanSaC · Semi-synthetic dataset · Benchmark

1 Introduction

To fit a model to noisy data in the presence of outliers, a standard regression method can easily fail and the RANdom SAmple Consensus algorithm (RanSaC) [9] was proposed as a solution. This algorithm try to discriminate inliers from outliers and estimate a model simultaneously. To do so, it compares residuals of datapoints to a user-defined threshold given a model. This model is estimated from a random minimal sample of data and gets scored based on the number of inliers it yields, its consensus. The higher this consensus, the most likely the right model has been selected. However, this method can fail if the outlier ratio is too high and most importantly, it requires *a priori* knowledge of the noise level of the inliers, or at least a good estimate of this value. Methods we call *adaptive*, *automatic* or *threshold-free* propose a solution to this issue by changing the quality criteria of models to some other measure that does not depend only on the inlier number and can estimate the inlier/outlier threshold.

A. A. de Sousa et al. (Eds.): VISIGRAPP 2022, CCIS 1815, pp. 1–20, 2023.
https://doi.org/10.1007/978-3-031-45725-8_1

Our first contribution is a semi-artificial data generation methodology that creates realistic and controlled data to precisely compare algorithms and see strengths and weaknesses of each. Usually, novel algorithms test on both real world data and artificial toy problems. However, in Multi-View Stereo (MVS) and Structure-from-Motion (SfM) it is expensive to get ground-truth and often relies on some algorithm that might introduce uncontrolled noise or bias. For instance, the KITTI [10] and the 7 scenes datasets [32] require calibrating an active sensor (LiDAR) to the passive one (camera). Another example is [6] that uses uncorrected matches as inliers. Artificial settings like the one proposed in [5], a plane estimation in 3D space, or [1], a random homography estimation between two 2D spaces, lack realism and do not give enough confidence in the generalization power of these experiments. Our solution presented in Sect. 5 answers that issue by using artificial matches based on real data.

Our second contribution is an extensive benchmark of different state-of-the-art adaptive RanSaC methods across different tasks. Through this benchmark we aim at comparing the different algorithms in a single setting; all algorithm have been integrated in a common pipeline so that the impact of the implementation of other elements can be removed. Contrary to previous RanSaC comparative studies like [4] we focus on adaptive methods and use our novel data generation technique to get more accurate results. It is also used to test the quality of the data generation methodology by testing it across multiple source datasets and comparing change and similarities in behavior depending on the setting.

RanSaC algorithms can be used in a variety of tasks but we focus our experiments around Multi-View Stereo and Structure-From-Motion tasks, namely homography estimation, fundamental and essential matrix fitting and the Perspective from n Points (PnP) problem. Those tasks are the core steps in 3D reconstruction pipelines, like in [25,31], and as such our benchmark compares the performance on these tasks. Improving the RanSaC algorithm should not only be able to provide a better model, but also better inliers, which are useful for the pipeline overall quality. Finally, datasets like [15] used to train 3D deep-learning estimators are created using those traditional methods, and thus improving the quality of them could help improving neural networks training.

This paper is an extension of a conference paper [30]. Compared to the latter, we introduced a new test case, the PnP problem. As we wrote, extending our method to this problem is the necessary next step to see whether we can improve software like ColMap [31] that is still state-of-the-art. We also propose a new version of Fast-AC-RanSaC, an automatic RanSaC algorithm that was used in the first paper and deemed unsatisfactory. We added the recent MAGSAC++ [2] to the benchmark, an improvement over MAGSAC [1] that was included in the first paper. For both MAGSAC and MAGSAC++, we also integrated their implementation in the same framework as all others, mainly to use more stable model estimators. Indeed, our previous benchmark indicated a high instability in MAGSAC result, with failure to estimate good models even in some easy cases, due to the numerical instability of the minimal solvers chosen by the authors.

Section 2 reviews the automatic RanSaC methods and those included in the benchmark are detailed in Sect. 3, Sect. 4 presents the data generation methodology and how to apply it to the different test cases, Sect. 5 presents the benchmark data, parameters, results and analysis and Sect. 6 concludes.

2 RanSaC Methods

2.1 Notation

Table 1. Notations. This table originates from the original paper [30].

	Definition	Description
k	$\in \mathbb{N}_{>0}$	dimension of data points
S	$= \mathbb{R}^k$	space of data points
$\mathcal{P}$	$\subset S$	set of input data points
d	$\in \mathbb{N}_{>0}$	degrees of freedom of a model
Θ	$\subset \mathbb{R}^d$	space of model parameters
θ	$\in \Theta$	parameter vector of a model
s	$\in \mathbb{N}_{>0}$	data sample size
Sa	$: 2^S \to S^s$	sampling function
F	$: S^s \to \Theta$	fitting function
p	$: [0,1] \to [0,1]$	proba. of sampling inliers only
D	$: S \times \Theta \to \mathbb{R}$	point-model residual function
σ	$\in \mathbb{R}$	inlier threshold
I	$: \Theta \times \mathbb{R} \to 2^{\mathcal{P}}$	inlier selector function
$\mathcal{I}$	$= I(\theta, \sigma) \subset \mathcal{P}$	set of model inliers
Q	$: 2^{\mathcal{P}} \times \Theta \to \mathbb{R}$	model quality function

The notations we use are the same as the original paper and are summarized in Table 1. The input of RanSaC algorithms are datapoint of dimension k, usually matches between two images where $k = 4$, or matches between putative 3D points and an image, where $k = 5$. We write $S = \mathbb{R}^k$, $k > 0$, the ambient space of the points and $\mathcal{P} \subset S$ the set of available input.

$\mathcal{P}$ contains both points originating from the true model, that we call inliers, even though they might not fit perfectly the model due to noise, and points that have no relation to the model, called outliers, that the algorithm will try to discriminate. The unknown proportion of inliers in the dataset is noted $\epsilon \in [0,1]$.

A model can be estimated on a sample of size d, the degree of freedom of the model, obtained with a sampler Sa that proposes s datapoints. Sa is usually a uniform sampler in $\mathcal{P}^s$ and thus the probability of drawing an uncontaminated sample is $p(\epsilon) = \epsilon^s$; however some algorithms presented in Sect. 2.2 do not use a uniform sampler. This sample is passed to a fitting function, or estimator F, which gives a solution in $\Theta \subset \mathbb{R}^d$, the parameter space. $d = 8$ for homographies, 7 for fundamental matrices because of rank 2 constraint, 5 for essential matrices, and 6 for PnP.

For a model θ, it is possible to compute its quality using the function Q. This function usually depends on the selected inliers of the model $\mathcal{I} = I(\theta)$, where I is the selector function, for example $Q(\mathcal{I}, \theta) = |\mathcal{I}|$ the number of inliers for standard RanSaC.

The classic selector of RanSaC $I(\theta, \sigma) = \{P \in \mathcal{P} : D(P, \theta) < \sigma\}$ depends on the inlier/outlier threshold σ and the computation of all residuals of datapoints $P \in \mathcal{P}$ with error function $D(P, \theta)$.

D varies with the model, I varies with the algorithm as the standard definition increases with σ and as such is not appropriate for an algorithm that would estimate σ and θ simultaneously. Another usual parameter of the presented algorithms are the confidence they have regarding some errors, like the type II error—the risk of missing a valid solution because of early termination—for classic RanSaC.

2.2   History of RanSaC Algorithms

Before presenting novel adaptative algorithms, Algorithm 1 presents the pseudo-code for the generic RanSaC from [9]. Most of the improvements have largely similar structure and mostly change a combination of Sa, I, Q. A few can propose widely different methods.

Algorithm 1. RanSaC algorithm. Algorithm originated from [30].

Input: $\mathcal{P}, Sa, F, p, Q, \sigma$
Input: confidence against type II error β, it_{max} (or min. inlier rate ϵ)
Output: Best model parameters and set of inliers
$\mathcal{I}_{max} = \emptyset, q_{max} = 0$;
$it = 0$ (and $it_{max} = \frac{ln(1-\beta)}{ln(1-p(\epsilon))}$ if ϵ is input);
while $it \leq it_{max}$ **do**
$\quad$ $sample = Sa(\mathcal{P}), \theta = F(sample)$;
$\quad$ $\mathcal{I} = I(\theta, \sigma), q = Q(\mathcal{I}, \theta)$;
$\quad$ **if** $q > q_{max}$ **then**
$\quad\quad$ $q_{max} = q, \theta_{max} = \theta, \mathcal{I}_{max} = \mathcal{I}$;
$\quad\quad$ $\epsilon = |\mathcal{I}|/|\mathcal{P}|, it_{max} = \frac{ln(1-\beta)}{ln(1-p(\epsilon))}$
$\quad$ $it = it + 1$;
return $\theta_{max}, \mathcal{I}_{max}$

Most authors, when designing a new RanSaC method, need to make assumption about the data or the models. They can be about the distribution of inliers or outliers, assuming some distribution of the points or their residuals, or a cross-model-consistency where patterns repeat across different models and can be related to detect valid models. Table 2 regroups such methods and summarizes the assumption and quantity measured by the quality function for the presented algorithms. For example RanSaC [9] is inlier consistent: all inlier residuals are counted and the quantity optimized is the number of inliers.

Different hypotheses can be used for the inlier consistent methods. For example, MUSE [20] estimates the noise level of all inliers set based on inlier residuals following a Gaussian distribution. This noise level is used as the quality measure of the model, smaller being better. [34] works with any unimodal distribution, though a Gaussian distribution is used in practice. With a threshold on the residual density, the inlier to inlier-threshold ratio gives the quality of a model.

Table 2. Overview of robust fitting methods with adaptive inlier criteria. Bracketed terms in the "Consistency assumption" column specify where the assumption is made.

Ref	Consistency assumption	Optimized function
[9]	Bounded residuals (inliers)	Inlier set size
[20]	Gaussian residual distribution (inliers)	Scale estimate
[34]	Gaussian (inliers)	Inlier/threshold
	Minimal residual density (transition)	
[8]	Gaussian (inliers)	Scale estimate
	Residuals correlate (cross-model)	
[3]	Low parameter variance (cross-model)	Variance
[21,22]	Problem specific (outlier)	Number of false alarms
[5]	Uniform (outliers)	Likelihood
[7]	Data-driven (outliers)	False discovery rate
[1]	Uniform (inliers) - Uniform (outliers)	Deviation
[2]	Uniform (inliers) - Uniform (outliers)	Deviation
[27]	Problem specific (outliers)	Greedy number of false alarms
[12]		Graph cuts energy
[33]	Residuals correlate (cross-model)	Inlier cluster merging cost
[18]	Residuals correlate (cross-model)	Residual cluster merging cost
[19]	Residuals correlate (cross-model)	Factorization error of residual matrix

Outlier consistent methods include A Contrario RanSaC (AC-RanSaC) [21,22] (first named ORSA in [23]) which assumes a background distribution for residual if the input is random, and checks the likeliness of getting a model. To do this, it tests all possible thresholds and ensures that a given model and threshold are selected only if the probability that they occur by chance is lower than some user defined confidence. The likelihood-ratio test [5] can also be used to assess the quality of a model against a uniform distribution of outlier residuals.

MAGSAC [1] and its newest improvement MAGSAC++ [2] make assumptions both on the inliers being uniformly distributed and the outliers being uniformly distributed on a different space. The quality function is based on the likelihood of a model given this hypothesis but the main improvement proposed is a refinement step to weigh the potential inliers instead of using a computed threshold.

StarSac [3] introduces cross-model-consistency by estimating multiple models for a given threshold and ranking the thresholds based on the variance over the parameters of the models. [8] proposes a mix between inlier and cross-model assumptions using a scale estimate as quality function. A weighted median absolute deviation is computed by increasing the weight and probability of a point to be inlier when it validates a sampled model.

In this paper only single model methods are considered; however, many threshold-free methods exist for such situations. Some still follow previous hypotheses, like [27] that uses multiple AC-RanSaC and merges results according to some criteria. Using cross-model-consistency, J-Linkage [33] and T-Linkage [18] cluster inliers and models to detect the good set of models. [12] uses graph cuts on an energy that depends on the total residual and number of models to compute a valid set of solutions.

3   Adaptative RanSaC Algorithms

We selected for our benchmark eight algorithms among those presented in Sect. 2.2, first RanSaC [9] which will be used as baseline, then MUSE [20], StaRSaC [3], A-Contrario RanSaC (AC-RanSaC) [22], Likelihood Ratio Test (LRT) [5], Marginalizing Sample Consensus (MAGSAC) [1] and two supposed improvements Fast-AC-RanSaC [25] and MAGSAC++ [2]. These algorithms where chosen as they are threshold-free methods and used for SfM and MVS tasks. We excluded multi-model specific methods like [12,18,33] as we concentrate our benchmark around the classification performance of the algorithms.

For the baseline, we used the results of RanSaC with a fixed σ in pixel. This baseline will be evaluated at two different thresholds to present the performance of non-adaptative methods even when the threshold is somewhat well chosen. The classic stopping formula to compute the number of iterations it_{max} of Algorithm 1 has been changed to have confidence β that at least $n = 5$ good samples have been drawn. The new formula is:

$$it_{max} = \frac{\log(1 - \beta)}{\log(1 - \epsilon^s)} + \frac{-\log\left(\sum_{i=0}^{n-1}\left(\frac{\epsilon^s}{1-\epsilon^s}\right)^i\right)}{\log(1 - \epsilon^s)} \tag{1}$$

where the first fraction is the usual stopping criteria of RanSaC and the second one is a positive value that increases the required number of iterations to reach this new confidence criterion. Its implementation was adapted from [24].

MUSE [20] is an adaptation of Least Median of Squares [14] that uses scale estimates as objective function to rank models using the standard iterative sampling of minimal samples of RanSaC. The article claims that the new objective function is more robust to higher outlier ratios. This algorithm does not include a stopping criteria when confidence β is reached, thus we added the usual RanSaC one as it adapts seamlessly to the framework. Implementation was adapted from https://github.com/vxl/vxl.

Likelihood Ratio Test (LRT) [5] introduces control over both the type I and type II errors. The type II error confidence β impacts the stopping criteria similarly to RanSaC. However, an early bailout strategy is implemented to reduce the number of residuals to compute when a model might not beat the so-far-the-best one, which requires a new parameter γ to control the increased risk. This early bailout strategy shifts the value of the stopping criteria:

$$it_{max} = \frac{\log(1 - \beta)}{\log(1 - \underline{\epsilon}^s \times \gamma)} \tag{2}$$

where $\underline{\epsilon}$ is the minimal value of the possible future inlier ratios to find a better model. The control over the type I error comes from the quality function of a model which is the likelihood for the dataset to be non-random at proposed σ.

$$Q = L(\epsilon, \sigma) = 2|\mathcal{P}| \left(\epsilon \log \frac{\epsilon}{p_\sigma} + (1 - \epsilon) \log \frac{1 - \epsilon}{1 - p_\sigma} \right), \tag{3}$$

with inlier ratio $\epsilon = k(\sigma)/|\mathcal{P}|$ and σ spanning a predefined list $\{\sigma_{min}, \ldots, \sigma_{max}\}$. We reimplemented this algorithm in [29].

StaRSaC [3] proposes the most intuitive solution to remove thresholds: simply launch RanSaC at different threshold values and select the best performing one according to a well chosen quality function Q. Q is defined as the variance over parameters. It is computed by launching $n_{starsac}$ RanSaC for each tested thresholds and computing the variance of the parameters of the estimated models $\theta_i(\sigma)$ for this threshold. A threshold that leads to less variance in model parameters should be an appropriate threshold.

$$Q(\sigma) = -\frac{1}{n_{starsac}} \left(\sum_{i=0}^{n_{starsac}} \left(\bar{\theta}_i(\sigma) - \theta_i(\sigma) \right)^2 \right) \tag{4}$$

where $\bar{\theta}_i(\sigma) = \frac{1}{n_{starsac}} \sum_{i=0}^{n_{starsac}} \theta_i(\sigma)$ is the mean of estimated parameters. To reduce runtime we reduced the range of tested thresholds σ to a smaller range around possible values. The selected range and the step size is the same we used for LRT defined above. We reimplemented this algorithm ourselves.

AC-RanSaC [21, 22] estimates the quality of a given model by considering all residuals as a potential threshold value. The best model will be the one with lowest Number of False Alarm (NFA), a measure of the type I Error.

$$Q = -NFA(\theta, \sigma) \sim \binom{|\mathcal{P}|}{k(\sigma)} \binom{k(\sigma)}{s} p_\sigma^{k(\sigma)-s}, \tag{5}$$

with $k(\sigma) = |I(\theta, \sigma)|$ the number of inliers at threshold σ and p_σ the relative area of the image zone defining inliers at σ. To accelerate computation the residuals are sorted in order to easily compute the NFA for each of them. AC-RanSaC always reserves the last 10% of the maximum number of iterations to improve the model by reducing the input dataset $\mathcal{P}$ to the so-far-the-best inlier set. The parameters of this method are σ_{max}, the maximum value of residual for which the NFA is computed and the upper bound of the NFA to consider the run successful NFA_{max}. However, the first parameter can technically be set to infinity with little increase in runtime if a good value cannot be guessed and a good value for the second is $NFA_{max} = 1$. Implementation was adapted from [24].

The Fast-AC-RanSaC we used in this paper is an improvement over our previous attempt in the original paper used in OpenMVG [25]. The main difference with traditional AC-RanSaC is the use of a histogram to classify errors and thus remove the need for a sorting step which slows the algorithm as discussed in Sect. 5.4. The residuals are thus just dispatched in n_{bin} in $\mathcal{O}(n)$ and the Number of False Alarms is computed at each value separating those bins B_i, $\forall i \in [n_{bin}]$:

$$NFA(\theta, B_i) \sim \binom{|\mathcal{P}|}{k(B_i)} \binom{k(B_i)}{s} p_\sigma^{k(B_i)-s}, \tag{6}$$

Our implementation was adapted from OpenMVG [25].

MAGSAC [1] makes hypotheses about the distribution of inliers and outliers, that they are uniform, and derives the likelihood of the model given these hypotheses as quality function. However, the main contribution of MAGSAC is to remove the need for an inlier/outlier threshold by introducing the σ-consensus method. The weights depend on various models estimated for different residual segmentations. This post-processing weighs a set of pseudo-inliers to fit a model with more confidence. It still requires parameters for the pseudo-inlier threshold σ_{max}, a reference threshold σ_{ref} and the number of segmentations to compute the weights of pseudo-inliers. The pseudo-inlier threshold σ_{max} has very low impact on the result. Implementation was adapted from [1].

MAGSAC++ [2] is a modification of the MAGSAC [1] algorithm. The main idea behind this algorithm is to remove entirely the need for inlier/outlier threshold by estimating a model with a weighted least square estimation. There is a threshold σ_{max} that determines the maximum residual a point can have to be considered inlier and thus have a weight in the estimation. MAGSAC++ uses a reweighted least square instead of multiple least square fittings. The computed weights are changed compared to the previous MAGSAC as well as the quality function, but the assumptions made on the inlier distribution and noise distribution are the same. Implementation was adapted from [2].

4   Data Generation Methodology

4.1   Models and Estimators

Four different problems are considered in this benchmark: homography estimation, fundamental matrix and essential matrix estimation, and the PnP problem. These estimation problems are all core tasks of Structure from Motion and Multi-View Reconstruction. All models except fundamental and essential matrix estimation require a different processing but the pipeline remains the same: a feature extraction and matching, a RanSaC step to select inliers from the matches and select the best parameters of the model thanks to a minimal estimator, and, usually, a refinement step at the end. Thus, to study the pros and cons of different threshold-free RanSaC algorithms we can use the same methodology for all models with little adaptation.

The homography estimation problem consists in estimating the projection from one image to the other originating from a rotation of the camera or a any movement around a flat scene. Correspondences are established between the two images and, as homographies maintain alignment it is possible to compute the deformation between these points. The fundamental and essential matrix estimation problems both consist in finding the relative pose of two cameras. The difference lies with the *a priori* knowledge of the intrinsic parameters of the camera for the essential matrix. Similarly to homography estimation, correspondences between the two images are established and then, using the epipolar constraint, it is possible to find the matrix.

The Perspective from n Points (PnP) problem consists in estimating the pose of a camera from correspondences between 3D points and their 2D image projection. From the correspondences, the position and rotation of the camera is estimated assuming the intrinsic camera parameters are known. This step is used to iteratively add views to an initial two-view estimation and obtain a complete reconstruction of a scene. The estimator used to compute the pose is the EPnPalgorithm [13]. This algorithm proposes an

$\mathcal{O}(n)$ non-iterative solution, compared to previous solutions that where either iterative and/or $\mathcal{O}(n^2)$ at least. The EPnPalgorithm rewrites the coordinates of the correspondences in the coordinate system of four control points. These control points are chosen to form a basis with the center of the data and its principal directions. Then, from expressing the projection from 2D to 3D in this new coordinate system, the camera pose can be computed as the right sum of null vectors of a derived matrix.

4.2 Semi-artificial Data Generation Method

Our proposed benchmark relies on semi-artificial data. Indeed, fully synthetic data are easy to control and generate but can be unrealistic and highly impacted by the generation choices. On the other hand, using data extracted from photographs is important to make sure the algorithm will succeed in real-life scenarios but it can be hard to compute reliable metrics when the ground-truth is hard to obtain. Thus it is hard to generalize results obtained on limited datasets with unknown noise and unknown outliers. Our solution uses real images models and data extracted from these to initialize our artificial dataset, giving us control over inlier noise and outlier distribution of synthetic data and the capacity to compute metrics reliably while retaining a realistic setup.

The pipeline used to generate a semi-artificial dataset can be used on any available dataset. If the dataset does not provide the matches, those can be computed using an *ad-hoc* algorithm like SIFT [17]. From the matches, containing both unknown inliers and outliers, a first model is estimated using a RanSaC algorithm. We chose AC-RanSaC [21, 22] at arbitrary precision and up to 10 000 iterations; our early experiments did not show any impact of the chosen algorithm and AC-RanSaC appeared to be the most stable one while its relative slowness was not an issue for this step of the pipeline. This first step creates an initial model and an inlier/outlier split. The model is considered "ground-truth": it is not the true model associated to the input data but it is realistic and thus can be used to generate new semi-artificial data. The outliers are discarded and the inliers are corrected to make "ground-truth" inliers using the "ground-truth" model.

This step creates a known model which can then be used to generate noisy inliers and true outliers in a known quantity and controlled distribution. To create noisy inliers, uniform noise is added to the "ground-truth" inliers. For matches, it is sufficient to add noise to one of the points, as this gives better control over the value of and distribution of the noise, for example avoiding cancelling if the same noise is added on both elements of the match. The choice of uniform noise for inliers has two reasons: no differences were observed in the initial tests between Gaussian and uniform noise and it would be extremely complicated to evaluate the true distribution of noise coming from SIFT matches or such. Given these noisy inliers, we have the true inlier/outlier threshold, by simply taking the maximum added noise.

Once our noisy inliers are generated, the outliers can be added. To create an outlier match, first a point is drawn at random on one side of the matches. Then, its projection is computed on the other side. This gives us an "inlier region" associated to the first point. A random point can thus be drawn outside this zone to generate a true outlier. However, drawing a match uniformly in pixel space outside the "inlier region" results in a poor distribution of errors as most matches end up very far from the model and thus do not offer a significant challenge to the RanSaC algorithms. A better method is to

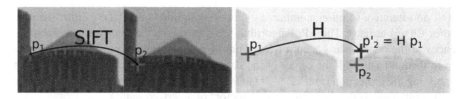

Fig. 1. From an imperfect match (p_1, p_2) considered inlier by AC-RanSaC, the "perfect match" (p_1, p_2') is constructed such that $p_2' = Hp_1$ using a realistic homography H given by AC-RanSaC. Figure originates from original paper [30].

Fig. 2. From an imperfect match (p_1, p_2) considered inlier by AC-RanSaC, the "perfect match" (p_1, p_2') is constructed using p_2' the orthogonal projection of p_2 on the epipolar line $\mathcal{L}_1 = Fp_1$ where F is a realistic fundamental matrix given by AC-RanSac. This does not guarantee that p_2' represents the same physical point as p_1, but that some 3D point at possibly different depth projects exactly at p_1 and p_2'. Figure originates from original paper [30].

draw uniformly the error of the match thus giving a good range of errors for the outliers and a realistic behavior for the RanSaC algorithms. The number of generated outliers varies during the benchmark in order to obtain a desired outlier ratio. However, to avoid slowing down the benchmark with situations where it is required to generate 9 times more outliers than inliers to get a 90% outlier ratio, the maximum number of matches is thresholded. If need be, inliers and outliers are removed in order to keep the desired ratio and less than 4000 matches.

The computation of an inlier or of the "inlier region" varies depending of the studied model. For homography estimation, inlier points in the first image are mapped into the second using the ground truth homography (Fig. 1) to create "ground-truth" inliers. Then inlier noise is added by a uniform 2D perturbation in $[-\sigma_{noise}, \sigma_{noise}]^2$ where the maximum inlier noise σ_{noise} varies during the benchmark. Once the inliers are drawn, to create outliers, a random point is drawn in the first image, then its "inlier region" in the second image is defined by a circle of radius σ_{noise} centered around the projection of the first point. The matching point is then drawn in a random, uniform, direction at a randomly, uniformly drawn distance from the "inlier region" (Fig. 3).

For fundamental and essential matrices, the inlier points on the second image are simply projected orthogonaly on the epipolar line computed with the "ground-truth" matrix associated to their matches in the first image to create "ground-truth" inliers (Fig. 2). Then the inlier noise is added in the second image perpendicularly to the epipolar line by drawing an uniform noise in $[-\sigma_{noise}, \sigma_{noise}]$. To compute the "inlier region" in the second image of a point from the first image to create an outlier, the zone of width $2\sigma_{noise}$ around the epipolar line is defined. Then, a random position is drawn along this line and from this direction, a random error perpendicular to the line (Fig. 4).

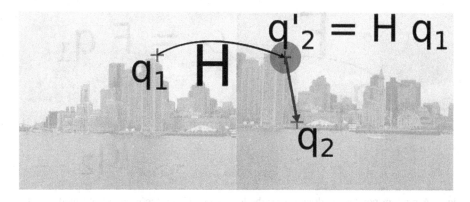

Fig. 3. A random point q_1 is drawn from the left image. Using the ground truth model H, its perfect match $q_2' = Hq_1$ is computed. Then a direction and a distance to q_2' are drawn uniformly in order to create q_2 so that it remains in the image and out of the inlier zone (marked in red) defined by the inlier noise level. Figure originates from original paper [30] (Color figure online).

For the PnP problem, the 3D points are projected on the 2D image to create the "ground-truth" inliers. The noise is added on the 2D image by a uniform 2D perturbation in $[-\sigma_{noise}, \sigma_{noise}]^2$. To create outliers, a bounding box is defined around the inlier 3D points as

$$[r_{aug} \min_{\forall i \in [n]} (x_i), r_{aug} \max_{\forall i \in [n]} (x_i)] \times$$
$$[r_{aug} \min_{\forall i \in [n]} (y_i), r_{aug} \max_{\forall i \in [n]} (y_i)] \times \qquad (7)$$
$$[r_{aug} \min_{\forall i \in [n]} (z_i), r_{aug} \max_{\forall i \in [n]} (z_i)]$$

where $r_{aug} = 1.1$ is a small factor to increase the range of outliers around the inliers. 3D points are then drawn in this bounding box. Then, following the same principle as for homographies, the 3D point is projected on the 2D image to create the "inlier region" and the outlier match is created by a random, uniform, direction at a randomly, uniformly drawn distance from this zone.

5   Benchmark and Results

5.1   Performance Measures

Thanks to the semi-artificial data generation method, we have access to the label of the matches and thus can compute precision and recall to evaluate the performance of the methods. Precision is computed as the number of correctly classified inliers over the number of detected inliers while recall its the same number over the true number of inliers. In the first paper we observed that, baring RanSaC, no algorithms presented compromise between precision and recall metrics depending on the dataset parameters. Thus the F1-Score is a good alternative to observe the results of the algorithms in a synthetic manner.

Fig. 4. A random point q_1 is drawn from the left image. Using the ground truth model F, the epipolar line $\mathcal{L}_1 = Fq_1$ is computed. Then position on this line and a distance to $\mathcal{L}_1$ are drawn uniformly in order to create q_2 so that it remains in the image and out of the inlier zone (marked in red) defined by the inlier noise level. Figure originates from original paper [30]. (Color figure online)

MAGSAC and MAGSAC++ do not provide an inlier/outlier classification but a weight on pseudo-inliers. As such, we introduce three metrics: Magsac-P, Magsac-R and Magsac-W. The first is the highest recall MAGSAC would get to obtain the same precision as AC-RanSaC. The second is the highest precision MAGSAC would get tot obtain the same recall as AC-RanSaC. The last is a weighted version of precision and recall.

The metrics are computed over different values of inlier noise levels and outliers to observe the classification performance and its evolution for the different algorithms. We also report runtime to evaluate its evolution across the different test cases for the different models.

5.2 Parameters

This section details the different elements related to the experiments: the datasets from which we extracted the input data for the generator, the solvers used for each task and the parameters of the generator and the different tested algorithms.

Datasets: The images used come from USAC [28]—10 image pairs for homographies estimation, 11 for fundamental matrix estimation and 6 for essential matrix estimation—Multi-H—24 image pairs for fundamental matrix estimation—, kusvod2—16 image pairs for fundamental matrix estimation—, homogr—16 image pairs for homographies estimation—[1] and megadepth [16]—16 images for the PnP problem were used.

Solvers: As minimal solvers F, we use the standard 4-point estimator for homography and 7-point estimator for fundamental matrix [11], the 5-point estimator for essential

---

[1] Multi-H, kusvod2 and homogr can be found at http://cmp.felk.cvut.cz/data/geometry2view/.

matrix [26] and the P3P algorithm for the PnP problem. For non-minimal solvers, least-square evaluation was used for two-view geometry problems and the EPNP [13] algorithm for PnP. For MAGSAC and MAGSAC++ weighted version of the non minimal solvers are required and we adapted the EPNP algorithm to work in a weighted case.

Data Generation Parameters: To average results across multiple runs we generate N_{gen} different datasets with same inlier noise σ_{noise} and outlier ratio $1 - \epsilon$ parameter for each image pair or 3D-2D matches. Each dataset is then evaluated N_{run} times. $N_{gen} = N_{run} = 5$ for a total of 25 different runs on which to compute the metrics. For inlier noise, we chose values in pixels that represent meaningful values, ranging from no noise (0) to 3 pixels by increments of 0.1. The outlier noise varied in $[0, 0.9]$ by increments of 0.1.

Algorithms Hyperparameters: When possible we extracted the parameters of the tested algorithms from their original publications, otherwise we chose value after some initials tests. Those values are summarized in Table 3.

Table 3. Hyperparameters of the tested algorithms, see Sect. 3 for definitions.

Parameter name	Value	Algorithms using it
Success confidence β	0.99	RanSaC, StarSac, MUSE, LRT, AC-RanSaC, Fast-AC-RanSaC
Inlier search cutoff σ_{max}	16 pixels	AC-RanSaC, Fast-AC-RanSaC, StarSaC and LRT
NFA maximum value NFA_{max}	1	AC-RanSaC, Fast-AC-RanSaC
Expected type I error α	0.01	LRT
Increase in type II error from early bailout γ	0.05	LRT
Number of data partitions p	10	MAGSAC, MAGSAC++
Pseudo-inlier threshold σ_{max}	10	MAGSAC, MAGSAC++
Reference threshold σ_{ref}	1	MAGSAC, MAGSAC++

5.3 Results

We exclude StaRSaC from the presented results as it extremely slow to run, with runtimes in the minutes for baseline or just above baseline levels of performance. All other adaptive methods performed better across all metrics and test cases (Fig. 5).

The first element we consider is runtime, as its value will impact the possible uses of the algorithm in real-time applications. It also reveals difference in behavior between algorithms, like MUSE, Fast-AC-RanSaC, AC-RanSaC and MAGSAC++ which are mostly not impacted by the noise level, and their speed depends mainly on the number of points considered whereas other algorithms, like LRT, RanSaC and MAGSAC can present huge differences of runtime between low and high noise levels. Regardless of the situation RanSaC, LRT and MUSE are usually the fastest algorithms except

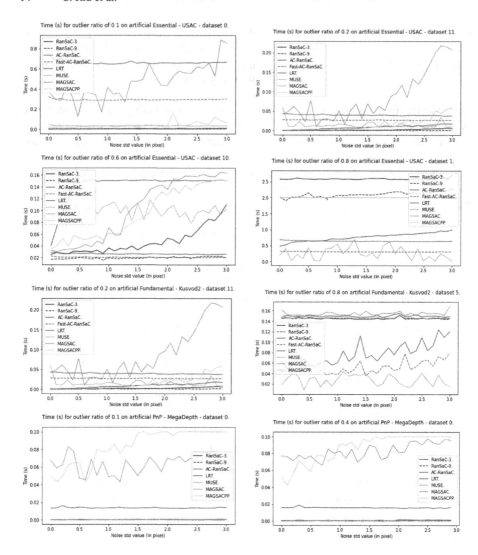

Fig. 5. Runtimes over different inlier noise levels and outlier ratios. The fitting problem, dataset name, and image pair number are in each graph title. `Ransac-σ` corresponds to RanSaC with threshold σ.

when reaching hard test scenarios. In those cases, LRT and RanSaC can have runtimes increase up to five seconds for a run while MUSE will keep a very low runtime. MAGSAC and MAGSAC++ have intermediate runtimes, lower for easy settings and higher for complex settings but with a small range of variations, especially for MAGSAC++ which is usually a bit faster than MAGSAC and with almost no runtime variation regarding the inlier noise. For two-view tasks they usually fail to terminate in a reasonable amount of time, and so are interrupted at 2 s for a run. AC-RanSaC usually is the slowest algorithm on easy settings, but, as its runtime is not impacted by inlier noise but mostly by the number of matches in the dataset, it can be competitive on complex algorithms when other algorithms show huge increase of their runtime. Fast-AC-RanSaC is usually twice as fast as Ac-RanSaC and is also not impacted by inlier noise. In easy settings its runtime is higher than most algorithms but it can be one of the fastest for the most complex settings.

When observing behaviors of algorithms, none of the three two-view geometry tasks presented a different challenge for the algorithms. A specific image pair or data generation parameter setup might prove more or less difficult but there was no major difference across homography, fundamental and essential matrix estimation. On the other hand, some algorithms presented huge change of performance when faced with the PnP problem.

Figures 6 and 7 illustrate the typical behaviors with low and high outlier ratios on a variety of estimation problems and datasets.

The two classic RanSaC show the expected behavior with good performance for easy settings that quickly degrade as the inlier noise and outlier ratio increase. On the one hand, the one with the lowest threshold has higher precision than the one with higher threshold with huge drops of performance for high noise or outlier ratio. On the other hand, concerning recall, the high threshold one performs better than the other and, moreover, its recall remains high while for a 3 pixels threshold, it drops significantly.

The MUSE algorithm offers quite poor performance, sometimes even below baseline in easy settings. However, its precision can remain high even in the most complex settings with more than 95% of good selections. This is due to selections of low thresholds by the algorithm, which negatively impacts its recall compared to other algorithms.

AC-RanSaC shows good performance across the benchmark, almost never showing significant drops in precision and small drops in recall for the most complex scenarios lowering the F1-Score.

For LRT, its performance is on par, on just below, the best performing algorithms for easy to medium settings. However, as the benchmark parameter increase, it gets closer to RanSaC performances with significant drops in F1-Score.

Fast-AC-RanSaC performs slightly worst than AC-RanSaC for the easiest settings, with good recall but lesser precision. Its performance is usually quite similar to that of LRT either slightly better or slightly worse depending on image pairs. This is due to a usually better recall but not always better precision from Fast-AC-RanSaC. It is also a bit more unstable with some runs where it fails to find a good model and stops on too high a threshold or a contaminated sample.

MAGSAC and its newest version MAGSAC++ have quite similar behavior. For all three methods to compute their precision and recall Sect. 5.1, they tend to perform better than most algorithms for all settings on two-view geometry tasks. They are the only algorithm that retain above 90% precision and above 80% recall even when presented with the highest inlier noise levels and outlier ratios. In those settings, MAGSAC++ obtains comparable or better results than MAGSAC but the difference between the two is small. However, for the PnP task, MAGSAC fails to produce satisfactory results. MAGSAC++ still performs slightly better but keeps a lot of failure cases. The precision of both algorithms remains somewhat stable but their recall can drop to extremely low values and fail to find any good model, even when lifting the runtime limitations.

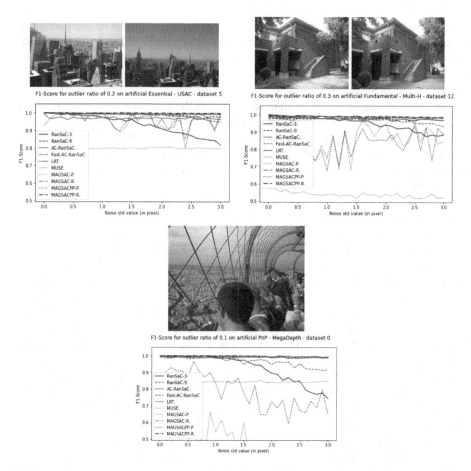

Fig. 6. Typical F1-score evolution over inlier noise for low outlier ratios. Estimation problem, dataset name and image pair number can be found in each graph's title. `Magsac-P`, `Magsac-R` and `Magsac-W` correspond to the metrics presented in Sect. 5.1.

5.4   Analysis and Comparison

As we observed similar behavior across different datasets, different images, our data generation methodology seems to be able to reveal intrinsic capacities of the tested algorithms. Indeed, while specific values might change, the ordering of algorithms, the drops in performance, the runtime evolution, are consistent across all test cases and depend on the data generation parameter and not the input task or images. The only difference being MAGSAC and MAGSAC++ for the $P n P$ problem, as discussed below.

StaRSaC and MUSE offer poor performance compared to other algorithms. The StaRSaC algorithm is just too slow to justify the small increase in performance compared to RanSaC, even when RanSaC's threshold is poorly chosen. MUSE performs better, with very high speed and high stability but, when compared to newer methods, it's classification performance is poorer than almost all newest methods.

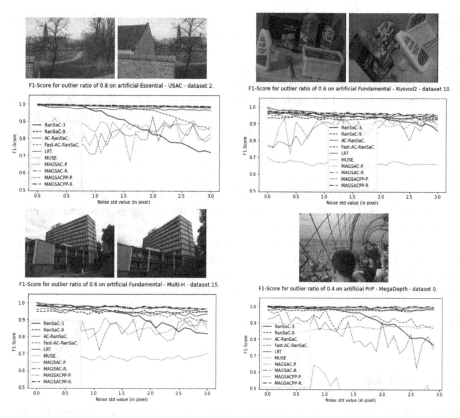

Fig. 7. Typical F1-score evolution over inlier noise for high outlier ratios. Estimation problem, dataset name and image pair number can be found in each graph's title. `Magsac-P`, `Magsac-R` and `Magsac-W` correspond to the metrics presented in Sect. 5.1.

Then, algorithms can be separated in two categories, fast and slow algorithms. This separation makes sense both in term of purpose, as algorithms that run in less than a tenth of a second can be used for real-time applications, and in term of performance as most slow algorithms perform better than faster ones. The runtime of an algorithm is mainly dependent on the computation of residuals and thus the number of iterations needed to reach a satisfactory model. Indeed, for most algorithms, the only two steps at each iteration are the computation of a model and the estimation of the quality of this model, through its residuals. The first step is usually very fast, almost instantaneous, while the second represents the bulk of the runtime. For some algorithms, some post-processing to compute the model quality might slow down the process. For example, for AC-RanSaC the sorting step required to compute the NFA at each possible threshold, and this easily takes as much time as the residual evaluation. It is also impacted by the reserved number of iterations, as it will always at least do 10% of the maximum number of allowed iterations. For MAGSAC and MAGSAC++ the addition of the σ-consensus step impacts runtime as well. However, if better model are chosen more often, it might speed up the process. For example, LRT is a fast algorithm in easy settings, as its early bailout strategy helps it skip useless computation of residuals. But for hard settings, it can be slowed down by missing too many good models. The new Fast-AC-RanSaC algorithm offers a good compromise for a fast algorithm as it is usually fast enough to perform real-time operations and its runtime is very stable across settings.

For fast algorithms LRT performs slightly worse than Fast-AC-RanSaC in a few cases, and is almost always faster for easy cases. As it is very sensitive to the complexity of the task, it might be better to use only when the setting is known and prefer the slowest but more stable Fast-AC-RanSaC when needing a fast algorithm.

For slow algorithms, AC-RanSaC is one of the slowest but most stable and consistent solution. Baring the most complex image pairs and generation parameters it always offers good precision and recall. MAGSAC is almost always slower or less effective or both than MAGSAC++, which is to be expected as the second is an improvement on the first one. For two-view geometry, MAGSAC++ performs almost always better than AC-RanSaC, producing good results even when other algorithms fail. It is also usually faster so it is a very stable and powerful solution. On the other hand, for the PnP problem, neither MAGSAC nor MAGSAC++ produce satisfactory results. The σ-consensus step seems to not adapt well to the EPNP estimator.

As a test conclusion, a user who needs speed should prefer Fast-AC-RanSaC, a user who needs precision AC-RanSaC and for robustness in two-view geometry tasks MAGSAC++.

6   Conclusion

In the field of robust estimation, many algorithms were proposed but few reliable and complete benchmarks were existing in the field of Structure from Motion and Multi-View Stereo, due to the complexity to get ground-truth. In this paper, we solve this problem with a semi-artificial generation method that offers a good referential to compare algorithms to each other and to study the behavior of a specific algorithms depending on the test case. Thanks to this new method we were able to improve algorithms like Fast-AC-RanSaC and validate the value of the improvement compared to other state-of-the-art algorithms.

RanSaC is known to struggle with high outlier ratios, especially when its inlier/outlier threshold is poorly chosen. Adaptive methods offer a solution to this problem, with no method proving superior overall but offering compromises between robustness, accuracy and speed. Fast-AC-RanSaC proposes a fast and robust algorithm that will provide good performance for its runtime. LRT is the most efficient in easy settings but will likely fail when faced with challenging cases. MAGSAC++ and AC-RanSaC offer good precision and recall across test cases, with a cost in runtime. For two-view geometry tasks, the first is the most performing, usually faster and more robust while for the PnP problem, the second performs largely better. The ability to reveal the specifics of each RanSaC algorithm shows that the data-generation method will be able to produce clearer benchmarks and conclusions when faced with new improvements.

Thanks to such observation, we plan on implementing the best performing algorithms in a reconstruction pipeline to see the impact of removing the user set threshold to compute the appropriate value at each step and hopefully improve the whole reconstruction.

References

1. Barath, D., Matas, J., Noskova, J.: MAGSAC: marginalizing sample consensus. In: Proceedings of the IEEE Conference on Computer Vision and Pattern Recognition (CVPR), pp. 10197–10205 (2019)
2. Barath, D., Noskova, J., Ivashechkin, M., Matas, J.: MAGSAC++, a fast, reliable and accurate robust estimator. In: Proceedings of the IEEE/CVF Conference on Computer Vision and Pattern Recognition (CVPR), pp. 1304–1312 (2020)
3. Choi, J., Medioni, G.: StaRSaC: stable random sample consensus for parameter estimation. In: 2009 IEEE Conference on Computer Vision and Pattern Recognition (CVPR), pp. 675–682 (2009). https://doi.org/10.1109/CVPR.2009.5206678
4. Choi, S., Kim, T., Yu, W.: Performance evaluation of RANSAC family. In: Proceedings of the British Machine Vision Conference (BMVC) (2009)
5. Cohen, A., Zach, C.: The likelihood-ratio test and efficient robust estimation. In: Proceedings of the IEEE International Conference on Computer Vision (ICCV), pp. 2282–2290 (2015). https://doi.org/10.1109/ICCV.2015.263
6. Cordts, M., et al.: The cityscapes dataset for semantic urban scene understanding. In: Proceedings of the IEEE Conference on Computer Vision and Pattern Recognition (CVPR) (2016)
7. Dehais, J., Anthimopoulos, M., Shevchik, S., Mougiakakou, S.: Two-view 3D reconstruction for food volume estimation. IEEE Trans. Multimedia 19(5), 1090–1099 (2017). https://doi.org/10.1109/TMM.2016.2642792
8. Fan, L., Pylvänäinen, T.: Robust scale estimation from ensemble inlier sets for random sample consensus methods. In: Forsyth, D., Torr, P., Zisserman, A. (eds.) ECCV 2008. LNCS, vol. 5304, pp. 182–195. Springer, Heidelberg (2008). https://doi.org/10.1007/978-3-540-88690-7_14
9. Fischler, M., Bolles, R.: Random sample consensus: a paradigm for model fitting with applications to image analysis and automated cartography. Commun. ACM 24(6), 381–395 (1981)
10. Geiger, A., Lenz, P., Urtasun, R.: Are we ready for autonomous driving? The kitti vision benchmark suite. In: Conference on Computer Vision and Pattern Recognition (CVPR) (2012)
11. Hartley, R., Zisserman, A.: Multiple View Geometry in Computer Vision, 2nd edn. Cambridge University Press, Cambridge (2004). ISBN 978-0521540513
12. Isack, H., Boykov, Y.: Energy-based geometric multi-model fitting. Int. J. Comput. Vis. (IJCV) 97(2), 123–147 (2012). https://doi.org/10.1007/s11263-011-0474-7
13. Lepetit, V., Moreno-Noguer, F., Fua, P.: EPnP: an accurate O(n) solution to the PNP problem. Int. J. Comput. Vision 81(2), 155–166 (2009)
14. Leroy, A.M., Rousseeuw, P.J.: Robust Regression and Outlier Detection. Wiley Series in Probability and Mathematical Statistics (1987)
15. Li, Z., Snavely, N.: MegaDepth: learning single-view depth prediction from internet photos. In: Proceedings of the IEEE Conference on Computer Vision and Pattern Recognition (CVPR), pp. 2041–2050 (2018)
16. Li, Z., Snavely, N.: Megadepth: learning single-view depth prediction from internet photos. In: Computer Vision and Pattern Recognition (CVPR) (2018)

17. Lowe, D.G.: Object recognition from local scale-invariant features. In: Proceedings of the Seventh IEEE International Conference on Computer Vision, vol. 2, pp. 1150–1157. IEEE (1999)
18. Magri, L., Fusiello, A.: T-linkage: a continuous relaxation of J-linkage for multi-model fitting. In: Proceedings of the IEEE Conference on Computer Vision and Pattern Recognition (CVPR), pp. 3954–3961 (2014). https://doi.org/10.1109/CVPR.2014.505
19. Magri, L., Fusiello, A.: Robust multiple model fitting with preference analysis and low-rank approximation. In: Proceedings of the British Machine Vision Conference (BMVC), pp. 20.1–20.12 (2015). https://doi.org/10.5244/C.29.20
20. Miller, J.V., Stewart, C.V.: MUSE: robust surface fitting using unbiased scale estimates. In: Proceedings of the IEEE Conference on Computer Vision and Pattern Recognition (CVPR), pp. 300–306 (1996). https://doi.org/10.1109/CVPR.1996.517089
21. Moisan, L., Moulon, P., Monasse, P.: Automatic homographic registration of a pair of images, with a contrario elimination of outliers. Image Process. On Line (IPOL) 2, 56–73 (2012)
22. Moisan, L., Moulon, P., Monasse, P.: Fundamental matrix of a stereo pair, with a contrario elimination of outliers. Image Process. On Line (IPOL) 6, 89–113 (2016)
23. Moisan, L., Stival, B.: A probabilistic criterion to detect rigid point matches between two images and estimate the fundamental matrix. Int. J. Comput. Vision (IJCV) 57(3), 201–218 (2004)
24. Moulon, P.: AC-RanSaC implementation (2012). https://github.com/pmoulon/IPOL_AC_RANSAC. Accessed 22 Jan 2021
25. Moulon, P., Monasse, P., Perrot, R., Marlet, R.: OpenMVG: open multiple view geometry. In: Kerautret, B., Colom, M., Monasse, P. (eds.) RRPR 2016. LNCS, vol. 10214, pp. 60–74. Springer, Cham (2017). https://doi.org/10.1007/978-3-319-56414-2_5
26. Nistér, D.: An efficient solution to the five-point relative pose problem. IEEE Trans. Pattern Anal. Mach. Intell. (PAMI) 26(6), 756–770 (2004)
27. Rabin, J., Delon, J., Gousseau, Y., Moisan, L.: MAC-RANSAC: a robust algorithm for the recognition of multiple objects. In: Proceedings of the Fifth International Symposium on 3D Data Processing, Visualization and Transmission (3DPVT), pp. 51–58 (2010)
28. Raguram, R., Chum, O., Pollefeys, M., Matas, J., Frahm, J.M.: USAC: a universal framework for random sample consensus. IEEE Trans. Pattern Anal. Mach. Intell. (PAMI) 35(8), 2022–2038 (2012)
29. Riu, C., Nozick, V., Monasse, P.: Automatic ransac by likelihood maximization. Image Process. On Line 12, 27–49 (2022)
30. Riu, C., Nozick, V., Monasse, P., Dehais, J.: Classification performance of ransac algorithms with automatic threshold estimation. In: 17th International Joint Conference on Computer Vision, Imaging and Computer Graphics Theory and Applications (VISIGRAPP 2022), vol. 5, pp. 723–733. Scitepress (2022)
31. Schonberger, J.L., Frahm, J.M.: Structure-from-motion revisited. In: Proceedings of the IEEE Conference on Computer Vision and Pattern Recognition (CVPR), pp. 4104–4113 (2016)
32. Shotton, J., Glocker, B., Zach, C., Izadi, S., Criminisi, A., Fitzgibbon, A.: Scene coordinate regression forests for camera relocalization in RGB-D images. In: Proceedings of the IEEE Conference on Computer Vision and Pattern Recognition, pp. 2930–2937 (2013)
33. Toldo, R., Fusiello, A.: Image-consistent patches from unstructured points with J-linkage. Image Vis. Comput. 31, 756–770 (2013)
34. Wang, H., Suter, D.: Robust adaptive-scale parametric model estimation for computer vision. IEEE Trans. Pattern Anal. Mach. Intell. (PAMI) 26(11), 1459–1474 (2004). https://doi.org/10.1109/TPAMI.2004.109

Semi-automated Generation of Accurate Ground-Truth for 3D Object Detection

M. H. Zwemer[1,2](✉)🔾, D. Scholte[2]🔾, and P. H. N. de With[1]🔾

[1] Department of Electrical Engineering, Eindhoven University, Eindhoven, The Netherlands
{m.zwemer,p.h.n.de.with}@tue.nl
[2] ViNotion BV, Eindhoven, The Netherlands
{matthijs.zwemer,dick.scholte}@vinotion.nl
https://vinotion.com/

Abstract. Visual algorithms for traffic surveillance systems typically locate and observe traffic movement by representing all traffic with 2D boxes. These 2D bounding boxes around vehicles are insufficient to generate accurate real-world locations. However, 3D annotation datasets are not available for training and evaluation of detection for traffic surveillance. Therefore, a new dataset for training the 3D detector is required. We propose and validate seven different annotation configurations for automated generation of 3D box annotations using only camera calibration, scene information (static vanishing points) and existing 2D annotations. The proposed novel Simple Box method does not require segmentation of vehicles and provides a more simple 3D box construction, which assumes a fixed predefined vehicle width and height. The existing KM3D CNN-based 3D detection model is adopted for traffic surveillance, which directly estimates 3D boxes around vehicles in the camera image, by training the detector on the newly generated dataset. The KM3D detector trained with the Simple Box configuration provides the best 3D object detection results, resulting in 51.9% AP3D on this data. The 3D object detector can estimate an accurate 3D box up to a distance of 125 m from the camera, with a median middle point mean error of only 0.5–1.0 m.

Keywords: 3D object detection · Semi-automated annotation · Traffic surveillance application

1 Introduction

Vehicle traffic is increasing worldwide and traffic congestion has become a major problem, especially in urban environments. Traffic surveillance systems are increasingly employed to improve traffic management and thereby reduce congestion and improve road and traffic safety. Such traffic surveillance systems commonly use networks of monocular cameras. Monitoring is automated by computer vision algorithms, which interpret the camera streams to determine several high-level metrics suitable for traffic management, such as the number of vehicles per traffic lane, the type of vehicles and the traffic flow.

M. H. Zwemer and D. Scholte—These authors contributed equally to this work.

A. A. de Sousa et al. (Eds.): VISIGRAPP 2022, CCIS 1815, pp. 21–50, 2023.
https://doi.org/10.1007/978-3-031-45725-8_2

Fig. 1. Vehicle localization using 2D and 3D bounding boxes. Note the difference between the estimated ground-plane location (red dot) for both 2D and 3D bounding boxes. Figure taken from Zwemer *et al.* [40] (Color figure online).

Typical traffic analysis systems for surveillance cameras use an object detector to localize vehicles followed by a tracking algorithm to follow vehicles over time. Object locations in computer vision are typically represented by a 2D box, fully capturing the object. The bottom midpoint of the box is then used to define the vehicle position at a single location (see the left-hand side in Fig. 1). The defined location of the vehicle is then considered the middle point of the ground surface of the object, thereby represented in a single point only. Using the camera calibration, this point discretely defined at the pixel level, can be converted to a real-world (GPS) location for further use in the traffic application. Although the computed GPS coordinates provide a good indication of the location of the vehicle, the coordinates are not very accurate and the dimensions and orientation of the vehicle are unknown. Furthermore, a single GPS-based location for each vehicle is not suitable for measurements such as near-collision detection, since accurate inter-vehicle distances should be available. The use of 3D bounding boxes for vehicles in GPS coordinates would enable such measurements. Therefore, a more accurate detection method would represent the object location by a 3D bounding box such that the complete ground plane of a vehicle is estimated in contrast to the current single-point definition (see the right-hand side in Fig. 1). The use of more accurate 3D location estimation enables more accurate measurements of vehicle speed, size and inter-vehicle distances.

Unfortunately, the amount of datasets for training and validating 3D bounding boxes is rather limited. One popular dataset focusing on 3D object detection is the KITTI dataset [13], containing stereo images and using depth information from LiDAR and camera calibrations. However, the in-car camera viewpoints are different from typical road-side surveillance viewpoints and no such large-scale 3D annotated dataset exists for surveillance situations. The lack of datasets with 3D annotations is a major challenge when developing 3D object detection techniques for new applications, especially because manual annotation is laborious and prone to errors.

In this work, we propose and evaluate several methods to convert 2D bounding-box labels to 3D boxes in existing datasets, containing monocular fixed-camera images in traffic surveillance scenarios. By first converting existing datasets from 2D to 3D annotations and afterwards training a 3D object detector, the use of scene-specific information is enabled and the existing 2D bounding-box annotations can be exploited.

To this end, a novel annotation-processing chain is proposed that converts existing 2D box labels to 3D boxes using labeled scene information. This labeled scene information is derived from 3D geometry aspects of the scene, such as (1) the vanishing points per region and (2) the estimated vanishing points per vehicle depending on the vehicle orientation. The use of vanishing points combined with camera-calibration parameters enables to derive 3D boxes, capturing the vehicle geometry in a realistic setting. This paper extends earlier work [40] by an extended validation of the annotation-processing chain, in which more configurations are evaluated and compared. In total, three additional configuration are added to the comparison. Furthermore, the utilized methods in the processing chain for creating 3D box annotations from 2D bounding boxes are explained in more detail and a more thorough literature overview is presented. The challenge is to automate this conversion using conventional computer vision techniques, without exploiting annotated data. A second aspect is the detection of vehicles in 3D. Because of the success of deep learning in 2D processing for vehicle detection, the aim is now to detect the vehicles directly in 3D, also offering an orientation. This relates to a further challenge of designing a CNN detector for 3D vehicles, that can be successfully trained with the automated 3D annotations. An in-depth evaluation of the 3D detector is carried out to determine (1) if the semi-automated pipeline for creating 3D annotations provides sufficient quality to train such a CNN detector and (2) whether a 3D detector can be successfully adapted and employed for traffic surveillance applications.

The previous challenges and considerations lead to the following key contributions of this work.

- An extensive literature overview of current 3D object detection methods and a proposal network for 3D vehicle detection.
- Multiple semi-supervised configurations are developed to automatically annotate 3D boxes from 2D boxes, using *a-priori* defined scene information.
- An unsupervised processing chain is proposed for directly creating 3D boxes without using 2D boxes, based on the same semi-supervised configurations.
- The proposed network for 3D detection is adapted towards the domain of traffic surveillance with multiple camera viewpoints. The adopted network is the KM3D network [20].
- An extensive evaluation of the proposed semi-supervised configurations is carried out on various traffic surveillance scenarios.

In this paper the aim is to create robust 3D annotations that can be used to successfully train the adopted KM3D detector. The first step is to convert 2D ground-truth with conventional computer vision algorithms to useful 3D annotations for semi-supervised learning. In this conversion step, data for learning is not needed and the conversion is based on an algorithmic description. The employed algorithms for creating the 3D annotations can be fine-tuned for each scene specifically, since they do not have to generalize to other scenes. The second step is to train a 3D detector on the generated 3D annotations from the first step so that training is solely based on the 3D data. The trained KM3D detector is expected to operate in 3D and on 3D annotations and should generalize for all surveillance applications. Finally, the 3D boxes generated with the semi-supervised configurations and the direct 3D detections of the KM3D detector are compared on a separate test set to measure the quality of the 3D bounding boxes.

The remainder of this paper is structured as follows. First, Sect. 2 presents an extensive literature overview. Second, in Sect. 3 the annotation-processing chain to create 3D boxes from 2D annotations is introduced. Section 4 contains the experiments and results based on the 2D to 3D conversions and the direct 3D detector. Section 5 discusses the conclusions.

2   Related Work on 3D Object Detection

2.1   Techniques for Early Object Detection

Most 3D object detectors depend on a combination of geometric constraints, labeled scene information and features computed on the image pixels. Early work uses a generic 3D vehicle model that is projected to 2D, given the vehicle orientation and camera calibration and then matches the projected template to the image. The authors of Sullivan *et al.* [33] use a 3D wire-frame model (mesh) and match it on detected edges in the image, while Nilsson and Ardö [26] exploit foreground/background segmentation to match a wire-frame model. Matching of a vehicle template is sensitive to the estimated vehicle position, the scale/size of the model, and the vehicle type (e.g. stationwagon vs. hatchback). Histogram of Oriented Gradients (HOG) [8] generalizes the viewpoint-specific wire-frame model to a single detection model. The authors of Wijnhoven and With [38] divide this single detection model into separate viewpoint-dependent models.

The research of Dubská *et al.* [10] proposes an automated camera calibration from vehicles in video. The obtained calibration is then used to compute 3D boxes for each vehicle from vehicle masks obtained by background modeling. The authors assume a single set of vanishing points per scene such that the orientation of vehicles is known, e.g. the road surface in the scenes are straight and the camera position is stationary. In Sochor *et al.* [31], the existing work is extended to improve vehicle classification using information from 3D boxes. Since the proposed method works on static 2D images and motion information is absent, the vehicle orientation cannot be estimated. Therefore, the authors propose a CNN to estimate the orientation of the vehicle. Employing the vehicle orientation and camera calibration, the 3D box is computed similar as in [10].

2.2   CNN-Based 3D Object Detection

In recent years, numerous 2D object detection algorithms have been proposed, such as Faster R-CNN [28] and Mask R-CNN [15]. Several 3D object detectors use the 2D bounding box as input for their network [6,7,16,17,27,37]. This means that any 2D object detector can be used as prior network. Other 3D object detectors use a 2D detector in parallel to depth map estimators [4,9,11,19,24], or extend the 2D detectors by means of feature extraction or keypoint estimation, such that 3D boxes can be estimated [23].

A. Depth Estimation. State-of-the-art performance for 3D object detectors is obtained for approaches that combine images from multiple cameras (stereo) and include LiDAR-based data, so that the CNN model can compute and use depth information. However, LiDAR scanners are heavy, require large quantities of energy, and are most of all highly expensive. Therefore, the trend is to develop methods that estimate depth without a LiDAR sensor, for example, with inverse perspective mapping [29,32,35] and pseudo-LiDAR [36,39] techniques. Inverse perspective mapping concerns converting camera images with a normal perspective view to a bird-eye-view perspective, in order to solve both occlusion and scale variation. Pseudo-LiDAR focuses on generation of a 3D point cloud, based on depth information from images and generally use stereo image sensors, since depth estimation from static monocular images has not proven to be very accurate.

B. Template Matching. Other CNN based methods are similar to the early vehicle template matching techniques. One particular example is the Deep MANTA [5] model proposed by Chabot *et al.*, which regresses 2D bounding-boxes, 2D keypoints, visibility aspects and dimensions for each object. These parameters are combined together for inference on a dataset of CAD models in order to find the best corresponding 3D template. In the same line of work, Mono3DOD [1] uses consecutive frames to create a road-plane reconstruction to improve detection and a 3D-RCNN [18] using extra depth information. Mono3D++ [16] extends this method and uses unsupervised monocular depth, shape priors and a ground-plane constraint as input. The inference time of Mono3D++ compared to the other methods in this category is superior, mainly due to the use of a morphable model. MonoGRNet [27] estimates key points and uses 5 predefined CAD models. The authors additionally regress the offset between the 2D and 3D bounding-box center.

C. Direct 3D Object Detection. A relatively new line of research focuses on estimating 3D bounding boxes directly from monocular images. In Chen *et al.* [6], the authors propose the Mono3D model that results in a major performance boost in monocular 3D object detection. The Mono3D detector creates candidate bounding boxes with typical physical sizes in the 3D space by assuming that they are located on a ground plane. These boxes are then projected on the image plane and scored by exploiting multiple features based on semantic segmentation into classes, instance semantic segmentation, contours, object shape, context, and location priors. The best-scoring object proposals are then further refined with a 2D detector based on Fast-RCNN [14]. The M3D-RPN model [2] improves this work by regressing anchors with 2D and 3D bounding boxes directly with a depth-aware convolution. The D4LCN network [9] improves this further by proposing a dynamic depth-dilated convolution. Although the depth is estimated from the same 2D images, it requires an additional depth-generation algorithm.

The authors of Mousavian *et al.* [25] use an existing 2D CNN detector and add a second CNN to estimate the object orientation and dimensions. The 3D box is then estimated as the best fit in the 2D box, given the orientation and dimensions. The RTM3D [21] and KM3D models [20] estimate 3D boxes from the 2D image directly in a single CNN. These models utilize CenterNet with a stacked hourglass architecture to find 8 key points and the object center, to ultimately define the 3D box. Whereas RTM3D utilizes the 2D/3D geometric relationship to recover the dimension, location, and orientation in 3D space, the KM3D model estimates these values directly, which is faster and can be jointly optimized.

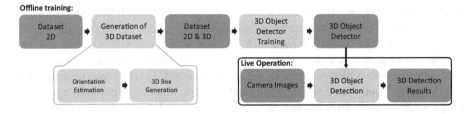

Fig. 2. Overview of the complete system for 3D object detection from datasets with 2D annotations. The left-hand side depicts the annotation-processing chain where 3D annotations are created semi-automatically, while the right-hand side depicts the training and deployment of a CNN for 3D object detection. Blue blocks indicate data and orange blocks depict a processing step. (Color figure online)

2.3   Conclusions on Related Work

This work focuses on monocular camera setups without available depth information, so that a depth estimator cannot be learned for the traffic surveillance problem. Although the template/CAD model-based techniques achieve high performance, finding the right template is computationally expensive and creating a template dataset is application-specific (and might be location) and a time-consuming task.

For the traffic surveillance scenario, we have adopted the KM3D detector [20], since this method only requires a camera calibration and a single image as input to perform 3D object detection. However, the KM3D detector requires training on a dataset with annotated 3D bounding boxes. To address this issue, this work proposes to create the 3D annotations from an existing dataset containing 2D annotations. The proposed method to convert 2D annotations to 3D annotations is based on the work of [10], since this method does not require 3D annotations for learning. However, instead of using the single-road direction (per scene) for each vehicle, we calculate the orientation of each vehicle independently. This enables to extend the single-road case to scenes with multiple vehicle orientations, such as road crossings, roundabouts and curved roads.

3   Semi-automated 3D Dataset Generation

This section presents a semi-automated technique to automatically estimate 3D boxes from scene knowledge and existing 2D annotated datasets for traffic surveillance. The creation of a 3D box from each 2D annotation is carried out in two consecutive steps (see Fig. 2). In the first step, the orientation of the vehicle in the 2D box is determined. In the second step, a 3D bounding box is constructed, based on the estimated orientation and the coordinates of the 2D bounding box. This step also requires a camera calibration, which should be generated only once for each unique scene. The camera calibration involves estimation of all internal and external camera parameters to form a camera projection matrix [3]. This matrix describes the mapping of a pinhole camera model from 3D points in the world to 2D image coordinates and vice versa.

The remainder of this section is structured as follows. First, several different methods are proposed for estimating the orientation in Sect. 3.1. Thereafter, Sect. 3.2

explains the method for constructing the 3D bounding box in detail. This part also elaborates on the method of Sochor *et al.* [30], which is similar to the proposed method, but requires the contours of the object in the form of a segmentation map instead of the 2D bounding box as input.

3.1 Orientation Estimation

The orientation of each vehicle is estimated prior to computing its 3D bounding box. When the orientation of a vehicle is known, only the location and dimensions remain to be estimated to construct a 3D box. The 3D box-construction step depends on a correct orientation estimation to robustly create the 3D boxes. In this section, four different methods for estimating the orientation are discussed, each with their own benefits and constraints. In the first method, the orientation is estimated based on the direction of the road. The second method estimates the orientation by computing the inertia axis of a segmentation mask of the object. The next method performs a line-fitting algorithm (called ray-casting) on a segmentation mask of the object. The last method is based on the Optical flow orientation of the object over time. An extensive comparison between the methods is presented later in the experiments section. Each of the four methods is now explained in detail.

A. Straight-Road Sections. This fist method exploits prior information about a scene. Since datasets for surveillance often consist of multiple images of the same scene, it can be considered a limited effort to manually annotate aspects of the scene. Hence, for each scene, the areas containing straight-road sections are marked and the direction of that straight-road section is annotated by finding the vanishing point. Figure 3 illustrates an example where the straight-road section is depicted by the blue area and the intersection of the yellow lines drawn parallel to the road section define the vanishing point (outside the image).

To estimate the orientation of a vehicle, we assume that the vehicle is driving in the correct direction and orientation with respect to these road sections. Hence, if a vehicle is located in the straight-road section, the orientation is equal to the orientation of the road surface. To this end, an overlap is calculated between each 2D-object bounding box and all the straight-road sections. If the bounding-box area is at least 50% overlapping with the annotated road-surface area, the orientation of the vehicle is assumed to be parallel with the direction of the considered road section (see Fig. 4a). If an object is not in a straight-road section, one of the other techniques explained in the following paragraphs should be used. Note that a straight-road section is not annotated when two straight-road sections intersect (simple crossing), since in these cases vehicles may turn and their orientation is not equal to the road direction.

Fig. 3. Example scene with configured horizon lines. Blue areas show the straight-road segments, yellow lines are used to find the vanishing points (image partially blurred for privacy reasons). Image taken from Zwemer *et al.* [40] (Color figure online).

B. Principal Component Analysis (PCA). This method requires a segmentation mask of the vehicle as input. This mask can be generated by any instance segmentation method, for example by Mask R-CNN [15] or Yolo-v7 [34]. Figure 5 shows an example segmentation map generated with Mask R-CNN. The individual segmentations are matched to the ground-truth annotations. If a vehicle is not present in the segmentation map for a ground-truth vehicle in the dataset, orientation estimation cannot be carried out. In these cases, a 3D bounding box cannot be generated.

The foreground points in the segmentation mask of a vehicle are then used as input for PCA. The first principal component corresponds to the orientation estimation, e.g. the inertia axis of the segmentation mask. Figure 4b illustrates an estimated orientation with PCA. If multiple sides of the vehicle are observed (e.g. front, top and side of the vehicle in Fig. 4b), the inertia axis of the segmentation will be based on several sides of the vehicle. This introduces an offset in the orientation estimation. This offset depends on the orientation of the vehicle, the tilt of the camera, and the location in the image (e.g. far field). Furthermore, this method is dependent on the quality of the segmentation map.

C. PCA with Ray-Casting. This method is similar to the previous implementation using PCA analysis, but extends it by additional post-processing using a ray-casting algorithm. Using solely PCA analysis, the method focuses on the inertia of the complete segmentation mask, while in the extended method with ray-casting the focus is on the bottom contour of the segmentation mask. The bottom contour of the segmentation mask typically equals the bottom part of the vehicle from the side, from front wheel until the back wheel. We assume that the bottom contour of the vehicle touches the

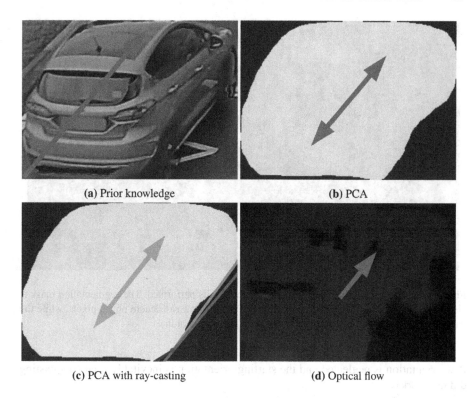

(a) Prior knowledge   (b) PCA

(c) PCA with ray-casting   (d) Optical flow

Fig. 4. Estimating the orientation of a vehicle in four different methods, as indicated underneath in (a)–(d). Images taken from Zwemer *et al.* [40]. (Color figure online)

ground plane for at least with two points (the wheels of the vehicle). A connected line between these points is touching the ground surface and is aligned with the orientation of the vehicle. To fit this line, the following two-step algorithm is proposed.

First, a line with the same orientation as the orientation from the above PCA is fitted to the bottom contour of the segmentation mask (when tilted right (left), this is at the bottom-right (left) corner). This line is shown by the red line in Fig. 4c. The point where this line intersects the segmentation contour is the starting point of a ray-casting algorithm.

Second, a ray-casting algorithm is applied to determine the edges of the contour, which can be observed and initialized from the intersection point onwards (see the green dot in Fig. 4c). The ray-casting algorithm searches for a line from the intersection point that intersects the segmentation contour at another point by evaluating multiple lines with small orientation changes. These orientation changes are carried out in two directions, clockwise and counter-clockwise. The two lines resulting from ray-casting are depicted at the bottom-right corner with dark blue and cyan lines in Fig. 4c. The orientation of the two resulting lines are compared to the original estimation from PCA. The newly found orientation that is closest to the orientation of PCA is adopted if it is similar to the initial orientation from PCA (maximum 25° difference), otherwise the

Fig. 5. Example scene on which instance segmentation is performed. The segmentation mask is visualized as an overlay on the original image. The yellow areas denote object pixels, while the dark areas are classified as background pixels. (Color figure online)

new orientation is neglected and the starting orientation is inevitably used (ray-casting did not work).

D. Optical Flow. The last orientation estimation method is based upon Optical flow between two consecutive frames over time. By measuring the direction of the flow, the driving direction can be derived. If we assume that vehicles are moving in the scene and that vehicles are always driving forward, the orientation of the vehicle is equal to the driving direction. The details of the Optical flow method are described below.

The Optical flow algorithm measures the apparent motion of objects in images caused by the displacement of the object or movement of the camera between two frames. In the case of static surveillance cameras, only the object movement influences the Optical flow fields. The result is a 2D vector field, where each vector shows the displacement of movement of points between the first and the second frame. We propose to use the Optical flow algorithm based on Farnebäck's algorithm [12] and have chosen to compute the Optical flow on the whole image with a 3 layer pyramid, where each layer is a factor of two smaller than the previous one. The averaging window size is 15 pixels.

The 2D box annotation of a vehicle is used to only select the Optical flow field that correspond to that vehicle. Then, only the flow vectors containing sufficient movement are selected by only keeping the flow vectors that have a magnitude of at least 50% of the highest magnitude in the flow field. The orientation is then estimated as the median of the remaining orientations of the Optical flow vectors. An example of Optical flow-based orientation estimation is visualized in Fig. 4d, where the background colors indicate the motion directions of points.

Although this method does not depend on a segmentation mask, it requires vehicles to move. So it does not work for parked vehicles or vehicles waiting for traffic lights.

3.2 3D Box Estimation

In this section, the 3D boxes are constructed for each vehicle from the estimated orientation and the 2D box annotation or segmentation of the vehicle. Two different methods are presented. The first method is based on the work of [10] and is called 'Segmentation fitting'. This method constructs the 3D bounding box, based a segmentation mask of a vehicle. The second method does not require a segmentation mask and instead uses the 2D box annotation of a vehicle and is called 'Simple Box'. Both methods rely on an estimated orientation, provided by one of the methods described in the previous section. Note that the methods for creating the 3D boxes in this section are only used to create annotations to train the actual detection model. The final detection method for live operation directly estimates the 3D box using the KM3D detector (see Fig. 2). The two methods for constructing the 3D boxes are now discussed in more detail.

A. Segmentation Fitting. The generation of 3D boxes based on segmentation uses the box-fitting algorithm of [10], where a 3D box is constructed using three vanishing points. The position of the three vanishing points depends on the orientation of the vehicle and the scene calibration and is determined as follows. The first vanishing point is located at the intersection of a line in the direction of the vehicle orientation and the horizon in the scene. The second point is the crossing of the horizon with a line orthogonal to the vehicle orientation. This orthogonal line is computed in the real-world domain using the camera-projection matrix. The third point is the vertical vanishing point of the scene, which results from camera calibration directly. An example of the three vanishing points for a vehicle in a scene is visualized in Fig. 6.

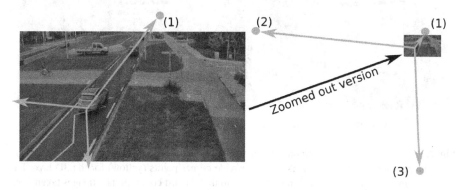

Fig. 6. Three vanishing points used in constructing the 3D box for the vehicle at the bottom of the image. Note that vanishing points (2) and (3) are located far outside of the image region, as shown in the zoomed out image on the right hand side.

The three vanishing points are used in the Segmentation-fitting algorithm to determine the corner points of the 3D bounding box. The algorithm is as follows (based on [10]). First, two lines are drawn originating at each of the three vanishing points along the sides of the contour of the vehicle, shown as the six red lines in Fig. 7a. At the intersections of these lines, six corner points of the 3D box are found, denoted by the numbered yellow dots (1–6). The remaining two corner points (7,8) are found as the intersection of lines from corner points 2, 3, 5 and 6 towards the vanishing points (denoted by the blue lines in Fig. 7b). The height of the different points at the top surface of the 3D box can vary between corner points because they are estimated individually. However, we assume the roof of a vehicle to be parallel to the ground surface and there-fore use the average height of these roof points in the final 3D box, as shown in Fig. 7d.

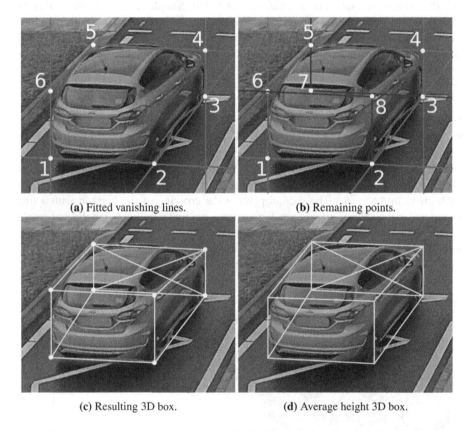

(a) Fitted vanishing lines.   (b) Remaining points.

(c) Resulting 3D box.   (d) Average height 3D box.

Fig. 7. Segmentation fitting based on the work of Dubská *et al.*where the vanishing lines (red) are fit to the contour (green). The intersections provide corner points (yellow) for the 3D box. The blue lines are the remaining vanishing lines used to find the last corner points. Images taken from Zwemer *et al.* [40]. (Color figure online)

B. Simple Box. Instead of using a segmentation mask for each vehicle, this section introduces a method to estimate a 3D box based on statistical vehicle dimensions. The method requires a 2D bounding box, camera calibration and the vehicle orientation, to convert this information to a 3D box. Furthermore, we assume a fixed vehicle width as a prior, despite this is a hard assumption it holds for most vehicles. The vehicle width is determined by the statistical average of 1.75 m. By fixing the vehicle width, only the length and height are to be determined from the 2D box.

The 3D box generation employs the same setup for the three vanishing points as the 'Segmentation-fitting' method. The implementation details are discussed in the following steps.

Final Algorithm of Simple Box. First, one of the two bottom corners of the annotated 2D box is defined as the starting point and the first corner point of the 3D box, depending on the estimated orientation (left- or right-facing car). The second corner point is located at the end of a line segment from the starting point towards the second vanishing point (orthogonal to the vehicle orientation) with the statistical vehicle width as its length. This is depicted by the blue line and the points 1 and 2 in Fig. 8a. These two points are the front-bottom corner points of the 3D box. The first back-corner point (3) is defined as the intersection of the orientation line along the length of the car at the ground plane and the 2D box. The last ground-plane point (4) is computed from the third point, by drawing a line segment with fixed length (statistical vehicle width) towards the second vanishing point. Now the bottom rectangle (at ground surface) of the 3D box is found and the only remaining unknown is the height of the 3D box, since we assume the roof of a vehicle to be parallel to the ground surface. The height is determined by measuring the distance between points (5) and (3) (Fig. 8a). The remaining corner points at the top of the 3D box are constructed from the ground-plane points (using the height) (see Fig. 8b). The final obtained 3D box is depicted in Fig. 8c.

  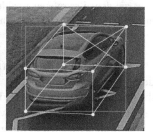

(a) Estimated ground-surface points based on vehicle width. (b) The remaining roof points estimated based on vanishing lines. (c) Resulting 3D box.

Fig. 8. Simple Box construction method for corner points (yellow) of the 3D box with the assumption that a car has a width of 1.75 m (blue arrows). The other 3D corner points are calculated through the estimated vanishing lines (red and cyan) and their intersections. Images taken from Zwemer *et al.* [40] (Color figure online).

Algorithmic Refinement. We have found that the vehicle height is often estimated too low, caused by small variations in the 2D box location and the orientation estimation of a vehicle. These variations and uncertainties in the measured size of the vehicle are addressed by a refinement step of the orientation, using a-priori average heuristics of the vehicle dimensions. This refinement step is as follows.

The estimated height of the vehicle is pragmatically adjusted when it is below a threshold T_{height}, by slightly modifying the orientation. The threshold $T_{height} = 1.25$ m is defined as the statistical average vehicle height $H_{avg} = 1.5$ m minus an empirically determined maximum offset $H_{variation} = 0.25$ m. The adjustment is carried out by updating the orientation estimation with one degree in a direction such that the estimated height becomes closer to the average vehicle height. The adapted direction depends on the orientation of the vehicle. After this one degree change, the final orientation is found.

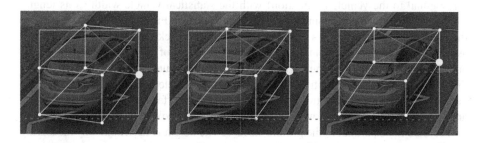

Fig. 9. Dummy example of the effect of changing the initial vehicle orientation clockwise (left image) and counter clockwise (right image) with respect to the initial orientation (middle image). The orientation causes the third corner point (large yellow dot) to be estimated lower or higher, causing the final 3D box to be higher and smaller or lower and wider, respectively. The red dotted lines are drawn as reference with respect to the original second and thirds corner points in the middle image. (Color figure online)

An example of the algorithmic refinement is briefly illustrated here. A vehicle dummy example is depicted in Fig. 9. In the image, it can be clearly observed that the third corner point shifts downwards by slightly changing the orientation clockwise, resulting in a higher 3D box while the box becomes narrower. Changing the orientation counter-clockwise (right image in Fig. 9) will result in a lower but wider vehicle box.

4   Experiments

The 3D box processing chain is evaluated with two different approaches. First, the output of the annotation-processing chain (without the 3D detector) is considered and the qualities of the computer vision generated 3D boxes are measured on a test set (see Evaluation 1 in Fig. 10). Hence, this evaluation considers the quality of the dataset. In the second approach, a 3D object detector (KM3D [20]) is trained on the generated 3D boxes from the first evaluation and the detection performance of the 3D object detector is evaluated (see Evaluation 2 in Fig. 10). Hence, Evaluation 2 concentrates on the detection performance. For the sake of completeness, the quality of the dataset is further evaluated as follows. In two additional experiments with the KM3D detector, a

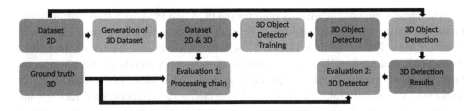

Fig. 10. Overview of the evaluation procedure. Evaluation 1 focuses on the performance of the annotation-processing chain, while Evaluation 2 validates the performance of the 3D object detection CNN trained on the generated data.

Table 1. Annotation-processing configurations to convert 2D annotations to a 3D dataset, based on the Segmentation fitting (Segm.) or the novel SimpleBox method.

Method	Orientation estimation				3D Box estimation	
	Straight	PCA	Ray-cast.	Opt. Flow	Segm.	Simple Box
Segm. PCA	✓	✓			✓	
Segm. RayCast	✓		✓		✓	
Segm. OptFlow	✓			✓	✓	
SimpleBox RayCast	✓		✓			✓
SimpleBox OptFlow	✓			✓		✓

cross-validation between our traffic surveillance and the public KITTI dataset [13] is presented, followed by an evaluation of an unsupervised approach of the annotation-processing chain.

4.1   Experimental Setup and Configuration

Annotation-Processing Configurations. The experiments are carried out on several different processing pipeline configurations, combining the orientation estimation methods and 3D box fitting techniques, as introduced in the previous section. Table 1 lists the combinations of the methods and the configuration name as used in the remainder of the experiments. Note that the orientation estimation method based on prior knowledge for straight-road sections is applied for all methods, since this method is stable and accurate for the annotated straight-road sections. For curved roads, three different estimations based on PCA, PCA with ray-casting, or Optical flow are created.

The first three configurations in Table 1 use a segmentation mask as input for the 'Segmentation-fitting' technique to estimate the 3D box. The orientation estimation in each of these three configurations is carried out with either PCA, PCA + Ray-casting, or Optical flow. The last two configurations are based on the Simple Box 3D box estimation technique, and apply ray-casting or Optical flow-based orientation estimation. For the ray-casting method, a segmentation map is required. However, it should be noted that the Simple Box method with Optical flow orientation estimation does not depend on an object segmentation map.

The same segmentation mask is used for the PCA and PCA with Ray-casting orientation estimation and for all Segmentation-fitting methods. Segmentation is carried out by either Mask R-CNN [15] or YOLOv7 [34]. Both networks are trained on the COCO dataset [22] and predict 2D boxes combined with the corresponding object segmentation. The detection threshold is empirically set to 0.75 for Mask R-CNN and 0.25 for YOLOv7. A minimum IoU threshold of 0.5 is applied to match between detections and ground-truth boxes. The performances of both segmentation methods are investigated in the first experiment later in this section.

For training the KM3D model, we have adopted the parameters, data preparation and augmentation process from the original implementation [20]. We have trained for 50 epochs using learning rate 1×10^{-4} and a batch size of 8.

Traffic Surveillance Dataset. The experiments are carried out on a proprietary traffic surveillance dataset annotated with 2D boxes. This dataset contains 25 different surveillance scenes of different traffic situations like roundabouts, straight-road sections and various crossings. The data are split in 20k training images and 5k validation images, with 60k and 15k vehicle annotations, respectively. The ground-truth set used for testing consists of 102 images with 509 3D-boxes which are manually annotated. This set contains 8 different surveillance scenes, which are outside the training and validation sets. In all experiments except the dataset cross-validation experiment, the train dataset from KITTI [13] is combined with the train part of our dataset to increase the amount of data.

Evaluation Metrics. In all experiments, the average precision 3D IoU (AP3D) and average orientation similarity (AOS) are measured, as defined by the KITTI benchmark metrics [13]. Similar to the KITTI evaluation, these metrics are computed for two different IoU thresholds of 50% and 70%. Next to these existing metrics, a novel metric is introduced that depicts the average location error E_{MME} of the center point on the ground plane in 3D-world coordinates (ignoring the vehicle width/height/length dimensions). This metric is called the Middle point Mean Error (MME) on the ground surface and is defined as:

$$E_{\mathrm{MME}} = \frac{1}{N} \sum_{i=0}^{N-1} \sqrt{(\hat{x}_i - x_i)^2 + (\hat{y}_i - y_i)^2}, \tag{1}$$

where N is the total number of true positive detections, $\hat{x}$ and $\hat{y}$ are the ground-truth x- and y-coordinates of the middle-point on the ground surface in real-world coordinates, where $\hat{x}$ and $\hat{y}$ are the estimated x- and y-coordinates, respectively.

4.2 Evaluation 1: Annotation-Processing Chain

The evaluation of the annotation-processing chain consists of two experiments. In the first experiment, the amount of vehicles is measured on which the orientation can be estimated directly based on their positions on a straight-road section. Furthermore, the amount of vehicles for which a segmentation can be created successfully is determined. Both counts indicate the fraction of vehicles for which a direct segmentation and orientation can be measured so that a 3D box can be established in an automated way.

This fraction has an impact on the second experiment, where the annotation-processing chain is evaluated on a test set by measuring the qualities of the generated 3D boxes.

Evaluation 1: Straight-Road Sections and Segmentation Masks. In all configurations, the orientation method based on prior knowledge on straight-road sections, is employed. It is interesting to measure how many samples are converted by exploiting this prior knowledge. Furthermore, the PCA, PCA with Ray-casting and Segmentation-fitting methods depend on the availability of a segmentation map. Therefore, the availability of the segmentation map is important. In this experiment, the amount of samples which are located on straight-road sections is measured and the amount of samples for which a segmentation map is generated successfully, is determined.

Table 2. Amount of samples that are located on straight-road sections and for which a segmentation can be generated successfully.

Method	Samples	Recall
Ground truth	509	100.0
Straight-road section	357	70.1
Segmentation by Mask R-CNN [15]	374	73.5
Segmentation by YOLOv7 [34]	426	83.7

Table 2 depicts the results on the measured amount of samples with successful segmentation and the recall. About 70% of the annotations are located on straight-road sections, and for these samples the orientation estimation is therefore determined by the prior-knowledge method. Mask R-CNN is able to create instance segmentations for 73.5% of the annotations, so the Segmentation-fitting method cannot be utilized for the remaining 26.5% of the samples. YOLOv7 is able to create instance segmentations for 83.8% of the annotations, which is significantly more than Mask R-CNN. Note that if a segmentation is required in the processing pipeline but it is unavailable, the annotation will be discarded and no 3D box is generated. Furthermore, it should be noted that the SimpleBox OptFlow configuration is the only configuration that does not depend on a segmentation mask, and therefore will generate 3D boxes for all ground-truth 2D boxes. The only exception is when no Optical flow field is present, e.g. for a stationary vehicle, since orientation cannot be estimated without motion.

3D Annotation-Processing Chain. This experiment evaluates the annotation-processing configurations, that create 3D annotations from the existing 2D annotated datasets. To this end, all network configurations are executed on the test dataset, where the 2D annotated boxes of the test dataset are used as input. The resulting 3D boxes generated by the different configurations are compared with the manually annotated 3D boxes in the test dataset.

Table 3. Comparison of 3D annotation-processing configurations without 3D object detector. The utilized segmentation method is indicated for each configuration that requires segmentation maps. The SimpleBox-based methods have higher performance than the Segmentation-fitting methods.

Processing configuration	Segmentation method	AP3D IoU = 0.7/IoU = 0.5			MME	AOS
		Easy	Moderate	Hard		
Segm. PCA	Mask R-CNN	5.9/42.1	5.7/37.6	3.3/23.3	0.80	84.7
Segm. RayCast	Mask R-CNN	6.0/41.9	5.8/31.7	3.3/22.9	0.80	84.9
Segm. RayCast	YOLOv7	16.4/48.1	11.6/36.2	7.0/22.7	0.91	88.2
Segm. OptFlow	Mask R-CNN	7.1/52.0	6.5/39.5	3.8/24.8	0.71	90.0
SimpleBox RayCast	Mask R-CNN	6.4/41.6	6.2/37.8	3.5/23.2	0.74	81.4
SimpleBox RayCast	YOLOv7	15.2/45.1	14.9/35.3	8.5/24.8	0.88	82.4
SimpleBox OptFlow	–	18.9/59.7	13.1/46.7	9.9/36.4	0.66	93.8

The results of the proposed configurations are shown in Table 3 and are first discussed with respect to the method for orientation estimation. Thereafter, the performances of the Segmentation fitting and SimpleBox methods are presented in detail.

A. Orientation Estimation. PCA and Ray-casting both depend on the segmentation map. For the Mask R-CNN-based segmentations, the Ray-casting technique (84.9%) results in a minor improvement in AOS score with respect to PCA (84.7%). The Ray-casting technique based on YOLOv7 outperforms the Mask R-CNN-based segmentations significantly. The Segm. OptFlow and SimpleBox OptFlow both use Optical flow as methods for orientation estimation and result in higher AOS scores with respect to PCA and Ray-casting. Therefore, it can be concluded that Optical flow outperforms the segmentation map-based methods. However, note that Optical flow cannot be computed when previous/next frames are not available in a dataset, in these cases the Ray-casting method with YOLOv7 can be used.

B. Segmentation Fitting. Visual inspection of the 3D generated box results of the Segmentation-fitting-based methods show that the main cause of errors is the width and length estimation, as shown in Fig. 11. In this example, the length is estimated 1 m too short. These errors are caused by segmentation maps that do not perfectly align with the actual object contours. The segmentation maps do not consistently include the headlights, wheels and other parts of the vehicles and sometimes include vehicle shadows. Although we always map the Mask-RCNN or YOLOv7 detection and segmentation outputs to the ground-truth 2D bounding boxes to ensure that false detections are not used as 3D ground truth, the processing dominantly relies on the quality of the generated segmentation maps. It can be observed that the YOLOv7 segmentation maps result in significantly higher quality 3D boxes in the Segmentation-fitting processing chain (Segm. RayCast Mask R-CNN vs. Segm. RayCast YOLOv7). This increase in performance is mainly caused by the number of samples for which a segmentation mask can be created by YOLOv7 with respect to Mask R-CNN, as measured in the previous experiment.

Fig. 11. Common error in Segmentation fitting where the length of the vehicle is estimated too short since the front of the 3D box only extends up to the front wheel of the vehicle.

C. Simple Box. The Simple Box configuration clearly results in the best AP3D score (IoU = 0.5) with 36.4% mAP for Hard objects, most accurate center-point estimation (MME = 0.66) and best orientation estimation (AOS = 93.8). Note that the detection performance for the strict IoU = 0.7 evaluation is too poor, probably because of inaccurate 3D box locations. However, the practical performance for IoU = 0.5 is representative for the application in video surveillance. Similar to the Segmentation-fitting configuration, Ray-casting on the YOLOv7 segmentation mask outperforms the Mask R-CNN-based method significantly.

From these results, we conclude that a 2D box annotation and the orientation information is sufficient to estimate a suitable, oriented 3D box. Visual inspection of the results show that errors commonly originate from 2D bounding boxes of which the bottom line is not touching the ground plane. In such a case, the starting point for the Simple Box method is too elevated and further away from the ground surface, so that the constructed 3D box is estimated farther away from the camera (see the examples in Fig. 12).

Fig. 12. Common errors in the SimpleBox method are caused by the 2D bounding box not touching the ground plane such that the 3D box will be estimated to far away on the ground plane. The dotted red line indicates the desired bottom of the 2D box and is the ground-plane location where the front/back of the vehicle is actually located. (Color figure online)

4.3   Evaluation 2: 3D Object Detector Trained on the Annotation-Processing Configurations

In this experiment, the KM3D detector is trained on the 3D annotations generated by the different annotation configurations. The performance of the KM3D detector is measured on the test dataset. After the first evaluation, several in-depth measurements are carried out to measure the errors of the estimated 3D box dimensions, the detection performance with respect to the distance from the camera and the middle-point mean error. The associated different experiments are now discussed in detail.

Trained 3D Object Detection Performance. The scores from the detection results are depicted in Table 4. Training of the 3D detector on the data generated by the 3D annotation configurations results in a significantly increased detection performance (increase of 12–18% AP3D) for all configurations with respect to the direct 3D annotation-processing results (see Table 3).

A. Orientation Estimation. The AOS is approximately 89% for all configurations. It shows that the model can estimate the orientation of the 3D box rather accurately and that the CNN model actually can learn the orientation from annotations with lower AOS scores (see Table 3 from the previous experiment).

Table 4. Detection performance results of 3D detectors trained on the data generated by the 3D annotation-generation procedure. The trained detectors have higher performance than the 3D annotation-generation procedures (see Table 3). The best performing detector is trained with annotations from the SimpleBox OptFlow method. Note that the IoU = 0.7/IoU = 0.5 performance values are indicated per column under AP3D with the left-side and right-side values of the '/' symbol, respectively.

Processing configuration	Segmentation method	AP3D IoU = 0.7/IoU = 0.5			MME	AOS
		Easy	Moderate	Hard		
Segm. PCA	Mask R-CNN	2.8/53.5	2.9/49.8	2.5/35.9	0.66	89.2
Segm. RayCast	Mask R-CNN	3.5/53.3	3.6/48.0	2.9/34.0	0.85	89.4
Segm. RayCast	YOLOv7	12.7/50.2	8.4/41.2	5.5/32.6	0.92	89.2
Segm. OptFlow	Mask R-CNN	4.2/62.8	5.6/51.0	3.8/42.9	0.66	89.5
SimpleBox RayCast	Mask R-CNN	5.9/63.0	5.8/51.1	3.8/41.5	0.72	88.4
SimpleBox RayCast	YOLOv7	19.6/60.5	19.7/46.3	11.8/32.6	0.88	88.4
SimpleBox OptFlow	–	26.2/73.4	19.9/62.9	15.6/51.9	0.70	89.6

B. Segmentation Fitting. It can be observed that the AP3D scores for IoU = 0.5 have improved significantly with respect to the annotations generated by the annotation configurations. However, the IoU = 0.7 scores are lower than the annotations generated by the annotation-processing configurations in the previous experiment. This can be caused by an improved detection rate of the CNN detector with respect to the annotation configurations, but a lower precision of the exact bounding-box localization.

C. Simple Box. Similar to the Segmentation-fitting method, the AP3D metric for IoU = 0.5 of the CNN model is significantly increased with respect to the annotation-processing results. However, the AP3D score for IoU = 0.7 is similar or has increased (SimpleBox OptFlow). An explanation for this effect can be that the SimpleBox Opt-Flow annotations used for training are more precise and therefore help the training to improve learning the localization aspect of the CNN detector.

In general, from the results we can conclude that the annotation quality of the dataset generated by the annotation-processing configurations is sufficient to successfully train a CNN model that generalizes over all the noisy input data. The trained CNN model results in higher 3D box estimation performance compared to the initial annotation-processing results.

In-depth Evaluation of the CNN Detector on SimpleBox OptFlow. The experiments will from now on focus on the in-depth results of the 3D detector trained with the 3D boxes generated by the SimpleBox OptFlow pipeline. First, the estimated vehicle dimensions are validated and next the effect on detection performance of objects farther away from the camera (smaller object pixel-area) is evaluated. Next, the mean Middle-point Mean Error (MME) is measured for all objects in the test set.

A. Vehicle Dimensions. In this experiment, the error distribution for each of the 3D box dimensions is measured. Figure 13 shows the error distributions for the estimated height, width and length dimensions on the test set. It can be observed that the distributions are symmetrical, since dimensions are evenly estimated too short or too large

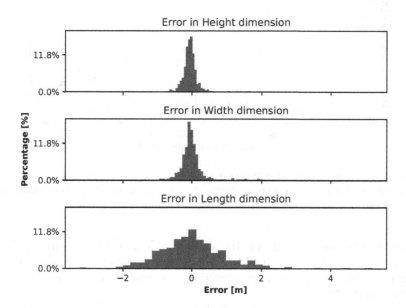

Fig. 13. Distributions of errors for height/width/length dimensions of the vehicles.

in each dimension. The mean errors with respect to the ground-truth are 0.05, 0.02 and 0.01 m for the height, length and width, respectively.

Note that the error in length estimation is larger than the errors in width and height. This can be explained by two aspects. First, note that the length of a vehicle is typically larger than the width/height dimensions, so that a relatively larger error in the length estimation is expected. Second, most vehicles in the dataset are driving towards or away from the camera and not many vehicles are driving from left to right. Estimating the length of the vehicle is therefore harder than estimating the width and height, since it is more sensitive for small localization errors in the image plane.

B. Distance From the Camera. This experiment investigates the effect of the distance of each vehicle to the camera on the accuracy of the 3D box estimation. The mean MME is computed for all detections in steps of 10-m distance from the camera.

Figure 14 illustrates the obtained results. The blue dots show the median values for each 10-m interval, the blue lines above/below represent the standard deviations of the errors of detections at larger/smaller distance. From the results, it can be observed that accurate position estimation is possible until about 130-m distance. The MME metric becomes inaccurate above 130-m distance. However, the test set lacks the images to validate this in more detail. Note that the manual generation of 3D ground-truth boxes also becomes more inaccurate at larger distance to the camera (and thus, lower resolution). Moreover, a small offset in image coordinates far away from the camera can lead to large errors in the real-world locations.

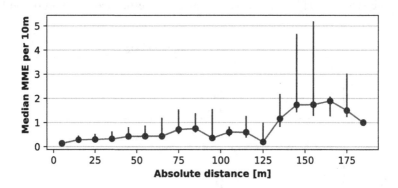

Fig. 14. Median of the Middle point Mean Error (MME) in steps of 10 m distance from the camera. Lines above and under the dots represent the standard deviations for errors estimated further away and nearby, respectively. Taken from Zwemer *et al.* [40].

C. Mean Middle-Point Mean Error. This experiment extends the previous experiment and measures the direction of the MME for all objects in the test set, resulting in a scatter plot in the ground-plane error directions, e.g. x and z coordinates. The results are shown in Fig. 15.

It can be observed that the errors in both the x and z-direction are scattered around the (0,0) coordinates, which means that there is no or very limited bias in the error and on average the ground-surface location is estimated correctly. From the previous experiment, it is known that the larger errors are caused by vehicles located far away from the camera. In these results, it can be observed that the MME error is caused by both an estimation error in the x and z-direction for these vehicles. So the localization error is probably caused by a lack of resolution in the estimated 3D boxes and/or in the ground-truth annotations.

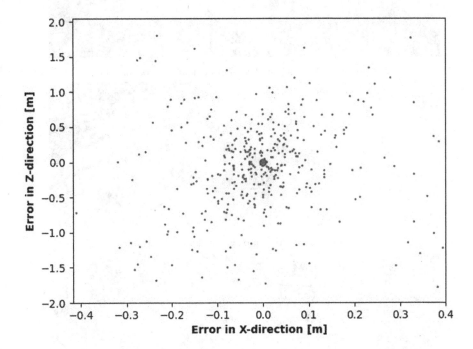

Fig. 15. Localization error of the middle point of each object on the ground-plane surface. The red dot indicates the absence of an error at the origin of the coordinate system. (Color figure online)

D. Visual Results. Some visual detection results of the 3D detector trained with annotations from Simple box are shown in Fig. 16. These images illustrate three limitations of the method. First, not every vehicle is estimated on the ground surface. Second, the orientation estimation of vehicles that are driving in a horizontal direction are prone to errors. Third, the height of the vehicles often seems estimated too low in value.

4.4 Cross-Validation on KITTI Dataset

This experiment performs a cross-validation on the datasets used for training and testing. To this end, the baseline KM3D detector trained on the KITTI dataset [13] is evaluated on the traffic surveillance test set and the KM3D detector is trained and evaluated on all combinations of the traffic surveillance dataset and the KITTI dataset. Although the KITTI dataset focuses on autonomous driving, this experiment will provide insight

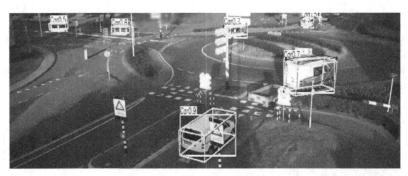

(a) Correct results in a complex scene containing a roundabout.

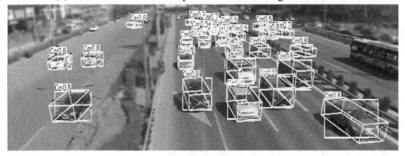

(b) Some faulty orientation estimations in the back.

(c) Horizontally oriented vehicle is estimated incorrectly (left).

(d) The height of the vehicle in the front is estimated to low.

Fig. 16. Detection results of KM3D trained with the annotations generated by the SimpleBox OptFlow configuration. The majority of the 3D bounding boxes are accurately estimated. Several localization issues are shown in (b–d). The subfigures are partially blurred for privacy reasons. Image taken from [40].

in the differences with our application. The training set annotations are generated using the SimpleBox OptFlow configuration.

Table 5. Cross-validation on the KITTI dataset with the KM3D detector. The 3D annotations for training are generated with the SimpleBox OptFlow configuration.

Train set	Test set	AP3D IoU = 0.5		
		Easy	Moderate	Hard
KITTI	KITTI	51.4	41.0	33.5
KITTI & Ours	KITTI	55.3	44.7	35.2
KITTI	Ours	5.2	3.87	2.3
Ours	Ours	66.0	60.1	43.4
KITTI & Ours	Ours	73.4	62.9	51.9

Table 5 depicts the obtained AP3D (IoU = 0.5) results of the cross-validation. The original results on the KITTI test set are similar to the original work [20]. Testing the KITTI-trained model on our dataset results in poor performance, probably caused by the difference in viewpoints between automotive and surveillance. Training on the combination of both datasets increases the AP3D with about 4% on the easy cases when evaluating on the KITTI dataset. The AP3D performance on our dataset significantly increases from 66.0% to 73.4%, when training only with our dataset or training with both KITTI and our dataset, respectively. Summarizing, although the two datasets contain different camera viewpoints, the detection model effectively exploits this information to generalize better.

4.5 Unsupervised Approach

This experiment investigates the effect of replacing the 2D box annotations with automatic detections such that an image can be annotated with 3D boxes without the requirement of initial 2D box annotations. To this end, the same Mask-RCNN network as previously used for creating segmentation masks is utilized to create 2D box detections for

Table 6. Detection performance when using the unsupervised SimpleBox OptFlow configuration (replacing 2D annotations with Mask-RCNN output). The unsupervised performance (US) is lower than when using the original 2D annotations.

Method	AP3D IoU = 0.5			MME
	Easy	Moderate	Hard	
SimpleBox OptFlow (reference)	59.7	46.7	36.4	0.66
SimpleBox OptFlow Unsupervised	37.4	31.5	15.6	0.76
SimpleBox OptFlow + KM3D (reference)	73.4	62.9	51.9	0.70
SimpleBox OptFlow Unsupervised + KM3D	67.3	55.8	40.7	0.65

each image in the training set. The resulting 2D detections are used in the SimpleBox OptFlow pipeline to create 3D annotations. This modified SimpleBox OptFlow pipeline is applied directly to our train and test set images. The KM3D detector is then trained on the train set and evaluated on the test set.

Table 6 depicts the results. The first two rows show the proposed unsupervised approach and the results of the annotation pipeline with the annotated 2D boxes (reference). It can be observed that the unsupervised approach results in a significant drop in performance with respect to the supervised reference implementation of 22.3% in AP3D score for the easy case.

When training the KM3D detector on the unsupervised pipeline, the performance significantly increases up to 67.3% AP3D. Compared to the supervised KM3D detector training (third row reference implementation in the Table), the AP3D difference is only 6–11%. Although the AP3D scores are significantly lower than the supervised approaches, this unsupervised configuration does not require any 2D annotation effort and is fully automatic. Visual inspection of the unsupervised pipeline shows that the 2D detection set generated by Mask-RCNN contains many false detections. This results in falsely annotated 3D boxes in the SimpleBox OptFlow pipeline and causes the KM3D detector to learn false objects. Further improvements of the 3D annotation quality, and thereby the 3D detector, are therefore expected when better performing 2D object detectors are employed.

5   Conclusion

This work has investigated the detection of 3D bounding boxes for objects using calibrated static monocular cameras in traffic surveillance scenes. Current object detection have difficulties in finding the correct orientation of the detected vehicle, which is problematic for the exact localization and tracking of the vehicle. The objective of this work is to draw an exact 3D bounding box around the vehicle that can disclose its unique localization on the ground plane and correct orientation. Therefore, we propose a system that constructs 3D box annotations from existing 2D annotated datasets, by exploiting camera-calibration information and simple scene annotations (static vanishing points). To this end, different configurations for a processing system have been proposed. Despite the different possibilities for solving this problem, the best solution is to directly generate the 3D box from the 2D annotations of the vehicles. In a second step, the 3D annotated dataset generated by this system is used to train the KM3D object detector to create object detection from self-supervised annotated data. The trained 3D detector can be directly integrated in surveillance systems, as inference only requires 2D images and camera calibration.

During the design and conducted experiments, the following findings have been noted.

Annotation-Processing Configurations. For optimization, seven different annotation-processing configurations have been validated, each containing orientation estimation and 3D construction components. In addition to combinations of existing components, we have proposed the novel SimpleBox OptFlow method. This method does not require segmentation of vehicles and provides a more simple 3D box construction, assuming prior-knowledge in the form of a fixed predefined vehicle width and a constant vehicle height. When comparing the different 3D annotation configurations, we have found that the SimpleBox OptFlow pipeline provides the best object annotation results, albeit all seven configurations result in accurate orientation estimation and localization. If the Optical flow for this configuration cannot be computed because of the lack of temporal data, the SimpleBox RayCast with YOLOv7 segmentation has proven to be the most accurate configuration. The experimental results have shown that this method depends on the quality of the generated segmentation mask and that the segmentation mask quality of YOLOv7 outperforms Mask R-CNN segmentation results.

CNN Object Detector Based on Semi-Automated Annotations. The extensive literature overview highlighted the power of the KM3D detector for traffic analysis. The KM3D CNN-based detection model developed for autonomous driving viewpoints has been adopted to the traffic surveillance scenarios. Using the 3D box annotations from SimpleBox OptFlow directly (without the 3D object detector), the AP3D score is 36.4% which improves to 51.9% AP3D when using KM3D trained on this data. The KM3D object detector generates more accurate 3D vehicle boxes than the vehicle annotations from the proposed automatic 3D annotation pipeline, due to its capacity to generalize. It can localize vehicles accurately within 1 m error in middle-point coordinates up to 125 m from the camera.

Cross-Validation on Datasets. Furthermore, we have found that the different viewpoints from the KITTI autonomous driving dataset increase performance when adding it to our generated surveillance dataset. Although the KITTI dataset contains different camera viewpoints, the detection model effectively exploits the dataset to generalize better.

Unsupervised Approach. The use of unsupervised annotation using existing 2D detectors can potentially increase the 3D detection performance even further. To this end, the 2D annotations are replaced by a 2D object detector, such that no initial annotations are required for the annotation-processing configurations. Although the results of the final detector performance are significantly lower, the obtained detection results are promising and expected to improve when a better 2D detector is employed.

The conducted experiments of this work show that it is possible to use a 2D dataset for the creation of a more informative 3D dataset for traffic surveillance purposes. It has been shown that the existing KM3D object detector trained on the created dataset generates more accurate 3D vehicle boxes than the vehicle annotations from the proposed automated 3D annotation pipeline, due to its capacity to generalize. The resulting 3D box detections are accurate (51.9% AP3D), both in middle-point locations of the vehicle and the obtained vehicle dimensions, up to about 125 m from the camera.

References

1. Ansari, J.A., Sharma, S., Majumdar, A., Jatavallabhula, K.M., Krishna, K.M.: The earth ain't flat: monocular reconstruction of vehicles on steep and graded roads from a moving camera. In: 2018 IEEE/RSJ International Conference on Intelligent Robots and Systems (IROS), pp. 8404–8410 (2018). https://api.semanticscholar.org/CorpusID:3761728

2. Brazil, G., Liu, X.: M3D-RPN: monocular 3D region proposal network for object detection. In: 2019 IEEE/CVF International Conference on Computer Vision (ICCV), pp. 9286–9295. IEEE Computer Society, Los Alamitos (2019). https://doi.ieeecomputersociety.org/10.1109/ICCV.2019.00938

3. Brouwers, G.M.Y.E., Zwemer, M.H., Wijnhoven, R.G.J., de With, P.H.N.: Automatic calibration of stationary surveillance cameras in the wild. In: Proceedings of the IEEE CVPR (2016). https://doi.org/10.1007/978-3-319-48881-3_52

4. Cai, Y., Li, B., Jiao, Z., Li, H., Zeng, X., Wang, X.: Monocular 3D object detection with decoupled structured polygon estimation and height-guided depth estimation. In: AAAI (2020). https://arxiv.org/abs/2002.01619

5. Chabot, F., Chaouch, M., Rabarisoa, J., Teulière, C., Chateau, T.: Deep MANTA: a coarse-to-fine many-task network for joint 2D and 3D vehicle analysis from monocular image. In: 2017 IEEE Conference on Computer Vision and Pattern Recognition (CVPR), pp. 1827–1836. IEEE Computer Society, Los Alamitos (2017). https://doi.ieeecomputersociety.org/10.1109/CVPR.2017.198

6. Chen, X., Kundu, K., Zhang, Z., Ma, H., Fidler, S., Urtasun, R.: Monocular 3D object detection for autonomous driving. In: Proceedings of the IEEE CVPR (2016). https://doi.org/10.1109/CVPR.2016.236

7. Choe, J., Joo, K., Rameau, F., Shim, G., Kweon, I.S.: Segment2Regress: monocular 3D vehicle localization in two stages. In: Robotics: Science and Systems (2019). https://doi.org/10.15607/RSS.2019.XV.016

8. Dalal, N., Triggs, B.: Histograms of oriented gradients for human detection. In: 2005 IEEE Computer Society Conference on Computer Vision and Pattern Recognition (CVPR 2005), vol. 1, pp. 886–893. IEEE (2005). https://doi.org/10.1109/CVPR.2005.177

9. Ding, M., Huo, Y., Yi, H., Wang, Z., Shi, J., Lu, Z., Luo, P.: Learning depth-guided convolutions for monocular 3D object detection. In: Proceedings of the IEEE/CVF Conference on CVPR (2020). https://arxiv.org/abs/1912.04799

10. Dubská, M., Herout, A., Sochor, J.: Automatic camera calibration for traffic understanding. In: BMVC, vol. 4, 6, p. 8 (2014). https://doi.org/10.5244/C.28.42

11. Fang, J., Zhou, L., Liu, G.: 3D bounding box estimation for autonomous vehicles by cascaded geometric constraints and depurated 2D detections using 3D results (2019). https://arxiv.org/abs/1909.01867

12. Farnebäck, G.: Two-frame motion estimation based on polynomial expansion. In: Bigun, J., Gustavsson, T. (eds.) SCIA 2003. LNCS, vol. 2749, pp. 363–370. Springer, Heidelberg (2003). https://doi.org/10.1007/3-540-45103-X_50

13. Geiger, A., Lenz, P., Urtasun, R.: Are we ready for autonomous driving? The kitti vision benchmark suite. In: Conference on CVPR (2012). https://doi.org/10.1109/CVPR.2012.6248074

14. Girshick, R.: Fast R-CNN. In: Proceedings of the IEEE International Conference on Computer Vision, pp. 1440–1448 (2015). https://arxiv.org/abs/1504.08083

15. He, K., Gkioxari, G., Dollár, P., Girshick, R.: Mask R-CNN. In: Proceedings of the IEEE ICCV (2017). https://arxiv.org/abs/1703.06870

16. He, T., Soatto, S.: Mono3D++: monocular 3D vehicle detection with two-scale 3D hypotheses and task priors. CoRR abs/1901.03446 (2019). https://arxiv.org/abs/1901.03446

17. Kehl, W., Manhardt, F., Tombari, F., Ilic, S., Navab, N.: SSD-6D: making RGB-based 3D detection and 6D pose estimation great again. In: Proceedings of the IEEE ICCV, pp. 1521–1529 (2017). https://arxiv.org/abs/1711.10006

18. Kundu, A., Li, Y., Rehg, J.M.: 3D-RCNN: instance-level 3D object reconstruction via render-and-compare. In: 2018 IEEE/CVF Conference on Computer Vision and Pattern Recognition, pp. 3559–3568 (2018). https://doi.org/10.1109/CVPR.2018.00375

19. Li, B., Ouyang, W., Sheng, L., Zeng, X., Wang, X.: GS3D: an efficient 3D object detection framework for autonomous driving, 2019 IEEE/CVF Conference on Computer Vision and Pattern Recognition (CVPR), pp. 1019–1028. IEEE Computer Society, Los Alamitos (2019). https://doi.ieeecomputersociety.org/10.1109/CVPR.2019.00111

20. Li, P.: Monocular 3D detection with geometric constraints embedding and semi-supervised training (2020). https://arxiv.org/abs/2009.00764

21. Li, P., Zhao, H., Liu, P., Cao, F.: RTM3D: real-time monocular 3D detection from object keypoints for autonomous driving. arXiv preprint arXiv:2001.03343 (2020)

22. Lin, T.-Y., et al.: Microsoft COCO: common objects in context. CoRR arXiv:abs/1405.0312 (2014). https://dblp.org/rec/bib/journals/corr/LinMBHPRDZ14

23. Liu, Z., Wu, Z., Tóth, R.: SMOKE: single-stage monocular 3D object detection via keypoint estimation. In: 2020 IEEE/CVF Conference on Computer Vision and Pattern Recognition Workshops (CVPRW), pp. 4289–4298 (2020). https://doi.org/10.1109/CVPRW50498.2020.00506

24. Ma, X., Wang, Z., Li, H., Zhang, P., Ouyang, W., Fan, X.: Accurate monocular 3D object detection via color-embedded 3D reconstruction for autonomous driving. In: Proceedings of the IEEE ICCV (2019). https://arxiv.org/abs/1903.11444

25. Mousavian, A., Anguelov, D., Flynn, J., Kosecka, J.: 3D bounding box estimation using deep learning and geometry. In: 2017 IEEE Conference on Computer Vision and Pattern Recognition (CVPR), pp. 5632–5640. IEEE Computer Society, Los Alamitos (2017). ISSN:1063-6919. https://doi.ieeecomputersociety.org/10.1109/CVPR.2017.597

26. Nilsson, M., Ardö, H.: In search of a car - utilizing a 3D model with context for object detection. In: Proceedings of the 9th International Conference on Computer Vision Theory and Applications - Volume 2: VISAPP, (VISIGRAPP 2014), pp. 419–424. INSTICC, SciTePress (2014). https://doi.org/10.5220/0004685304190424

27. Qin, Z., Wang, J., Lu, Y.: Monogrnet: a geometric reasoning network for monocular 3D object localization. In: Proceedings of the AAAI Conference on Artificial Intelligence (2019). https://arxiv.org/abs/1811.10247

28. Ren, S., He, K., Girshick, R., Sun, J.: Faster R-CNN: towards real-time object detection with region proposal networks. arXiv preprint arXiv:1506.01497 (2015)

29. Roddick, T., Kendall, A., Cipolla, R.: Orthographic feature transform for monocular 3D object detection. arXiv:1811.08188 (2018)

30. Sochor, J., Juránek, R., Herout, A.: Traffic surveillance camera calibration by 3D model bounding box alignment for accurate vehicle speed measurement. Comput. Vis. Image Underst. **161**, 87–98 (2017). https://arxiv.org/abs/1702.06451

31. Sochor, J., Špaňhel, J., Herout, A.: Boxcars: Improving fine-grained recognition of vehicles using 3-D bounding boxes in traffic surveillance. IEEE Trans. Intell. Transp. Syst. **20**(1), 97–108 (2018). https://arxiv.org/abs/1703.00686

32. Srivastava, S., Jurie, F., Sharma, G.: Learning 2D to 3D lifting for object detection in 3D for autonomous vehicles. arXiv preprint arXiv:1904.08494 (2019)

33. Sullivan, G.D., Baker, K.D., Worrall, A.D., Attwood, C., Remagnino, P.: Model-based vehicle detection and classification using orthographic approximations. Image Vis. Comput. **15**(8), 649–654 (1997). https://doi.org/10.1016/S0262-8856(97)00009-7

34. Wang, C.Y., Bochkovskiy, A., Liao, H.Y.M.: YOLOv7: trainable bag-of-freebies sets new state-of-the-art for real-time object detectors. arXiv preprint arXiv:2207.02696 (2022)

35. Wang, X., Yin, W., Kong, T., Jiang, Y., Li, L., Shen, C.: Task-aware monocular depth estimation for 3D object detection. In: Proceedings of the AAAI Conference on Artificial Intelligence (2020). https://arxiv.org/abs/1909.07701

36. Wang, Y., Chao, W., Garg, D., Hariharan, B., Campbell, M., Weinberger, K.Q.: Pseudo-lidar from visual depth estimation: bridging the gap in 3D object detection for autonomous driving. CoRR abs/1812.07179 (2018). https://arxiv.org/abs/1812.07179

37. Weber, M., Fürst, M., Zöllner, J.M.: Direct 3D detection of vehicles in monocular images with a CNN based 3D decoder. In: 2019 IEEE Intelligent Vehicles Symposium (IV), pp. 417–423 (2019). https://doi.org/10.1109/IVS.2019.8814198

38. Wijnhoven, R.G.J., de With, P.H.N.: Unsupervised sub-categorization for object detection: finding cars from a driving vehicle. In: 2011 IEEE ICCV Workshops, pp. 2077–2083. IEEE (2011). https://doi.org/10.1109/ICCVW.2011.6130504

39. You, Y., et al.: Pseudo-lidar++: accurate depth for 3D object detection in autonomous driving. CoRR abs/1906.06310 (2019). https://arxiv.org/abs/1906.06310

40. Zwemer, M.H., Scholte, D., Wijnhoven, R.G.J., de With, P.H.N.: 3D detection of vehicles from 2D images in traffic surveillance. In: Proceedings of the 17th International Joint Conference on Computer Vision, Imaging and Computer Graphics Theory and Applications - Volume 4: VISAPP, pp. 97–106. INSTICC, SciTePress (2022). https://doi.org/10.5220/0010783600003124

A Quantitative and Qualitative Analysis on a GAN-Based Face Mask Removal on Masked Images and Videos

Hitoshi Yoshihashi[1]([✉]), Naoto Ienaga[2], and Maki Sugimoto[1]

[1] Graduate School of Information and Computer Science, Keio University,
Yokohama, Kanagawa, Japan
`hitoshi.yoshihashi@imlab.ics.keio.ac.jp`
[2] Faculty of Engineering, Information and Systems, University of Tsukuba,
Tsukuba, Ibaraki, Japan

Abstract. In 2020 and beyond, there are more and more opportunities to communicate with others while wearing a face mask. Since masks hide the mouth and facial muscles, it becomes more challenging to convey facial expressions to others while wearing a face mask. In this study, we propose using generative adversarial networks (GAN) to complement facial regions hidden by masks on images and videos. We defined the custom loss function that focuses on the error of the feature point coordinates of the face and the pixels in the masked region. As a result, we were able to generate higher-quality images than existing methods. Even when the input was video-based, our approach generated high-quality videos with fewer jittering and pixel errors than existing methods.

Keywords: Face completion · Inpainting · Generative adversarial networks · Face mask

1 Introduction

Since 2020, when the pandemic became a global problem, people are increasingly conversing with others while wearing masks. When communicating with others, humans have a habit of focusing on cues that appear on the face, such as the eyes, mouth area, and facial muscles, to read the mind of others. When we wear a mask, these important cues are partially lost. For example, masks do not hide the area around the eyes, so we can look at the eyes and predict emotions, but we need to see the mouth and facial muscles to read detailed changes in facial expressions. It has been reported that it is 10–20% more difficult to convey a smile when wearing a mask than when not wearing a mask [14]. Thus, we can expect smoother communication even in masked situations if we can compensate for the hidden areas (Fig. 1).

In this study, we propose a method to complete the facial area hidden by masks, essential cues for communication facilitation, with human face images and videos. If our approach can generate high-quality unmasked videos, we can apply that to actual use cases. Thus, we apply both image and video-based datasets to our method to verify the robustness and extensibility.

A. A. de Sousa et al. (Eds.): VISIGRAPP 2022, CCIS 1815, pp. 51–65, 2023.
https://doi.org/10.1007/978-3-031-45725-8_3

Mask Video   Ours   Real Video

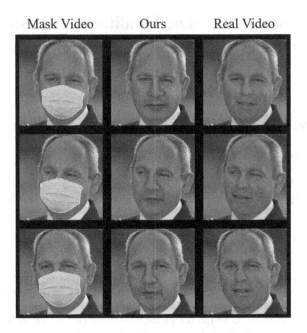

Fig. 1. Examples of Mask Removal Results Using Our Method.

2   Related Works

2.1   Inpainting

Inpainting is a technique for restoring a scratch or hole in a part of an image. Inpainting attempts to restore the original image from the pixels surrounding the missing area using a mask image representing the area in black and white.

A deep learning-based inpainting method was first proposed in 2012 [17]. The method outperformed previous methods in removing white Gaussian noise and inpainting using a denoising autoencoder. Still, it was not able to remove noise in patterns not present in the training data.

DeepFill [19,20] used generative adversarial networks (GAN) [4], which consist of a generator and a discriminator. A generator outputs a plausible image, and a discriminator determines whether the input image is an image derived from the training data (true) or an image created by the generator (false). Both networks compete with each other in the learning process. The generator aims to generate new data of the same quality as the training data. The discriminator aims to be able to perform binary classification based on the probability distribution of true and false images.

Traditionally, fast marching inpainting methods that cut and paste pixels around a hole in an image have been common [13]. DeepFill, however, used a GAN-based inpainting method. Such methods learn many pairs of correct images (targets) and images that need to be corrected (sources). If the trained model is given a source image, it attempts to predict the target image.

These methods can repair irregular scratches or holes in an image. However, the repair may fail if huge holes are concentrated in one area of the image, such as in a face mask.

2.2 Face Completion

Research is also being conducted on face completion, which repairs missing portions of human face images. For example, using convolutional neural networks (CNN), face images with missing area were fixed [5]. Also, there were GAN-based methods to repair face images with randomly pasted squares [3] or to estimate the eyes of a person wearing a head-mounted display [16].

Pix2pix [6] is a GAN that learns the correspondence between two images and generates another corresponding image given one image. For example, if it learns the pair of a completed face image and a distorted face image, it can generate a completed one when a distorted one is given using the trained model.

These methods are similar to learning-based inpainting but are designed and trained to repair facial images. As a result, they can successfully repair a large hole in a part of the image. However, they did not aim to estimate the facial regions hidden by the mask.

A study aimed to estimate the masked region was conducted [15]. Using DeepFill with various custom loss functions applied to it as a baseline, it filled masked areas. However, the quality of the generated images, especially the skin tone of the masked regions, had room for improvement.

3 Method

3.1 Pix2pix-Based Inpainting

In this study, we used pix2pix as the baseline. In pix2pix, images are given to the generator as condition vectors since it uses conditional GAN (CGAN) [11]. Pix2pix brings a randomly assigned noise vector closer to the probability distribution of the correct image by referring to and comparing vectorized values of images.

The pix2pix generator uses U-Net [12] to perform precise pixel-by-pixel image transformation. The loss function of the pix2pix generator is the sum of D_{fake} (0–1 values returned by the discriminator) and the L_1 reconstruction error term.

$$G_{loss} = -\log D_{fake} + L_1 \times 100 \qquad (1)$$

To minimize the value of G_{loss}, the generator aims to make D_{fake} close to 1 and L_1 close to 0. L_1 is assigned the average of the absolute error of the pixel values of the generated and real images.

The pix2pix discriminator is similar to the discriminator used in the vanilla GAN [4], but it is designed to discriminate whether an image is true or false by using N × N data (patches), which is a portion of the whole image. The loss function of the discriminator is calculated by using D_{fake} and D_{real} (0–1 values returned by the discriminator for true pairs).

$$D_{loss} = -(\log D_{real} + \log(1 - D_{fake})) \qquad (2)$$

To minimize the value of D_{loss}, the discriminator aims to make D_{real} close to 1 and D_{fake} close to 0.

This study proposes a pix2pix-based method that complements pixels in the masked region for unknown mask images by learning pairs of face images with and without a mask.

3.2 Custom Loss Function

In this study, two terms are added to the loss function of the generator (Eq. 1), and G_{loss} is redefined as follows, where λ_1 to λ_3 are hyperparameters.

$$G_{loss} = -\log D_{fake} + L_1 \times \lambda_1 + C_1 \times \lambda_2 + C_2 \times \lambda_3 \tag{3}$$

C_1 is a term to feed back the error of the face-feature point coordinates to the generator. For the output (generated) image O and the real (ground truth) image R, the feature point coordinates of 17 points on the face contour (the large blue points shown in Fig. 3) are obtained. The error of these coordinates are fed back to the generator. C_1 is defined as follows, where O_n and R_n are the feature point coordinates of the output image and the real image.

$$C_1 = \frac{\sum_{n=1}^{17}(|O_n - R_n|)}{17} \tag{4}$$

C_2 is a term to feed back the error of pixel values in the masked region to the generator. In the existing L_1 reconstruction error term, all pixels in the image are included in the calculation, but in C_2, only pixels in the masked region are included in the calculation. C_2 is defined as follows, where nr, ng, and nb are the 256-level RGB pixel values at pixel n, and x is the number of pixels in the masked region.

$$C_2 = \frac{\sum_{n=1}^{x}(|O_{nr} - R_{nr}|^2 + |O_{ng} - R_{ng}|^2 + |O_{nb} - R_{nb}|^2)}{x} \tag{5}$$

3.3 System Overview

In this study, pix2pix was used as the baseline for the system shown in Fig. 2. The blue arrows are the newly added parts in this study.

First, each generated image is saved as an image file and processed using the OpenCV library so that the generated image can be compared with the real image of the training data.

Next, we added two new custom terms to the generator loss function equation. One of the custom terms is the average of the squared error of the pixel values restricted to the masked region, and the other is the average error in the feature point coordinates predicted from the face contour.

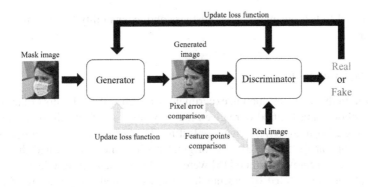

Fig. 2. System Overview. (Color figure online)

3.4 Predicting Feature Points on a Face

Dlib [9] was used to obtain feature point coordinates. Dlib is a library that detects face regions and feature points on input images. Learning the correspondence between faces and feature points can detect feature points of unknown face images. However, when dlib's feature point detection program is run on a face image with a mask attached, the coordinates of all feature points cannot be obtained correctly because the nose and mouth are hidden. This is because the model loaded by dlib is trained only for face images without masks. Therefore, we retrained the model using 30 face images with and without masks in equal proportions. We generated the mask images by using MaskTheFace [2], the same tool used in the experiment section. The retrained model did not fail to predict feature points around the nose and mouth for mask images, as shown in Fig. 3.

Because the images generated during the training process still had parts of the face hidden by masks, it was necessary to retrain the model to avoid failing to predict feature points.

4   Experiment

We experimented to see if the proposed system accurately complemented the masked region. We conducted two experiments: the image evaluation and the video evaluation. The image evaluation experiment was conducted to test if our method can generate higher-quality images than existing methods. The video evaluation experiment

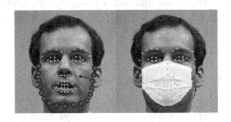

Fig. 3. Example of Predicting Feature Points on a Face Image (Left) and a Mask Image (Right). (Color figure online)

was conducted to test our method's robustness and extensibility by applying a video-based dataset.

4.1 Image Evaluation

Procedure. In the image evaluation experiment, we prepared 7931 pairs of face images with and without a mask. 5600 were given to the system for 300 epochs of training, and the remaining 2331 images were given for testing. The fast marching inpainting method (OpenCV's inpaint function [13]), the original pix2pix method [6], and the existing GAN-based mask removal method [15] were tested with the same test data.

The dataset was created by pasting face masks on real images using MaskThe-Face [2]. We pasted seven mask patterns shown in Fig. 7. The details of our test dataset are shown in Table 1. We applied the alignment of Stylegan2encoder [8] to all images in the dataset to correct the face positions and feature point coordinates. Each image file was resized to 256×256.

For quantitative evaluation metrics, we used mean squared error (MSE), peak signal-to-noise ratio (PSNR), structural similarity (SSIM), and learned perceptual image patch similarity (LPIPS) [21] to evaluate the generated images. The unit for PSNR is decibel (dB). MSE, SSIM, and LPIPS have no units. MSE was calculated by taking the squared error of each pixel's value in the real and generated images in the masked region. PSNR was calculated from the ratio of the maximum power of a signal to the power of the noise. SSIM was calculated from the structural similarity between the real and generated images. LPIPS was calculated from the perceptual loss of the generated images compared with the real images. For PSNR and SSIM, higher values mean better quality. For MSE and LPIPS, lower values mean better quality.

We also used these quantitative measures to determine how many epochs to train the model for the proposed method. As shown in the table, we decided to train the model in 300 epochs because both SSIM and LPIPS showed the best values (Table 2).

We designed facial expression identification and quality evaluation experiments using the generated images, and qualitative evaluation indices were calculated. Participants (10 total, eight males and two females, 20–24 years old) were asked to view ten images from each method, including real images, and to judge facial expressions (neutral, happy, angry, sad, surprise) and quality (7-point scale, one being the worst and seven the best).

As qualitative measures, we used human-rated quality score (HQS), accuracy, and duration, since a quick and correct understanding of facial expressions is essential for communication. The HQS was derived by taking the average of the scores of each method. The accuracy was derived by taking the average percentage of correct

Table 1. The Details of the Test Dataset.

Dataset	Number of Images	Example of Images
FFHQ [7]	1400	Fig. 4
KDEF [10]	588	Figs. 5 and 6
UTKFace [22]	343	Fig. 4

Table 2. Transition in Quantitative Metrics by Number of Epochs [18].

Metric	10	30	60	100	300
MSE	2.59×10^3	$\mathbf{2.23 \times 10^3}$	2.25×10^3	2.24×10^3	2.32×10^3
PSNR (dB)	2.76×10^1	2.87×10^1	$\mathbf{2.88 \times 10^1}$	$\mathbf{2.88 \times 10^1}$	$\mathbf{2.88 \times 10^1}$
SSIM	9.01×10^{-1}	9.16×10^{-1}	9.22×10^{-1}	9.24×10^{-1}	$\mathbf{9.26 \times 10^{-1}}$
LPIPS	9.07×10^{-2}	6.26×10^{-2}	5.56×10^{-2}	5.22×10^{-2}	$\mathbf{4.59 \times 10^{-2}}$

Mask Image   Telea's   Isola's   Din's   Ours   Real Image

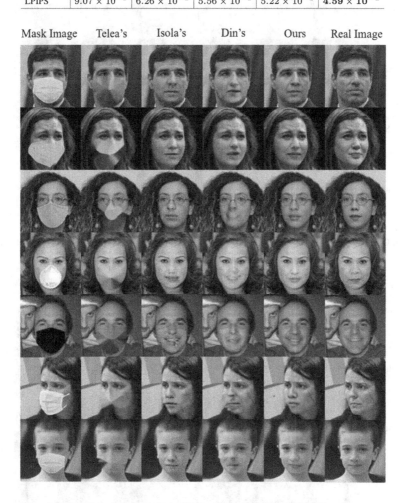

Fig. 4. Examples of Mask Removal Results on FFHQ and UTKFace Dataset.

responses for the facial expressions selected by the subject for the ten images of each method. The duration was derived by taking the average of the total time participants took to select the correct expression for the ten images of each method.

Results. The output results of the test data for each method are shown in Figs. 4, 5, and 6. In the case of our method, less mask pixels remained and little noise was generated, resulting in high quality facial images.

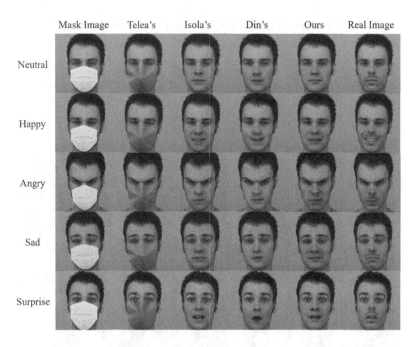

Fig. 5. Comparison Among Each Facial Expression of the Same Man on KDEF Dataset [18].

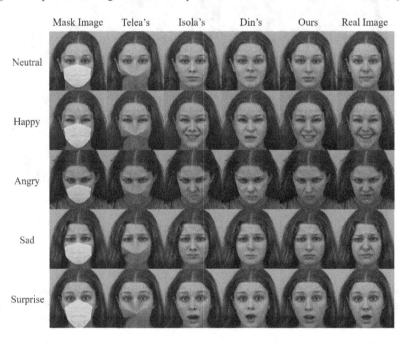

Fig. 6. Comparison Among Each Facial Expression of the Same Woman on KDEF Dataset [18].

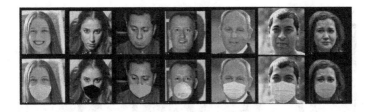

Fig. 7. The Base Images Used for Generating the Video-based Dataset.

The results of quantitative metrics for each method are shown in Table 3. In all four metrics, our method outperformed the others (For MSE and LPIPS, smaller is better). Our method improved MSE by 22.7%, PSNR by 6.27%, SSIM by 1.94%, and LPIPS by 10.9% compared with Din's method.

The results of qualitative metrics for each method are shown in Table 4. For the HQS and the accuracy, our method had the next highest values after the real image.

Wilcoxon rank-sum test was conducted for HQS, and Tukey's multiple comparison test was conducted for the accuracy and the duration to investigate which methods had significant differences (5% significant level). For the HQS, there were significant differences between all method pairs except for Din's-Ours. HQS of our method was significantly higher than that of Isola's, but was significantly lower than that of the real image. For accuracy, there were significant differences only between Din's and the real image. For the duration, there was no significant difference among the methods.

4.2 Video Evaluation

Procedure. In the image evaluation experiment, we created a video-based dataset using MyHeritage Deep Nostalgia [1], which generates a short video from a face image. We used seven images shown in Fig. 7 and generated seven videos. Each generated video was 10 s long on average. The video-based test dataset was created by pasting mask patterns to each frame of the generated videos. A total of 2018 frames were given to the system for testing to compare the quality of generated frames among each method.

For evaluating video-based results, we used frame-by-frame structural similarity (F-SSIM) in addition to the four quantitative evaluation metrics used in the image evaluation. F-SSIM was calculated from the value of SSIM between the current and previous frames. Thus, higher F-SSIM means that the video had less frequency of jittering.

Table 3. Results of the Quantitative Evaluation Experiment [18].

Metric	Telea's	Isola's	Din's	Ours
MSE	6.75×10^3	2.69×10^3	3.00×10^3	$\mathbf{2.32 \times 10^3}$
PSNR (dB)	2.40×10^1	2.76×10^1	2.71×10^1	$\mathbf{2.88 \times 10^1}$
SSIM	9.07×10^{-1}	8.96×10^{-1}	9.08×10^{-1}	$\mathbf{9.26 \times 10^{-1}}$
LPIPS	9.16×10^{-2}	5.47×10^{-2}	5.15×10^{-2}	$\mathbf{4.59 \times 10^{-2}}$

Mask Video   Telea's   Isola's   Din's   Ours   Real Video

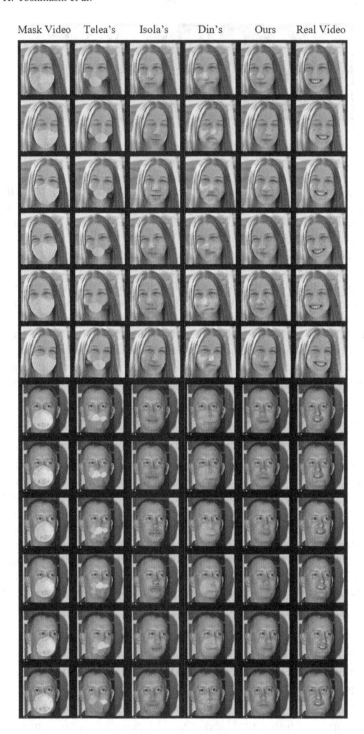

Fig. 8. Examples of Mask Removal Results on Video-based Dataset.

Table 4. Results of the Qualitative Evaluation Experiment [18].

Metric	Telea's	Isola's	Din's	Ours	Real Image
HQS	1.41 ± 0.49	2.70 ± 0.79	4.54 ± 0.96	$\mathbf{4.78 \pm 1.08}$	6.04 ± 1.04
Accuracy (%)	$\mathbf{96.00 \pm 5.16}$	95.00 ± 7.07	89.00 ± 5.68	94.00 ± 5.16	97.00 ± 4.83
Duration (sec)	60.20 ± 24.22	60.10 ± 18.36	56.90 ± 10.67	$\mathbf{54.10 \pm 7.58}$	47.00 ± 5.96

Results. The output results of the video-based test data for each method are shown in Fig. 8. In the case of our method, fewer mask pixels remained, and little noise was generated, resulting in an image of high quality.

The results of quantitative metrics of the video-based test data for each method are shown in Table 5. In all five metrics, our method outperformed the others. Our method improved MSE by 36.7%, PSNR by 8.75%, SSIM by 0.767%, LPIPS by 6.86%, F-SSIM by 0.419% compared with Din's method.

5 Discussion

5.1 Quality of Generated Images

Our method generated high-quality face images as shown in Tables 3 and 4 using the test dataset, which consists of synthesized mask images.

In addition to this, the method were applied to real-world cases. To verify the robustness of our approach, we compared the results of each method on a dataset consisting of real-world images with face masks. As a result, our method generated high-quality images in most cases, as shown in Fig. 9. We also found that our approach can be applied to real-world images, although it produced a blurrier impression than the image generated by the synthetic mask image dataset. In addition, our method was still able to complete the masked region when the image was showing the side view of the face. However, if the masked area was too large, our approach did not partially complete the area.

In the generated images in Fig. 9, our method showed less error in facial color and geometry since our network was trained with focusing on the masked region. On the other hand, the networks of the other methods were trained only with all image-based loss functions such as L_1 reconstruction error and structural similarity (not focusing on the masked region). Thus, whether focusing on the masked region or not made the difference between our method and the other methods.

Table 5. Results of the Quantitative Evaluation Experiment on Video-based Dataset.

Metric	Telea's	Isola's	Din's	Ours
MSE	9.63×10^3	3.11×10^3	3.79×10^3	$\mathbf{2.40 \times 10^3}$
PSNR (dB)	2.38×10^1	2.72×10^1	2.63×10^1	$\mathbf{2.86 \times 10^1}$
SSIM	9.10×10^{-1}	8.66×10^{-1}	9.13×10^{-1}	$\mathbf{9.20 \times 10^{-1}}$
LPIPS	8.03×10^{-2}	4.95×10^{-2}	4.20×10^{-2}	$\mathbf{3.87 \times 10^{-2}}$
F-SSIM	9.52×10^{-1}	9.54×10^{-1}	9.54×10^{-1}	$\mathbf{9.58 \times 10^{-1}}$

Mask Image   Telea's   Isola's   Din's   Ours

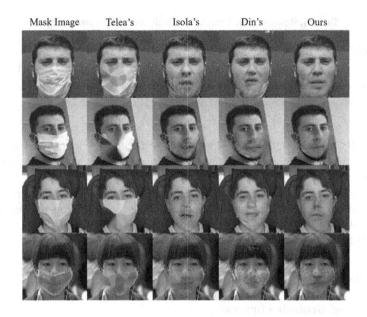

Fig. 9. Examples of Mask Removal Results on Real-World Dataset.

5.2 Discriminating Facial Expressions

As shown in Table 6, the qualitative evaluation of our method showed that it was accurate for all expressions except happiness. In addition, Din's method had difficulty with the happy image. Many participants misidentified the happy image as neutral because the mouth was not smiling.

Considering the accuracy of Telea's method, which cannot use the mouth as a cue, it is inferred that it is challenging to recognize surprise with the eyes alone. However, for other facial expressions, Telea's method showed high accuracy, suggesting that cues around the eyes, especially the angle of the eyebrows, may contribute to the discrimination of facial expressions.

Table 6. The Accuracy (%) of Each Facial Expression in Qualitative Evaluation [18].

Facial Expression	Telea's	Isola's	Din's	Ours	Real Image	Average
Neutral	100	100	100	100	90.0	98.0
Happy	95.0	85.0	55.0	75.0	100	82.0
Angry	100	95.0	100	100	100	99.0
Sad	95.0	95.0	90.0	95.0	95.0	94.0
Surprise	90.0	100	100	100	100	98.0
Average	96.0	95.0	89.0	94.0	97.0	94.2

5.3 Generating Smooth Videos

As shown in Fig. 8, our method was able to generate high-quality images on the sequential video-based dataset. However, when we merged all the generated frames into one video, the complemented area was slightly jittering. This problem was probably caused by needing to consider the temporal information, such as the continuity among the previous, current, and following frames. If the temporal information was considered during the learning process, the results on video-based inputs can be improved.

5.4 Additional Quantitative Analyses

In the custom term C_1 of the loss function, we checked whether the values of the evaluation metrics can be further improved by considering the coordinates of the 20 feature points that exist around the mouth.

Table 7. Comparison of Evaluation Metrics When Adding 20 Feature Points Around the Mouth.

Metric	17 Points	37 Points
MSE	2319.373	**2280.771**
PSNR (dB)	28.789	**28.843**
SSIM	0.926	**0.928**
LPIPS	**0.0459**	0.0492

From Table 7, the three indices except for LPIPS were slightly improved, but the results were not significantly changed by considering the feature point coordinates of the mouth.

We also checked if increasing the training dataset to 12,600 pairs can further improve the results.

Table 8. Comparison of Evaluation Metrics When Augmenting the Training Dataset.

Metric	5,600 Pairs	12,600 Pairs
MSE	2280.771	**2047.970**
PSNR (dB)	28.843	**29.348**
SSIM	0.928	**0.931**
LPIPS	0.0492	**0.0434**

From Table 8, MSE improved by 10.21%, PSNR by 1.75%, SSIM by 0.03%, and LPIPS by 11.79%, suggesting that the expansion of the training dataset did improve the results.

Furthermore, we considered the possibility that the training may not have converged at 300 epochs due to the extension of the training dataset. We checked whether training in 600 epochs can further improve the values of the evaluation metrics.

From Table 9, SSIM and LPIPS improved slightly, but the results did not change significantly as the number of epochs during learning was increased, suggesting that training had already converged at 300 epochs.

Table 9. Comparison of Evaluation Metrics When Increasing the Number of Epochs.

Metric	300 Epochs	600 Epochs
MSE	**2047.970**	2060.726
PSNR (dB)	**29.348**	29.326
SSIM	0.931	**0.932**
LPIPS	0.0434	**0.0424**

6   Limitations

Our study has two limitations. One is that the results can be poor if the given face image wears a different mask far from the ones used in the training dataset. The other is that we see slight jittering on the output videos. Therefore, future work should include developing a more robust network that can handle mask input and real-time face completion considering temporal information for smoother video-based processing.

7   Conclusion

In this study, we proposed a machine learning-based approach that considers the errors between facial landmarks and pixels and complements the areas hidden by the face mask. Using a GAN-based model as a baseline and modifying the loss function equation of the generator, the error between the coordinates of facial feature points and the pixel values of the masked area was calculated and updated to produce a higher-quality image than existing methods. We examined the performance of the network on facial images and sequential video-based dataset.

Our method may have the potential to support face-to-face communication with people who have difficulties predicting the facial expressions of others with face masks.

References

1. Myheritage deep nostalgia. https://www.myheritage.jp/deep-nostalgia
2. Anwar, A., Raychowdhury, A.: Masked face recognition for secure authentication. arXiv abs/2008.11104 (2020)
3. Cai, J., Han, H., Shan, S., Chen, X.: FCSR-GAN: joint face completion and super-resolution via multi-task learning. IEEE Trans. Biom. Behav. Identity Sci. **2**(2), 109–121 (2020). https://doi.org/10.1109/TBIOM.2019.2951063

4. Goodfellow, I., et al.: Generative adversarial nets. In: Advances in Neural Information Processing Systems, vol. 27, pp. 2672–2680. Curran Associates, Inc. (2014)
5. Iizuka, S., Simo-Serra, E., Ishikawa, H.: Globally and locally consistent image completion. ACM Trans. Graph. **36**(4), 107:1–107:14 (2017). (Proc. of SIGGRAPH 2017)
6. Isola, P., Zhu, J., Zhou, T., Efros, A.A.: Image-to-image translation with conditional adversarial networks. In: 2017 IEEE Conference on Computer Vision and Pattern Recognition, pp. 5967–5976 (2017). https://doi.org/10.1109/CVPR.2017.632
7. Karras, T., Laine, S., Aila, T.: A style-based generator architecture for generative adversarial networks. In: 2019 IEEE/CVF Conference on Computer Vision and Pattern Recognition, pp. 4396–4405 (2019). https://doi.org/10.1109/CVPR.2019.00453
8. Karras, T., Laine, S., Aittala, M., Hellsten, J., Lehtinen, J., Aila, T.: Analyzing and improving the image quality of stylegan. In: 2020 IEEE/CVF Conference on Computer Vision and Pattern Recognition, pp. 8107–8116 (2020). https://doi.org/10.1109/CVPR42600.2020.00813
9. King, D.E.: Dlib-ml: a machine learning toolkit. J. Mach. Learn. Res. **10**(60), 1755–1758 (2009)
10. Lundqvist, D., Flykt, A., Öhman, A.: The Karolinska Directed Emotional Faces. Karolinska Institutet (1998)
11. Mirza, M., Osindero, S.: Conditional generative adversarial nets. arXiv abs/1411.1784 (2014)
12. Ronneberger, O., Fischer, P., Brox, T.: U-Net: convolutional networks for biomedical image segmentation. In: Navab, N., Hornegger, J., Wells, W.M., Frangi, A.F. (eds.) MICCAI 2015. LNCS, vol. 9351, pp. 234–241. Springer, Cham (2015). https://doi.org/10.1007/978-3-319-24574-4_28
13. Telea, A.: An image inpainting technique based on the fast marching method. J. Graph. Tools **9**, 23–34 (2004). https://doi.org/10.1080/10867651.2004.10487596
14. Tsujimura, Y., Nishimura, S., Iijima, A., Kobayashi, R., Miyajima, N.: Comparing different levels of smiling with and without a surgical mask. J. Compr. Nurs. Res. **19**(2), 3–9 (2020). https://doi.org/10.14943/95250
15. Ud Din, N., Javed, K., Bae, S., Yi, J.: A novel GAN-based network for unmasking of masked face. IEEE Access **8**, 44276–44287 (2020). https://doi.org/10.1109/ACCESS.2020.2977386
16. Wang, M., Wen, X., Hu, S.: Faithful face image completion for HMD occlusion removal. In: 2019 IEEE International Symposium on Mixed and Augmented Reality Adjunct, pp. 251–256 (2019). https://doi.org/10.1109/ISMAR-Adjunct.2019.00-36
17. Xie, J., Xu, L., Chen, E.: Image denoising and inpainting with deep neural networks. In: Advances in Neural Information Processing Systems, vol. 25, pp. 341–349 (2012)
18. Yoshihashi, H., Ienaga, N., Sugimoto, M.: Gan-based face mask removal using facial landmarks and pixel errors in masked region. In: the 17th International Joint Conference on Computer Vision, Imaging and Computer Graphics Theory and Applications, vol. 5, pp. 125–133 (2022). https://doi.org/10.5220/0010827500003124
19. Yu, J., Lin, Z., Yang, J., Shen, X., Lu, X., Huang, T.: Free-form image inpainting with gated convolution. In: 2019 IEEE/CVF International Conference on Computer Vision, pp. 4470–4479 (2019). https://doi.org/10.1109/ICCV.2019.00457
20. Yu, J., Lin, Z., Yang, J., Shen, X., Lu, X., Huang, T.S.: Generative image inpainting with contextual attention. In: 2018 IEEE/CVF Conference on Computer Vision and Pattern Recognition, pp. 5505–5514 (2018). https://doi.org/10.1109/CVPR.2018.00577
21. Zhang, R., Isola, P., Efros, A.A., Shechtman, E., Wang, O.: The unreasonable effectiveness of deep features as a perceptual metric. In: 2018 IEEE/CVF Conference on Computer Vision and Pattern Recognition, pp. 586–595 (2018). https://doi.org/10.1109/CVPR.2018.00068
22. Zhang, Z., Song, Y., Qi, H.: Age progression/regression by conditional adversarial autoencoder. In: 2017 IEEE Conference on Computer Vision and Pattern Recognition, pp. 4352–4360 (2017). https://doi.org/10.1109/CVPR.2017.463

Dense Material Segmentation
with Context-Aware Network

Yuwen Heng⬦, Yihong Wu⬦, Srinandan Dasmahapatra,
and Hansung Kim$^{(\boxtimes)}$⬦

Vision, Learning and Control (VLC) Research Group,
School of Electronics and Computer Science (ECS), University of Southampton,
Southampton, UK
{y.heng,yihongwu,h.kim}@soton.ac.uk, sd@ecs.soton.ac.uk

Abstract. The dense material segmentation task aims at recognising the material for every pixel in daily images. It is beneficial to applications such as robot manipulation and spatial audio synthesis. Modern deep-learning methods combine material features with contextual features. Material features can generalise to unseen images regardless of appearance properties such as material shape and colour. Contextual features can reduce the segmentation uncertainty by providing extra global or semi-global information about the image. Recent studies proposed to crop the images into patches, which forces the network to learn material features from local visual clues. Typical contextual information includes extracted feature maps from networks targeting object and place related tasks. However, due to the lack of contextual labels, existing methods use pre-trained networks to provide contextual features. As a consequence, the trained networks do not give a promising performance. Their accuracy is below 70%, and the predicted segments have coarse boundaries. Considering this problem, this chapter introduces the Context-Aware Material Segmentation Network (CAM-SegNet). The CAM-SegNet is a hybrid network architecture to simultaneously learn from contextual and material features jointly with labelled materials. The effectiveness of the CAM-SegNet is demonstrated by training the network to learn boundary-related contextual features. Since the existing material datasets are sparsely labelled, a self-training approach is adopted to fill in the unlabelled pixels. Experiments show that CAM-SegNet can identify materials correctly, even with similar appearances. The network improves the pixel accuracy by 3–20% and raises the Mean IoU by 6–28%.

Keywords: Dense material segmentation · Material recognition ·
Deep learning · Scene understanding · Image segmentation

1 Introduction

The dense material segmentation task aims to recognise the physical material categories (*e.g.* metal, plastic, stone, etc.) for each pixel in the input image. The

---

Supported by the University of Southampton.

A. A. de Sousa et al. (Eds.): VISIGRAPP 2022, CCIS 1815, pp. 66–88, 2023.
https://doi.org/10.1007/978-3-031-45725-8_4

material cues can provide critical information to many applications, such as robot manipulation [38,54] and spatial audio synthesis [6,22,30]. One example is to teach a robot to perform actions such as "cut" with a tool. This action indicates that the robot should grasp a knife at the wooden grip and cut with the metal blade [38]. For scenarios that can harm the human body, e.g.nuclear garbage collection, robots need material labels to put the waste into corresponding bins [53]. Materials can also estimate the acoustic properties (how sound interacts with surroundings [9]) from physical material categories to synthesise immersive sound with spatial audio reflections and reverberation [22,30,43]. Moreover, physically based rendering (PBR) [19], which is the technique used to synthesise realistic camera or LiDAR outputs, requires the material labels to decide the surface reflectivity in applications such as autonomous driving simulation [12].

One of the main challenges in the dense material segmentation task is that materials could have a variety of appearances, including colour, shape, and transparency [14]. The appearances vary when viewed in different contexts, such as objects and places [37]. For example, a metal knife is glossy under bright lighting conditions, but a rusted metal mirror can be dull. In order to achieve high accuracy, an ideal network should know all possible combinations; thus, a large dataset is necessary. However, the similarity between the appearances of different materials can make annotation work challenging. Even humans cannot identify a material precisely from rectangular RGB images, especially when the material is covered with a coat of paint [2]. Consequently, material datasets are often sparsely labelled regarding the number of images and the integrity of labelled material regions. For example, the training set segments in the Local Material Database (LMD) [36,37] cover only a tiny region of the material, as shown in the ground truth images in Fig. 5.

As suggested by [36,37], a possible solution is to combine material features and contextual features [3,18,34,36,37]. Material features allow the network to identify the categories despite their varied appearances, and contextual features can limit the possible categories of materials that appear in a given scene. Taking Fig. 1 as an example, given that the picture is taken in a kitchen, then the cupboard is probably made of wood. Here the kitchen and cupboard provide the contextual features that semantically describe the scene of the image and the object to which the material belongs. When zooming in on the cupboard, the tree-grain pattern, which is a unique texture of wood, describes the appearance of the material. The texture is one of the material features that humans can name. In turn, the generalisable features of wood can be used to infer labels for areas of the kitchen image that are also made of wood.

Unfortunately, combining material and contextual features remains a challenging task. [36,37] proposed a multi-branch network architecture [51,52]. The network adopts one branch to extract material features from image patches, and multiple pre-trained branches targeting object segmentation and scene recognition tasks to extract contextual features. The material and contextual features are concatenated to predict the material labels. They hold the belief that training a network with small image patches cropped from material regions without contextual cues can force the network to learn from the visual properties of materials. Although their work contributed a feasible method to achieve dense

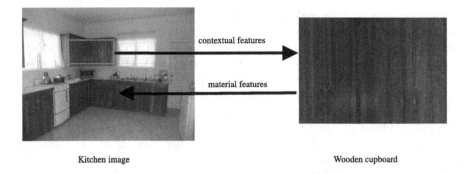

Kitchen image   Wooden cupboard

Fig. 1. The kitchen image with a wooden cupboard.

material segmentation with a neural network, the network design is still imma-
ture. The pre-trained branches that provide contextual features are not fine-
tuned together with the material branch since dedicated material datasets do
not contain contextual labels.

In order to boost the performance in dense material segmentation, this
chapter illustrates a redesigned hybrid network architecture, the CAM-SegNet.
Instead of integrating fully untangled material and contextual features, the
CAM-SegNet demonstrates that a carefully designed mechanism to combine
these features during training can improve the segmentation performance. The
CAM-SegNet consists of global, local and composite branches. The global branch
is responsible for extracting contextual features from the entire image, while
the local branch is designed to learn the material features from image patches.
Finally, the composite branch produces the material predictions from merged
features. This chapter demonstrates the efficiency of CAM-SegNet by adjusting the global branch to extract boundary-related contextual features with the
loss function that measures the alignment between generated and ground truth
material boundaries.

Since existing datasets are sparsely labelled, a self-training approach is
adopted to augment the datasets with predicted labels. The networks are evaluated on the sparse LMD test set and the dense LMD (DLMD) test set. The
DLMD contains eight densely labelled indoor scene images. The CAM-SegNet
achieves an improvement of 3–20% in pixel accuracy (Pixel Acc) and 6–28% in
Mean Intersection over Union (Mean IoU) against the state-of-the-art (SOTA)
network architectures and single-branch approaches in the control group. Moreover, the BCAM-SegNet can ensure that accuracy does not decline with the
iterative self-training approach.

The main features of CAM-SegNet are the following:

– A CAM-SegNet to combine extracted boundary features with material features.
– A self-training approach to augment sparsely labelled datasets to provide
  boundary features for the Boundary CAM-SegNet.

This chapter is an extended version of the conference paper [18], with
extra introduction of material segmentation applications, additional related work

explanation, detailed network architecture explanation, and some new segmented image analysis.

2 Related Works

This section reviews recent material datasets and relevant image segmentation techniques based on deep learning, such as Fully Convolutional Network (FCN) and global-local training.

2.1 Material Segmentation Datasets

In the computer vision domain, the material can be considered as an additional property of an object. Knowing what an object is made of provides one more clue to identify the object. Therefore, some researchers chose to add material segments to existing object segmentation datasets. For instance, [13] enhanced the Pascal dataset[1] [11,56] extended the NYU dataset[2] [39], both with eight material attributes. These material attributes contain both material categories and material traits. For example, the attributed Pascal contains four material categories, such as "metal" and "plastic", and four material traits, such as "furry" and "shiny". Their work makes it possible to segment materials with neuron networks. However, the limited number of material categories is not enough for applications such as room acoustic rendering [22].

In order to fulfill the needs of a dedicated material segmentation dataset, [2] created the OpenSurfaces[3]. It is the first large-scale, high-resolution material dataset that contains more than one hundred thousand segments belonging to 45 categories. However, it is highly unbalanced, and some categories, such as "sponge", contain only a few samples. [3] further extended the OpenSurfaces with more image samples in the unbalanced categories and then organised the dataset into 23 mutually exclusive material categories. They named this new dataset Material in Context (MINC[4]). However, the MINC contains only labelled pixels rather than segments in the training set. As a consequence, it is not trivial to train a neural network with it in an end-to-end manner.

Recently, [37] released the Local Material Database (LMD[5]), which contains 5,845 images with material segments that each covers a single category. The authors carefully chose 16 material categories without controversial ones such as "carpet" and "sky" in the OpenSurfaces and MINC. The well-annotated segments and dedicated material categories make LMD the most suitable material dataset for effective deep learning methods. The drawback is that this dataset is coarsely labelled. First of all, the number of samples is insufficient since the LMD is very diverse in terms of material categories and scenes. Second, the

---

[1] https://vision.cs.uiuc.edu/attributes/.

[2] https://kylezheng.org/research-projects/densesegattobj/.

[3] http://opensurfaces.cs.cornell.edu/.

[4] http://opensurfaces.cs.cornell.edu/publications/minc/.

[5] https://vision.ist.i.kyoto-u.ac.jp/codeanddata/localmatdb/.

ground truth segments do not cover all pixels belonging to the same category, as shown in Fig. 5. Accordingly, it is difficult for networks to recognise the materials precisely, especially for pixels near the boundary.

2.2 Fully Convolutional Network

Before stepping into the material segmentation task, this section first introduces the concepts of neural networks. From the perspective of mathematics, a basic neural network can be considered as a series of matrix multiplications followed by non-linear transformations [28]. These operations are applied to the input data in a hierarchical fashion. In other words, a neural network constructs a complex non-linear mapping $f_\theta(x) = \hat{y}$ that links the input x to its predicted label $\hat{y}$. The training process of a network is to tune the parameters θ in the matrix in a certain way so that the average loss $\bar{l}(y, \hat{y})$ is minimised. Here the loss function measures the difference between $\hat{y}$ and its corresponding ground-truth label y for all the training samples in a dataset. This chapter prefers using a particular network named the Fully Convolutional Network (FCN) in the semantic segmentation realm. It consists of convolutional (Conv) kernels that perform the sum of Hadamard product (also known as element-wise product) on patch regions of the input data.

[29] proposed the first FCN architecture trained end-to-end to achieve dense segmentation. The FCN fully adopts Conv kernels so that it takes images of arbitrary size as input. [33] further improved this architecture to a more elegant U-shaped network (U-Net), which contains a downsampling encoder to extract features, and an upsampling decoder to recover the shape and make predictions. The U-Net also contains skip-connections that copy and paste extracted features from the encoder, which may ease the optimisation problem [27]. This U-Net architecture won the 2015 ISBI neuronal structures segmentation challenge. Since then, the encoder-encoder FCN architecture and its successors tend to dominate 2D and 3D segmentation challenges, such as the Cityscapes task [5,15,44] and the SemanticKITTI benchmark [31,60]. They show that FCN can make dense segmentation predictions with high accuracy as well as good segment boundaries. The introduced CAM-SegNet also follow this encoder-decoder FCN architecture.

2.3 Material Segmentation with FCN

Recent achievements in material segmentation using datasets mentioned in Sect. 2.1 are also based on the FCN architecture. Since every dataset has its flaws, extra processes are necessary to segment images densely. For the MINC that contains only pixel labels, [3] trained a classifier to recognise the central point of the image patch, which covers about 5%[6] of the area of the whole image. After that, they replaced the fully connected (FC) kernel with an equivalent Conv kernel [29] and removed the global pooling layer to work as a sliding-window segmentation network. Finally, the nearest-neighbour interpolation operation upsamples

---

[6] The patch size is 23.3% of the smaller image dimension and can cover up to 5.29% of the area of the image.

the predicted segments to the same size as the input images. Although their best attempt achieved an accuracy of 79.8%, more advanced network structures are not suitable for the MINC since its training set contains no labelled segments.

For the LMD, since the training set contains single-material segments, it is possible to achieve dense material segmentation with an end-to-end FCN network. [35] claimed that for the material segmentation task, it is better to train an FCN network with cropped image patches (without contextual cues about object and scene) to force the network to focus on the generalisable material features. [36] then discovered that integrating contextual information can reduce the uncertainty in identifying materials. They proposed an FCN network which takes 48 × 48 image patches as input and concatenated contextual features before the final layer. The contextual features are extracted from two parallel network branches, pre-trained on the ADE20K[7] [58] and the SUN[8] [47,48] separately. Although their method improved the segmentation performance, it runs three branches in parallel and costs unacceptable computing resources for real-time applications. Moreover, since the contextual branches are not fine-tuned with the LMD, they may not be able to extract high-quality contextual features. In contrast, the CAM-SegNet adopts the boundary information, which does not require extra labels. It also shares the features between the material branch and the contextual branch so that they can jointly learn the features together. The training strategies discussed above all utilised the Conditional Random Field (CRF) to refine the segmentation result to get a clear boundary between different materials. This chapter will introduce CRF further in Sect. 2.5.

2.4   Global and Local Training

Global and local training is an approach to combine features extracted from full-size images by the global branch and image patches by the local branch. [7] adopted this approach to preserve local details when processing down-sampled images. Due to the memory bottleneck when processing high-resolution patches, they split these patches into multiple batches and gather the full feature maps with several forward steps. This method makes the feature combining process complicated and costs more training time. To reduce the training time, [51] removed trainable parameters by sharing the weights between local and global branches. [46] alleviated the training burden by proposing only critical patches to refine the global segmentation. Likewise, [20] proposed to crop the extracted global feature maps into equal blocks as the local features. For the dense material segmentation task, the CAM-SegNet compensates for the lost features when training with a single branch alone. According to [34], the network trained with original images tends to ignore material properties, while the network trained with patches drops contextual cues. Moreover, the LMD contains no high-resolution images so that the CAM-SegNet can jointly train the global and local branches in an end-to-end manner without a severe training burden.

---

[7] https://groups.csail.mit.edu/vision/datasets/ADE20K/.

[8] https://vision.princeton.edu/projects/2010/SUN/.

2.5 Boundary Refinement

For the dense material segmentation task, the network-based methods may not predict the pixels near the boundary accurately due to the lack of training labels to measure the boundary quality [36]. One possible solution is to use the Conditional Random Fields (CRF) in addition to the FCN (Sect. 2.2) to refine the segmentation quality. Another possible way to refine the boundary is to use the boundary loss [4], which measures the proportion of overlapping boundary pixels between ground truth segments and predicted segments.

Conditional Random Fields. CRF is a powerful tool to predict labels with the consideration of neighbouring pixels [42]. For image segmentation task, CRF optimises two penalties: the single pixel prediction should be the same as ground truth label (also known as the unary term), and the assumption that adjacent pixels should have the same class label (the pairwise term, as shown in Eq. 1). Here $\hat{y}$ is the predicted label for a pixel, w_p is the weight of this pairwise term in the loss function, δ is the Potts label compatibility function. $\delta = 1$ if $\hat{y_i} \neq \hat{y_j}$ else 0. k is the unit Gaussian kernel, which measures the difference between $\mathbf{f}_i$ and $\mathbf{f}_j$, where $\mathbf{f}$ is decided by the pixel position and raw pixel value in the original image.

$$\psi_{ij}(\hat{y_i}, \hat{y_j}) = w_p \delta(\hat{y_i} \neq \hat{y_j}) k(\mathbf{f}_i - \mathbf{f}_j) \tag{1}$$

The research of CRF focuses on how to decide that two pixels are neighbours and should be classified as the same category. [23] proposed the well-known dense-CRF, which assumes that a pixel is adjacent to all other pixels. Although dense-CRF is powerful for material segmentation [3], the parameters cannot be optimised together with the network. Moreover, tuning the parameters manually can be a time-consuming task. According to the supplemental code in [3], the CRF refined predictions are sensitive to the parameter choices. To cope with the problem, [57] implemented the dense-CRF model as a recurrent neural network (CRFasRNN) so that the CRF parameters can be optimised together with the network. However, it is difficult to accelerate the training process of the CRFasRNN with GPU [45].

This chapter evaluates two GPU trainable CRF variants, the Convolutional CRF (Conv-CRF) [45] and the Pixel-adaptive Convolutional CRF (PAC-CRF) [41], to speed up the training process. [45] managed to implement a GPU trainable Conv-CRF, with the locality assumption that the pairwise term (Eq. 1) is zero if the same Conv kernel does not cover the two pixels. They proved that the Conv-CRF segmentation performance is still comparable with the dense-CRF with the local assumption. At the same time, [41] proposed another GPU-trainable PAC-CRF. The PAC-CRF obeys the locality assumption and considers long-range dependency with the dilated kernel. Although PAC-CRF can predict segments more accurately compared with Conv-CRF [41], it consumes more memory and requires longer computing time. For the CAM-SegNet, Sect. 5.3 evaluates both of these two CRF methods and shows that the PAC-CRF can be affected by the material texture and can give wrong predictions.

Boundary Loss Function. Another method to refine the boundary is to use a loss function that measures the quality of the segmentation boundary. One straightforward choice is the IoU between ground truth segments and predicted segments for each material category. Another way is to measure the overlapping between boundary pixels for each category. However, both methods are count-based, which is not differentiable, and thus cannot be used to train networks directly. [32] proposed a Soft IoU loss, which adopts the continuous predicted output from the sigmoid layer in the IoU function. [4] utilised the max pooling operation to generate the segment boundaries for both ground truth segments as well as predicted segments after the sigmoid layer. Then they use pixel-wise multiplication to extract the overlapping pixels between them. To avoid the non-differentiable operation argmax, these two losses are defined directly on the extracted feature maps. This chapter adopts the boundary loss in [4] to train the networks since it is explicitly designed to refine the boundaries.

Although experiments in [4,21] have shown that this boundary loss can help the network to optimise the predictions near the boundaries, the loss value may not decrease when used in isolation since it does not contribute to the segmentation accuracy directly. Therefore, the local branch features, designed to achieve high accuracy, are passed to the global branch to ensure the BCAM-SegNet can extract boundary features steadily. Moreover, the boundary loss function assumes that the ground truth segments should cover all adjacent pixels belonging to the same category. As a consequence, the boundary loss cannot be used for the MINC and LMD databases directly. Section 2.6 introduces a solution, the self-training strategy, which can provide pseudo labels for the unlabelled pixels.

2.6   Self-training

Semi-supervised learning is one possible way to improve the segmentation results with sparsely labelled datasets. It utilises both labelled and unlabeled pixels during training. Among all semi-supervised learning approaches [59], self-training is the most simple yet efficient one to fill in unlabelled pixels with generated pseudo labels. Recent experiments show that this approach can achieve state-of-the-art segmentation performance with limited labelled samples [8,24,61]. Although the self-training method may introduce more misclassified labels as noise to the dataset compared with more robust methods based on a discriminator to control pseudo label quality [40], the noise can also prevent the network from overfitting [16, p. 241] since the LMD is a small dataset. Therefore, this chapter chooses the self-training method to generate pseudo labels and provide the boundary information for the CAM-SegNet. The experiments show that the self-training approach is not the factor that improves performance. Instead, the combined boundary and material features are the reason why the CAM-SegNet can perform well.

3   CAM-SegNet Architecture

This section presents the architecture of the CAM-SegNet, which is designed for the dense material segmentation task. Figure 2 illustrates the overall net-

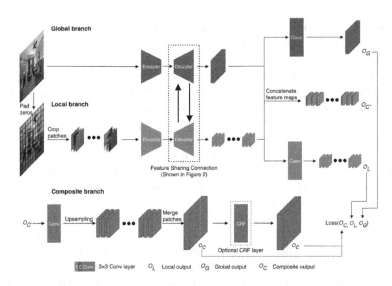

Fig. 2. CAM-SegNet architecture [18]. The feature maps in the decoders are shared between the global and local branches. After the encoder-decoder component, the feature maps at the same spatial location are concatenated together and passed into the composite branch, which upsamples the feature maps to the same size as the original input image. The composite output can be refined by an optional CRF layer.

work structure. The network contains three branches. Its global branch extracts global-related features from the original image, and the local branch learns material features from cropped patches. The encoders of these two branches downsample the feature maps and extract features independently. The decoders work together to recover the feature map size with the feature-sharing connection gradually. The decoders also generate the global branch output O_G and the local branch output O_L. Then O'_C is formed by cropping and concatenating O_G to O_L. The composite branch takes O'_C as input and processes O'_C through a series of Conv layers. The processed feature maps are merged and upsampled to generate the composite output O_C. The composite branch stays with the cropped patches to ensure that the overall network focuses on learning material information hidden in image patches. Finally, the optional CRF layer can be used to refine the composite output O_C. When training the network, the global and local branch outputs O_G, O_L are used to make the network learn contextual and material features by applying specific loss functions. When inferring new images, only the composite output O_C is kept to generate the final segmentation.

3.1   Feature Sharing Connection

The decoders in Fig. 2 gradually upsample the feature maps with three blocks of convolutional layers. At the input of each block, the feature maps are shared between the global and local branches through the feature-sharing connec-

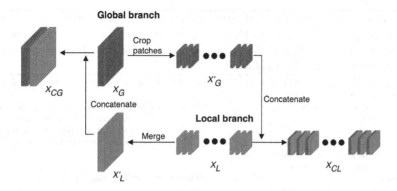

Fig. 3. The feature-sharing connection between the decoders [18]. X_{CG} is the concatenated global branch feature maps, while X_{CL} is the concatenated local branch feature maps.

tion to train the local and global branches collaboratively. The feature-sharing connection architecture is detailed in Fig. 3. The feature maps are defined as $X_G \in \mathbb{R}^{c \times h_G \times w_G}$ for the global branch, and $X_L \in \mathbb{R}^{b \times c \times h_L \times w_L}$ for the local branch. Here c represents the number of channels, h, w are the height and width of the feature maps, and b is the number of patches cropped from X_G. First, the global branch feature maps X_G are cropped into patches with the same size as X_L, $X'_G \in \mathbb{R}^{b \times c \times h_L \times w_L}$. These cropped patches are concatenated with the local branch feature maps X_L. Then the feature maps X_L from the local branch are merged together to produce $X'_L \in \mathbb{R}^{c \times h_G \times w_G}$, whose resolution is the same as X_G. Finally, the merged feature maps X'_L are concatenated with the global branch feature maps X_G. After concatenating the feature maps, the concatenated features X_{CG} and X_{CL} are produced with doubled channel number $2c$. To ensure that the matched global and local feature maps are learning from the same image region, the patch cropping method used to crop the input images is adopted, as described in Algorithm 1. The feature merging process is precisely the reversed cropping operation, and the overlapping pixels between patches are averaged.

Algorithm 1. This algorithm is designed to calculate the parameters when cropping the input images or feature maps. The same parameters are used to merge the patches to ensure the feature value at the corresponding position describes the same image region in the global and the local branch.

```
 1: procedure GETPATCHINFO(PatchSize, S)          ▷ S is the height or width of the original image
 2:     Initialize
 3:         num_patch ← 0                          ▷ Number of patches cropped alone one dimension
 4:         stride ← 0                                      ▷ Number of pixels to next patch
 5:         pad ← 0                                ▷ Number of zeros to pad at a particular dimension
 6:     if S mod patch_size equal 0 then                ▷ When the patches accurately cover the image
 7:         num_patch ← S divide patch_size
 8:         stride ← patch_size
 9:     else                                        ▷ Allow padding and overlapping for one more patch
10:         num_patch ← (S divide patch_size) plus 1
11:         stride ← (S divide num_patch) plus 1
12:         pad ← (stride multiply (num_patch minus 1)) plus patch_size minus S
13:     end if
14:     return num_patch, stride, pad
15: end procedure
```

3.2 Context-Aware Dense Material Segmentation

The CAM-SegNet generates three outputs (O_G, O_L, O_C) from the global, local and composite branches. By optimising the branches to achieve different tasks, it is convenient to control the features extracted from each branch. The total loss function L_{total} [18] applied to CAM-SegNet outputs can be represented as

$$L_{total} = L_{global}(O_G, Y_{1/4}) + L_{local}(O_L, Y_{1/4}) + L_{composite}(O_C, Y) \tag{2}$$

where Y is the ground truth segment, and $Y_{1/4}$ is the quarterly downsampled ground truth segment. The downsampled ground truth reduces the memory capacity needed during training. Since the output of the composite branch, O_C, is designed to produce a final prediction, its size is the same as the input image. The objective of the CAM-SegNet is to generate dense material segmentation with combined contextual and material features. According to Schwartz and Nishino [34, 36, 37], cropped image patches without contextual cues can force the network to learn local material features. Since the local branch takes image patches as input, it is optimised to predict material categories correctly with the focal loss [26], i.e., $L_{focal} = \frac{1}{N} \sum_i -(1 - p_i)^3 log(p_i)$. Here N is the number of pixels in O_L, and p_i is the estimated probability of pixel i for the correct category. Similarly, the global branch is optimised to extract contextual features from the full image. However, as a supervised training task, traditional contextual labels (e.g.objects or places) are needed to train the network. Although these features can reduce the material segmentation uncertainty [36], the cost of annotating extra labels is not desired.

Instead of annotating images with contextual labels, the CAM-SegNet optimises the global branch to refine the material boundaries. For pixels along the boundaries of material category c, let R^c, P^c be the recall and precision score. To provide boundary-related features, the boundary loss [4], $L_{boundary} = \sum_c 1 - \frac{2R^c P^c}{R^c + P^c}$, is applied to the global branch output O_G, which measures the alignment of the predicted material boundaries and the ground-truth segment boundaries. Since the boundary information is lost in the image patches, the features extracted from the global branch should be able to improve the segmentation quality, especially for pixels near the boundary between different materials.

Ideally, the composite branch should be able to predict material labels correctly with clean boundary between different materials. Therefore, we set the composite branch loss function $L_{composite}$ to $L_{boundary}(O_C, Y) + L_{focal}(O_C, Y)$ to ensure that it is optimized to achieve both objectives.

3.3   Self-training Approach

Since the LMD is a sparsely annotated dataset, not all training segments cover the whole material region. Consequently, the detected ground truth material boundary may not properly separate different materials and can mislead the boundary loss [4]. Therefore, we decide to fill in the missing labels with the self-training approach [61]. The idea behind self-training is to treat the pseudo labels generated by a teacher network as ground truth labels, and use the augmented dataset to train another student network. For the CAM-SegNet, this chapter assumes that the LMD augmented with pseudo labels can provide necessary information to validate the boundary loss. There are four stages in the detailed teacher-student self-training approach:

1. The initial teacher model is trained by optimising all three branches to achieve high segmentation accuracy. At this step, no boundary loss is applied.
2. The initial teacher model generates O_C in Fig. 2 for the unlabelled pixels. The labelled pixels are filled in with provided ground truth.
3. The generated feature maps are refined by the CRF layers to obtain better material boundaries. The LMD is then augmented with refined pseudo-labels.
4. A new student CAM-SegNet is trained with the augmented LMD and the boundary loss is enabled.

The aforementioned self-training process can be repeated [8,24,61] many times to improve the pseudo label quality and achieve an acceptable performance. When repeating the process, the student model trained at round t is considered as the new teacher model, to produce a new augmented dataset with the second and third stages. Then this dataset is used to produce a new student model, S_{t+1} with the forth stage. However, the self-training approach may not work well if the initial teacher model is not good enough to predict most of the labels correctly. According to Bank et al. [1], an initial accuracy below 70% may not improve the network performance. Since the reported material segmentation accuracy is merely above or below 70% [3,36,37], it is not expected to achieve a significant improvement with the self-training approach. Instead, this chapter wants to illustrate that the additional boundary information can improve the segment boundary quality, and the self-training approach is one of the possible options to provide such information. The results in Table 3 show that the CAM-SegNet performs better with the boundary information produced by the self-training approach.

4   CAM-SegNet Experiment Configurations

4.1   Dataset

This chapter evaluates the CAM-SegNet on the local material database (LMD) [36,37]. Following their suggestions, this chapter crops the images into 48 × 48 patches. The full dataset is randomly split into three splits: training (70%), validation (15%) and test (15%). Since the LMD is sparsely labelled, it is worth pointing out that the LMD test set can only reflect the network performance on inner points of the material regions. Therefore, this chapter exhaustively labelled eight indoor images in the LMD test set to evaluate how the network performs on dense segmentation task. These eight images are referred as DLMD in the evaluations.

4.2   Evaluation Metrics

The network performance is evaluated with the per-pixel average accuracy (Pixel Acc) and the mean intersection over union value (Mean IoU). We want to emphasise that IoU is not a suitable metric since it assumes that the ground truth segments are densely labelled. For the LMD, The intersection between predicted and ground truth segments would be smaller than it should be. Consequently, the IoU score may worsen when the network performs better. To illustrate the advantage of the CAM-SegNet, this chapter chooses to evaluate three more networks: DeepLabV3+ [5], BiSeNetV2 [50], and PSPNet [55], implemented by [49]. The training procedures of these networks are adopted from their original papers.

4.3   Implementation Details

In the experiments, the ResNet-50 [17] pre-trained on ImageNet [10] is used as the network encoder for the CAM-SegNet and the three baseline models. The Feature Pyramid Network (FPN) [25] is used as the CAM-SegNet decoder. Between the encoder and the decoder, the skip connections are added to keep the low layer information [7]. However, the suggested patch size 48 is not divisible by 32, which is the encoder downsampling factor. One way is to pad the feature map with zeros at the input of the fourth stage of ResNet-50, but this method can cause a spatial mismatch problem between the local and global feature maps. Therefore, the stride of the last convolutional layer is changed from 2 to 1 and the new downsampling factor is 16. Since the recent study of dense material segmentation [36,37] did not release the training configurations, this chapter follows the work in [3] and normalises the images by subtracting the mean (124, 117, 104) for the R, G, B channels respectively. The trainable Conv-CRF [45] is adopted to refine the segmentation quality. The network training procedure contains three steps:

1. The Adam optimiser with a learning rate of 0.00002 is used to train the network without a CRF layer.
2. The network parameters are frozen to train the CRF layer with a learning rate of 0.001.
3. The network is refined with the CRF layer with a learning rate of 0.0000001.

Each stage is trained for 40 epochs and the network that achieves the highest Pixel Acc is reported. Since the images have different resolutions, the batch training is not easy. In the experiment, the network gradients are accumulated to achieve an equivalent batch size of 32. According to [7], a mean squared error regularisation term between the global and local outputs can help the network to learn from both branches. This regularisation term is removed after step 1 to encourage the global and local branches to learn more diverse features. The self-training approach is repeated three times.

5   CAM-SegNet Performance Analysis

5.1   Quantitative Analysis

Table 1 reports the performance that compares the CAM-SegNet against the baseline models. CAM-SegNet achieves the best performance in Pixel Acc as well as Mean IoU. When evaluated on the LMD, the CAM-SegNet achieves a 3.25% improvement in Pixel Acc and 27.90% improvement in Mean IoU, compared with the second-highest score achieved by DeepLabV3+. In order to illustrate the model performance evaluated with densely labelled segments, seven common materials that exist in indoor scenes from DLMD are chosen to report the per-category Pixel Acc values. One discovery is that DeepLabV3+, BiSeNetV2 and PSPNet got low scores on materials that cover a small area of the image, such as foliage (plants for decoration) and paper. Another observation is that these three networks can achieve comparable performance for categories that usually cover a large area of the image, such as plaster (material of the wall and ceiling) and wood (usually wooden furniture).

One explanation for the low scores may be that these networks focus too much on global features and fail to learn from local material features such as texture. In detail, the PSPNet relies on the pooling layers with multiple window sizes to learn from multi-scale features. The pooling layers summarise the features in the window region, and the detail of the local information can be lost. The DeepLabV3+ uses dilated convolutional layers, which pursue global information instead of local. Although BiSeNetV2 adopts two branches to learn from local and global features, they all take full-size images as input, and the intermediate

Table 1. Quantitative evaluation results for the CAM-SegNet and baseline models [18]. The values are reported as percentage. The highest value for each evaluation metrics is in bold font. Seven common indoor materials are selected to report the performance Pixel Acc. The Pixel Acc is evaluated on both LMD (the second column) and DLMD (the first column). Since LMD test set provides sparsely labelled images, it is not meaningful to report Mean IoU on LMD. Therefore, Mean IoU is reported on DLMD only.

Models	ceramic	fabric	foliage	glass	paper	plaster	wood	Pixel Acc		Mean IoU
DeepLabV3+	**97.68**	27.56	0.00	48.91	0.00	**88.94**	73.69	71.37	67.09	32.04
BiSeNetV2	18.86	3.07	0.00	23.00	0.34	58.68	70.77	45.66	37.66	15.08
PSPNet	55.59	0.12	0.00	**66.73**	1.47	79.25	73.76	50.12	52.11	23.39
CAM-SegNet (ours)	92.65	**32.72**	**88.81**	21.99	**30.67**	87.77	**93.82**	**71.65**	**69.27**	**40.98**

layers do not communicate during training. The local features can fade out during training, especially when the image resolution is low. Consequently, these networks depend on global features and may not recognise small material regions well. In contrast, the CAM-SegNet adopts full-size images and cropped patches to learn from the global and local features, which are combined and co-trained. The dedicated branches enable the CAM-SegNet to recognise materials that are hard to identify (foliage and paper) for the baseline models.

5.2 Qualitative Analysis

Since this chapter mainly focuses on dense material segmentation for indoor scenes, this section qualitatively evaluates the segmentation results only with images taken in indoor scenes such as kitchens and living rooms. Figure 4 compares the segmentation quality of the CAM-SegNet with the DeepLabV3+, which is the second-best model. From the segmented images, it is clear that the CAM-SegNet can adequately segment the boundary between the ceramic floor and the wooden cupboard in the kitchen image. The segmented toilet image shows that CAM-SegNet successfully separates the ceramic close-stool from the wall covered with plaster. The qualitative discovery is consistent with the Mean IoU score, indicating that CAM-SegNet is better at recognising pixels around material boundaries than DeepLabV3+.

5.3 Ablation Study

Table 2 and 3 report the evaluated effectiveness of the CAM-SegNet components. The components include the network architecture designs, the loss function configurations, and the CRF layer choices. For fairness, all models are trained with the same training procedure as the CAM-SegNet. In detail, to show the advantages of the two-branch architecture, two single-branch models are trained with full-size images and image patches separately. They are referred to as the Global and Local models, respectively.

Since the LMD is a sparsely labelled dataset, it is not straightforward to study how the boundary information influences the network performance without the self-training approach. Therefore, this chapter chooses to retrain the CAM-SegNet by replacing the boundary loss with focal loss [26] and following the same self-training procedure described in Sect. 3.3. The trained model is named the Self-Adaptive CAM-SegNet (SACAM-SegNet), which indicates that the global branch decides what contextual features to learn from the full image. To avoid confusion, the CAM-SegNet trained to extract boundary features is referred to as the Boundary CAM-SegNet or BCAM-SegNet.

Table 2 shows the study of the SACAM-SegNet without the boundary information and the self-training approach. The SACAM-SegNet improves 12–20% on Pixel Acc and 6–19% on Mean IoU, compared with single branch models. The excellent performance of the SACAM-SegNet indicates that the hybrid design is profitable. As for the CRF choices, although PAC-CRF refined models tend to get higher Pixel Acc, Conv-CRF refined models can achieve higher Mean IoU. Their performance indicates that the Conv-CRF should be the suitable choice if the boundary quality is preferred.

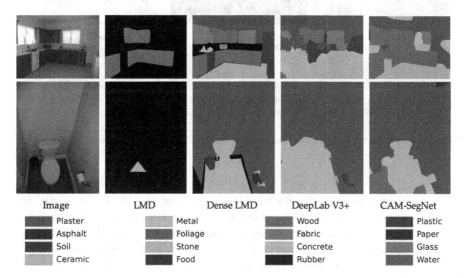

| Image | LMD | Dense LMD | DeepLab V3+ | CAM-SegNet |

Plaster	Metal	Wood	Plastic
Asphalt	Foliage	Fabric	Paper
Soil	Stone	Concrete	Glass
Ceramic	Food	Rubber	Water

Fig. 4. Qualitative comparison [18]. The sparsely labelled images are taken from LMD test set, and densely labelled with all known material categories manually.

Table 2. Quantitative results for the SACAM-SegNet and single branch models [18]. Our network outperforms single branch models.

Metric	CRF Layer	Local	Global	SACAM-SegNet
Pixel Acc	PAC-CRF	61.95	60.58	**69.25**
	Conv-CRF	58.07	55.67	**66.83**
Mean IoU	PAC-CRF	27.07	30.52	**32.25**
	Conv-CRF	31.77	32.25	**34.16**

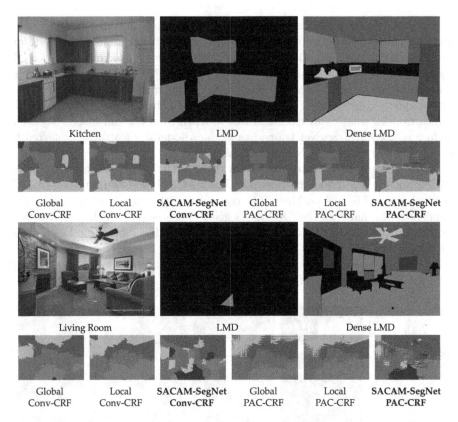

Fig. 5. Dense material segmentation results for Kitchen and Living Room images [18].

Figure 5 shows that the SACAM-SegNet can produce correct labels for pixels that are hard to recognise for the Global or Local models. For example, the SACAM-SegNet can correctly label the kitchen window as glass. Moreover, the CAM-SegNet can ignore object boundaries and cover all adjacent pixels belonging to the same material category. A good example is the ceiling and the wall of the living room picture. Surprisingly, the SACAM-SegNet can distinguish between the scene outside the window and the scene drawing in the painting in the living room and successfully classify them as glass and paper, respectively. However, it is also noticed that the PAC-CRF refined SACAM-SegNet tends to predict wrong labels if the material region has rich textural clues. For example, the striped curtain covers the window in the kitchen. The PAC-CRF forces the network to label pixels between the stripes to different categories. This behaviour is not desired since it can give wrong boundary information. That is the reason why this chapter chooses to use a Conv-CRF refined model to generate the pseudo labels.

Table 3 compares the performance between SACAM-SegNet and BCAM-SegNet with the self-training approach. Without boundary loss, the SACAM-

Table 3. Quantitative performance of the CAM-SegNet trained on augmented LMD with the self-training approach [18].

Models	SACAM-SegNet		BCAM-SegNet	
	Pixel Acc	Mean IoU	Pixel Acc	Mean IoU
Student 1	66.42%	37.93	67.38%	39.26
Student 2	67.26%	38.97	68.18%	39.81
Student 3	64.85%	32.19	**69.27%**	**40.98**

SegNet performs worse compared with the BCAM-SegNet. This shows that self-training alone does not result in the good performance of the BCAM-SegNet. The boundary information can stabilise the CAM-SegNet to learn from noisy pseudo labels and gradually correct the pseudo labels to achieve higher accuracy. More segmentation images generated by the SACAM-SegNet refigned by the Conv-CRF [45] layer are shown in Fig. 6. Extra segmentation images generated by the three BCAM-SegNet student models trained with the self-training

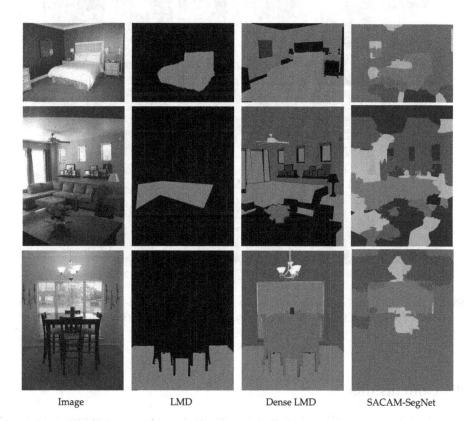

Image   LMD   Dense LMD   SACAM-SegNet

Fig. 6. Dense material segmentation results for the SACAM-SegNet, refined by the Conv-CRF layer. The second column images are the ground truth segments in the LMD [36,37], and the third column images are manually labelled dense segments.

approach are shown in Fig. 7. Our BCAM-SegNet managed to refine the material boundaries for some images, such as the window in the first image, and the ceramic close-stool in the sixth image.

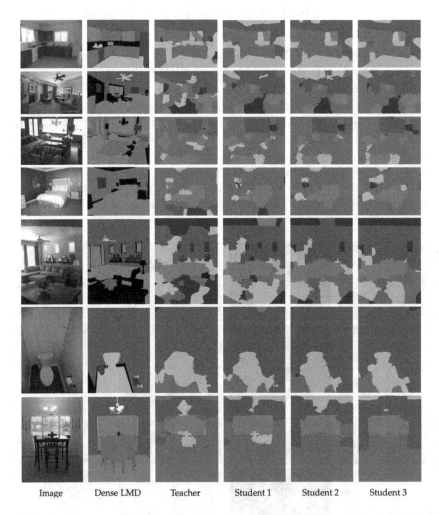

Image   Dense LMD   Teacher   Student 1   Student 2   Student 3

Fig. 7. Dense material segmentation results generated by BCAM-SegNet, refined with the Conv-CRF layer. The self-training approach is repeated three times to train Student 1, 2, and 3.

6   Conclusions

This chapter introduced a hybrid network architecture and training procedure to combine contextual features and material features. The effectiveness of the CAM-SegNet is validated with boundary contextual features. We illustrate that the combined features can help the network to recognise materials at different scales and assign the pixels around the boundaries to the correct categories. Having shown that the material segmentation tasks rely on features extracted from cropped patches, we believe it is possible to improve the network performance one step further by adjusting the patch size. In the future, we plan to investigate how to effectively extract material features from patches cropped into multiple sizes.

Acknowledgements. This work was supported by the EPSRC Programme Grant Immersive Audio-Visual 3D Scene Reproduction Using a Single 360 Camera (EP/V03538X/1).

References

1. Bank, D., Greenfeld, D., Hyams, G.: Improved training for self training by confidence assessments. In: Arai, K., Kapoor, S., Bhatia, R. (eds.) SAI 2018. AISC, vol. 858, pp. 163–173. Springer, Cham (2019). https://doi.org/10.1007/978-3-030-01174-1_13
2. Bell, S., Upchurch, P., Snavely, N., Bala, K.: OpenSurfaces: a richly annotated catalog of surface appearance. ACM Trans. Graph. (TOG) **32**(4), 1–17 (2013)
3. Bell, S., Upchurch, P., Snavely, N., Bala, K.: Material recognition in the wild with the materials in context database. In: Proceedings of the IEEE Conference on Computer Vision and Pattern Recognition, pp. 3479–3487 (2015)
4. Bokhovkin, A., Burnaev, E.: Boundary loss for remote sensing imagery semantic segmentation. In: Lu, H., Tang, H., Wang, Z. (eds.) ISNN 2019. LNCS, vol. 11555, pp. 388–401. Springer, Cham (2019). https://doi.org/10.1007/978-3-030-22808-8_38
5. Chen, L.C., Zhu, Y., Papandreou, G., Schroff, F., Adam, H.: Encoder-decoder with atrous separable convolution for semantic image segmentation. In: Proceedings of the European Conference on Computer Vision (ECCV), pp. 801–818 (2018)
6. Chen, L., Tang, W., John, N.W., Wan, T.R., Zhang, J.J.: Context-aware mixed reality: a learning-based framework for semantic-level interaction. In: Computer Graphics Forum, vol. 39, pp. 484–496. Wiley Online Library (2020)
7. Chen, W., Jiang, Z., Wang, Z., Cui, K., Qian, X.: Collaborative global-local networks for memory-efficient segmentation of ultra-high resolution images. In: Proceedings of the IEEE/CVF Conference on Computer Vision and Pattern Recognition, pp. 8924–8933 (2019)
8. Cheng, H., Gu, C., Wu, K.: Weakly-supervised semantic segmentation via self-training. In: Journal of Physics: Conference Series, vol. 1487, p. 012001. IOP Publishing (2020)
9. Delany, M., Bazley, E.: Acoustical properties of fibrous absorbent materials. Appl. Acoust. **3**(2), 105–116 (1970)
10. Deng, J., Dong, W., Socher, R., Li, L.J., Li, K., Fei-Fei, L.: Imagenet: a large-scale hierarchical image database. In: 2009 IEEE Conference on Computer Vision and Pattern Recognition, pp. 248–255. IEEE (2009)
11. Everingham, M., et al.: The 2005 PASCAL visual object classes challenge. In: Quiñonero-Candela, J., Dagan, I., Magnini, B., d'Alché-Buc, F. (eds.) MLCW 2005. LNCS (LNAI), vol. 3944, pp. 117–176. Springer, Heidelberg (2006). https://doi.org/10.1007/11736790_8

12. Eversberg, L., Lambrecht, J.: Generating images with physics-based rendering for an industrial object detection task: realism versus domain randomization. Sensors **21**(23), 7901 (2021)
13. Farhadi, A., Endres, I., Hoiem, D., Forsyth, D.: Describing objects by their attributes. In: 2009 IEEE Conference on Computer Vision and Pattern Recognition, pp. 1778–1785. IEEE (2009)
14. Fleming, R.W.: Visual perception of materials and their properties. Vision. Res. **94**, 62–75 (2014). https://doi.org/10.1016/j.visres.2013.11.004
15. Ghiasi, G., Fowlkes, C.C.: Laplacian pyramid reconstruction and refinement for semantic segmentation. In: Leibe, B., Matas, J., Sebe, N., Welling, M. (eds.) ECCV 2016. LNCS, vol. 9907, pp. 519–534. Springer, Cham (2016). https://doi.org/10.1007/978-3-319-46487-9_32
16. Goodfellow, I., Bengio, Y., Courville, A.: Deep Learning. MIT Press, Cambridge (2016)
17. He, K., Zhang, X., Ren, S., Sun, J.: Deep residual learning for image recognition. In: Proceedings of the IEEE Conference on Computer Vision and Pattern Recognition, pp. 770–778 (2016)
18. Heng, Y., Wu, Y., Kim, H., Dasmahapatra, S.: Cam-segnet: a context-aware dense material segmentation network for sparsely labelled datasets. In: 17th International Conference on Computer Vision Theory and Applications (VISAPP), vol. 5, pp. 190–201 (2022)
19. Hodaň, T., et al.: Photorealistic image synthesis for object instance detection. In: 2019 IEEE International Conference on Image Processing (ICIP), pp. 66–70. IEEE (2019)
20. Iodice, S., Mikolajczyk, K.: Text attribute aggregation and visual feature decomposition for person search. In: BMVC (2020)
21. Kang, J., Fernandez-Beltran, R., Sun, X., Ni, J., Plaza, A.: Deep learning-based building footprint extraction with missing annotations. IEEE Geosci. Remote Sens. Lett. **19**, 1–5 (2021)
22. Kim, H., Remaggi, L., Jackson, P.J., Hilton, A.: Immersive spatial audio reproduction for VR/AR using room acoustic modelling from 360 images. In: 2019 IEEE Conference on Virtual Reality and 3D User Interfaces (VR), pp. 120–126. IEEE (2019)
23. Krähenbühl, P., Koltun, V.: Parameter learning and convergent inference for dense random fields. In: International Conference on Machine Learning, pp. 513–521. PMLR (2013)
24. Le, T.H.N., Luu, K., Savvides, M.: Fast and robust self-training beard/moustache detection and segmentation. In: 2015 International Conference on Biometrics (ICB), pp. 507–512. IEEE (2015)
25. Lin, T.Y., Dollár, P., Girshick, R., He, K., Hariharan, B., Belongie, S.: Feature pyramid networks for object detection. In: Proceedings of the IEEE Conference on Computer Vision and Pattern Recognition, pp. 2117–2125 (2017)
26. Lin, T.Y., Goyal, P., Girshick, R., He, K., Dollár, P.: Focal loss for dense object detection. In: Proceedings of the IEEE International Conference on Computer Vision, pp. 2980–2988 (2017)
27. Liu, F., Ren, X., Zhang, Z., Sun, X., Zou, Y.: Rethinking skip connection with layer normalization. In: Proceedings of the 28th International Conference on Computational Linguistics, pp. 3586–3598 (2020)
28. Liu, Z., Chow, P., Xu, J., Jiang, J., Dou, Y., Zhou, J.: A uniform architecture design for accelerating 2D and 3D CNNs on FPGAs. Electronics **8**(1), 65 (2019)

29. Long, J., Shelhamer, E., Darrell, T.: Fully convolutional networks for semantic segmentation. In: Proceedings of the IEEE Conference on Computer Vision and Pattern Recognition, pp. 3431–3440 (2015)
30. McDonagh, A., Lemley, J., Cassidy, R., Corcoran, P.: Synthesizing game audio using deep neural networks. In: 2018 IEEE Games, Entertainment, Media Conference (GEM), pp. 1–9. IEEE (2018)
31. Milioto, A., Vizzo, I., Behley, J., Stachniss, C.: Rangenet++: fast and accurate lidar semantic segmentation. In: 2019 IEEE/RSJ International Conference on Intelligent Robots and Systems (IROS), pp. 4213–4220. IEEE (2019)
32. Rahman, M.A., Wang, Y.: Optimizing intersection-over-union in deep neural networks for image segmentation. In: Bebis, G., et al. (eds.) ISVC 2016. LNCS, vol. 10072, pp. 234–244. Springer, Cham (2016). https://doi.org/10.1007/978-3-319-50835-1_22
33. Ronneberger, O., Fischer, P., Brox, T.: U-Net: convolutional networks for biomedical image segmentation. In: Navab, N., Hornegger, J., Wells, W.M., Frangi, A.F. (eds.) MICCAI 2015. LNCS, vol. 9351, pp. 234–241. Springer, Cham (2015). https://doi.org/10.1007/978-3-319-24574-4_28
34. Schwartz, G.: Visual Material Recognition. Drexel University (2018)
35. Schwartz, G., Nishino, K.: Visual material traits: recognizing per-pixel material context. In: Proceedings of the IEEE International Conference on Computer Vision Workshops, pp. 883–890 (2013)
36. Schwartz, G., Nishino, K.: Material recognition from local appearance in global context. In: Biology and Artificial Vision (Workshop held in conjunction with ECCV 2016) (2016)
37. Schwartz, G., Nishino, K.: Recognizing material properties from images. IEEE Trans. Pattern Anal. Mach. Intell. **42**(8), 1981–1995 (2020). https://doi.org/10.1109/TPAMI.2019.2907850
38. Shrivatsav, N., Nair, L., Chernova, S.: Tool substitution with shape and material reasoning using dual neural networks. arXiv preprint arXiv:1911.04521 (2019)
39. Silberman, N., Hoiem, D., Kohli, P., Fergus, R.: Indoor segmentation and support inference from RGBD images. In: Fitzgibbon, A., Lazebnik, S., Perona, P., Sato, Y., Schmid, C. (eds.) ECCV 2012. LNCS, vol. 7576, pp. 746–760. Springer, Heidelberg (2012). https://doi.org/10.1007/978-3-642-33715-4_54
40. Souly, N., Spampinato, C., Shah, M.: Semi supervised semantic segmentation using generative adversarial network. In: Proceedings of the IEEE International Conference on Computer Vision, pp. 5688–5696 (2017)
41. Su, H., Jampani, V., Sun, D., Gallo, O., Learned-Miller, E., Kautz, J.: Pixel-adaptive convolutional neural networks. In: Proceedings of the IEEE/CVF Conference on Computer Vision and Pattern Recognition, pp. 11166–11175 (2019)
42. Sutton, C., McCallum, A.: An introduction to conditional random fields for relational learning. In: Introduction to Statistical Relational Learning, vol. 2, pp. 93–128 (2006)
43. Tang, Z., Bryan, N.J., Li, D., Langlois, T.R., Manocha, D.: Scene-aware audio rendering via deep acoustic analysis. IEEE Trans. Visual Comput. Graphics **26**(5), 1991–2001 (2020)
44. Tao, A., Sapra, K., Catanzaro, B.: Hierarchical multi-scale attention for semantic segmentation. arXiv preprint arXiv:2005.10821 (2020)
45. Teichmann, M., Cipolla, R.: Convolutional crfs for semantic segmentation. In: BMVC (2019)

46. Wu, T., Lei, Z., Lin, B., Li, C., Qu, Y., Xie, Y.: Patch proposal network for fast semantic segmentation of high-resolution images. In: Proceedings of the AAAI Conference on Artificial Intelligence, vol. 34, pp. 12402–12409 (2020)
47. Xiao, J., Ehinger, K.A., Hays, J., Torralba, A., Oliva, A.: Sun database: exploring a large collection of scene categories. Int. J. Comput. Vision 119(1), 3–22 (2016)
48. Xiao, J., Hays, J., Ehinger, K.A., Oliva, A., Torralba, A.: Sun database: large-scale scene recognition from abbey to zoo. In: 2010 IEEE Computer Society Conference on Computer Vision and Pattern Recognition, pp. 3485–3492. IEEE (2010)
49. Yakubovskiy, P.: Segmentation models pytorch (2020). https://github.com/qubvel/segmentation_models.pytorch
50. Yu, C., Gao, C., Wang, J., Yu, G., Shen, C., Sang, N.: Bisenet v2: bilateral network with guided aggregation for real-time semantic segmentation. arXiv preprint arXiv:2004.02147 (2020)
51. Zhang, H., Liao, Y., Yang, H., Yang, G., Zhang, L.: A local-global dual-stream network for building extraction from very-high-resolution remote sensing images. IEEE Trans. Neural Netw. Learn. Syst. 33(3), 1269–1283 (2020)
52. Zhang, H., Shao, J., Salakhutdinov, R.: Deep neural networks with multi-branch architectures are intrinsically less non-convex. In: The 22nd International Conference on Artificial Intelligence and Statistics, pp. 1099–1109. PMLR (2019)
53. Zhao, C., Sun, L., Stolkin, R.: A fully end-to-end deep learning approach for real-time simultaneous 3D reconstruction and material recognition. In: 2017 18th International Conference on Advanced Robotics (ICAR), pp. 75–82. IEEE (2017)
54. Zhao, C., Sun, L., Stolkin, R.: Simultaneous material segmentation and 3D reconstruction in industrial scenarios. Front. Robot. AI 7, 52 (2020)
55. Zhao, H., Shi, J., Qi, X., Wang, X., Jia, J.: Pyramid scene parsing network. In: Proceedings of the IEEE Conference on Computer Vision and Pattern Recognition, pp. 2881–2890 (2017)
56. Zheng, S., et al.: Dense semantic image segmentation with objects and attributes. In: Proceedings of the IEEE Conference on Computer Vision and Pattern Recognition, pp. 3214–3221 (2014)
57. Zheng, S., et al.: Conditional random fields as recurrent neural networks. In: Proceedings of the IEEE International Conference on Computer Vision, pp. 1529–1537 (2015)
58. Zhou, B., Zhao, H., Puig, X., Fidler, S., Barriuso, A., Torralba, A.: Scene parsing through ADE20K dataset. In: Proceedings of the IEEE Conference on Computer Vision and Pattern Recognition, pp. 633–641 (2017)
59. Zhu, X.J.: Semi-supervised learning literature survey (2005)
60. Zhu, X., et al.: Cylindrical and asymmetrical 3D convolution networks for lidar segmentation. arXiv preprint arXiv:2011.10033 (2020)
61. Zoph, B., et al.: Rethinking pre-training and self-training. arXiv preprint arXiv:2006.06882 (2020)

Partial Alignment of Time Series for Action and Activity Prediction

Victoria Manousaki[1(✉)] and Antonis Argyros[1,2]

[1] Computer Science Department, University of Crete, Heraklion, Greece
{vmanous,argyros}@ics.forth.gr
[2] Institute of Computer Science, Foundation for Research and Technology - Hellas (FORTH), Heraklion, Greece

Abstract. The temporal alignment of two complete action/activity sequences has been the focus of interest in many research works. However, the problem of partially aligning an incomplete sequence to a complete one has not been sufficiently explored. Very effective alignment algorithms such as Dynamic Time Warping (DTW) and Soft Dynamic Time Warping (S-DTW) are not capable of handling incomplete sequences. To overcome this limitation the Open-End DTW (OE-DTW) and the Open-Begin-End DTW (OBE-DTW) algorithms were introduced. The OE-DTW has the capability to align sequences with common begin points but unknown ending points, while the OBE-DTW has the ability to align unsegmented sequences. We focus on two new alignment algorithms, namely the Open-End Soft DTW (OE-S-DTW) and the Open-Begin-End Soft DTW (OBE-S-DTW) which combine the partial alignment capabilities of OE-DTW and OBE-DTW with those of Soft DTW (S-DTW). Specifically, these algorithms have the segregational capabilities of DTW combined with the soft-minimum operator of the S-DTW algorithm that results in improved, differentiable alignment in the case of continuous, unsegmented actions/activities. The developed algorithms are well-suited tools for addressing the problem of action prediction. By properly matching and aligning an on-going, incomplete action/activity sequence to prototype, complete ones, we may gain insight in what comes next in the on-going action/activity. The proposed algorithms are evaluated on the MHAD, MHAD101-v/-s, MSR Daily Activities and CAD-120 datasets and are shown to outperform relevant state of the art approaches.

Keywords: Segregational soft dynamic time warping · Temporal alignment · Action prediction · Activity prediction · Duration prognosis · Graphs

1 Introduction

The visual observations of different executions of the same activity may vary considerably when performed by different or even the same subject. Variations are further attributed to changes in the environment, the manipulated objects the observation viewpoints and several other causes. A video showing an action/activity execution can be represented as a time series of frames, each of which is represented in a point in a multidimensional feature space. Given time-series representations of certain

© The Author(s), under exclusive license to Springer Nature Switzerland AG 2023
A. A. de Sousa et al. (Eds.): VISIGRAPP 2022, CCIS 1815, pp. 89–107, 2023.
https://doi.org/10.1007/978-3-031-45725-8_5

actions/activities, temporal alignment algorithms have been used for matching different executions in time in order to support the solution of problems such as action quality assessment [25], action co-segmentation [20], fine-grained frame retrieval [11] etc.

The Dynamic Time Warping (DTW) [26] algorithm is a commonly employed time series alignment algorithm. DTW requires that the test and reference action/activity executions need to be trimmed in order to be aligned. The alignment of two sequences is achieved by finding the minimum-cost warping path between them. The alignment path provides a one-to-one alignment between the frames of the two sequences. The Soft Dynamic Time Warping (S-DTW) [7] algorithm is a variant of the baseline DTW algorithm which finds their alignment by calculating the soft-minimum cost of all possible path-based alignments.

Both DTW and S-DTW are able to align only trimmed/segmented sequences. When the starting and ending points of the time series are known, these algorithms can provide meaningful alignments. But there are cases where the executions are not trimmed or there can be prefix or suffix noise. In such scenarios, the DTW and S-DTW algorithms fail to achieve satisfactory alignment of the input sequences. Such situations may occur, for example, when an ongoing, incomplete action needs to be matched with a completed, reference one, or when the two actions to be matched occur between other actions. Such untrimmed/unsegmented inputs can be aligned by two other DTW variants, the Open-End DTW [28] and Open-Begin-End DTW [28]. The OE-DTW is designed for aligning two sequences with known starting point but have unknown ending points. On the contrary, the OBE-DTW algorithm is not anchored to either points thus is able to align the unsegmented input without any boundary constraints.

In this paper we explore the use of two new S-DTW variants, the Open-End Soft DTW (OE-S-DTW) and Open-Begin-End Soft DTW (OBE-S-DTW). These alignment algorithms were proposed by Manousaki et al. [16] for the problem of aligning segmented and unsegmented action executions. These two variants combine the merits of OE-DTW and OBE-DTW to that of S-DTW. Specifically, similarly to OE-DTW and OBE-DTW they have reduced requirements on the knowledge of the sequence endpoints (i.e., relaxed sequence boundary constraints) and similarly to S-DTW they are differentiable. Thus, these DTW variants can be used for aligning unsegmented sequences and also as a loss function for training deep neural networks. Currently, they have been used in the framework of Manousaki et al. [16] as a tool for solving the problem of action prediction.

In this paper we build on top of the OE-S-DTW and OBE-S-DTW algorithms and we provide the following additional investigations and contributions:

– We extend the experimental evaluation of the framework of Manousaki et al. [16] by providing additional evaluations of the OE-S-DTW and OBE-S-DTW alignment algorithms on the problem of short-term human action prediction and action duration prognosis in standard datasets and in comparison to existing state of the art methods. More specifically, we present results on the duration prediction problem on the MSR Daily Activities [29] and CAD120 [13] datasets. We also evaluate the efficiency of the alignment algorithms on a new challenging action prediction scenario involving a reversed observation of the input actions.

- Differently from [16] where the evaluation of the OBE-S-DTW and OE-S-DTW algorithms is focused on the prediction of actions, we evaluate these algorithms using activities, too, that are composed of long (and therefore more complex) sequences of actions. In that direction, we evaluate OBE-S-DTW and OE-S-DTW not only using trimmed actions of the MHAD101-s/-v [22] and CAD120 [13] datasets, but also activities of the CAD120 dataset.
- In [16], the OE-S-DTW and OBE-S-DTW algorithms have been used for action prediction in a closest match-based action prediction framework. In this paper we extend the experimental evaluation of these two variants by utilizing and comparing them also in a graph-based framework for action and activity prediction [18].

2   Related Work

The temporal alignment of sequences is a problem that has been explored for many years and remains of interest until today. A classical approach is the Dynamic Time Warping [26] algorithm which is capable of aligning segmented sequences by finding the minimum-cost warping path between them. The warping path is calculated upon the distance matrix which contains all the frame-wise distances between the two sequences to be aligned. The DTW score is based on the summation of all path-related values in the distance matrix. The DTW algorithm poses boundary constraints on the warping path which means that the sequences to be aligned must start and end at known frames i.e. the first frame of the first sequence will be matched to the first frame of the second sequence. DTW has been used in a variety of problems such as action cosegmentation [22], representation learning [10], etc.

The boundary constraints of DTW have been relaxed by the work of Tormene et al. [28] who proposed the Open-End DTW (OE-DTW) algorithm. The OE-DTW variant is capable of aligning sequences that have a known common start point but unknown endpoints. This relaxation of the endpoint constraint is useful when the sequences to be matched are partially observed or when other actions appear after the end of the sequence. The OE-DTW score is provided by the summation of all values of the minimum-cost alignment path. The difference to the DTW algorithm is that the alignment path that starts at the top-left point of the distance matrix should not necessarily end at the bottom-right cell of that matrix, thus permitting a certain sequence to match with a part of a reference one. OE-DTW has been used to compare motion curves for the rehabilitation of post-stroke patients [27] as well as for the evaluation of the user's motion in visual observations of humans with Kinect [32].

Tormene et al. [28] also proposed the Open-Begin-End (OBE-DTW) [28] that aligns two unsegmented sequences, i.e., two sequences of unknown starting and ending points. The matching path defined by OBE-DTW does not necessarily have to start and end at the top-left and bottom-right cells of the distance matrix. OBE-DTW has been used in many contexts for unsegmented sequence alignment e.g., for the problem of classifying motion from depth cameras [12].

While the DTW algorithm considers the minimum-cost alignment path of the sequences, the Soft Dynamic Time Warping (S-DTW) [7] variant considers the soft-minimum of the distribution of all costs spanned by all possible alignments between two segmented sequences. This alignment score contains the summation of all path-based values. The S-DTW algorithm has been used by [11] as temporal alignment loss for training a neural network to learn better video representations. The differentiable alignment of S-DTW has also been used by Chang et al. [6] for the alignment and segmentation of actions by using the videos and the transcripts of the actions.

Segmental DTW [23] seeks for the minimum-cost sub-sequence alignment of pairs of unsegmented inputs. Segmental DTW decomposes the distance matrix in sets of overlapping areas and finds the local end-to-end alignments in these areas resulting in sub-sequence matching. Segmental DTW has been used in the context of action co-segmentation [19] in motion-capture data or video between pairs of actions for the detecting of commonalities of varying length, different actors, etc.

The Ordered Temporal Alignment Module (OTAM) [5] aligns segmented sequences of fixed length by using the soft-minimum operator and calculating all possible path-based alignments. The alignment score is given by aligning the sequences end-to-end using S-DTW, while the alignment path is retrieved by an OBE-DTW approximation. Cao et al. [5] used the OTAM alignment for few-shot video classification of fixed-length trimmed videos.

Finally, the Drop Dynamic Time Warping (Drop-DTW) [8] algorithm is a variant of DTW based on images where outliers are dropped during the alignment of sequences. Differently from OBE-DTW where the unrelated parts can be at the prefix or the suffix of an action, this DTW approximation is very useful in cases where the sequences to be aligned have unrelated parts anywhere inside the sequences. By eliminating all the irrelevant parts Drop-DTW results in more meaningful alignments.

3   Temporal Alignment of Action/Activity Sequences

Let $Q = (q_1, \ldots q_l) \in \mathbb{R}^{n \times l}$ represent a test action/activity sequence that needs to be aligned with a reference sequence $Y = (y_1, \ldots, y_m) \in \mathbb{R}^{n \times m}$. The distance matrix $D(Q, Y) = [d(q_i, y_i)]_{ij} \in \mathbb{R}^{l \times m}$ contains all Euclidean pair-wise frame distances $d(q, y)$ of frames q and y. The cumulative matrix that is based on D and represents all path-based alignments P of Q and Y, is denoted as $C(Q, Y) = \{\langle p, D(Q, Y) \rangle, p \in P_{l,m}\}$ where P represents all the alignments connecting the upper-left to the lower-right of the distance matrix. Using this notation, we proceed with presenting the employed action/activity sequence alignment methods.

3.1   Alignment Methods - Segmented Sequences

Dynamic Time Warping (DTW) [26]: The DTW algorithm aligns two sequences in their entirety by finding their minimum alignment cost. The distance matrix $D(Q, Y)$ is used to create the cumulative matrix $C(Q, Y)$. The minimum alignment cost is provided at the bottom-right cell of the cumulative matrix. Due to the variability of the sequence sizes the alignment score needs to be normalized by the length of the test sequence. The alignment cost provided by DTW is defined as:

$$DTW(Q, Y) = min_{p \in P} C(Q, Y). \tag{1}$$

Soft Dynamic Time Warping (S-DTW) [7]: The DTW algorithm has some limitations such as not being differentiable and getting stuck in local minima due to the min operator. S-DTW is a powerful extension of the original DTW algorithm which is differentiable and introduces a smoothing parameter γ that can help avoid local minima depending on the values of the smoothing parameter. In order to do so, the S-DTW takes into account all possible alignment paths contrary to DTW which calculates only the minimum cost alignment path. The limitations are alleviated by changing the minimum operator with the soft-minimum operator (see Eq. (3)). The cumulative matrix $C(x_i, y_j) = D(x_i, y_j) + min^\gamma(C(x_{i-1}, y_j), C(x_{i-1}, y_{j-1}), C(x_i, y_{j-1}))$ is calculated as in DTW by allowing horizontal, diagonal and vertical moves. The cumulative matrix is padded at the top with a row and at the left with a column so that $C_{i,0} = C_{0,j} = \infty$ for all $i, j \neq 0$ and $C_{0,0} = 0$. The S-DTW alignment cost between two sequences is defined as:

$$SDTW_\gamma(X, Y) = min^\gamma_{p \in P} C(X, Y), \qquad (2)$$

with

$$min\,\gamma(p_1, \ldots, p_k) = \begin{cases} min_{i \leq k}\, p_i, & \gamma = 0, \\ -\gamma \log \sum_{i=1}^{k} e^{p_i / \gamma} & \gamma > 0, \end{cases} \qquad (3)$$

where $\gamma \geq 0$ is a smoothing hyper-parameter. When γ is equal to zero, the DTW score is calculated.

3.2 Alignment Methods - Unsegmented Sequences

Open-End Dynamic Time Warping (OE-DTW) [28]: DTW [26] is designed and used for aligning two sequences from start to finish. When the sequences have unknown end points, DTW produces poor alignment results. A DTW variant was created to address this problem called OE-DTW. The cumulative matrix C is calculated as

$$C(x_i, y_j) = D(x_i, y_j) + min(C(x_{i-1}, y_j), C(x_{i-1}, y_{j-1}), C(x_{i-1}, y_{j-2})). \qquad (4)$$

Essentially, the alignment cost becomes the minimum value of the last row of the cumulative matrix. As explained earlier, the values need to be normalized by the size of the test sequence. Thus, the alignment cost of OE-DTW is defined as:

$$OE\text{-}DTW(X, Y) = min_{j=1,\ldots,m} DTW(X, Y_j). \qquad (5)$$

Open-Begin-End Dynamic Time Warping (OBE-DTW) [28]: There can be sequences that do not share the same beginning and ending or one sequence appears anywhere inside the other. To solve this alignment problem a variant of the DTW algorithm was created namely OBE-DTW. To calculate the alignment cost based on this variant, a row with zero values is appended at the beginning of the distance matrix and the computations are performed as in OE-DTW. The computed cumulative matrix is denoted as $C'(X, Y)$ and the alignment cost is the minimum value of the last row which were previously normalized by the length of the test sequence. The back-tracing

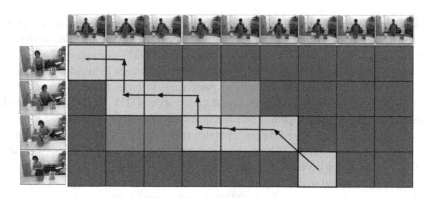

Fig. 1. Graphical illustration of the OE-S-DTW algorithm. On the horizontal axis we can observe a man performing an activity. On the vertical axis a woman is performing the same activity which is not yet completed. The light pink boxes represent the possible alignment paths while the black arrows represent a possible path. The two sequences share the same starting point but end at different points. The OE-S-DTW algorithm is able to match the partially observed activity with a part of the completely observed one. (Color figure online)

of the minimum-cost path starts from the minimum value of the last row and ends at the first zero-valued row. The OBE-DTW alignment cost is denoted as:

$$OBE\text{-}DTW(X, Y) = min_{j=1,...,m} C'(X, Y_j). \tag{6}$$

Open-End Soft DTW (OE-S-DTW) [16]: The OE-S-DTW is a newly proposed algorithm that combines the merits of the OE-DTW and S-DTW algorithms. This is a differentiable alignment algorithm that can align sequences that share the same beginning but do not share the same ending points. The distance matrix is calculated by using the pairwise distances of the reference and test sequences X and Y, respectively. The cumulative matrix is calculated as in S-DTW by using the min^γ operator as follows:

$$C(x_i, y_j) = D(x_i, y_j) + min^\gamma(C(x_{i-1}, y_j), C(x_{i-1}, y_{j-1}), C(x_i, y_{j-1})). \tag{7}$$

The scores at the last row are normalized by the query's size and the cost of alignment is the minimum of the last row. As in OE-DTW, the alignment path may terminate at any point of the last row of the cumulative matrix. Finally, the gradient is calculated from that point backwards to the common start point to find the alignment between the two sequences. The final OE-S-DTW score is also normalised by the size of the matched reference as follows:

$$OE\text{-}S\text{-}DTW(X, Y) = min^\gamma_{j=1,...,m} SDTW_\gamma(X, Y_j). \tag{8}$$

A graphical illustration of the OE-S-DTW algorithm is presented in Fig. 1.

Open-Begin-End Soft Dynamic Time Warping (OBE-S-DTW) [16]: OBE-S-DTW is an alignment algorithm that combines the beneficial properties of the OBE-DTW and S-DTW. The distance matrix $D'(X, Y)$ is created by appending the distance matrix

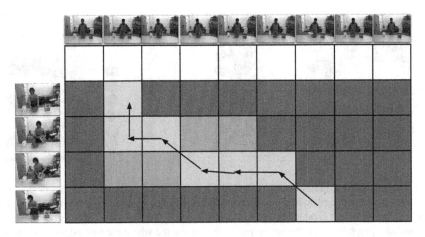

Fig. 2. Graphical illustration of the OBE-S-DTW algorithm. The activity illustrated at the left (rows) matches a part of the activity illustrated on the top (columns). At the top a zero-valued row is added. The light blue boxes represent all possible alignments while the black arrows show a possible warping path. (Color figure online)

$D(X, Y)$ with a row of zero values at the beginning. Following that, the cumulative matrix denoted as C' is calculated by using the soft-minimum operator as follows:

$$C'(x_i, y_j) = D'(x_i, y_j) + min^\gamma(C'(x_{i-1}, y_j), C'(x_{i-1}, y_{j-1}), C'(x_i, y_{j-1})). \quad (9)$$

The last row of the cumulative matrix is normalized by the test sequence size and the alignment cost is found at the minimum value of the last row. Then, the gradient is computed from that point towards the zero-valued row. The size of the matched reference corresponds to that range. The calculated gradient gives the possibility to consider all possible alignments (see Fig. 2). Once the alignment path is obtained, we normalize the alignment cost with the size of the matching part of the reference sequence. The OBE-S-DTW alignment cost is defined as:

$$OBE\text{-}S\text{-}DTW(X, Y) = min^\gamma_{j=1,...,m} C'(X, Y_j). \quad (10)$$

An illustration of the OBE-S-DTW algorithm is provided in Fig. 2.

3.3 Action and Activity Prediction

Alignment-Based Action and Activity Prediction. The action/activity prediction problem is denoted as the problem of predicting the correct label of a partially observed action/activity execution. Our intention is to solve the problem of action and activity prediction by matching reference and test action executions. To do so, prototype executions are aligned with incomplete executions and the inference of the label is done by reporting the label of the closest matching prototype execution to the incomplete one as in Manousaki et al. [17]. More specifically, we fuse the human and object representations by calculating the weighted sum of the respective distance matrices. If the actions

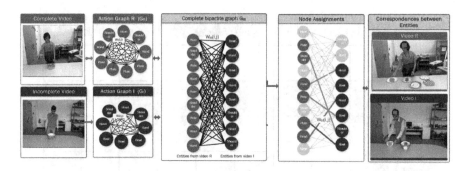

Fig. 3. Illustration of the graph-based framework for action/activity prediction. We assume a complete video (reference) and an incomplete/partially observed (test) one. First, the fully connected graphs of each video are created based on the video entities. On the basis of these graphs, a complete bipartite graph between the action graphs is constructed where the new edges describe the semantic and motion dissimilarity between the nodes of the two graphs. By calculating the Graph Edit Distance (GED), we are able to quantify their dissimilarity and to correspond nodes between the two original action graphs.

do not contain objects then only the human pose representations are used. The weights depend on the manipulated/closest object class. Further details on how to transform an input video into a multidimensional times series can be found in [17].

Having represented the action/activity executions as multi-dimensional time series, our goal is to align the Z prototype actions/activities with labels $L(P_i)$ with the incomplete action/activity A and infer the label $L(A)$. More specifically, a set of prototype actions/activities will be aligned temporally with the incomplete action/activity. The minimum alignment cost denoted as $MAC(P, A)$ will determine which prototype action/activity P^i has the minimum alignment cost with A. Formally,

$$L(A) = L\left(arg\ min_{1 \leq i \leq Z}\left(MAC(A, P^i)\right)\right). \tag{11}$$

Graph-Based Action and Activity Prediction. The OE-S-DTW and OBE-S-DTW alignment algorithms can be exploited in another, graph-based framework for action and activity prediction. Specifically, we explore the work of [18] where they use graphs to solve the activity and next-active-object prediction problem. According to this approach, each activity is represented as a graph. The nodes of the graph represent the entities that participate in an activity, i.e., the joints of the human body of the acting person and the visible scene objects. The nodes hold the semantic label of the corresponding entity and its motion information (2D/3D trajectory). The semantic dissimilarity of the entities as well their motion dissimilarity are encoded on the edges of the graph. More specifically, the semantic dissimilarity of two entities is calculated based on the Wordnet [9] lexical database and the Natural Language Toolkit [14] to calculate the Wu-Palmer distance metric [31]. The motion dissimilarity is calculated using either the OE-S-DTW or the OBE-S-DTW algorithms based on the 2D/3D trajectories of the corresponding entities. Thus, the edges carry the weighted sum of the motion and the semantic dissimilarity that they connect.

Then, matching and aligning actions amounts to matching the graphs representing them. To do so, a complete bipartite graph is created between the graph nodes of a prototype and an incomplete video. As illustrated in Fig. 3, in this new graph the edges hold the semantic and motion dissimilarities of the connected entities between the two graphs. The dissimilarity of these graphs is calculated using the Graph Edit Distance (GED) [1]. In order to disregard action-irrelevant objects, the BP-GED is normalized by the number of pairs of matched objects (MO). Thus, the dissimilarity $D(G_I, G_R)$ of the graph of incomplete video G_I and the graph of the reference video G_R is defined as:

$$D(G_I, G_R) = BP\text{-}GED(G_I, G_R)/MO. \tag{12}$$

It is noted that while [17] can handle up to only one object per activity, this graph-based approach does not pose any relevant constraint.

The BP-GED is calculated thus providing us with the node correspondences between the pair of graphs. For activity prediction, the above process is performed between the test activity and all the reference activities. The test activity takes the label of the reference activity that gives rise to the smallest BP-GED. A detailed explanation of this graph-based action/activity prediction algorithm can be found in [18].

4   Experimental Results

4.1   Datasets

The assessment of the considered methods is performed on benchmark datasets for action/activity prediction. These datasets contain actions and activities in trimmed and untrimmed sequences performed by different subjects manipulating a variety of objects. Each action is represented by the poses of human/object and the class of the manipulated objects using various features, as described in the following.

CAD-120 Dataset [13]: The CAD-120 dataset contains long and complex activities of human-object interactions. The activities are performed by male and female subjects and filmed from varying viewpoints. Moreover, the same actions are performed with different objects in order to induce variability in the executions. These activities can be trimmed in actions based on the provided ground truth data. The dataset provides annotations regarding the activity and action labels, object labels, affordance labels and temporal segmentation of activities. The activities are: arranging objects, cleaning objects, having meal, making cereal, microwaving food, picking objects, stacking objects, taking food, taking medicine and un-stacking objects. The action labels are: reach, move, pour, eat, drink, open, place, close, clean. The comparative evaluation is done based on the experimental split adopted in [18, 30].

In each video, we consider the upper body joints of the acting person as well as the manipulated objects as in [18, 30]. Specifically, the 3D locations of the 8 upper body joints are employed, as well as the distance moved by each joint and their displacement. As object features we employ their 3D centroid location, the distance between the object centroid and each of the 8 upper body human joints. Also, the distance moved by the object (i.e., the displacement of the object's centroid).

MSR Daily Activity 3D Dataset [29]: The MSR Daily Activity 3D Dataset contains actions performed by different subjects in an indoor environment. A small part of these trimmed actions do not contain human-object interactions but the majority does. The actions are performed twice by all subjects, the first time by standing up while the second by sitting on a sofa. The actions contained in the dataset are: cheering up, sitting still, playing a game, walking, lie down on the sofa, playing the guitar, reading a book, standing up, drinking, sitting down, eating, tossing paper, speaking on cellphone, writing on paper, using a laptop and using a vacuum cleaner. Again, we follow the evaluation split used in [17,18,24].

In the MSR Daily Activity dataset the estimation of the lower body positions are very noisy, so following the related works [16,18] we take into consideration only the upper body. The representation consists of a 45-dimensional feature vector containing the 3D joint angles and the 3D skeletal joint position relative to the body center. The dataset does not provide object classes and object positions, so we acquired them using YoloV4 [4].

MHAD101-s/-v Datasets [21]: The MHAD101-s/-v Datasets are constructed based on actions in the MHAD dataset. The MHAD dataset contains 11 trimmed human actions which mainly do not contain human-object interactions with the exception of one action. The actions are performed with different execution styles and speeds. The actions are: waving two hands, clapping, throwing a ball, sit down and stand up, sit down, stand up, jumping in place, jumping jacks, bending, punching, waving one hand. These actions are used in the MHAD101-s/-v to form longer sequences of actions starting from sequences containing from 3 to 7 actions in a row. The concatenated actions exclude the action sit down/stand up as the combination of these two actions results in ambiguities and confusion. From the 101 pairs of action sequences contained in the dataset we use only the first 50 paired sequences where each sequence consists of 3 concatenated action clips (triplets) and the paired sequences have exactly 1 in common. We used only the first 50 pairs of action sequences. By splitting these 50 pairs, we obtained 100 action sequences where each of them contains 3 concatenated actions. An important aspect is that the style and duration variability are enforced by using different subjects in forming different triplets.

The MHAD101-s is constructed using skeletal data and features. We employ the same human body representation as in [15,17] based on the 3D skeletal data of the 30 human joints provided from a motion capture system. The employed features are body-centered and camera-centered providing a 60-dimensional vector plus four angles representing the angles encoding the fore- and the back- arms and upper- and lower legs. The MHAD101-v dataset contains the RGB videos of the same triplets as in MHAD101-s. We then extract features from the VGG-16 network as in [3]. We took into account all the available frames without down-sampling to 30fps.

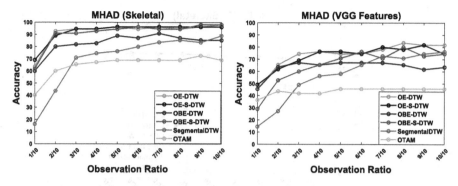

Fig. 4. Action prediction accuracy in trimmed videos as a function of observation ratio involving skeletal (left) and VGG (right) features on the MHAD dataset.

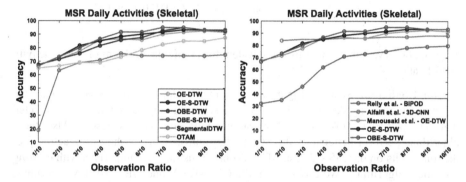

Fig. 5. Action prediction accuracy in trimmed videos as a function of the observation ratio involving skeletal features in the MSR Daily Activities dataset. (Left) a comparison of the OBE-S-DTW and OE-S-DTW with other alignment algorithms, (right) a comparative evaluation of the proposed algorithms with the state-of-art on action prediction on the MSR dataset.

4.2 Alignment-Based Prediction in Segmented Sequences

Action Prediction: The OE-S-DTW and OBE-S-DTW algorithms are employed for solving the problem of action and activity prediction in trimmed sequences. For this reason we evaluate them on the trimmed action executions of the MHAD (skeletal & VGG features), MSR (skeletal features) and CAD120 (skeletal features) datasets and on the activities of the CAD120 (skeletal features) dataset. These algorithms are evaluated by employing the framework of Manousaki et al. [16] as described in Sect. 3.3 which aligns test and reference action sequences and classifies them based on the closest match.

Performance Metrics: To assess our method we use the standard observation split of a certain test action/activity in parts of 10% in the range [0, 100%]. At every successive such split, we match the (partially) observed test sequence to the reference ones and we calculate the agreement between the predicted activity/action label and the ground truth label. An observation ratio of 100% means that the whole test sequence

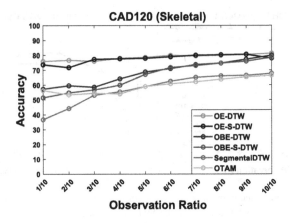

Fig. 6. Action prediction results on the CAD120 dataset.

has been observed, therefore this is equivalent to solving the problem of action/activity classification.

Action Prediction Results: Figure 4 shows the results of action prediction on the MHAD dataset using skeletal and VGG features. For this segmented input it is expected that the Open-End DTW and S-DTW variants will have the best results. Also, these algorithms perform better than the SOTA algorithms. Figure 5 shows the action prediction results on the MSR dataset. The left plot illustrates a comparison with existing alignment algorithms. We observe that the OE-S-DTW and OBE-S-DTW algorithms have the best results across all observation ratios. The right plot of the same figure shows a comparison of OE-S-DTW and OBE-S-DTW with the state-of-art work on action prediction on the MSR dataset of Alfaifi et al. [2], Manousaki et al. [17] and Reily et al. [24]. For an observation ratio greater than 40% the OBE-S-DTW outperforms all other algorithms. Finally, Fig. 6 shows a comparison of the OBE-S-DTW and OE-S-DTW algorithms with the OE-DTW [28], OBE-DTW [28], Segmental-DTW [19] and OTAM [5] algorithms on the actions of the CAD120 dataset.

Activity Prediction Results: On top of the results presented in [16], we also evaluate the framework of Manousaki et al. [16] on the activities of the CAD120 dataset. To do so, we use compare the performance of the OE-S-DTW and the OBE-S-DTW methods to several competitive methods [2,2,5,19,24] and the works of Wu et al. [30] and Manousaki et al. [18] that hold the state-of-art results. As it can be observed in Fig. 7 the OE-S-DTW alignment algorithm performs generally better than the OBE-S-DTW. This happens due to the fact that most of the activities start from the same pose so the OE-S-DTW that has the starting point constraint aligns the sequences more accurately. Generally, the alignment of activities using the framework of [16] has low performance compared to the state-of-art. This happens because the activities are more complex compared to actions. Additionally this method has the drawback of taking into account only one object while in these activities several objects are used.

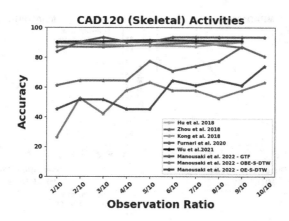

Fig. 7. Activity prediction results on the CAD120 dataset.

4.3   Alignment-Based Action Prediction in Unsegmented Sequences

Action Prediction: The OBE-S-DTW algorithm is capable of finding an action any-where inside a long sequence of actions as shown in [16] for the MHAD101-s/-v datasets. This was achieved by checking whether the OBE-S-DTW can recognize an unsegmented action that appears between some other prefix and suffix actions. We com-plement those experiments here by observing action triplets not only from start to finish as in [16] but also backwards (from the suffix to the prefix). It is noted that in each observed triplet, the prefix/suffix actions are excluded from the set of the prototype actions.

Performance Metrics: The prefix and suffix actions are progressively observed in thirds while the middle action is observed in tenths. This protocol is used to acquire finer performance measures for the action of interest. Accuracy is used as the metric for action prediction of the middle action. F1-score, precision, recall and Intersection-over-Union (IoU) are calculated for all observation ratios.

Action Prediction Results: Figure 8 shows the F1-score, recall, precision and IoU scores for the OBE-DTW and OBE-S-DTW algorithms which are the better algorithms overall for aligning unsegmented sequences. From this plot we can observe that the OBE-S-DTW provides better alignments.

A comparison of the OBE-S-DTW and OE-S-DTW with the OE-DTW [28], OBE-DTW [28], SegmentalDTW [23] and OTAM [5] is provided in Fig. 9 (left) for the MHAD101-s and in Fig. 9 (right) for the MHAD101-v dataset. As it can be observed, the OBE-S-DTW has the best performance overall.

As mentioned earlier, on top of the results presented in Manousaki et al. [16], we evaluate the performance of the OE-DTW and OBE-S-DTW algorithms on reversed action triplets. In Fig. 10 (left) we observe how the algorithms performs for the MHAD101-s dataset while observing the triplet from start to end (deep red and deep blue lines) and how they perform while observing the triplet from the end to the start (light red and light blue lines). In Fig. 10, the two vertical black lines denote the

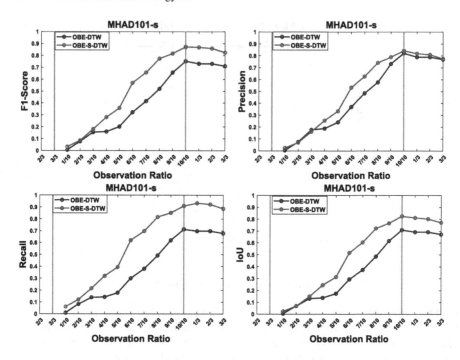

Fig. 8. Performance metrics for OBE-DTW and OBE-S-DTW on the MHAD101-s dataset.

ground-truth start and end of the middle action. High accuracy during the prefix denotes the ability of the algorithm to recognize that the algorithm correctly identifies that the sought action has not yet started. High accuracy during the suffix denotes the successful recognition of the middle action inside the triplet. We can observe a symmetrical effect in the results which means that observing the triplet from start to end or vice versa does not have a significant impact on the algorithms. Also, the OBE-S-DTW algorithm consistently outperforms the OBE-DTW algorithm. The same holds for the MHAD101-v dataset as it can be observed in Fig. 10 (right).

4.4 Graph-Based Activity Prediction

We evaluate the performance of OE-S-DTW and OBE-S-DTW on the problem of activity prediction when employed in the graph-based framework of Manousaki et al. [18]. As it can be observed in Fig. 11 the OBE-S-DTW algorithm helps the GTF method achieve much better results compared to the use of the OE-S-DTW algorithm. This method considers multiple objects for the task of activity prediction. The motion weights with the use of OE-S-DTW and OBE-S-DTW are calculated for each pair of nodes in the action graphs and the bipartite graph. The boundary constraint of OE-S-DTW is not an advantage in this setting where objects can be used in different points in time and in mixed order.

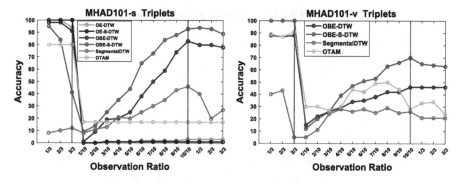

Fig. 9. Aligning unsegmented action sequences on the MHAD101-s and MHAD101-v datasets by comparing the OBE-S-DTW and OBE-DTW algorithms to other pre-existing alignment algorithms while observing the triplets from the prefix to the suffix. Vertical lines depict the limits of the middle action.

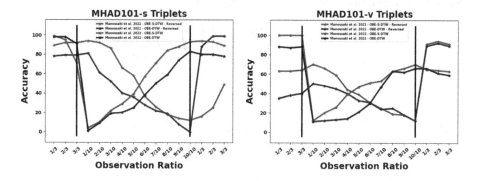

Fig. 10. Aligning unsegmented action sequences on the MHAD101-s/-v datasets using the OBE-S-DTW and OBE-DTW algorithms. Dark red and blue lines depict the accuracy of the alignment algorithms while observing the triplets from the prefix to the suffix. The light (red and blue) lines depict the observation of the triplet from the suffix to the prefix. (Color figure online)

4.5 Duration Prognosis

Knowing the label of an ongoing action before its completion is a very useful capability. In certain situations, it is equally important to be able to predict the time at which the currently observed action/activity will end. As proposed in [16], action duration prognosis is defined as the prediction of the time remaining until the completion of the currently observed action. Currently in the framework of [16] the duration prognosis has been evaluated only on the MHAD101-s dataset (see also Fig. 12). We extend this evaluation by performing duration prognosis of actions and activities on the MSR and CAD120 datasets, respectively.

Performance Metrics: For a given observation ratio, we report the end-frame prediction error which is defined as the discrepancy of the estimated end of a certain action/activity from its ground truth end, as a percentage of the test action length. When

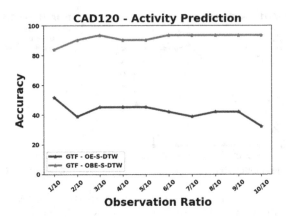

Fig. 11. Activity prediction results on the CAD120 dataset using the graph based method presented in [18]. The OBE-S-DTW and OE-S-DTW algorithms were used to quantify the motion dissimilarity of the entities involved in the considered activities.

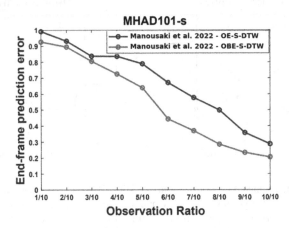

Fig. 12. End-frame prediction error calculated for all observation ratios of the middle actions of the triplets of MHAD101-s.

an action/activity is wrongly classified by the algorithm, then a prediction error of 1.0 (100%) is added.

Action Duration Prognosis Results: Figure 12 shows the results of duration prognosis on the triplets of the MHAD101-s dataset, as presented in [16]. We can observe that the OBE-S-DTW has smaller error rates across all observation ratios compared to OBE-DTW.

We also report the evaluation of duration prognosis on the actions of the MSR dataset. Figure 13 (left) show the relevant action prediction results while in Fig. 13 (right) the results of the duration prognosis are presented. The OBE-S-DTW is the best choice for this dataset across the different frameworks. The higher the action prediction accuracy, the lower the duration prognosis error. As the observation ratios increase

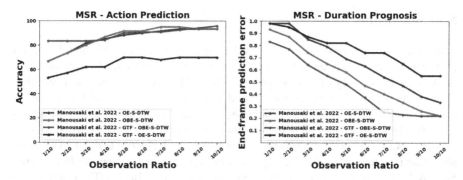

Fig. 13. (Left) Action prediction results for the MSR Daily Activities dataset. (Right) Prognosis of the duration of the partially observed actions for the MSR Daily Activities dataset.

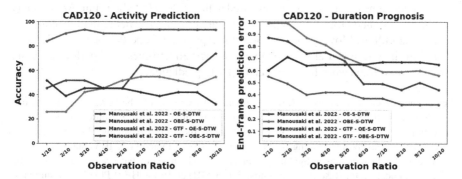

Fig. 14. (Left) Activity prediction results for the CAD120 dataset. (Right) Prognosis of the duration of the partially observed activities of the CAD120 dataset.

more meaningful alignments are established thus matching with actions of similar temporal duration. While the prediction accuracy of the different frameworks is similar, we observe differences in the end-frame prediction error. This happens because the test actions get classified to different reference actions thus having variability in their predicted temporal duration.

Activity Duration Prognosis Results: Complementary to the duration prognosis for actions, we extend the experimental evaluation of duration prognosis on the activities of the CAD120 dataset. In Fig. 14 we present the results of activity prediction and duration prognosis of the framework of [16] and the GTF framework [18] on the CAD120 dataset. As it can be observed, the OE-S-DTW performs better than the OBE-S-DTW in the framework of [16] while the opposite holds true for the GTF framework. As explained earlier, these frameworks handle different numbers of objects. Thus, depending on the framework, the dataset and its characteristics, different alignment algorithms should be employed. Moreover, moving forward onto the timeline we can see that the end-frame prediction error is decreasing for both algorithms, as they observe a larger portion of the test activity.

5 Conclusions

In this paper we presented an extensive evaluation of the OBE-S-DTW and OE-S-DTW alignment algorithms on the task of human action prediction and duration prediction on the MHAD, MSR Daily Activities, CAD-120 and MHAD101-s/-v datasets. These algorithms were deployed for the alignment and matching of segmented and unsegmented action executions. We opted to extend the use of these algorithms for the task of activity prediction by incorporating them in different frameworks and testing them on the activities of the CAD120 dataset. Our experimental evaluation showed that the OE-S-DTW algorithm is better suited for the alignment of segmented sequences while the OBE-S-DTW for the alignment of unsegmented sequences. The OBE-S-DTW is a powerful algorithm that can identify actions as parts of unsegmented sequences. We showed that the OBE-S-DTW algorithm can align/match sequences with similar duration thus having low end-frame prediction error compared to the OBE-DTW algorithm. Additionally, the OE-S-DTW and OBE-S-DTW algorithms are proven to be better than several competitive algorithms. Moving forward, we will exploit the properties of these alignment algorithms in a deep neural network to assess their effectiveness and performance in a learning-based framework for action and activity prediction.

Acknowledgements. This research was co-financed by Greece and the European Union (European Social Fund-ESF) through the Operational Programme "Human Resources Development, Education and Lifelong Learning" in the context of the Act "Enhancing Human Resources Research Potential by undertaking a Doctoral Research" Sub-action 2: IKY Scholarship Programme for PhD candidates in the Greek Universities. The research work was supported by the Hellenic Foundation for Research and Innovation (HFRI) under the HFRI PhD Fellowship grant (Fellowship Number: 1592) and by HFRI under the "1st Call for H.F.R.I Research Projects to support Faculty members and Researchers and the procurement of high-cost research equipment", project I.C.Humans, number 91.

References

1. Abu-Aisheh, Z., Raveaux, R., Ramel, J.Y., Martineau, P.: An exact graph edit distance algorithm for solving pattern recognition problems. In: ICPRAM (2015)
2. Alfaifi, R., Artoli, A.: Human action prediction with 3D-CNN. SN Comput. Sci. 1, 1–15 (2020)
3. Bacharidis, K., Argyros, A.: Improving deep learning approaches for human activity recognition based on natural language processing of action labels. In: IJCNN. IEEE (2020)
4. Bochkovskiy, A., Wang, C., Liao, H.: Yolov4: optimal speed and accuracy of object detection. arXiv:2004.10934 (2020)
5. Cao, K., Ji, J., Cao, Z., Chang, C.Y., Niebles, J.C.: Few-shot video classification via temporal alignment. In: CVPR (2020)
6. Chang, C.Y., Huang, D.A., Sui, Y., Fei-Fei, L., Niebles, J.C.: D3TW: discriminative differentiable dynamic time warping for weakly supervised action alignment and segmentation. In: CVPR (2019)
7. Cuturi, M., Blondel, M.: Soft-DTW: a differentiable loss function for time-series. arXiv:1703.01541 (2017)
8. Dvornik, N., Hadji, I., Derpanis, K.G., Garg, A., Jepson, A.D.: Drop-DTW: aligning common signal between sequences while dropping outliers. arXiv preprint arXiv:2108.11996 (2021)

9. Fellbaum, C.: Wordnet and wordnets (2005)
10. Hadji, I., Derpanis, K.G., Jepson, A.D.: Representation learning via global temporal alignment and cycle-consistency. arXiv preprint arXiv:2105.05217 (2021)
11. Haresh, S., et al.: Learning by aligning videos in time. arXiv preprint arXiv:2103.17260 (2021)
12. Kim, D., Jang, M., Yoon, Y., Kim, J.: Classification of dance motions with depth cameras using subsequence dynamic time warping. In: SPPR. IEEE (2015)
13. Koppula, H., Gupta, R., Saxena, A.: Learning human activities and object affordances from RGB-D videos. Int. J. Robot. Res. **32**(8), 951–970 (2013)
14. Loper, E., Bird, S.: NLTK: the natural language toolkit. arXiv preprint CS/0205028 (2002)
15. Manousaki, V., Papoutsakis, K., Argyros, A.: Evaluating method design options for action classification based on bags of visual words. In: VISAPP (2018)
16. Manousaki, V., Argyros, A.A.: Segregational soft dynamic time warping and its application to action prediction. In: VISIGRAPP (5: VISAPP), pp. 226–235 (2022)
17. Manousaki, V., Papoutsakis, K., Argyros, A.: Action prediction during human-object interaction based on DTW and early fusion of human and object representations. In: Vincze, M., Patten, T., Christensen, H.I., Nalpantidis, L., Liu, M. (eds.) ICVS 2021. LNCS, vol. 12899, pp. 169–179. Springer, Cham (2021). https://doi.org/10.1007/978-3-030-87156-7_14
18. Manousaki, V., Papoutsakis, K., Argyros, A.: Graphing the future: activity and next active object prediction using graph-based activity representations. In: 17th International Symposium on Visual Computing (2022)
19. Panagiotakis, C., Papoutsakis, K., Argyros, A.: A graph-based approach for detecting common actions in motion capture data and videos. Pattern Recognit. **79**, 1–11 (2018)
20. Papoutsakis, K., Panagiotakis, C., Argyros, A.: Temporal action co-segmentation in 3D motion capture data and videos (2017)
21. Papoutsakis, K., Panagiotakis, C., Argyros, A.A.: Temporal action co-segmentation in 3D motion capture data and videos. In: CVPR 2017. IEEE (2017)
22. Papoutsakis, K., Panagiotakis, C., Argyros, A.A.: Temporal action co-segmentation in 3D motion capture data and videos. In: CVPR (2017)
23. Park, A.S., Glass, J.R.: Unsupervised pattern discovery in speech. IEEE Trans. Audio Speech Lang. Process. **16**(1), 186–197 (2007)
24. Reily, B., Han, F., Parker, L., Zhang, H.: Skeleton-based bio-inspired human activity prediction for real-time human-robot interaction. Auton. Robots **42**, 1281–1298 (2018)
25. Roditakis, K., Makris, A., Argyros, A.: Towards improved and interpretable action quality assessment with self-supervised alignment (2021)
26. Sakoe, H., Chiba, S.: Dynamic programming algorithm optimization for spoken word recognition. IEEE Trans. Acoust. Speech Signal Process. **26**(1), 43–49 (1978)
27. Schez-Sobrino, S., Monekosso, D.N., Remagnino, P., Vallejo, D., Glez-Morcillo, C.: Automatic recognition of physical exercises performed by stroke survivors to improve remote rehabilitation. In: MAPR (2019)
28. Tormene, P., Giorgino, T., Quaglini, S., Stefanelli, M.: Matching incomplete time series with dynamic time warping: an algorithm and an application to post-stroke rehabilitation. Artif. Intell. Med. **45**(1), 11–34 (2009)
29. Wang, J., Liu, Z., Wu, Y., Yuan, J.: Mining actionlet ensemble for action recognition with depth cameras. In: IEEE CVPR (2012)
30. Wu, X., Wang, R., Hou, J., Lin, H., Luo, J.: Spatial-temporal relation reasoning for action prediction in videos. Int. J. Comput. Vision **129**(5), 1484–1505 (2021)
31. Wu, Z., Palmer, M.: Verb semantics and lexical selection. arXiv preprint CMP-LG/9406033 (1994)
32. Yang, C.K., Tondowidjojo, R.: Kinect V2 based real-time motion comparison with retargeting and color code feedback. In: IEEE GCCE (2019)

Automatic Bi-LSTM Architecture Search Using Bayesian Optimisation for Vehicle Activity Recognition

Rahulan Radhakrishnan[1]($\boxtimes$)(iD) and Alaa AlZoubi[2](iD)

[1] School of Computing, The University of Buckingham, Buckingham, U.K.
rahulan.radhakrishna@buckingham.ac.uk
[2] School of Computing and Engineering, University of Derby, Derby, U.K.
a.alzoubi@derby.ac.uk

Abstract. This paper presents a novel method to find optimal Bidirectional Long-Short Term Memory Neural Network (Bi-LSTM) using Bayesian Optimisation method for vehicle trajectory classification. We extend our previous approach to be able to classify a larger number of vehicle trajectories collected from different sources in a single Bi-LSTM network. We also explored the use of deep learning visual explainability by highlighting the parts of the activity (or trajectory) contribute to the classification decision of the network. In particular, Qualitative Trajectory Calculus (QTC), spatio-temporal calculus, method is used to encode the relative movement between vehicles as a trajectory of QTC states. We then develop a Bi-LSTM network (called VNet) to classify QTC trajectories that represent vehicle pairwise activities. Existing Bi-LSTM networks for vehicle activity analysis are manually designed without considering the optimisation of the whole architecture nor its trainable hyperparameters. Therefore, we adapt Bayesian Optimisation method to search for an optimal Bi-LSTM architecture for classifying QTC trajectories of vehicle interaction. To test the validity of the proposed VNet, four datasets of 8237 trajectories of 9 unique vehicle activities in different traffic scenarios are used. We further compare our VNet model's performance with the state-of-the-art methods. The results on the combined dataset (accuracy of 98.21%) showed that the proposed method generates light and most robust Bi-LSTM model. We also demonstrate that Activation Map is a promising approach for visualising the Bi-LSTM model decisions for vehicle activity recognition.

Keywords: Vehicle activity classification · Qualitative trajectory calculus · Long-short term memory neural network · Automatic LSTM architecture design · Bayesian optimisation · Activation map

1 Introduction

The development of computer vision and machine learning as methods for detecting and analysing objects activities based on their movements have attracted increasing research interests in many applications such as vehicle movements analysis. Learning and understanding the surrounding environment is vital for the moving vehicles to make

© The Author(s), under exclusive license to Springer Nature Switzerland AG 2023
A. A. de Sousa et al. (Eds.): VISIGRAPP 2022, CCIS 1815, pp. 108–134, 2023.
https://doi.org/10.1007/978-3-031-45725-8_6

rational and intelligent decisions in several applications including collision avoidance, self-driving and surveillance. Dangerous road scenarios such as collisions and overtaking can be avoided if the behaviours of the surrounding vehicles are captured accurately. The research field where the actions of one or more vehicles are recognized using the analysis of their interactions overtime is known as vehicle activity analysis. It can be categorized into three types: 1) single activity where the vehicle performs motion behaviours on its own; 2) pair or group activity where the vehicle interacts with one or more other moving vehicles; and 3) stationary obstacles (e.g. stalled vehicles). Previous research concerned with pair-activity analysis (a special case of group activity analysis) have been focused on two main approaches: quantitative and qualitative methods. The quantitative methods such as [14,23,29] use sequences of real-valued features (e.g. vehicle position, orientation or speed) to describe and capture behaviours and interactions between the vehicles. On the other hand, a smaller body of work [4,6] has been directed specifically at using qualitative features (e.g. symbolic representation). These methods have shown high performance for activity classification in general and vehicle trajectory classification in particular. The high performance and low complexity of these methods have motivated the researchers to investigate the qualitative representations with deep learning methods for vehicle trajectory analysis. Qualitative methods (e.g. QTC [46] "a calculus for representing and reasoning about movements of objects in a qualitative framework") have several advantages: abstract the real values of the trajectories, use symbolic representation, compact, computationally less expensive, and more human understandable than quantitative methods.

Few previous studies for single and multiple vehicle activity classification and prediction have been developed using different techniques such as Bayesian Networks [27] and Hidden Markov Models [9,14,19]. The promising performance of the LSTM method in classifying temporal data with long term dependencies has increased the interest on using such technique for vehicle activity analysis task. Few previous works attempted to manually design LSTM network with quantitative methods to classify group vehicles activities [23]. The manual design of LSTM architectures has several limitations: i) the optimisation process (trial-and-error) is time consuming; ii) it requires architectural domain expertise; iii) error prone; and iv) the complex structure of the LSTM architecture includes gates and memory cells to store long term dependencies of sequential data. Thus, it requires a methodical way of tuning its hyperparameters to get the optimal architecture rather than using manual designing or brute force methods such as Grid Search and Random Search. Bayesian Optimisation has been used for optimising LSTM networks in applications such as image caption generation [42] and forecasting [47]. Such optimiser can be adapted to design the LSTM architectures for vehicle trajectory classification task. However, the use of symbolic features to represent the interaction between vehicles with LSTM for vehicle activity analysis task still remains to be an open investigation area which we tried to explore in our previous work [37].

In this study, we present our novel approach for vehicle pair-activity classification using QTC, Bi-LSTM and Bayesian Optimisation. Our method consists of three main components: encode the relative motion (interactions) between the vehicles using QTC and one-hot vectors representations; automatic design and search for a generic optimal Bi-LSTM architecture for vehicle activity classification using Bayesian Optimisation technique; and build Bi-LSTM model (called VNet) for vehicle pair activity recognition. Figure 1 shows an overview of our method. We evidence the overall generality of our approach with evaluations against five datasets.

This article is an extension to our work previously presented in [37]. We extended our study in three folds: Firstly, we have extended the experiment by evaluating our method on a new vehicle activity dataset (NGSIM [44]) which consists of 980 trajectories for two classes (Follow and Preceding). Secondly, we have further extended the experiment by evaluating our approach on a new dataset which combines vehicle activity trajectories from four different data sources. Section 5.2 shows our approach is now able to accurately distinguish between 8237 different pairwise activities, without compromising on accuracy. This new added experiments demonstrated that our method can be used for applications with a wide range of scenarios collected from different settings. Finally, we have explored the deep learning 'visual explanations' solution to gain insight into the function of Bi-LSTM layers and the classification decision of the models trained on vehicle trajectories. In particular, in Sect. 6, we demonstrate that the classification decisions of our VNet model [37] in such safety critical tasks is required and we discuss the possibilities of understanding the decisions of the model by visualizing the activation map of Bi-LSTM hidden units.

The remainder of this paper is organised as follows: In Sect. 2 we present background work, focusing on Trajectory Representation Techniques, Trajectory Analysis, LSTM and Bayesian optimisation. Our proposed method is presented in full in Sect. 3. Section 4 and 5 provide details of the datasets and experimental results respectively. Discussing the explainability of the model classification decision is presented in Sect. 6. Our concluding remarks are presented in Sect. 7.

2   Related Work

In this section, we briefly review the state of the art trajectory representation and analysing techniques and the optimisation methods used for automatic design of deep learning architectures.

2.1   Trajectory Representation and Analysis

The rapid growth of sensing devices and wireless communication and the advancement of computing devices and machine learning techniques has highly benefited the analysis of trajectories of moving objects [12]. Numerous interesting studies have been conducted in the field of trajectory analysis under different domains: Human - Human Interaction [48], fish behaviour analysis [4], Sports player interaction [8], Game based interaction [33], Dance movements [10], Human - Robot Interaction [17,21], Ball trajectory analysis [28] and Vehicle Activity recognition [4,7,29,37]. Vehicle is a specific type of moving object that maneuvers in a controlled environment (road traffic environment). Similar to other moving objects, approach towards vehicle activity analysis can be grouped under three categories based on the number of vehicles/objects involved in the interaction: single-vehicle activities [3,23,49], pair vehicle activities [4,6,7,48], and group vehicle activities [16,24,29]. An extensive review on vehicle trajectory analysis with respect to trajectory extraction, representation, and the method of analysis from surveillance videos is provided by Ahmed et al. [2].

Finding the appropriate method for feature extraction and representation is crucial for the success of any trajectory-based activity analysis. In general, feature representation methods can be categorised into two types: Qualitative Features and Quantitative Features. Majority of the previous studies use quantitative features to represent the trajectories. However, recently researchers have shown their interest in qualitative features as well. Qualitative Trajectory Calculus (QTC) [46] has been the most favoured qualitative feature for trajectory-based activity analysis. Almost all the studies on qualitative method have utilised either a variant of QTC (QTC_B, QTC_C, QTC_{Full}) or a modified version of QTC (QTC_S, QTC_{BC}) [8] as their feature representation method. Among them, QTC_C has been widely used in applications such as Gaming Interactions [33], Human - Robot Interaction [21] and Dance Movement Analysis [11]. However, there is no such unanimity among the studies in quantitative method. Common motion descriptors such as Position, Displacement, Velocity and Heading Angle have been used as quantitative features as well as statistical measures such as Causality Ratio, Feedback Ratio and Heat Map. Among them, Position feature, Velocity and Heading Angle have been widely used in the analysis of vehicle trajectories [15, 16, 23, 25, 49]

Several attempts have been made to classify single and pair vehicle activities using quantitative features with different techniques such as Heatmap, Hidden Markov Model (HMM) and LSTM. Studies of [23], Philips et al. [36] and Zyner et al. [49] focuses on classifying single vehicle activities using manually designed LSTM network with quantitative features. Among them, the studies of Khosroshahi et al. [23] and Philips et al. [36] strongly emphasises the importance of finding the optimal hyper-parameters and proper input features in the success of developing an LSTM model for vehicle activity classification. Studies of Lin et al. [29] and Deo et al. [14, 16] focus on classifying pair-wise vehicle activities. A heat-map based algorithm was proposed by Lin et al. for the recognition of pair activities [29]. They developed their own surface fitting method to classify their heat maps. This method was evaluated in one of the dataset (Traffic Dataset) we used in this study and they have shown that their heat map approach was able to classify the vehicle trajectories with an accuracy of 95.8%. The study of Deo et al. initially proposed an algorithm using Hidden Markov Model for vehicle maneuver classification [14]. Their HMM maneuver recognition module was trained using the position coordinates and instantaneous velocities as input features and achieved an overall accuracy of 84.24%. They further expanded their study to develop an LSTM network for the same problem and showed that their LSTM network outperforming their previous HMM based solution [15, 16]. However, the very first model for pair activity classification was developed for human pair activity classification [48]. They used causality and feedback ratio as their input and built a Support Vector Machine (SVM) model that was able to achieve an accuracy of 92.1%. This method was used as a benchmark study by Lin et al. [29] on the Traffic Dataset.

The possibilities of using qualitative methods for vehicle activity analysis were initially explored by AlZoubi et al. [4] in 2018. AlZoubi et al. used Qualitative Trajectory Calculus (QTC) as their qualitative feature extraction technique and developed their own similarity measuring metric called Normalized Weighted Sequence Alignment (NWSA) to classify the trajectories [4]. They evaluated their algorithm on the Traffic Dataset which was previously used by [29] in their heat map approach. They were able to outperform the heat map approach by achieving an average accuracy of 96.56%. In 2020, AlZoubi et al. further expanded their study by replacing their similarity measuring method with a DCNN model (TrajNet) as the classifier for QTC sequences [6]. TrajNet was built using transfer learning from the well established classification CNN AlexNet. Using this deep learning approach, they were able to further improve the accuracy upto 98.84% on the Traffic Dataset. They also created a Simulation dataset named Vehicle-Obstacle Interaction (VOI) dataset [4] with three classes (Left Overtake, Right Overtake and Crash) which is also one of the dataset we used in this study.

Studies of AlZoubi et al. has shown that their QTC based deep learning (DCNN) approach outperforming all the other state-of-the art qualitative and quantitative techniques for vehicle trajectory classification in a particular dataset. On the other hand, the qualitative study of Panzner et al. clearly indicates that QTC with LSTM has a potential in classifying pair activities in gaming application [33]. Their manually designed LSTM architecture contains a single LSTM layer with 128 hidden units. Thus, it motivates us to investigate the potential of an automatically designed LSTM with QTC features for vehicle trajectory analysis. We adopt the quantitative and qualitative methods of [4,29,30,32,48] and [6] as benchmark techniques to compare our method.

2.2 Deep Neural Network Optimisation

Performance of deep learning algorithms such as CNN and LSTM highly relies on their architectures [40]. However, existing architectures such as VGG [40], EfficientNet [43], and LSTM [33] are all manually designed by experts who have rich domain knowledge in CNNs or they rely on trial-and-error approach. Neural Architecture Search (NAS) is one of the automatic architecture design approach that has been successfully deployed in medical image classification [1] and object recognition in natural images [35]. However, NAS does not consider the modelling-hyperparameters such as optimiser and number of epochs. Bayesian Optimisation (BO) is a state-of-the-art framework in optimising complex and computationally expensive deep neural networks including CNN and LSTM [18]. It works under the principles of Bayes Theorem and Gaussian Processes. The optimisation mainly depends on the acquisition function that determines the next exploration point. Expected Improvement is one such acquisition function that considers both mean and variance of the posterior model when choosing the next best point [20]. Bayesian Optimisation has achieved state-of-the-art results in optimising deep neural networks in the fields of speech recognition [13], image classification [41,42] and natural language processing [31]. Few attempts have been made to use Bayesian Optimisation to optimise LSTM in the domains of time series forecasting [22,47] and image caption generation [42]. However, there are no LSTM that has been automatically designed for vehicle activity classification.

3   Method

Our method of vehicle activity recognition consists of three major components.

- Qualitative representation (QTC trajectory) of pair-wise vehicle activities.

– Automatic Bi-LSTM architecture search and design using Bayesian Optimisation.
– Modelling of optimal Bi-LSTM architecture for qualitative vehicle trajectory classification.

Initially, pair wise vehicle trajectories are represented as QTC sequences and then they are transformed into a two-dimensional matrix using one hot vector representation. An automatically designed Bi-LSTM architecture was developed to classify these QTC coded vehicle trajectories into relevant vehicle activities. Bayesian Optimisation was used for the automatic optimisation of the Bi-LSTM architecture. Figure 1 shows an overview of the main components of our method.

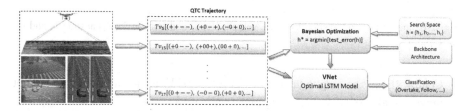

Fig. 1. Our Proposed Method [37].

3.1   Qualitative Feature Representation

The 2D positions of the vehicles are given in the form of x, y coordinates in all the datasets. Thus, we used those position coordinates to encode the relative motion between the two vehicles as a sequence of QTC states. We utilized both QTC_C and QTC_{Full} variants in this study.

Definition 1. Given the x, y position coordinates of two interacting vehicles between the time interval t_1 to t_k, the trajectories of those two vehicles V_{1i} and V_{2i} are defined as:

$$V_{1i} = \{(x_1, y_1), ..., (x_t, y_t), ..., (x_k, y_k)\},$$
$$V_{2i} = \{(x'_1, y'_1), ..., (x'_t, y'_t), ..., (x'_k, y'_k)\},$$

Where x_t and y_t are the position coordinates of the first interacting vehicle at time t. Likewise, x'_t and y'_t are the position coordinates of the second interacting vehicle. k represents the total number of time steps in the trajectories. As described in Sect. 2, QTC states are defined as different combination of QTC codes. QTC_C and QTC_{Full} states are represented using four and six codes respectively. In the context of pair vehicle interactions, using the two interacting vehicles V_1 and V_2, the six QTC codes are as follows:

– Code 1: If V_1 is moving towards V_2: "−"; If V_1 is neither moving towards nor away from V_2: "0"; If V_1 is moving away V_2: "+".
– Code 2: "−", "0" and "+" indicate the same as Code 1 but with V_1 and V_2 swapped.
– Code 3: If V_1 is moving slower than V_2: "−", If V_1 and V_2 are either not moving or moving at the same speed: "0", If V_1 is moving faster V_2: "+".

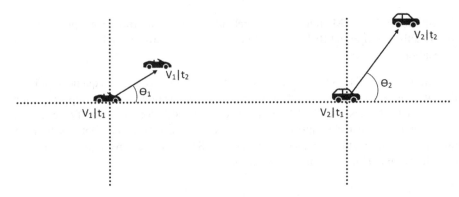

Fig. 2. Example of an interaction between Vehicle 1 (V_1) and Vehicle 2 (V_2) at time t_1 and t_2: QTC_{Full} $(-,+,-,+,-,-)$.

- Code 4: If V_1 is moving to the left of $\overrightarrow{V_1V_2}$: "$-$", If V_1 is moving along $\overrightarrow{V_1V_2}$ or not moving at all: "0", If V_1 is moving to the right of $\overrightarrow{V_1V_2}$: "+"
- Code 5: "$-$", "0" and "+" indicates the same as the code 4 but with V_1 and V_2 swapped
- Code 6: If $\theta1 < \theta2$: "$-$", If $\theta1 = \theta2$: "0", If $\theta1 > \theta2$: "+"

Between time t_1 and t_2, QTC_C state S_1 is constructed using the relevant symbols of Code 1, Code 2, Code 4 and Code 5. Similarly, QTC_{Full} state is formed using Code 1, Code 2, Code 4, Code 5, Code 3 and Code 6 in order. The example given in Fig. 2 generates $(-,+,-,+)$ and $(-,+,-,+,-,-)$ as QTC_C state and QTC_{Full} state respectively. Thus, the pair-wise trajectory is defined as a sequence of corresponding QTC_C (or QTC_{Full}) states: $Tv_i = \{S_1, ..., S_R, ...S_N\}$, where S_R is the QTC_C (or QTC_{Full}) state representation of the relative motion of the two vehicles V_1 and V_2 from time t to $t + 1$ in trajectory Tv_i and N is the total number of observations in Tv_i ($N = k - 1$). In this paper, QTC_C variant was used to do the optimal architecture search because of the limited computational resources. However, both QTC_C and QTC_{Full} were used to model the network.

The trajectory Tv_i which is a time varying sequence of QTC_C (or QTC_{Full}) states, is represented as a one dimensional sequence of characters $Ch_i = \{Ch_1, ..., Ch_R, ..., Ch_N\}$ in text format. For instance, the first $(- - --)$ and last $(+ + + +)$ states of QTC_C are represented as Ch_1 and Ch_{81} respectively. However, this character representation loses high level information such as the range of QTC states and states that are not present in each time frame. It only provides the QTC_C (or QTC_{Full}) state that is present in that time frame. Thus, we converted this character representation of QTC sequence (Ch_i) into a one hot encoded sequence without losing the location information. To avoid the formation of any rankings between the QTC states, one-hot encoding was selected over ordinal encoding. For example, QTC State 81 is not higher or lower than QTC State 1. Thus, the one hot vector representation of trajectory Tv_i generates a 2D matrix (Mv_i) with size ($Q * N$); where Q is the number of possible QTC states (range) and N is the total number of observations in Tv_i. Figure 3 presents an example of conversion from QTC_C trajectory to One Hot Vector Representation. This One Hot

Vector Representation is used as the sequential input for the Bi-LSTM model presented in Sect. 3.2.

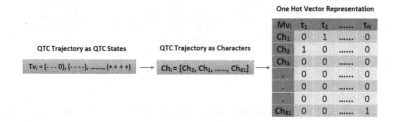

Fig. 3. QTC Trajectory to One Hot Vector Representation.

3.2 Automatic Bi-LSTM Architecture Search

A key contribution of our method is the automatic design of Bi-LSTM architecture with less operator intervention. Our method of automatic design of Bi-LSTM involves three main steps. First of all, we define a Bi-LSTM backbone architecture with optimisable hyperparameters and their search space. Then, we perform automatic architecture search using Bayesian optimisation to identify best performing architectures. Finally, we use our selection policy to identify the generic optimal Bi-LSTM architecture and training parameters for vehicle activity classification using QTC trajectories.

Bi-LSTM Backbone Architecture: Our design of Bi-LSTM backbone architecture consists of six layers: Sequence Input Layer (SI), Bi-directional LSTM Layer ($LSTM$), Dropout Layer (DL), Fully Connected Layer (FL), SoftMax Layer (SM), and Classification Layer (OL) in sequential order. The input layer was defined with an input size of $(Q * N)$ based on the one hot vector representation of QTC trajectories (Sect. 3.1). Input layer was followed by L number of pairs of (Bi-LSTM + Dropout) Layers. The number of hidden units in the Bi-LSTM layer is expressed by m and the dropout rate of the dropout layer is represented by p. Depending on the number of (Bi-LSTM + Dropout) layer pairs (value of L), m and p can have multiple values. For example, if there are two pairs of Bi-LSTM + Dropout layers ($L = 2$), then there will be two values for m and p:(m_1, m_2), (p_1, p_2). L, m and p constitutes the architecture hyperparameters and their values were determined by the Bayesian optimiser. A fully connected layer with C number of classes was then added after the (Bi-LSTM + Dropout) layer pairs where C is the number of vehicle activities in the datasets. It is followed by a softmax layer and a classification output layer which completes the backbone architecture. The classification layer calculates the cross entropy loss of each class by taking the probability distribution produced by the softmax layer to determine the class of the input. Figure 4 shows the backbone architecture with its architecture-hyperparameters.

Hyperparameters and Search Space: Optimisation of Bi-LSTM models involve several hyperparameters with large range of search spaces. Therefore, identifying the most impactful hyperparameters and suitable search spaces becomes vital. The performance

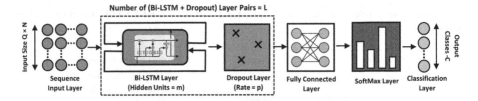

Fig. 4. Proposed Bi-LSTM Backbone Architecture [37].

of the model as well as the computational expense of the search rely on the appropriate selection of hyperparameters and their search space. However, all the studies conducted so far on vehicle trajectory analysis using LSTM, selected the optimal hyperparameters empirically [3,16,24,34]. The study by Reimers and Gurevych [38] on sequence labelling task has identified the hyperparameters that needs to be tuned for Bi-LSTM in order to produce better performance. Their results showed the impact of several hyperparameters (e.g. Number of Bi-LSTM Layers, Number of Hidden Units, Mini Batch Size) on the performance of their Bi-LSTM model [38]. In [38], the optimiser which governs the whole training process was given a high impact factor than the learning rate. In this paper, we define six hyperparameters for the optimisation of our Bi-LSTM model. These hyperparameters can be categorized as architecture-hyperparameters and modelling-hyperparameters. Those six hyperparameters and their search space are listed below. The search space boundaries of the hyperparameters were selected considering the best performing values of previous studies and their suitability to our method, features and datasets.

1. Architecture-Hyperparameters
   - Number of (Bi-LSTM + Dropout) Layers (L) - $\{1, 2, 3\}$
   - Number of Hidden Units (m) - $[8 - 512]$
   - Dropout Rate (p) - $\{0, 25, 50, 75\}\%$
2. Modelling-Hyperparameters
   - Number of Epochs (Epo) - $[1 - 400]$
   - Mini Batch Size (MB) - $\{2, 4, 8, 16\}$
   - Optimiser (Opt) - $\{SGDM, Adam, RMSprop\}$

Bayesian Optimisation: Given our definition of hyperparameters and their search space, we performed Bayesian Optimisation to tune the hyperparameters of our Bi-LSTM network. In Bayesian Optimisation, a hyperparameter setting h is known as one set of possible values of optimisable hyperparameters (L, m, p, Epo, MB and Opt). Thus, it is defined as $h = \{h_1, ..., h_j, ..., h_z\}$ where h_j is the value of optimisable hyperparameter j in hyperparameter setting h and z is the total number of hyperparameters that are being optimised. z is equal to 6 in our case. Besides that, Bayesian optimiser requires an objective function $f(h)$ which it minimise in each iteration. We set the objective function $f(h)$ as the classification error of the test set when modelling the backbone architecture with hyperparameter setting h.

$$f(h) = \text{Classification Error}(h) \tag{1}$$

Firstly, Bayesian optimiser randomly selects r number of hyperparameter settings. r is known as the initial seed points that the Bayesian optimiser randomly examines before starting the methodical search process. r was set to 4 in our experiment. Using those hyperparameter settings, Bayesian optimiser models the backbone architecture to calculate the objective function $f(h)$ which is the classification error of the test set. Using the values of the objective function, Bayesian optimiser builds the surrogate model $G(h)$ which is based on Gaussian Process Regression. After the initialisation of the surrogate model, Bayesian optimiser starts to select the next hyperparameter setting using an acquisition function. We defined the acquisition function as *Expected Improvement*. *Expected Improvement* chooses the next hyperparameter setting as the one that has the highest expected improvement over the current best observed point of the objective function. The Expected Improvement for hyperparameter setting h is,

$$EI(h) = \mathbf{E}(max(G(h) - f^*(h), 0)) \tag{2}$$

where $G(h)$ is the current posterior distribution of the surrogate model and $f^*(h)$ is the best observed point of the objective function thus far. On each iteration, the h that maximises the $EI(h)$ is selected as the next hyperparameter setting for evaluation. After each iteration, the surrogate model was updated with the newly evaluated point. The search process is continued until the maximum number of evaluation e_{max} which is 30 in our case. The values r and e_{max} were defined empirically in this study. Our Optimisation process is further explained in Algorithm 1.

Algorithm 1. Bayesian Optimisation [37].

Input: Hyperparameter Search Space h
Input: Objective Function $f(h)$
Input: Max No of Evaluation n_{max}
Input: Initial Seed Points r
Output: Optimal hyperparameter setting h^*
Output: Classification Error of Optimal hyperparameter setting d^*

   Select: initial hyperparameter settings $h_0 \in h$ for r number of points
   Evaluate: the initial classification error $d_0 = f(h_0)$
   Set $h^* = h_0$ and $d^* = d^0$
   for n = 1 to e_{max} **do**
   Select: a new hyperparameter configuration $h_n \in h$ by optimising the acquisition function $D(h_n)$

$$h_n = argmax(D(h_n))$$

   where,

$$D(h_n) = EI(h_n) = \mathbf{E}(max(f^*(h) - G(h_n), 0))$$

   Evaluate: f for h_n to obtain the classification error $d_n = f(h_n)$ for hyperparameter setting h_n
   Update: the surrogate model
      if d_n ¡ d^* **then** $h^* = h_n$ and $d^* = d_n$
      end if
   end for
Output: h^* and d^*

3.3   Optimal Architecture Selection

The optimal architecture selection process was carried out under two stages. Initially the best architectures were selected within the datasets and then between the datasets. As further explained in the Sect. 5.1, we used two real world datasets under 5-fold cross validation protocol (5 groups of 80% training and 20% test sets) to find the generic optimal architecture for vehicle activity recognition. Firstly, we performed Bayesian optimisation on each fold of the dataset and generated 30 Bi-LSTM architectures per fold (150 architectures per dataset). We used two criteria in optimal architecture selection: High Classification Accuracy and Low Architecture Complexity. Architecture complexity is determined using the total number of trainable parameters (T.P) an architecture contains. Trainable parameters of Bi-LSTM layer and Fully Connected layer constitutes the total number of trainable parameters (T.P) of our generated architecture as illustrated in Eq. 3.

$$T.P = 2(4m(Q + m + 1)) + C(2m + 1) \tag{3}$$

where 4 represents the four activation function unit equations of the LSTM cell and 2 represents the duality of Bi-LSTM layer.

In the first stage, the architecture(s) that provided the highest classification accuracy from Bayesian Optimisation search were selected from each fold. Given that Bayesian Optimisation method can produce multiple architectures with highest classification accuracy, we decided to include all of them in our selection process. As a result, multiple high performing architectures (highest classification accuracy) were found in each fold. Hence, the architecture complexity of those high performing architectures were compared in order to select the best architecture from each fold. After the selection of first stage, we end up with 5 best architectures from each dataset (1 per fold). In the second stage of selection, we compare the similarities of the best architectures between the datasets. A simple similarity measure was used to perform this selection. It determines how identical (or similar) two architectures are by comparing the values of architecture hyperparameters (L, m and p) between the two architectures. Using this similarity measure, we identify the two optimal architectures from two datasets (one each from the datasets) which are exactly the same/closely matched. If they are exactly the same, we use that architecture as the generic optimal architecture. If they are closely matched we select the architecture generated from the larger and complex dataset between those to architectures.

3.4   VNet Modelling

Given the feature representation (one hot vector in Sect. 3.1) of pair vehicle trajectories and the optimal architecture (Sect. 3.3), we train VNet models for classification of different vehicle activities using four datasets. Based on the number of activities in the given dataset, we update the number of classes C of the fully connected layer. Apart from that, learning rate and momentum of the training were set as 0.01 and 0.9 respectively. The overall average classification accuracy, class wise standard deviation and the class wise classification accuracy were used to evaluate the performance of the models.

4   Vehicle Activity Datasets

We used four publicly available vehicle-vehicle and vehicle-obstacle pair interaction datasets namely Traffic Motion Dataset (Traffic Dataset) [29], Vehicle Obstacle Interaction Dataset (VOI Dataset) [5], Highway Drone Dataset (HighD Dataset) [26] and Next Generation Simulation Open Data (NGSIM Dataset) [44], to evaluate the effectiveness of our model and compare it against the state of the art approaches on the same datasets. All four datasets were gathered under different settings such as using drone camera, static camera, surveillance camera and simulator. In order to further validate our approach, we combined all four datasets together to built a challenging fifth dataset which had different kind of vehicle pair activities collected under different settings, locations and different road traffic environment. A detailed description of each of these dataset is provided below.

4.1   Highway Drone Dataset

Highway Drone (HighD Dataset) Dataset [26] was recorded on highways of Germany by hovering a drone camera on top of the highways as shown in Fig. 5(a). The data was collected from six different locations of German highways that vary in number of lanes, the level of traffic (light and heavy) and speed limit. It contains vehicle trajectories of more than 110,500 vehicles in the form of x, y position coordinates and the behaviour of each vehicle has with its surrounding vehicles at each time step. Using these information, we extracted five unique vehicle pair activities: Follow, Precede, Left Overtake, Left Overtake (Complex) and Right Overtake. Definition of each of these activities are presented in Table 1. Among the extracted pair vehicle trajectories, we selected a total of 6805 pair-trajectories (1361 trajectories per class) in order to avoid class imbalance as well as to reduce the required computational resources to model the Bi-LSTM network. The length of the trajectories varies between 11 time steps to 1911 time steps. Among the 6805 selected pair-trajectories, we separated 1805 pair-trajectories (361 pair-trajectories per class) which were extracted from different highways and different acquisition sessions compared to the rest of the 5000 trajectories, as unseen trajectories for external testing. Out of the 5000 pair-trajectories allocated for modelling the Bi-LSTM network, we only used 500 of them (100 pair-trajectories per class) to optimise the architecture considering the computational expense of the automatic architecture search. However, all 5000 pair-trajectories were used to model the selected generic optimal architecture.

4.2   Traffic Dataset

The traffic dataset is a dataset of 175 pair vehicle trajectories extracted from 20 surveillance videos recorded from different surveillance cameras placed in a road junction [29]. The dataset contains x, y positions of pair of vehicles for each time step and all the pair-trajectories had been sampled to have a fixed length of 20 time steps. Further, it has been annotated with five unique vehicle pair activities and each activity has 35 pair-trajectories in the dataset. Table 2 provides the names and the definition of all five activities, and Fig. 6 shows samples of each activity.

Table 1. Definition of pair-wise vehicle activities generated from HighD Dataset [26].

Activity	Definition
Follow	One vehicle followed by another vehicle on the same lane
Precede	One vehicle preceded by another vehicle on the same lane
Left Overtake	One vehicle is overtaken by another vehicle on the left lane
Left Overtake (Complex)	One vehicle is followed by another vehicle on the same lane and then it is successfully overtaken by that vehicle using the left lane
Right Overtake	One vehicle is overtaken by another vehicle on the right lane

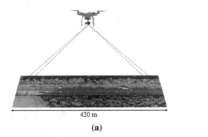
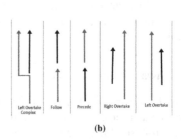

(a)   (b)

Fig. 5. HighD Dataset [26] examples of (a) Moving Vehicles Captured from a Drone Camera. (b) Pair-wise Manoeuvres.

Table 2. Definition of pair-wise vehicle activities in Traffic Dataset [29].

Activity	Definition
Turn	One vehicle moves straight and another vehicle in another lane turns right
Follow	One vehicle followed by another vehicle on the same lane
Side	Two vehicles go side by side in two lanes
Pass	One vehicle passes the crossroad and another vehicle in the other direction waits for green light
Confront	Two vehicles in opposite directions go by each other
Overtake	A vehicle is overtaken by another vehicle
BothTurn	Two vehicles move in opposite directions and turn right at same time

| Turn | Follow | Pass | Overtake | Bothturn |

Fig. 6. Example Pair-wise Manoeuvres of Traffic Dataset [29].

4.3 Vehicle Obstacle Interaction Dataset

Vehicle Obstacle Interaction (VOI) dataset is a synthetic dataset that is acquired through a simulation environment developed using Virtual Battlespace 3 with Logitech G29

Table 3. Definition of pair-wise vehicle activities in VOI Dataset [5].

Activity	Definition
Left Pass	The vehicle successfully passes the object on the left
Right Pass	The vehicle successfully passes the object on the right
Crash	The vehicle and the obstacle collide

Fig. 7. Example Pair-wise Manoeuvres of VOI dataset [5].

Driving Force Racing Wheel and Pedals [26]. The simulated model is a replica of a six lane highway of Dubai. This dataset gives importance to close proximity maneuverings and contains dangerous vehicle activities such as crash which rarely gets captured in real life scenario. The dataset consists of 277 pair vehicle trajectories and it has been labelled with three classes: Left Pass (104 pair-trajectories), Right Pass (106 pair-trajectories) and Crash (67 pair-trajectories). The definitions of these activities are provided in Table 3. The position of each vehicle is given in the form of x, y coordinates and the lengths of the pair trajectories in the dataset vary between 10 and 71 time steps. Figure 7 shows example trajectories of each activity.

4.4 Next Generation Simulation Dataset

The Next Generation Simulation Dataset (NGSIM) is one of the largest publicly available vehicle trajectory dataset which was collected by the Federal Highway Administration of United States using a network of synchronised digital video cameras as shown in Fig. 8(a) [44]. The dataset was collected from four different highways of United States: Southbound US 101, Lankershim Boulevard in Los Angeles, eastbound I-80 in Emeryville and Peachtree Street in Atlanta. It contains vehicle trajectories of more than 3000 vehicles with their x, y position coordinates and the references of the vehicles that are in front and back of the Eco vehicle. Using this information, we extracted 960 pair vehicle trajectories representing two pair vehicle activities: Follow (480) and Preceding (480). The definition of these activities are exactly similar to the definitions of Follow and Preceding of HighD Dataset (Sect. 4.1). The length of the pair-trajectories vary between 10 and 797 time steps. We kept this dataset as external dataset for the VNet models trained on the combined dataset (Sect. 4.5).

4.5 Combined Dataset

We built the combined dataset by integrating three datasets presented in Sects. 4.1, 4.2, 4.3. We merged and split the common classes with careful consideration. The commonality between classes have been captured based on the definition of each class in each

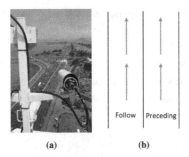

Fig. 8. NGSIM Dataset [44] examples of (a) Moving Vehicles Captured from a Digital Video Camera. (b) Pair-wise Manoeuvres.

dataset. Initially, we split the Pass and Overtake classes of Traffic dataset into (Left Pass, Right Pass) and (Left Overtake, Right Overtake) in order to match the classes of the other datasets. Then we combined the similar classes from each dataset. Follow and Right Overtake class samples of HighD Dataset and Traffic Dataset were combined together. Similarly, Left Pass and Right Pass class samples of Traffic Dataset and VOI Dataset were combined together. Further, Left Overtake and Left Overtake (Complex) classes of HighD dataset were combined together as a single class since both those classes perform the same activity of one vehicle overtaking another vehicle on the left. Apart from that, all the other classes were used as the same as the original dataset. Thereby, we preserved the ground truths of all classes as their original. Thus, the combined dataset consists of 952 pair vehicle trajectories of 9 activities: Follow (135), Left Pass (138), Right Pass (107), Turn (35), Both Turn (35), Crash (67), Preceding (100), Right Overtake (135) and Left Overtake (200).

5   Experiments and Results

In this section, we evaluate the effectiveness of our method of vehicle activity classification using comparative experiments. All the experiments were conducted on an Intel Core i7 laptop, CPU@1.80 GHz with 8.0 GB RAM and 2 GB GPU of NVIDIA GeForce MX130. We use two common metrics to evaluate the performance of our method: Overall Classification Accuracy and Standard Deviation. We initially present the outcome of our automatic Bi-LSTM architecture search process. The evaluations that are carried out to identify the generic optimal architecture are provided here. Then, we present the results of the comparative experiments we conducted on the optimal Bi-LSTM architecture using four different datasets as well as the challenging combined dataset.

5.1   Optimal Architecture Selection

Highway Dataset and Traffic Dataset which are the two real world datasets with multiple activities, were chosen to perform the automatic Bi-LSTM optimal architecture selection process. Even though, the traffic dataset was used completely (175 pair trajectories), we only used 500 pair trajectories (100 each per activity) from the 5000 trajectories which were allocated for modelling. This selection of datasets was made considering the computational expense, limited hardware resources, time constraints as well as to keep few datasets as completely external to evaluate the generality of the automatic architecture search process. In addition, these two datasets has variety of activities with large number of samples for each class. Bayesian optimisation was performed on these datasets in order to find the optimal hyperparameters for the backbone Bi-LSTM architecture proposed in Sect. 3.2.

Initially, the backbone Bi-LSTM architecture, optimisable hyperparameters and their search spaces were defined as explained in Sect. 3.2. Then, both Traffic Dataset (175 trajectories) and HighD Dataset (500 trajectories) were split into 5 non overlapping folds of training and test set. The classification error rate of the test set of each fold was determined as the objective function for the optimisation. Bayesian Optimiser takes the optimisable hyperparameters, their search space and the training and test set of each fold as input. The classification error rate of the test set of the fold was set as the objective function for the Bayesian Optimiser. The search carried out for 150 iterations (30 iterations per fold) individually on both the datasets. For each iteration, Bayesian optimiser produced a Bi-LSTM architecture which resulted in 300 architectures overall. Then, our selection process was applied to identify the generic optimal architecture among those 300 architectures. Firstly, the architectures with the highest classification accuracy in each fold were selected. In all 5 folds, 47 architectures were identified from the HighD Dataset with the highest classification accuracy. However, only 6 architectures were produced from the Traffic Dataset with highest classification accuracy across all 5 folds. For example, fold 1 of HighD Dataset provided 7 architectures with 99.00% accuracy which is the highest classification accuracy achieved from that fold. On the other hand, fold 1 of Traffic Dataset produced one single architecture with the highest accuracy of 91.84%. Since multiple architectures from each fold have achieved the highest classification accuracy, the complexity of the architectures were compared to identify the best architecture of each fold. Table 4 provides the summary of the best models of HighD Dataset and Traffic Dataset from each fold. Among the selected models of each fold, model 2, 3 and 4 produced the best classification accuracy (100%) for HighD Dataset. In Traffic dataset, model 2 achieved the best classification accuracy (93.88%). Therefore, we compared the similarity in architecture among those 4 best performing models of the datasets. Interestingly, BO search has produced exactly the same optimal Bi-LSTM architecture from both real-world datasets. This is one of the key findings of our study. Architectures of Model 2 of both the datasets are constructed of a single Bi-LSTM layer with 74 hidden units and a dropout layer with 50% dropout rate. They share the same L, m and p hyperparameters. Thus, this architecture was selected as the generic optimal architecture for vehicle activity classification during our optimisation. In terms of modelling-hyperparameters, we used the Epochs (Epo), Minibatch size (MB) and Optimiser (Opt) of Model 2 of HighD Dataset which are 232, 8 and SGDM respectively to train the VNet models. This selection was made considering the size and the challenging nature of HighD Dataset which is 25 times larger and has trajectories that varies in length (11–1911 time steps) when compared to Traffic dataset.

5.2 Evaluation of the Optimal Architecture

The selected optimal architecture consists of a single Bi-LSTM Layer with 74 hidden units followed by a dropout layer with 50% dropout rate and a fully connected layer with

Table 4. Summary of the Best Performing Architectures: D.S - Dataset, Arc - Architecture, Acc - Accuracy, S.D - Class-wise Standard Deviation, T.Par - Trainable Parameters, Opt - Optimiser, L - Number of (Bi-LSTM + Dropout) Layer Pairs, m - Number of Hidden Units, p - Dropout Percentage, MB - Mini Batch Size, Epo - Number of Epochs [37].

D.S	Arc	Acc(%)	S.D	T.Par	Opt	L	m	p	MB	Epo
HighD	1	99.00	2.24	9149	RMSprop	1	12	25%	8	23
	2	**100.00**	**0.00**	**93097**	**sgdm**	**1**	**74**	**50%**	**8**	**232**
	3	100.00	0.00	184909	adam	1	116	0%	8	381
	4	100.00	0.00	36865	sgdm	1	38	50%	8	165
	5	99.00	2.24	23819	sgdm	1	27	0%	16	379
Traffic	1	91.84	11.25	35749	sgdm	1	37	25%	8	283
	2	**93.88**	**11.25**	**93395**	**sgdm**	**1**	**74**	**50%**	**4**	**376**
	3	89.80	10.81	28465	sgdm	1	31	75%	4	372
	4	91.84	11.25	187909	sgdm	1	117	75%	8	395
	5	85.71	31.94	5879	sgdm	1	8	50%	8	69

Table 5. Comparison between Our Proposed Method with State-of-the-art TrajNet Method on HighD Dataset: Ave. Acc. - Average Accuracy, S.D - Standard Deviation [37].

Model	Modelling		External Testing	
	VNet	Trajnet	VNet	Trajnet
Follow	99.80%	98.00%	100%	99.34%
Left Overtake	100%	97.00%	100%	97.40%
Left Overtake (Complex)	99.20%	98.00%	99.36%	98.44%
Preceding	100%	100%	100%	99.90%
Right Overtake	100%	100%	100%	99.76%
Ave Acc.	**99.80%**	**98.60%**	**99.87%**	**98.98%**
S.D	**0.35%**	**1.34%**	**0.29%**	**1.05%**

C number of classes in the dataset. It uses Stochastic Gradient Descent with Momentum (SGDM) as the optimiser and 232 epochs and a mini batch size of 8 for training. Firstly, we used the provided x, y position coordinate pairs of each vehicle as inputs, generated corresponding QTC trajectories, and constructed the one-hot vector representations for all four datasets as well as the combined dataset presented in Sect. 4. Then, we evaluated the performance of the selected optimal architecture with 5-fold cross validation.

Experiment 1: Evaluations on Highway Drone Dataset. The optimal Bi-LSTM architecture was trained with 4000 pair trajectories and tested with 1000 pair trajectories for each fold during the modelling. The five models produced an average modelling accuracy of 99.80% with a standard deviation of 0.35%. On the external test set of 1805 trajectories, the models performed even better reaching an average accuracy of

Table 6. Average Classification Accuracy of Different Algorithms on the Traffic Dataset [37].

Type	VNet	[6]	[4]	[29]	[48]	[32]	[30]
Turn	100%	97.10%	97.10%	97.10%	98.00%	83.10%	89.30%
Follow	100%	100%	94.30%	88.60%	77.10%	61.90%	84.60%
Pass	100%	100%	100%	100%	88.30%	82.40%	84.50%
Bothturn	97.14%	100%	97.10%	97.10%	98.80%	97.10%	95.80%
Overtake	97.14%	97.10%	94.30%	94.30%	52.90%	38.30%	63.40%
Ave. Acc.	**98.86%**	**98.84%**	**96.56%**	**95.42%**	**83.02%**	**72.76%**	**83.52%**

99.87% with a standard deviation of 0.29%. We evaluated the model using both QTC_C and QTC_{Full} and the results did not vary much. The data used for training and unseen test were generated from different highways. Further, we only used 10% of the training data to find the optimal Bi-LSTM architecture (500 pair trajectories). The high classification accuracy on the unseen dataset shows the generality and robustness of our proposed method over different activities. It also shows how representative QTC has been, as a qualitative feature. Majority of the misclassifications were caused by Left Overtake (Complex) activity being classified as either Follow or Left Overtake activity. Left Overtake (Complex) is a complex behaviour where initially the second vehicle follows the first vehicle and then overtakes it from the left. Thus, it is combination of two non-complex behaviours: Follow and Left Overtake. The misclassified Left Overtake (Complex) trajectories are comparatively small in sequence length and one of the non-complex behaviour (Follow or Left Overtake) is under represented in those trajectories which lead to their misclassification.

'TrajNet' which uses QTC with a DCNN was selected as a benchmark qualitative method to compare against our model because TrajNet has already proven to outperform all the other qualitative and quantitative methods [4, 29, 30, 32, 48] on other datasets. Thus, we evaluated the TrajNet using the same HighD dataset split and the TrajNet achieved an average modelling accuracy of 98.60% and an unseen test accuracy of 98.98%. Thus, it is evident that VNet performs better than TrajNet here. Even though, the difference between the two models is 1.2% in 5-fold cross validation, that 1.2% represents 60 pair trajectories. Table 5 shows the performance of both TrajNet and VNet during modelling and unseen test. Both in modelling and external testing, VNet has shown relatively less variance (low standard deviation) between the models than TrajNet. Further, Left Overtake (Complex) is a complex activities that incorporates two simple activities: Follow and Left Overtake. Comparatively, TrajNet finds it difficult to differentiate such incorporation of multiple activities.

Experiment 2: Evaluations on Traffic Dataset. We split the Traffic Dataset into training and test set at a ratio of 80% to 20%. Similar experiments were conducted using both QTC_C and QTC_{Full} and our model was able to classify the dataset with an average accuracy of 98.86% (std = 1.56%). The performance of our model was compared against six state of the art pair activity classification methods [4, 6, 29, 30, 32, 48] applied on this dataset. Among them, TrajNet and NWSA are qualitative methods and the rest of them are quantitative methods. However, our VNet model outperforms all of them convincingly as shown in Table 6.

Experiment 3: Evaluations on VOI Dataset. Accurate detection of dangerous close proximity activities is vital for our model to gain traction as a mainstream analysis method. These type of activities are inevitable during vehicle interaction. Thus, evaluated VNet on this publicly available dataset of close proximity maneuvers [5]. Our VNet model achieved the highest possible average accuracy (100%) on this dataset when evaluated using 5-fold cross validation. This result is similar to the performance TrajNet on this dataset. Besides that, high performance on this dataset shows well our optimal architecture search and selection process has worked since this dataset was completely external and not part of the optimal architecture selection process. This shows that our Bi-LSTM architecture is generic and can be used to model vehicle interactions collected from different settings.

Experiment 4: Evaluations on Combined Dataset. As described in Sect. 4.5, this combined dataset is a combination 3 pair vehicle activity datasets collected from different settings and road types and it is particularly challenging because it contains simple and complex vehicle activities with high sequence length range (10 to 1911). Therefore, we conducted similar evaluations on this dataset to demonstrate the generality of our approach. Similar to other datasets, 5-folds cross validation protocol was followed and our VNet model was able to classify the combined dataset with an average accuracy of 98.21%. For comparison, we modelled the state of the art qualitative approach TrajNet [6] using the same 5-fold split. However, TrajNet (Accuracy = 98.10%) could not match the performance our VNet model. The issues of TrajNet in distinguishing between similar kind simple and complex of activities got further exposed in this evaluation. TrajNet struggled to classify activities such as (Left Overtake, Left Pass) and (Right Overtake, Right Pass). In those activities TrajNet (Accuracy = 98.24%) performs poorly compared to our VNet model (Accuracy 99.52%). Evaluations on both HighD Dataset (Sect. 4.1) and Traffic Dataset (Sect. 4.2) validates the superiority of VNet in differentiating similar kind of activities such as Left Overtake, Left Pass and Left Overtake Complex compared to VNet.

Experiment 5: Evaluations on NGSIM Dataset. Similar to the previous experiments, the pair trajectories of NGSIM dataset was split into training and test set at a ratio of 80% to 20%. The training set was used to model our Bi-LSTM network and the test set was then classified by the trained model. Our models were able to classify the dataset with an average accuracy of 100% under 5-folds cross validation protocol. In order to further validate our approach, we used the full NGSIM dataset (960 pair trajectories) as a completely external dataset for the VNet models we built using the combined dataset presented in Experiment 4. The models achieved an average overall accuracy of 99.69% with subclass accuracy of 99.38% and 100% for Follow and Preceding respectively. Majority of the confusion occurred between Follow and Left Overtake classes. It is understandable because some of the Left Overtake class samples has a segment where one vehicle follows the other. This results show how effectively QTC has extracted the relative motion between the vehicles and how well our Bi-LSTM models are optimised since this dataset was collected from highways of a country that is entirely different from the samples we used to train the VNet models of combined data. However, the models were able to achieve a very high accuracy on the external dataset with those two classes.

Table 7. Average Classification Accuracy of Manually Designed LSTM (Handcrafted) [33], TrajNet [6] and Our VNet across all the datasets: H.LSTM - Handcrafted LSTM, Comb. - Combined Dataset [37].

Method	HighD	Traffic	VOI	Comb.
H. LSTM	21.30%	72.00%	89.12%	26.79%
TrajNet	98.60%	98.84%	100%	98.10%
VNet	99.80%	98.86%	100%	98.21%

Experiment 6: Evaluations on Manually Designed Bi-LSTM Architecture. One of the major component of our approach is the automatic optimisation of Bi-LSTM architecture and modelling-hyperparameters. To provide more evidence on the performance of our proposed method and the importance of automatic designing of LSTM architecture, we compared the performance of our auto-optimised Bi-LSTM architecture against a manually designed LSTM architecture presented in [33]. For this, we selected the manually designed LSTM architecture developed for QTC features in [33] as a benchmark. It was chosen as benchmark, since it is the only approach that uses LSTM with QTC and there are no existing LSTM architecture that has been specifically designed for vehicle pair activity recognition. The models of manually designed architecture achieved an average accuracy of 89.12%, 72%, 21.30%, and 26.79% on VOI, Traffic, HighD, and Combined datasets respectively under the same evaluation protocol. Poor LSTM architecture design and modelling-hyperparameter selection are reason behind the substandard performance of these models. The results clearly shows the importance of careful design of Bi-LSTM architecture and methodical selection of modelling-hyperparameters in achieving a successful vehicle activity classification model. Further, the models also show contrasting results across different datasets. It performs reasonably well with VOI dataset but performs really poor with HighD and Combined datasets. It shows the non generalised nature of the architecture. Table 7 shows the results of the model [33] compared against state-of-the-art TrajNet model and our auto-optimised Bi-LSTM model. Our VNet model outperforms existing methods including the manually optimised LSTM across all the datasets.

6 Discussion

In this study, we evaluated a large number of Bi-LSTM models trained on different vehicle trajectory datasets for vehicle activity classification task. The models were also able to deliver high performance by making good predictive decisions. However, interpreting the decisions of these Bi-LSTM models is crucial for the acceptance of such a system in critical applications such as self driving, collision avoidance and security

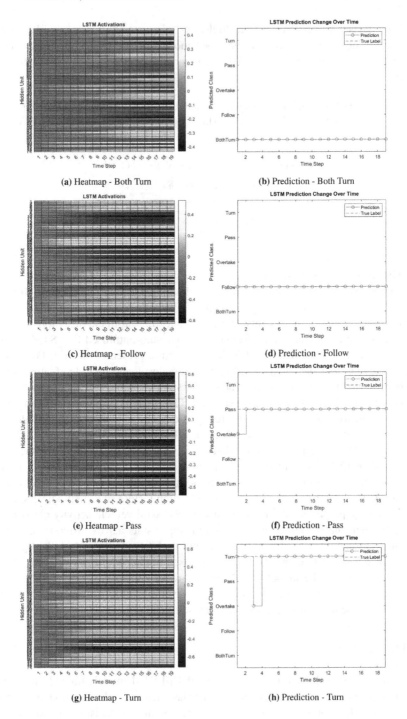

(a) Heatmap - Both Turn

(b) Prediction - Both Turn

(c) Heatmap - Follow

(d) Prediction - Follow

(e) Heatmap - Pass

(f) Prediction - Pass

(g) Heatmap - Turn

(h) Prediction - Turn

Fig. 9. LSTM Hidden Unit Activation Change and LSTM Prediction Change over time for Both Turn, Follow, Pass and Turn Activities of Traffic Dataset.

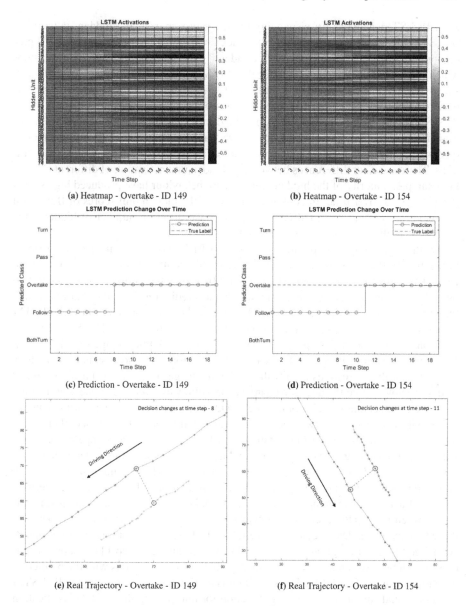

Fig. 10. Comparison between two samples (ID 149 and ID 154) of Overtake Activity in Traffic Dataset.

surveillance. In this section, we try to establish if the visualisation of features learned by our Bi-LSTM models can be used to understand the classification decision of the models. Class Activation Map (CAM) is one of the latest and powerful technique used in computer vision to identify the contribution of each region of the image in the classification decision in image classification task [39]. Similar understanding can be built for a Bi-LSTM network by visualizing the activation map of the hidden units of the Bi-LSTM model [45]. By examining the hidden unit activation map and Bi-LSTM predictions for each class over time, we can identify the hidden units and the time steps which mostly influence the decision of the Bi-LSTM for that particular class. Figure 9 shows the heatmap representation of Bi-LSTM hidden unit activation and Bi-LSTM prediction change over time for four activities of Traffic dataset (Both Turn, Follow, Pass and Turn). The activation maps provided in this section are generated from our evaluations of Traffic dataset using qualitative features. Thus, there are 74 hidden units (generic optimal architecture) and 19 time steps (Traffic dataset) in the heatmap illustrations. There are clear differences between the hidden unit activation of different classes. For example, majority of the hidden units of Turn behaviour have produced high scores (bright regions) over time. In contrast, majority of the hidden unit scores of Both Turn behaviour are around zero. Different activities have different number of hidden units generating really low scores (dark regions).

Further, examining the prediction change of Bi-LSTM over time can also help us in identifying the parts (or actions) that have highly contributed to the decision of the Bi-LSTM from the original trajectory. Figure 10 shows the comparison between two overtake samples of traffic dataset in which the prediction decision changes at different time steps. In overtake sample ID 149, the classification decision of Bi-LSTM changes from Follow to Overtake at time step 8 (Image (c) of Fig. 10). Similarly, the decision changes at time step 11 for overtake sample ID 154 (Image (d) of Fig. 10). Mapping those time steps with the real world trajectories of those samples can show us the region that is responsible for the decision change. Images (e) and (f) of Fig. 10 evidently show us that the decision change from Follow to Overtake happens at the time step where the second vehicle comes side by side to the first vehicle. Up until that point, the activity between those two vehicles has remained to be Follow. Since, there is no Side behaviour in this experiment, rationale behind this decision change corresponds with human reasoning as well as the ground truth of these activities. Interestingly, our model has learned this features on its own. Verification of these understandings with human reasoning can lead us to develop models with rational decision making. Further, Bi-LSTM activation heatmaps of these two overtake samples also show high similarities between them. However, we can also notice a shift in the darker regions between those two heatmaps. Dark regions of overtake ID 149 starts earlier (around time step 8) compared to the dark regions of overtake ID 154 (around time step 11). It shows a shift of 3 time steps between these two heatmaps which also corresponds with the prediction decision change of Bi-LSTM. The study in this section demonstrates that the Bi-LSTM decision visualisation is a promising direction for interpreting the model classification decision of vehicles activity analysis.

7   Conclusion

In this paper, we have presented a novel vehicle pair activity recognition method using qualitative feature representation QTC with sequential deep learning algorithm Bi-LSTM. Our method encodes the relative motion between two vehicles using the QTC and uses one-hot vector to represent the QTC trajectories. In addition, we proposed an automatic neural network architecture search method using Bayesian Optimisation to find the optimal Bi-LSTM architecture and modelling hyperparameters for the vehicle pair activity classification task. Our method has outperformed all the existing qualitative [4,6] and quantitative [29,30,32,48] algorithms for pair activity classification in four publicly available vehicle activity datasets. Our approach achieved an average classification accuracy of 98.21% on a challenging combined dataset that comprises the three datasets. Further, our model trained on combined dataset was able to classify a completely external dataset with an average accuracy of 99.69%. The results clearly show how well our method is generalised while still giving optimal results. Further, we also observed that Bayesian Optimisation with our selection policy providing same generic optimal architectures for vehicle activity classification from two different datasets. It indicates the effectiveness of Bayesian Optimisation in automatically designing generalised Bi-LSTM architectures. We have also explored Class Activation Map visualization method on Bi-LSTM models trained using vehicle trajectories. Our preliminary investigation has shown different visualization output of vehicle activities (e.g. Both Turn, Follow, Pass and Turn). This observation of Bi-LSTM decision behavior helps in identifying the actions that have contributed to the model final classification decision.

Intrigued by the performance of our approach based on Bi-LSTM with Bayesian Optimisation, we intend to further expand our investigation using quantitative features with our Bayesian optimised Bi-LSTM approach. It will provide the platform to compare the advantages and disadvantages of both qualitative and quantitative features under the same experimental framework. We would also like to extend our investigation on Bi-LSTM decision understanding. We identified that analysing the Bi-LSTM Activation Maps and the outputs of Bi-LSTM cells in each time step in order to identify the trajectory regions that contribute to the Bi-LSTM classification decision as the first step towards Bi-LSTM decision understanding. Further, we also want to explore other powerful sequential modelling techniques such as transformers, causal and dilated convolutional neural networks for vehicle activity classification in future.

References

1. Ahmed, M., Du, H., AlZoubi, A.: An ENAS based approach for constructing deep learning models for breast cancer recognition from ultrasound images. arXiv preprint arXiv:2005.13695 (2020)
2. Ahmed, S.A., Dogra, D.P., Kar, S., Roy, P.P.: Trajectory-based surveillance analysis: a survey. IEEE Trans. Circuits Syst. Video Technol. **29**(7), 1985–1997 (2018)
3. Altché, F., de La Fortelle, A.: An LSTM network for highway trajectory prediction. In: 2017 IEEE 20th International Conference on Intelligent Transportation Systems (ITSC), pp. 353–359 (2017). https://doi.org/10.1109/ITSC.2017.8317913
4. AlZoubi, A., Al-Diri, B., Pike, T., Kleinhappel, T., Dickinson, P.: Pair-activity analysis from video using qualitative trajectory calculus. IEEE Trans. Circuits Syst. Video Technol. **28**(8), 1850–1863 (2017)
5. Alzoubi, A., Nam, D.: Vehicle Obstacle Interaction Dataset (VOIDataset), October 2018. https://doi.org/10.17862/cranfield.rd.6270233.v2

6. AlZoubi, A., Nam, D.: Vehicle activity recognition using DCNN. In: Cláudio, A.P., et al. (eds.) VISIGRAPP 2019. CCIS, vol. 1182, pp. 566–588. Springer, Cham (2020). https://doi. org/10.1007/978-3-030-41590-7_24

7. AlZoubi, A., Nam, D.: Vehicle activity recognition using mapped QTC trajectories. In: Proceedings of the 14th International Joint Conference on Computer Vision, Imaging and Computer Graphics Theory and Applications - Volume 5: VISAPP, pp. 27–38. INSTICC, SciTePress (2019). https://doi.org/10.5220/0007307600270038

8. Beernaerts, J., De Baets, B., Lenoir, M., De Mey, K., Van de Weghe, N.: Analysing team formations in football with the static qualitative trajectory calculus. In: Proceedings of the 7th icSPORTS International Conference on Sports Science Research and Technology Support, Seville, Spain, pp. 20–21 (2018)

9. Berndt, H., Dietmayer, K.: Driver intention inference with vehicle onboard sensors. In: 2009 IEEE International Conference on Vehicular Electronics and Safety (ICVES), pp. 102–107. IEEE (2009)

10. Chavoshi, S.H., et al.: Knowledge discovery in choreographic data using relative motion matrices and dynamic time warping. Appl. Geogr. **47**, 111–124 (2014)

11. Chavoshi, S.H., De Baets, B., Neutens, T., De Tré, G., Van de Weghe, N.: Exploring dance movement data using sequence alignment methods. PLoS ONE **10**(7), e0132452 (2015)

12. Chen, L., Özsu, M.T., Oria, V.: Robust and fast similarity search for moving object trajectories. In: Proceedings of the 2005 ACM SIGMOD International Conference on Management of Data, pp. 491–502 (2005)

13. Dahl, G.E., Sainath, T.N., Hinton, G.E.: Improving deep neural networks for LVCSR using rectified linear units and dropout. In: 2013 IEEE International Conference on Acoustics, Speech and Signal Processing, pp. 8609–8613. IEEE (2013)

14. Deo, N., Rangesh, A., Trivedi, M.M.: How would surround vehicles move? A unified framework for maneuver classification and motion prediction. IEEE Trans. Intell. Veh. **3**(2), 129–140 (2018)

15. Deo, N., Trivedi, M.M.: Convolutional social pooling for vehicle trajectory prediction. In: Proceedings of the IEEE Conference on Computer Vision and Pattern Recognition Workshops, pp. 1468–1476 (2018)

16. Deo, N., Trivedi, M.M.: Multi-modal trajectory prediction of surrounding vehicles with maneuver based LSTMS. In: 2018 IEEE Intelligent Vehicles Symposium (IV), pp. 1179–1184. IEEE (2018)

17. Dondrup, C., Bellotto, N., Hanheide, M., Eder, K., Leonards, U.: A computational model of human-robot spatial interactions based on a qualitative trajectory calculus. Robotics **4**(1), 63–102 (2015)

18. Feurer, M., Hutter, F.: Hyperparameter optimization. In: Hutter, F., Kotthoff, L., Vanschoren, J. (eds.) Automated Machine Learning. TSSCML, pp. 3–33. Springer, Cham (2019). https:// doi.org/10.1007/978-3-030-05318-5_1

19. Framing, C.E., Heßeler, F.J., Abel, D.: Infrastructure-based vehicle maneuver estimation with intersection-specific models. In: 2018 26th Mediterranean Conference on Control and Automation (MED), pp. 253–258. IEEE (2018)

20. Frazier, P.I.: A tutorial on Bayesian optimization (2018)

21. Hanheide, M., Peters, A., Bellotto, N.: Analysis of human-robot spatial behaviour applying a qualitative trajectory calculus. In: 2012 IEEE RO-MAN: The 21st IEEE International Symposium on Robot and Human Interactive Communication, pp. 689–694. IEEE (2012)

22. Kaselimi, M., Doulamis, N., Doulamis, A., Voulodimos, A., Protopapadakis, E.: Bayesian-optimized bidirectional LSTM regression model for non-intrusive load monitoring. In: ICASSP 2019–2019 IEEE International Conference on Acoustics, Speech and Signal Processing (ICASSP), pp. 2747–2751. IEEE (2019)

23. Khosroshahi, A., Ohn-Bar, E., Trivedi, M.M.: Surround vehicles trajectory analysis with recurrent neural networks. In: 2016 IEEE 19th International Conference on Intelligent Transportation Systems (ITSC), pp. 2267–2272. IEEE (2016)

24. Kim, B., Kang, C.M., Kim, J., Lee, S.H., Chung, C.C., Choi, J.W.: Probabilistic vehicle trajectory prediction over occupancy grid map via recurrent neural network. In: 2017 IEEE 20th International Conference on Intelligent Transportation Systems (ITSC), pp. 399–404 (2017). https://doi.org/10.1109/ITSC.2017.8317943

25. Kim, T.Y., Cho, S.B.: Particle swarm optimization-based CNN-LSTM networks for forecasting energy consumption. In: 2019 IEEE Congress on Evolutionary Computation (CEC), pp. 1510–1516. IEEE (2019)

26. Krajewski, R., Bock, J., Kloeker, L., Eckstein, L.: The highD dataset: a drone dataset of naturalistic vehicle trajectories on German highways for validation of highly automated driving systems. In: 2018 IEEE 21st International Conference on Intelligent Transportation Systems (ITSC) (2018)

27. Lefèvre, S., Laugier, C., Ibañez-Guzmán, J.: Exploiting map information for driver intention estimation at road intersections. In: 2011 IEEE Intelligent Vehicles Symposium (IV), pp. 583–588. IEEE (2011)

28. Lenik, P., Krzeszowski, T., Przednowek, K., Lenik, J.: The analysis of basketball free throw trajectory using PSO algorithm. In: icSPORTS, pp. 250–256 (2015)

29. Lin, W., Chu, H., Wu, J., Sheng, B., Chen, Z.: A heat-map-based algorithm for recognizing group activities in videos. IEEE Trans. Circuits Syst. Video Technol. 23(11), 1980–1992 (2013)

30. Lin, W., Sun, M.T., Poovendran, R., Zhang, Z.: Group event detection with a varying number of group members for video surveillance. IEEE Trans. Circuits Syst. Video Technol. 20(8), 1057–1067 (2010)

31. Melis, G., Dyer, C., Blunsom, P.: On the state of the art of evaluation in neural language models. arXiv preprint arXiv:1707.05589 (2017)

32. Ni, B., Yan, S., Kassim, A.: Recognizing human group activities with localized causalities. In: 2009 IEEE Conference on Computer Vision and Pattern Recognition, pp. 1470–1477. IEEE (2009)

33. Panzner, M., Cimiano, P.: Comparing hidden Markov models and long short term memory neural networks for learning action representations. In: Pardalos, P.M., Conca, P., Giuffrida, G., Nicosia, G. (eds.) MOD 2016. LNCS, vol. 10122, pp. 94–105. Springer, Cham (2016). https://doi.org/10.1007/978-3-319-51469-7_8

34. Park, S.H., Kim, B., Kang, C.M., Chung, C.C., Choi, J.W.: Sequence-to-sequence prediction of vehicle trajectory via LSTM encoder-decoder architecture. In: 2018 IEEE Intelligent Vehicles Symposium (IV), pp. 1672–1678. IEEE (2018)

35. Pham, H., Guan, M., Zoph, B., Le, Q., Dean, J.: Efficient neural architecture search via parameters sharing. In: International Conference on Machine Learning, pp. 4095–4104. PMLR (2018)

36. Phillips, D.J., Wheeler, T.A., Kochenderfer, M.J.: Generalizable intention prediction of human drivers at intersections. In: 2017 IEEE Intelligent Vehicles Symposium (IV), pp. 1665–1670 (2017). https://doi.org/10.1109/IVS.2017.7995948

37. Radhakrishnan, R., AlZoubi, A.: Vehicle pair activity classification using QTC and long short term memory neural network. In: VISIGRAPP (5: VISAPP), pp. 236–247 (2022)

38. Reimers, N., Gurevych, I.: Optimal hyperparameters for deep LSTM-networks for sequence labeling tasks. arXiv preprint arXiv:1707.06799 (2017)

39. Selvaraju, R.R., Cogswell, M., Das, A., Vedantam, R., Parikh, D., Batra, D.: Grad-CAM: visual explanations from deep networks via gradient-based localization. In: Proceedings of the IEEE International Conference on Computer Vision, pp. 618–626 (2017)

40. Simonyan, K., Zisserman, A.: Very deep convolutional networks for large-scale image recognition. arXiv preprint arXiv:1409.1556 (2014)
41. Snoek, J., Larochelle, H., Adams, R.P.: Practical Bayesian optimization of machine learning algorithms. In: Advances in Neural Information Processing Systems, vol. 25 (2012)
42. Snoek, J., et al.: Scalable Bayesian optimization using deep neural networks. In: International Conference on Machine Learning, pp. 2171–2180. PMLR (2015)
43. Tan, M., Le, Q.: EfficientNet: rethinking model scaling for convolutional neural networks. In: International Conference on Machine Learning, pp. 6105–6114. PMLR (2019)
44. U.S. Department of Transportation Federal Highway Administration: Next generation simulation (NGSIM) vehicle trajectories and supporting data (2016)
45. Van Der Westhuizen, J., Lasenby, J.: Techniques for visualizing LSTMS applied to electrocardiograms. arXiv preprint arXiv:1705.08153 (2017)
46. Van de Weghe, N.: Representing and reasoning about moving objects: a qualitative approach. Ph.D. thesis, Ghent University (2004)
47. Yang, T., Li, B., Xun, Q.: LSTM-attention-embedding model-based day-ahead prediction of photovoltaic power output using Bayesian optimization. IEEE Access 7, 171471–171484 (2019)
48. Zhou, Y., Yan, S., Huang, T.S.: Pair-activity classification by bi-trajectories analysis. In: 2008 IEEE Conference on Computer Vision and Pattern Recognition, pp. 1–8. IEEE (2008)
49. Zyner, A., Worrall, S., Nebot, E.: A recurrent neural network solution for predicting driver intention at unsignalized intersections. IEEE Robot. Autom. Lett. 3(3), 1759–1764 (2018). https://doi.org/10.1109/LRA.2018.2805314

ANTENNA: Visual Analytics of Mobility Derived from Cellphone Data

Pedro Silva(✉), Catarina Maçãs, João Correia, Penousal Machado, and Evgheni Polisciuc

CISUC, Department of Informatics Engineering, University of Coimbra, Coimbra, Portugal
{pedros,cmacas,jncor,machado,evgheni}@dei.uc.pt

Abstract. Nowadays, it is possible to characterise, visualise, and analyse urban mobility using digital footprints, in particular, cellphones. However, movement patterns from vast heterogeneous datasets must be parsed, filtered, and aggregated using dynamic and scalable methods. ANTENNA, is a visual analytic tool that depicts trajectories of movement gathered from mobile cellphone data, enabling the discovery and analysis of its patterns. The data is processed in real time, transforming raw records of cellphone connections into trajectories, that can be used to infer mass movements of crowds. The proposed visualisation tool is prepared to deal with different analytical scenarios, presenting distinct visualisation strategies for various ranges of tasks. We conducted user testing with experts from many fields to validate ANTENNA. According to the results, ANTENNA proved to be beneficial for each one of the tested scenarios.

Keywords: Urban mobility · Flow visualisation · Spatio-temporal data · Origin-destination visualisation · Visual analytics

1 Introduction

Transportation systems are not only a key factor for economic sustainability and social welfare but also a key dimension in the smart city agenda. A smart city is a place where traditional networks and services are made more efficient for the benefit of its inhabitants and businesses, through the use of digital and telecommunication technologies. The wide deployment of pervasive computing devices (e.g., smartphones, GPS devices, digital cameras), increasing storage and processing capacity of computing, and improvements in sensing and modelling capabilities, just to name a few, offer opportunities for digital transformation in cities. For example, it is now possible to collect and store the necessary data to estimate and calibrate urban mobility, which data can be further visualised, in real-time, to provide a better understanding of the functioning of cities, and generate powerful insights in several contexts like economical, social, and public policy. Understanding personal travel patterns and modelling travel demand is essential to plan sustainable urban transportation systems to fulfil the citizens' mobility needs. To do this effectively and timely, urban and transportation planners need a dynamic way to profile the movement of people and vehicles.

ⓒ The Author(s), under exclusive license to Springer Nature Switzerland AG 2023
A. A. de Sousa et al. (Eds.): VISIGRAPP 2022, CCIS 1815, pp. 135–160, 2023.
https://doi.org/10.1007/978-3-031-45725-8_7

Urban movements are generally profiled using information about land use patterns. However, unlike transportation and land use infrastructures, which rarely alter after being put in place, urban movements frequently shift. Contrary to traditional research methods which were costly and quickly became outdated, ubiquitous systems (e.g., wireless networks and mobile devices) [27] can now provide massive amounts of data on human digital traces that allow for dynamic mobility profiling and real-time location information. All of these mobility data, along with cutting-edge geoprocessing, data fusion, and visualisation techniques, open up fresh possibilities for determining activity destinations and connecting online and offline activities through user interactions, which can improve the models of land use and transportation. Mining individuals' mobility patterns is an emergent research area [16,29,37,42,46] for predicting future movements, destinations [9,23,27,50], or city planning [31], for instance. Nonetheless, the inconsistency and incompleteness of the retrieved data may lead to various challenges in finding mobility patterns exclusively through modern practices that rely solely on data mining [27,31]. From the literature review, it is clear that automatically collected data from mobile phone records has the advantage of large size and long observation time periods. However, it has several weaknesses, such as low spatial resolution, inconsistent temporal samples, and noise from interchangeable connections to multiple cells.

In this paper, we present a system for transforming sequences of cell tower's connections into logical trajectories—reducing inconsistencies in data and identifying the locations of stay and passage—and for the visualization of such data in an easy to use web-interface. Our pipeline for the data transformation is divided into two main parts: temporal aggregation and trajectory extraction, which tackles several challenges of transforming raw cell phone data into analysable trajectories. Namely, the difficulties range from cleaning the cell phone data records to extracting sequential events [53] and from converting these events into sequences of trips and activity locations [61] and to matching these trips and locations to the geographic map [41]. In short, temporal aggregation removes the noise from available data by filtering and aggregating data by time and user. Trajectory extraction, as well as map matching, occurs after the temporal aggregation step and uses additional information from the pre-processed data to infer trajectories. Finally, our approach employs technologies to work with large amounts of data in distributed and scalable fashion (e.g., Spark and Hadoop), allowing near real-time visualisation and analysis of clutter-free mobility patterns—one of the biggest problems when dealing with such amounts of mobile phone data without pre-processing and storing [54].

To address the interaction and exploration of the trajectories and the mobility of crowds, in cooperation with Altice Labs, we developed ANTENNA a visual analytics tool. The main goal of this tool is to provide the means to visualise, analyse, and identify inter- and intra-urban mobility patterns, promoting the application of measures for sustainable urban mobility. More specifically, the visualisation allows (i) the identification of the most common trajectories; (ii) quantitative analysis of how many people move from/towards a specified reference areas; (iii) identification of how many people do the same trajectory, or have the same origin/destiny points; (iv) identification and categorisation of different geographic locations; (v) comparison among different periods of time, identifying areas of greater affluence throughout time. A demonstration video of the tool can be accessed on this link https://bit.ly/3CT16Vu.

This article, in comparison with the original paper [47], presents the entire architecture of our system and the pipeline implemented to process the raw data into the final trajectories. Concerning the contributions to temporal aggregation and trajectory extraction, we emphasise the combination of multiple existing methods in one single pipeline to produce a functional visualization of mobility data in real time, such as noise filtering, clustering, segmentation, and stay points identification.

2 Related Work

This section provides an overview of the related techniques on reconstruction of trajectories from cellphone data, as well as the methods for visual analysis of movement in urban spaces.

2.1 Reconstruction and Extraction of Trajectories

Several works have been done to tackle the issue of reconstructing trajectory. Although the approaches vary, for instance, Hunter et al. [22] introduce path influence filter based on random sampling, Mazhelis [33] suggests a probabilistic approach based on Bayesian inference, Ochieng et al. [35] present another probabilistic method based on Kalman filter, Horn et al. [21] compared it with Recursive filtering, Newson and Krumm [34] propose an algorithm based on Hidden Markov Model, in general, the underlying idea is similar – try to find the relationship between the trajectory and the road network. This is usually done through the technique known as *map matching* – matching measured latitude/longitude points to roads [41].

Most trajectory reconstruction works use GPS locations from either a vehicle or a person. If measuring GPS coordinates inaccuracy contributes to noisy trajectory estimation, the problem increases when trying to estimate a cellphone data knowing only the GPS location of the connected cell tower. A simple method was presented by Wang et al. [55], where the authors cluster consecutive locations according to their geographical distance and then use these clusters as locations of origin and destination of a trajectory. Vajakas et al. [53] present a trajectory reconstruction method that consists of cell pair routing with ping-pong suppression. In short, the method proceeds twofold: first, ambiguous cellphone connections are removed from the cell trajectory; then, the algorithm generates possible trajectories from the resulted sequence. Similarly, Song et al. [48] propose a model with similar steps – first, data pre-processing, which includes raw data clustering, detection of important locations, and commute trajectory extraction; second, map matching, which consist of mapping commute trajectories to the real world roads. Schlaich et al. [45] proceed in a similar fashion – first extract the trajectory, and then match it with the map. Widhalm et al. [57] proposes a method that combines low-pass filters with an incremental algorithm to transform a sequence of call events into the pass-by (trip) and stay (activity) locations, with their respective duration.

In regards to trajectory extraction from time-sequenced mobile network data, the methods vary. In general, the data cleaning process starts by performing multiples checks and groupings, such as, determine whether the following data entry is an actual movement by analysing the overlapping shapes of cell towers [53]; check if the movement is possible during the indicated time and perform temporal clustering [53]; identify pass-by locations [24,61]; check for forward and backward ping-pong events using the variants of ABAB technique [15,45,53]. Also, some approaches subdivide the trajectory into smaller sub-trajectories, creating so-called virtual locations [9,53], which can be classified as locations of interest where the user performs some activity or stay locations [48,57]. To remove outliers, the work of Widhalm et al. [57] suggests a recursive "Look-Ahead" filter – the combination of geographic distance with the temporal distance between two consecutive records to determine the speed of movement and compare it against some threshold.

To sum-up, we identified several groups of methods that can be applied during the process of trajectory extraction: noise filtering (e.g., Kalman filter, ping-pong filter), clustering (e.g., spatial and temporal), segmentation (i.e., subdivide trajectory into smaller logical segments), stay points identification (e.g., locations of long or short stay duration).

2.2   Visual Analytics of Movement

The visual analytics of movement has its own state-of-the-art techniques, which are well-established approaches concerning visual analysis of movement data [4]. Andrienko and Andrienko identified four directions of visual analysis: (i) *looking at trajectories*, (ii) *looking inside trajectories*, (iii) *bird's-eye view on movement*, and (iv) *investigating movement in context*.

The first category, *looking at trajectories*, is characterised by the strong focus on trajectories of moving objects analysed as a whole by resorting to different graphical means. Representing trajectories with linear symbols (lines) in static and animated maps [5,14,28] and space-time cubes (STC) [25,26] are the most common techniques. Arcs are also used to show flow [10,38]. However, these methods may suffer from visual occlusions and clutter [6]. Clustering trajectories, more known as progressive clustering method, is another popular technique to deal with large amounts of data [3,43] and to reduce visual clutter [11]. As such, ANTENNA takes the advantage of aggregation techniques while using linear symbols to represent trajectories.

Concerning the variation of movement characteristics along the trajectory, *looking inside trajectories*, are used to support the detection of segments with specific movement characteristics. Attribute values can be represented by colouring or shading [49,52], as well as placing glyphs onto the segments [56]. Furthermore, a trajectory can be considered as a sequence of spatial events [1], and techniques such as presented in [2] can be used to extract and cluster movement data. We apply variable colouring and shading in ANTENNA to distinguish sections of trajectories with major activity influx.

The techniques under *bird's-eye view on movement* mainly focus on providing an overview of the distribution of movement in space and time through the means of generalisation and aggregation such as flow maps [11,13], or thematic maps [12,39,59]. Origin-destination (OD) matrix [17,30] and Small multiple maps are another techniques to show flows [18,58]. Apart from clustering techniques, kernel density estimation method can be applied on trajectories to display density fields on a map by using colour or shading [39] and an illumination model [44]. In ANTENNA we implemented an aggregation method that is based on a hexagonal grid, which subdivides into hexagonal areas that are served as aggregation bins and shown with glyphs.

Movement data can also be analysed within the context, focusing on the relations and interaction between moving objects and the environment [51]. Interaction techniques, for instance "staining" (i.e., the user marks a certain area of the context and relationships with moving objects emerge) [8] or by computing distances of moving objects to a selected element and visualising the result on a timeline [36], can be employed to explore movement in context. Similar ideas are presented in [1], which consist of computing spatial and temporal distances from moving objects to items in the environment and representing them as attributes linked to trajectory positions. ANTENNA provides the user with a functionality that consists of updating the map according to the hovered bar on the timeline, which in turn is a representation of aggregated data shown on the map.

3   System Overview

The ANTENNA system is a three-tiered system with three major parts: frontend *presentation tier*, backend *application tier* and datasource *database tier* (Fig. 1). It is constructed to be able to process different requests in a parallel and scalable way, and to read from dynamic distributed datasources. The frontend of the system serves to request or cancel a visual query and visualise its results. The first entry point on the server, i.e. backend, is the REST API module. The frontend request a visual query that is submitted via the REST API. The REST API receives and processes the request, passing to the backend's Worker unit which starts processing the information of the query and uses the available data to construct the result[1]. The worker uses pre-processed information

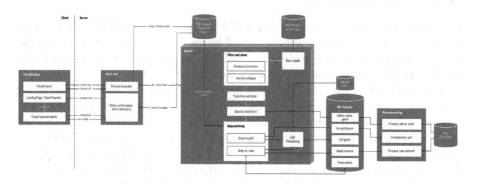

Fig. 1. Representation of the ANTENNA architecture. The important modules are visualisation, REST API, the datasource, and the worker.

---

[1] Note that the REST API module works in an asynchronous way, i.e., once a visual query is submitted it delivers the response for the visual query submission and becomes available to accept new visual queries.

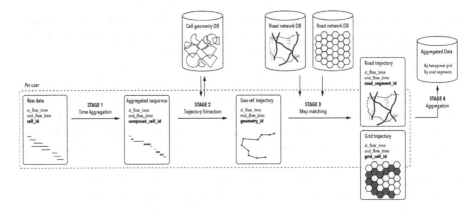

Fig. 2. The processing pipeline executed inside the worker unit. The vertical rectangles illustrate the input/output data, attributes, and schematic structure. In each stage the data is transformed into different spatio-temporal forms, and at the end is persisted in the database for further visualization.

to enrich the data and construct the response data for the frontend to build the visualisation. During the analysis of the query, the system performs temporal and spatial aggregation and filtering (discussed later in Sect. 4.2). The final result is stored in the database tier and the frontend provides a way to consult and see the information of the query.

The processing pipeline (Fig. 2) consists of four stages: i) time aggregation, ii) trajectory extraction, iii) map matching, and iv) data aggregation. Each stage of the pipeline will be discussed in detail in the respective sections.

3.1 Backend and Frontend

To implement the backend, we resorted to Flask, Pandas, and PySpark in Python programming language. In summary, the visual query API submits the query and the worker unit starts processing the request. Once the request is done and processed by the worker unit, it is saved into the database so it can be visualised later.

The REST API serves the purpose of exposing different methods to manage the visual query resource. It comes as an executable server created using python's Flask module. As such, the following resources are exposed: Query and QueryList. For the Query resource we have the following methods: (i) POST - Creates a new visual query; (ii) GET - Gets the information on a visual query that was submitted; (iii) DELETE - Removes and cancels the visual query. As for the QueryList, the only method that exists is the GET, which retrieves the information on all visual queries that were submitted.

The worker is responsible for constructing the visual query response, which are executed by the Apache Spark engine on a computer cluster, with the goal of processing the data in real and useful time. The process is divided into two main parts: time aggregation and trajectory extraction. In short, time aggregation processes the available data by filtering and aggregating data by time and by user. Trajectory extraction occurs after the time aggregation algorithm step and uses information from the pre-processing data and the time aggregation to infer trajectories.

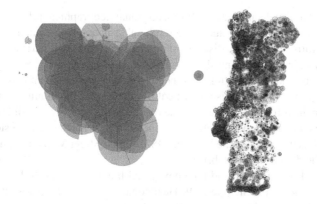

Fig. 3. Cellphone towers overlap issue (left) and the entire network of towers (right).

The frontend consists of the query page and the visualization page, which will be discussed later in Sect. 5.

4 Data

The dataset provided by Altice[2] contains per-user sequences of cell connection events. The time span ranges from December of 2018 to January of 2019, and covers the entire area of Aveiro city, in Portugal. Each event is a time interval that indicates the beginning and the end of the connection to a cell tower. The data entries have an average interval of 10 min between them. In some cases, simultaneous connections from the same user to two cell towers can occur. This results in an added temporal uncertainty associated to user positioning in space-time. Further, the cell towers are characterised by their GPS location, and the sector of coverage (angle and radius). Multiple towers can appear within the range of other towers, which further decrease the positioning accuracy (see Fig. 3).

4.1 Database

The database is used for diverse purposes (e.g., storing geometries of administrative units and road network), taking advantage of the PostGres engine for storing and processing geospatial geometries. Some tables are created and filled before the execution of the system (e.g., the submitted queries, query results), some are created and filled before the initialisation of the system (e.g., tables with the hexagonal grid, roads, cells towers, and administrative units geometries), and others are filled dynamically at execution time (e.g., roads cache). The database includes: (i) Geometries of the cells; (ii) Hexagonal grid geometries; (iii) Road network and the cache; (iv) Administrative unit geometries; and (v) Queries and the results;

Besides the existence of the datatables we need to preprocess some information related to the problem, which will be described in the following subsections.

---

[2] A telecommunication operator in Portugal.

The frontend visualisation depends on additional geographical information, such as the country's road network, hexagonal hierarchical grid, and the geometries of the country's administrative units (e.g., districts, municipalities, and civil parishes). These data are optionally calculated during the installation/setup phase, and can be recalculated every time the official information is updated (e.g., a new significant road constructed, civil parishes join), although it is not critical for the correct functioning of the system.

We rely on the information of a routable road network to depict possible routes that a user could have taken to reach location A to location B. It is noted that, instead of using the workshop's data, we used the Portugal OSM (Open Street Maps) road network (this project uses the data from Geofabrik).

A hexagonal hierarchical grid (aka hexagonal binning), developed by CDV lab, is used as an aggregation technique [40]. Hexagonal binning is a process that produces hexagonal grids of variable resolution to subdivide space according to the density of data points in geographical space. Similar to quadtrees the hexagonal tree uses a hierarchical structure with hexagons on the leaves and a composition of seven copies at higher levels of the tree. The hexagonal grid provides a higher level visualisation, and therefore analysis of geographical data (see Sect. 5.3). A more detailed description of this technique can be found in.

The geometries of the administrative units are used as origin/destination filters to visualise only the activities that start at the origin and/or end at destination areas (see Sect. 5.4). There are three levels of administrative units: (i) districts, (ii) municipalities, and (iii) civil parishes. The system uses this information in two instances: (i) in the visual query page (see Sect. 5.2) and (ii) in the spatial constraints module. The shapefiles for the Portugal administrative units were taken from GADM.

4.2 Processing Pipeline

The frontend visualisation depends on additional geographical information, such as the country's road network, the geometries of the hexagonal grid, and the geometries of the country's administrative units (e.g., districts, municipalities, and civil parishes). This data is prepared on the setup phase, and can be renewed every time the official information is updated (e.g., new road constructed, civil parishes joined), although it is not critical for the correct functioning of the system. We rely on the information of a routable road network to depict possible routes that a user could have taken to reach from location A to location B. For that we used the Portugal OSM (Open Street Maps) road network, in particular the data retrieved from Geofabrik [32].

Hexagonal hierarchical grid is used as an aggregation technique, which is a grid of variable resolution that subdivide space according to the density of data points [40]. Similar to quadtrees the hexagonal tree uses a hierarchical structure with hexagons on the leaves and a composition of seven copies at higher levels of the tree. The hexagonal grid enables a higher level analysis, and therefore a broader understanding of mobility patterns.

The geometries of the administrative units[3] are used as origin/destination filters to visualise only the activities that start at the origin and/or end at the destination areas (see

---

[3] The shapefiles for the Portugal administrative units were taken from GADM.

Sect. 5.3). There are three levels of administrative units: (i) districts, (ii) municipalities, and (iii) civil parishes. The system uses this information in two instances: (i) in the visual query page and (ii) as a spatial constraint in the processing module (detailed in Sect. 4.2).

Time Aggregation. A time aggregation algorithm is used to summarise the data in terms of user versus time per antenna (cell unit), and it is the first stage of the pipeline (Fig. 2). The algorithm proceeds as follows:

1. Retrieve the information during the time interval defined in the visual query. The algorithm at this point expects the following information from the datasource layer: $user\_id$, $start\_flow$, end_flow, $cell\_id$. During this step the $start\_flow$ and end_flow will be filtered by the start time and end time of the visual query.
2. The information from step 1 is aggregated by user.
3. After aggregating by user, the worker processes the information by sorting it by $start\_flow$ in ascending order. The values are then aggregated by interaction with the different antenna cells ($cell\_id$).
4. For each $cell\_id$ we collapse the timelines by analysing pairs of consecutive timelines by joining timelines that are between a $start\_flow$ and end_flow interval given a certain predefined threshold.
5. After doing step 4 for all antennas we sort the information again by $start\_time$ and, in this step, we check overlaps between the different antennas timelines. For instance, as an abstraction, consider A and B, their intersection AB as interactions between different antennas, and a sequence of interactions denoted as: $X \rightarrow Y$ meaning that the first event was X then Y. If the timeline of A and B intersection we can have three situations: 1) B intersects A and has an end_flow lower than A, which creates the new $composite\_id$ AB and the timeline would be, $A \rightarrow AB \rightarrow B$; 2) B intersects A and has an end_flow later than A, leading to $A \rightarrow AB \rightarrow B$ or; 3) B intersects A and the end_flow of B and A are equal, which will generate: $A \rightarrow AB$. Note that in this step we can be adding more information, i.e. more rows to the dataset to be analysed by the next modules.
6. The information is gathered in a single sequence of events with the following structure: $user\_id$, $start\_flow$, end_flow, $composite\_cell\_id$; ordered by $start\_flow$ in ascending mode.

In the end, the newly constructed time sequence is fed to the trajectory extraction module to extract and map the trajectories based on the user interactions with the antennas at the geographic level.

Trajectory Extraction. The trajectory extraction module is responsible for transforming sequences of events into meaningful paths that the user might have taken with identified stay points. The algorithm takes into account the shapes of the cell towers and assumes a constant movement speed of a user since the transportation mode is not considered in our approach. Additionally, the algorithm assumes a minimum time for an activity inside a location to consider it as a stay point.

The algorithm proceeds in the following 6 steps:

1. *Combine multiple activities within the same cell.* This step consists of identifying multiple activities within the same cell and combining them into a single event, regardless of the duration of each activity. For instance, consider a sequence of activities AAABBAABCC, where each letter character means a unique cell. This step yields the following sequence ABABC.
2. *Remove "ping-pongs" using "ABAB" rule.* In the cases, when a user stays within the coverage of multiple cells, the cellphone may alternately connect to cells A and B. This step removes the so-called ping-pong effect, cleaning and reducing the sequence of activities even more.
3. *Infer arrival and departure times.* In this step, each activity in the sequence is enriched with two additional timestamps. Having the approximate coverage radius of a cell and assuming a constant movement speed (e.g., 30 km/h) [57], the algorithm calculates the time that a user needs to traverse the cell. From this information, we infer the approximate time the user arrived and departed to/from the cell's range.
4. *Infer locations.* Until this step, the algorithm acts upon the cell IDs, regardless of their locations in the geographic space. This step infers the approximate location of a user taking into account the shape of a cell and its location, and the time passed between the connections to the consecutive cells. For instance, a user connects to cell A and 5 min later to cell B, where cells A and B overlap. So, we can say that a user moved from cell A to the overlapping part of cells A and B.
5. *Clustering.* In this step, all the locations within a certain distance (e.g., 500 m) are clustered, respecting the temporal order of activities in a sequence. This way, we remove unnecessary ping-pongs to the cells that are close to each other and lower the positioning error.
6. *Split sequences of activities into logic trajectories by points of stay.* If a user performs his/her activities for more than 30 min within the same location, the algorithm considers that location as a stay point and splits the sequence at that point. In the end, the initial sequence of activities transforms into a sequence of trajectories, composed of temporally ordered sequences of locations.

Map Matching. Having the trajectories computed, which consist of sequences of locations ordered by the time of activity, we proceed to map them to the real-world road network. Depending on the visualization mode (e.g., road or grid), the trajectories are projected to the road network or hexagonal grid, respectively. The projection is done in a twofold approach: (i) sequence of locations becomes a sequence of segments/edges (e.g., ABAC becomes AB, BA, and AC); (ii) then each segment is projected into the road network. In the second step, the start and end node of an edge is attributed to the closest vertex of the road map or a centroid of the containing hexagon grid cell, depending on the visualisation mode. The projection onto the grid is a straightforward connection to the closest grid cells. In contrast, the projection onto the road network is more sophisticated, which uses a pgRouting[4] module to find the shortest route between start and end nodes, and stores the found path to the cache so not to repeat the calculations if the same edge is being processed. At this point, the algorithm acts upon a graph, with nodes being the projected locations, and edges being the segments of each

---

[4] https://pgrouting.org/.

individual trajectory. Finally, the statistics are calculated per edge and node, having a total number of activities on an edge, a total number of users that pass and stay on each node, and the total number of activities on an edge and time interval, which is specified in the visual query. In the end, the graph is stored in the database and can be consulted and visualised on the frontend.

5   ANTENNA's Visualization

In this section we start by enumerating the tasks and design requirements of the tool and then we present the visualization designed based on the stipulated objectives.

5.1   Tasks and Design Requirements

The collaboration with Altice's analysts aided us to derive a set of tasks to support the analysis of the trajectory data. The main goal of these tasks is to facilitate the understanding of how people move, at any given time, from location A to location B. The resulting tasks, which will be used as primary guidelines for designing ANTENNA, are the following:

T1 Identify the Traffic Flow Within a City. Identification of the most likely roads used within a city. For this task, a higher level of detail was achieved by projecting sequences of trips onto the Portuguese roads. The road segments are selected depending on their proximity to the connection between locations A and B;

T2 Identify Periods of Time with Different Traffic Volumes. Identification of important periods of time according to the traffic activity. To facilitate this task, all trips were aggregated by different time periods and the amount was represented in a timeline, with the aid of bar charts;

T3 Analyse the Trips Between Larger Geographic Areas. Identification of the trips between different cities. This task requires a higher aggregation of locations, as its main goal is to give an overview of the trajectories. To aggregate the different locations, a dynamic hexagonal grid (Sect. 5.3) was implemented that, depending on the zoom level, can have more or less granularity [40];

T4 Analyse the Trips from, to, or Between Specific Areas. This task refers to the aggregation and visualisation of all trajectories depending on their departing, arriving, or both points. This task is defined in the visual query page and visualised in the visualisation page;

T5 Distinguish Urban Locations. Characterisation of the different locations depending on the trajectory's characteristics if the users only pass by, stay, or leave certain cell towers.

From these tasks, it was possible to determine the design requirements:

DR1 Enable the User to Zoom and Pan the Map. To have different levels of detail, the user should be able to pan the map and zoom in on areas with higher densities of transitions;

DR2 Enable interaction with the Timeline. To analyse the differences in traffic flow according to time, the visualisation should provide the means to select different periods of time and to visualise them on the map;

DR3 Distinguish the Directionality of the Trajectories. To comprehend how people move, a visual cue should be given so it is possible to distinguish different directions;

DR4 Visualise the Mobility Between Cities. The user should be able to perceive the movements between locations, being these aggregated at a higher level (hexagonal grid) or a lower level (road map);

DR5 Characterise the Geographic Areas According to their Mobility Impact. Visual cues should be given so the user can understand the type of mobility in different locations.

5.2 Visual Query

The starting point of our tool is the definition of the visual query and its submission to the query queue. The query is defined by graphical means and enables the user to define parameters such as: (i) start and end date and time; (ii) aggregation time intervals; (iii) spatial aggregation for trajectories—by hexagonal grid or road network; (iv) selection of origin/destination regions; and (v) group aggregation mode.

After the query is completed, the backend returns the processed data, a set of trajectories, that can then be consulted and represented according to the aggregation mode chosen on the visual query process (**DR1**). When analysing the trajectories, a timeline is also shown at the bottom of the interactive map (Fig. 4) to enable the consultation of a specific time within the visualisation entire period of time, by updating the map as the user interacts with a time block (**DR2**). More details about all these visual components, can be consulted in [47]. In the following subsections, we detail how the trajectories are visualised in both grid and road aggregation modes.

5.3 Grid Aggregation Mode

In the spatial grid aggregation mode, the locations of the cell towers are projected onto an invisible hexagonal grid (Fig. 5). Therefore, the centre of each hexagonal cell can represent one or more cell towers that are placed within the grid. This strategy was defined to reduce visual clutter and provide a higher level of analysis of geographical data (**DR4**), enabling an overview rather than exact estimation of the data values.

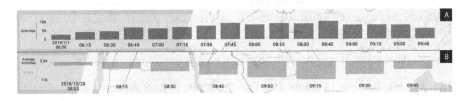

Fig. 4. Two timeline designs: (A) represent the distribution of activities aggregate per time intervals; (B) shows the distribution of trips made as a group, also aggregated by temporal blocks [47].

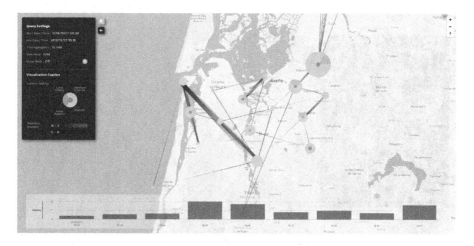

Fig. 5. Grid aggregation mode. Aggregated activities are encoded with lines and the characteristics of the geographic locations are summarised by the glyph nodes. At the bottom, the timeline shows the temporal distribution of activities [47]. (Color figure online)

Furthermore, it is noticeable in Fig. 6, the visual improvements obtained with our visualisation due to the cleaning of the noise present in the data.

The transitions between antennas are defined by an edge. In this projection mode, the edge is represented by a straight line. The edge's direction is represented through colour and is emphasised by a gradient along the edge, with decreasing fading towards the endpoint, based on practices studied in [19,20]. We coloured the edges in red and purple for North-South and South-North directions, respectively, and placed them side by side when exist connection in both directions between two antennas [11]. Additionally, the line thickness represents the number of trips made between two antennas in a given direction by unique users. The user can visualise more information about each edge's activity by hovering it with the mouse. Through this interaction, a tooltip with the edge's activity distribution along time and some statistics are displayed as shown in Fig. 7.

When in the grid mode, the antennas, are represented with a pie chart. The pie chart is represent three types of behaviours: pass-by, arrival-and-stay, and stay-and-departure, distinguished by colour (Fig. 8). The activities of passage are represented in grey. The stay activities, which are subdivided into arrival and departure, are coloured in cyan and yellow, respectively. The distinction between passage and stay behaviours is made by the time that a user is connected to a cell tower. If it is less than 30 min it is considered as a passage behaviour, otherwise, it is a stay. This threshold was stipulated based on studies made in [60]. Additionally, at the centre of the pie chart, we represent the self-connections, through an orange circle. A self-connection is defined when the beginning and the end of the connections are made within the range of the same antenna (see Fig. 9). The angle of each slice represents the percentage of connections of each behaviour[5]. Similarly, the radius of the self-connection circle is defined according to its

---

[5] An antenna may not exhibit the 3 types of behaviours previously described.

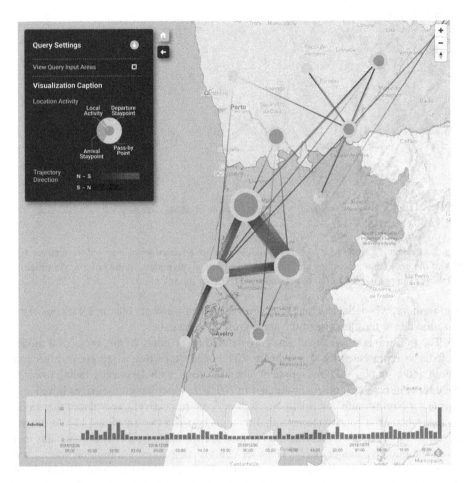

Fig. 6. Grid aggregation mode before (left) and after (right) our trajectory extraction data using noise filtering methods [47].

Fig. 7. Label displayed by interacting with an edge. It shows the activities distribution over time and additional statistical data [47].

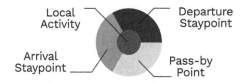

Fig. 8. Glyph design. The cyan, yellow, and grey colours encode arrival, departure, and pass-by locations, respectively. The orange represent local activities [47] (Color figure online).

Fig. 9. Example of different glyphs representing geographic areas with different types of mobility behaviour: (from left to right) arrival/departure location with local activities, mostly a pass-by location, arrival and pass-by location, mixed behaviour with little local activity, arrival only, and mixed behaviour with some local activities [47].

Fig. 10. Schematic representation of an edge. Line colour depicts direction, while semi-circles represent the start and end points. Line width encodes the number of unique trips [47].

percentual activity over the antenna. The radius of the pie chart is defined by the total number of activities, encompassing also the self-connections.

With the multiple glyph-profiles obtained it is possible to quickly characterise a certain location as a passage and/or stay point. By representing these patterns we aim to ease the understanding of the urban dynamics, their inhabitants' behaviours, and the types of activities per region, revealing urban structures such as streets congestion [27].

5.4 Road Aggregation Mode

To enable detailed analysis of the most used roads (**DR4**), we aggregate the trajectories at the road level. For that, we project the extracted trajectories onto the Portuguese road network, using a distance-based map matching approach [41]. The matching road segments are returned to the *presentation* tier along with the attached quantitative information (the number of distinct trips), and are used as a geometry descriptor for rendering of the trajectories.

To represent the directionality, we used red and purple plan colours, for representing south-north and north-south directions, respectively (Fig. 10). Also, the directionality is dictated by the relative position of the start and end points. If the end point of the trajectory is further north than its starting point, the trajectory is coloured in purple, otherwise, it is coloured in red, which is aligned with (**DR3**). Line thickness represent the number of unique trips made in a given direction. Furthermore, we use transparency to highlight the impact of the most used roads, i.e., the higher the number of trips, the more opaque the trajectories will be. The use of opacity is also due to the need to discriminate possible overlapping trajectory paths [7].

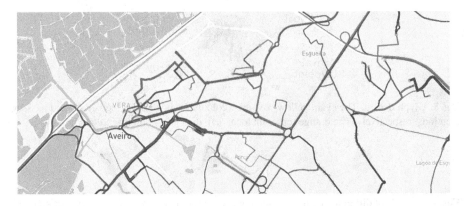

Fig. 11. Trips in the centre of the Aveiro city. An example of the arrival activities, denoted by the cyan colour of the endpoints and the predominant colour of the lines [47].

As for the start and end points, we represent them with a semicircle painted with yellow and cyan colours, respectively. This is done to overpass the reading issues caused by trajectory overlapping, easing the identification of the start and end points, as well as the directionality **DR5**. Furthermore, the semicircles are positioned in such a way that their combination in the locations that have both starting and ending points can form a full circle (see Fig. 10). These circles suggest the locations of shared activities, such as arrivals or departures (Fig. 11).

6   Usage Scenarios

In this section, we describe two usage scenarios, encompassing both aggregation modes and exposing their main advantages and purposes. In the first, we present a high-level analysis to study inter-urban movements. The second is focused on a lower level analysis, where a more accurate assessment of urban mobility is intended[6].

6.1   Scenario 1: Inter-Urban Movements

To analyse how people travel from two different cities known for their New Year's Eve festivities, we visualised the trips made from Oporto to Aveiro, in the last 4 days of 2018 (Fig. 5). We used the origin-destination filters during the query creation and set Oporto as the origin district (Fig. 5, cyan area) and Aveiro as the district of arrival (Fig. 5, orange area).

We chose the grid aggregation since the intention was to understand the flows between the two urban areas and not the exact roads used (**T4**). This way, we could reduce the visual clutter by aggregating overlapping trajectories into a single edge. The time interval of 1 h was defined empirically after previous tests with different time intervals.

---

[6] Other scenarios can be visualised in the demo videos at the following link https://bit.ly/3BTcoaY.

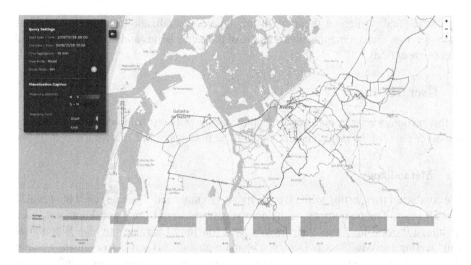

Fig. 12. Result of a visual query depicting the trajectories in road mode for the city of Aveiro. The trajectories are aggregated by grouped activities. The query details can be consulted in the side sheet, located at the top-left corner [47].

By interacting with the timeline, it was possible to detect daily patterns throughout the first three days—increased activity at morning hours, lunchtime (12 h–14 h), and end of work hours (18 h–20 h) but also identify an increase in activity and movement towards Barra's beach. Through this interaction, it was possible to identify different traffic volumes in different periods of time (**T2**), understand the transitions between cities (**T3**) and detect uncommon behaviours.

6.2   Scenario 2: Group Movements

To make a more detailed analysis and perceive which roads are the most used (**T1**) during the hours of entry to work, we defined a reduced time interval (8 h–10 h) and chose the road aggregation. We selected the group mode option to view only the shared trajectories to understand where mass activities happened, suggesting possible congested routes (Fig. 12).

In this visualization we could detect homogeneous group activities throughout the city. We noticed a considerable set of trajectories ending in the northernmost region of the city centre, indicated by the major number of arrival activities (cyan semi-circles), suggesting the existence of a commercial area. Through the transparency of trajectories, we were able to identify the most used roads at this time of day, seeing an increase in group activities throughout the morning and a decrease towards the end of the morning (working hours).

It was also possible to perceive an interesting activity showing the transition from another city, near a municipal stadium, to the municipal stadium of Aveiro, suggesting the occurrence of a sport event. Analysing trajectories starting outside the city of interest may be useful to understand which access roads may be used to enter the city and thus strategically improve them. With this type of visualization, the users can focus on congestion management analysis and road affluence issues and take sustainable and preventive actions.

7 User Testing

In this section, we cover our user evaluation starting with our methodology followed by the description of the tasks, and ending with the findings of our study.

7.1 Methodology

We conducted user testing with 20 participants (15 male and 5 female) aged between 21 and 28 years. The participants include university students from several domains, such as Image Processing, Data Visualisation, and Machine Learning but also Biomedical Engineering and Multimedia Design. The main goal of this test is to evaluate whether the participants can understand both aggregation modes and retrieve correct information from the visualisation by interacting with ANTENNA. The tests were composed of *five tasks*.

At the beginning of each test, an introduction was made to contextualise our tool, its main purpose and visual elements for both aggregation modes with screenshots of some examples. After this, a sheet containing the tasks was given to the participants. All tests were performed with the same setup. If a task is composed of two queries, the queries are presented separately during the test, so the response to one does not influence the other. All tasks were timed and executed in the same order. During each task, participants were encouraged to think out loud, so we could comprehend their rational and understand if the interaction techniques influenced their interpretations.

7.2 Tasks

To evaluate the visualisation's visual elements, we based the test's tasks on the task abstraction defined in Sect. 5.1.

The first two tasks focus on road aggregation. To validate the trajectory representation, in Task 1, we asked the participants to *indicate the most used roads*. To validate the timeline, in Task 2, we asked the participants to *indicate which roads are the most used in the time interval with more activities*. Task 2 was performed with two queries, one with group aggregation (Task 2-Groups) and the other without (Task 2-No Groups). Task 3 focuses on grid aggregation. To evaluate its effectiveness for high-level analyses and validate the edge and node representations, we presented the trajectories between two districts and asked the participants to *indicate main points of access for both districts*. Task 4 evaluates the usefulness of the road aggregation over the grid aggregation. For that purpose, two identical queries with the two aggregation modes were used (Task 4-Grid and Task 4-Road). For both queries, we asked the participants to *identify areas with high levels of movements*. Task 5 focuses on the glyph. We used a query that presented various types of behaviours. To perceive the glyph's effectiveness and if insights about the urban topology could be inferred, we asked the participants to *identify a specific glyph fulfilling a set of requirements* and to *characterise three urban areas with distinct glyph compositions*.

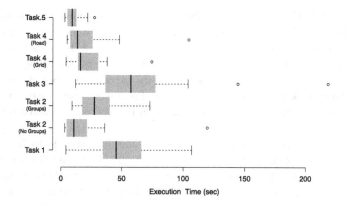

Fig. 13. Box-plot of the execution times for each task [47].

The participants answered freely and were not constrained, allowing us to obtain the most information possible. To verify the consistency within the given answers or if a major deviation occurred, a ground truth answer was defined for each task.

7.3   Results

The participants' performance provided positive insights about the aggregation modes and the visual tool itself. In Fig. 13, we can see a positively skewed distribution of the participants' execution times since their median is closer to the bottom of the boxplot, revealing a high concentration of results with short execution times. Most participants revealed no major difficulties in completing the tasks. However, their learning curve and exploration times varied to a great extent, originating outliers (Fig. 13). Some participants gave quick answers without exploring the visualisation while others explored it thoroughly before providing their answers. The learning curve can be analysed by the time taken in the first three tasks, as their goals were the same but for different scenarios. Being the first task the participants' first point of contact with the visualisation, it took additional time to interpret it. The execution times for the following two tasks improved considerably, even presenting more complex scenarios to analyse, corroborating a smooth and fast learning curve. Task 3 presents higher values of execution times as it is the most ambiguous question in the test due to the interpretation of an access point. From Fig. 14, we can see that Task 3 that contains the most distinct number of answers. Concerning the remaining tasks, the majority of the participants completed them with no difficulties and in less time, requiring much less inspection. For all tasks, the majority of the participants indicated, at least, one correct answer, with the exception of task 5, where one participant answered incorrectly.

In Fig. 14, we represent the number of different answers for each task and we can see that most answers are within the set of correct answers. It is important to note that the majority of the tasks implied the ordered listing of the visualisation elements (e.g., "Identify the most used roads"). For this reason, some participants continued to point out elements that are not within the correct answer set even though it is no longer required. In Fig. 15, we can see the participants distribution per number of given answers. Tasks 1 and 3 have the most distinct number of answers supporting the results retrieved from the distributions for these tasks (Fig. 13). For both queries of Task 4 the majority of participants gave the same number of answers. Analysing both Figs. 14 and 15, we can see that most participants gave the expected number of answers, with the exception of Task 1, Task 3, and Task 4-Grid. From these results, we can verify that all participants who provided fewer answers than the desired, contained only correct answers.

According to the participants' feedback, we found that the majority found the tool useful and intuitive for completing the tasks, as they quickly began to interpret the visualisations correctly. In terms of difficulties, all participants referred to the impossibility of interacting with the trajectories within specific periods of time in the timeline. Due to the participants' diverse interpretations, we can refer that the glyphs were the most complex visual element in ANTENNA.

8   Discussion

In this section, we discuss the usefulness and advantages of both aggregation modes and the effectiveness of ANTENNA for the scenarios presented. Then, the results from the user tests are analysed to assess the users understanding of the application.

Usage Scenarios. Section 6 enabled the understanding of real usage scenarios for both aggregation modes and their combination with other parameters, such as spatial and temporal aggregation filters. The grid aggregation was found as more efficient for an overview analysis. Its main advantages are: (i) the reduction of visual clutter; (ii) the visual highlight of areas according to the type of activity (e.g., residential, commercial, passage); and (iii) the highlight of inter-region flow patterns. Also, the glyphs provided a quick and general interpretation of its region's behaviours. The road aggregation was found as more efficient for more detailed and precise analysis. Its main advantages are: (i) the understanding of road affluence; (ii) the highlight of everyday movement patterns (i.e., travels to work, recreation); and (iii) the highlight of intra-region flow patterns.

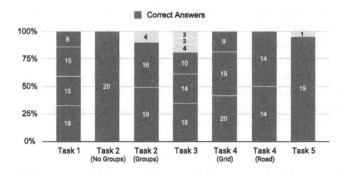

Fig. 14. Answer distribution for each task. Dark grey bars represent answers within the set of correct answers. The count value for each answer is inside the bars [47].

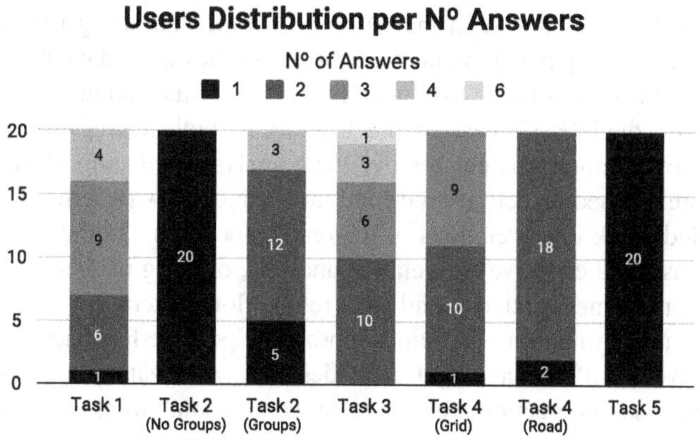

Fig. 15. Participants distribution per number of answers for each task. The number of participants is inside each bar [47].

Also, the representations of the start and end points of the trips facilitated the reading of directionality. The unexpected results for both aggregation modes, enabled the users to get additional insights, revealing the added value of these types of visualisation approaches.

User Evaluation. Given the results of the user evaluation and the participants' positive feedback about both aggregation modes, we consider that their visualisation modes present the data correctly and are intuitive as they are based on interaction techniques commonly used in similar web mapping tools. The last task revealed interesting insights about the glyphs due to their varied interpretations. For example, one participant did not consider the grey area of the glyph as being representative of information, as it was too similar to the map base colour. Also, some participants had difficulties in characterising the areas according to the glyphs representation. However, the participants reported that after some adaptation, the glyphs could characterise different areas, enabling them to distinguish residential from work areas.

9   Conclusion

In this paper, we presented ANTENNA, an analytical tool that combines multiple methods of temporal aggregation and trajectory extraction to transform sequences of cell connections into analysable mobility patterns. The system processes large amounts of raw data in useful time, enabling nearly real-time analysis of urban mobility. This is due to the architectural design and the methods for distributed computation, which also ensures the scalability of our approach. ANTENNA was tested using a dataset of cell phone connections provided by our collaboration with a telecommunication provider, Altice.

The primary objective of the presented work was to summarise and make the data easier to interpret, enabling faster analysis of inter- and/or intra-urban mobility. We implemented a three-tiered system that i) processes the data using time aggregation, trajectory extraction, map matching methods; ii) stores the output data into the database; and iii) presents the results to the user in an interactive visualization.

The research findings showcased the benefits of both aggregation modes. Grid aggregation proved more efficient for overview analysis, reducing visual clutter and highlighting areas based on activity type and inter-region flow patterns. The associated glyphs provided quick interpretations of regional behaviours. On the other hand, road aggregation was more effective for detailed analysis, offering insights into road affluence, everyday movement patterns, and intra-region flow patterns.

In terms of user evaluation, participants provided positive feedback on the correctness and intuitiveness of both aggregation modes. The visualization modes were aligned with commonly used interaction techniques in web mapping tools. However, the evaluation also revealed challenges in the glyphs' interpretation and encountered some difficulties in characterizing areas based on glyph representation, revealing some visual challenges to be tackled in future work. These findings contribute to the understanding of the effectiveness of our visualization modes and highlight the importance of adaptive tools that could accommodate and adapt accordingly to users' needs in the context of urban mobility studies.

The major challenges and limitations of the work are in the improvement of backend functionalities, such as detection of pendulum movements, user profiling, communication among dockers, and enhancement of the trajectory extractor algorithm for better analysis of mobility data. The original idea of visually identifying pendulum movements faced limitations due to complex path calculations in the "road mode" visualization, multiple directions on large roads, and the variability of routes taken by individuals. Future work aims to develop machine learning algorithms to detect pendulum movements and integrate them into the visualization system.

The lack of a direct PDF export option in the frontend limits the tool's usability. The ability to export a PDF document that includes the visualization model, statistics, and a summary of specific queries would enhance interaction and reporting capabilities. Additionally, leveraging the current architecture for visual analytics, such as integrating machine learning models for urban mobility forecasting and representing the impact of social events, would provide valuable insights for urban planners and decision-makers. Improving the trajectory extraction algorithm to identify transportation modes would enhance accuracy and enable more efficient analysis of public transportation usage in urban planning. Overall, leveraging the existing visualization system would further enhance the value of mobile network data.

To our knowledge, we have advanced the state of the art in urban mobility by developing a visual analytics tool with two visualisation modes appropriate for a variety of mobility study scenarios in a single tool, streamlining the users' analyses processes. We also note that our system architecture made it possible to explore this type of data in useful and practicable times due to a functional combination of cleaning and pre-processing data techniques.

References

1. Andrienko, G., Andrienko, N., Heurich, M.: An event-based conceptual model for context-aware movement analysis. Int. J. Geogr. Inf. Sci. **25**(9), 1347–1370 (2011)
2. Andrienko, G., Andrienko, N., Hurter, C., Rinzivillo, S., Wrobel, S.: From movement tracks through events to places: extracting and characterizing significant places from mobility data. In: 2011 IEEE Conference on Visual Analytics Science and Technology (VAST), pp. 161–170. IEEE (2011)
3. Andrienko, G., Andrienko, N., Wrobel, S.: Visual analytics tools for analysis of movement data. ACM SIGKDD Explor. Newsl. **9**(2), 38–46 (2007)
4. Andrienko, N., Andrienko, G.: Visual analytics of movement: an overview of methods, tools and procedures. Inf. Vis. **12**(1), 3–24 (2013)
5. Andrienko, N., Andrienko, G., Gatalsky, P.: Supporting visual exploration of object movement. In: Proceedings of the Working Conference on Advanced Visual Interfaces, pp. 217–220 (2000)
6. Bach, B., Dragicevic, P., Archambault, D., Hurter, C., Carpendale, S.: A descriptive framework for temporal data visualizations based on generalized space-time cubes. In: Computer Graphics Forum, vol. 36, pp. 36–61. Wiley Online Library (2017)
7. Bach, B., Perin, C., Ren, Q., Dragicevic, P.: Ways of visualizing data on curves (2018)
8. Bouvier, D.J., Oates, B.: Evacuation traces mini challenge award: innovative trace visualization staining for information discovery. In: 2008 IEEE Symposium on Visual Analytics Science and Technology, pp. 219–220. IEEE (2008)
9. Calabrese, F., Diao, M., Di Lorenzo, G., Ferreira, J., Jr., Ratti, C.: Understanding individual mobility patterns from urban sensing data: a mobile phone trace example. Transp. Res. Part C Emerg. Technol. **26**, 301–313 (2013)
10. Chua, A., Marcheggiani, E., Servillo, L., Vande Moere, A.: FlowSampler: visual analysis of urban flows in geolocated social media data. In: Aiello, L.M., McFarland, D. (eds.) SocInfo 2014. LNCS, vol. 8852, pp. 5–17. Springer, Cham (2015). https://doi.org/10.1007/978-3-319-15168-7_2
11. Chua, A., Servillo, L., Marcheggiani, E., Moere, A.V.: Mapping Cilento: using geotagged social media data to characterize tourist flows in Southern Italy. Tour. Manage. **57**, 295–310 (2016)
12. Cornel, D., et al.: Composite flow maps. In: Computer Graphics Forum, vol. 35, pp. 461–470. Wiley Online Library (2016)
13. Dent, B.: Cartography: Thematic Map Design, vol. 1. WCB/McGraw-Hill (1999)
14. Enguehard, R.A., Hoeber, O., Devillers, R.: Interactive exploration of movement data: a case study of geovisual analytics for fishing vessel analysis. Inf. Vis. **12**(1), 65–84 (2013)
15. Fiadino, P., Valerio, D., Ricciato, F., Hummel, K.A.: Steps towards the extraction of vehicular mobility patterns from 3G signaling data. In: Pescapè, A., Salgarelli, L., Dimitropoulos, X. (eds.) TMA 2012. LNCS, vol. 7189, pp. 66–80. Springer, Heidelberg (2012). https://doi.org/10.1007/978-3-642-28534-9_7
16. Gonzalez, M.C., Hidalgo, C.A., Barabasi, A.L.: Understanding individual human mobility patterns. nature **453**(7196), 779–782 (2008)
17. Guo, D.: Visual analytics of spatial interaction patterns for pandemic decision support. Int. J. Geogr. Inf. Sci. **21**(8), 859–877 (2007)
18. Guo, D., Chen, J., MacEachren, A.M., Liao, K.: A visualization system for space-time and multivariate patterns (vis-stamp). IEEE Trans. Vis. Comput. Graph. **12**(6), 1461–1474 (2006)
19. Holten, D., Isenberg, P., Van Wijk, J.J., Fekete, J.D.: An extended evaluation of the readability of tapered, animated, and textured directed-edge representations in node-link graphs. In: 2011 IEEE Pacific Visualization Symposium, pp. 195–202. IEEE (2011)

20. Holten, D., Van Wijk, J.J.: A user study on visualizing directed edges in graphs. In: Proceedings of the SIGCHI Conference on Human Factors in Computing Systems, pp. 2299–2308. ACM (2009)
21. Horn, C., Klampfl, S., Cik, M., Reiter, T.: Detecting outliers in cell phone data: correcting trajectories to improve traffic modeling. Transp. Res. Rec. **2405**(1), 49–56 (2014)
22. Hunter, T., Abbeel, P., Bayen, A.: The path inference filter: model-based low-latency map matching of probe vehicle data. IEEE Trans. Intell. Transp. Syst. **15**(2), 507–529 (2013)
23. Jain, A., Murty, M., Flynn, P.: Estimating origin-destination flows using mobile phone location data. ACM Comput. Surv. **31**(3), 264–323 (1999)
24. Jiang, S., Fiore, G.A., Yang, Y., Ferreira, J., Jr., Frazzoli, E., González, M.C.: A review of urban computing for mobile phone traces: current methods, challenges and opportunities. In: Proceedings of the 2nd ACM SIGKDD International Workshop on Urban Computing, pp. 1–9 (2013)
25. Kapler, T., Wright, W.: Geotime information visualization. Inf. Vis. **4**(2), 136–146 (2005)
26. Kraak, M.J.: The space-time cube revisited from a geovisualization perspective. In: Proceedings of the 21st International Cartographic Conference, pp. 1988–1996. Citeseer (2003)
27. Krings, G., Calabrese, F., Ratti, C., Blondel, V.D.: Urban gravity: a model for inter-city telecommunication flows. J. Stat. Mech. Theor. Exp. **2009**(07), L07003 (2009)
28. Krüger, R., Thom, D., Wörner, M., Bosch, H., Ertl, T.: TrajectoryLenses - a set-based filtering and exploration technique for long-term trajectory data. Comput. Graph. Forum **32**, 451–460 (2013)
29. Lin, M., Hsu, W.J.: Mining GPS data for mobility patterns: a survey. Pervasive Mob. Comput. **12**, 1–16 (2014)
30. Lu, M., Wang, Z., Liang, J., Yuan, X.: OD-Wheel: visual design to explore OD patterns of a central region. In: 2015 IEEE Pacific Visualization Symposium (PacificVis), pp. 87–91. IEEE (2015)
31. Makse, H.A., Havlin, S., Stanley, H.E.: Modelling urban growth patterns. nature **377**(6550), 608 (1995)
32. OpenStreetMap (2020). https://www.geofabrik.de/
33. Mazhelis, O.: Using recursive Bayesian estimation for matching GPS measurements to imperfect road network data. In: 13th International IEEE Conference on Intelligent Transportation Systems, pp. 1492–1497. IEEE (2010)
34. Newson, P., Krumm, J.: Hidden Markov map matching through noise and sparseness. In: Proceedings of the 17th ACM SIGSPATIAL International Conference on Advances in Geographic Information Systems, pp. 336–343 (2009)
35. Ochieng, W.Y., Quddus, M., Noland, R.B.: Map-matching in complex urban road networks. Rev. Bras. Cartogr. **55**(2), 1–14 (2003)
36. Orellana, D., Wachowicz, M., Andrienko, N., Andrienko, G.: Uncovering interaction patterns in mobile outdoor gaming. In: 2009 International Conference on Advanced Geographic Information Systems & Web Services, pp. 177–182. IEEE (2009)
37. Polisciuc, E., Alves, A., Bento, C., Machado, P.: Visualizing urban mobility. In: ACM SIGGRAPH 2013 Posters, SIGGRAPH 2013, Association for Computing Machinery, New York (2013). https://doi.org/10.1145/2503385.2503511
38. Polisciuc, E., et al.: Arc and swarm-based representations of customer's flows among supermarkets. In: IVAPP, pp. 300–306 (2015)
39. Polisciuc, E., Cruz, P., Amaro, H., Maças, C., Machado, P.: Flow map of products transported among warehouses and supermarkets. In: VISIGRAPP (2: IVAPP), pp. 179–188 (2016)
40. Polisciuc, E., Maçãs, C., Assunção, F., Machado, P.: Hexagonal gridded maps and information layers: a novel approach for the exploration and analysis of retail data. In: SIGGRAPH ASIA 2016 Symposium on Visualization, p. 6. ACM (2016)

41. Quddus, M.A., Ochieng, W.Y., Noland, R.B.: Current map-matching algorithms for transport applications: state-of-the art and future research directions. Transp. Res. Part C Emerg. Technol. **15**(5), 312–328 (2007)
42. Ratti, C., Frenchman, D., Pulselli, R.M., Williams, S.: Mobile landscapes: using location data from cell phones for urban analysis. Environ. Plann. B. Plann. Des. **33**(5), 727–748 (2006)
43. Rinzivillo, S., Pedreschi, D., Nanni, M., Giannotti, F., Andrienko, N., Andrienko, G.: Visually driven analysis of movement data by progressive clustering. Inf. Vis. **7**(3–4), 225–239 (2008)
44. Scheepens, R., Willems, N., Van de Wetering, H., Andrienko, G., Andrienko, N., Van Wijk, J.J.: Composite density maps for multivariate trajectories. IEEE Trans. Vis. Comput. Graph. **17**(12), 2518–2527 (2011)
45. Schlaich, J., Otterstätter, T., Friedrich, M., et al.: Generating trajectories from mobile phone data. In: Proceedings of the 89th Annual Meeting Compendium of Papers, Transportation Research Board of the National Academies. Citeseer (2010)
46. Schneider, C.M., Belik, V., Couronné, T., Smoreda, Z., González, M.C.: Unravelling daily human mobility motifs. J. R. Soc. Interface **10**(84), 20130246 (2013)
47. Silva, P., Maças, C., Correia, J., Machado, P., Polisciuc, E.: ANTENNA: a tool for visual analysis of urban mobility based on cell phone data. In: VISIGRAPP (3: IVAPP), pp. 88–100 (2022)
48. Song, X., Ouyang, Y., Du, B., Wang, J., Xiong, Z.: Recovering individual's commute routes based on mobile phone data. Mob. Inf. Syst. **2017**, 1–11 (2017)
49. Spretke, D., Bak, P., Janetzko, H., Kranstauber, B., Mansmann, F., Davidson, S.: Exploration through enrichment: a visual analytics approach for animal movement. In: Proceedings of the 19th ACM SIGSPATIAL International Conference on Advances in Geographic Information Systems, pp. 421–424 (2011)
50. Tettamanti, T., Varga, I.: Mobile phone location area based traffic flow estimation in urban road traffic. In: Advances in Civil and Environmental Engineering, vol. 1, no. 1, pp. 1–15. Columbia International Publishing (2014)
51. Tomaszewski, B., MacEachren, A.M.: Geo-historical context support for information foraging and sensemaking: conceptual model, implementation, and assessment. In: 2010 IEEE Symposium on Visual Analytics Science and Technology, pp. 139–146. IEEE (2010)
52. Tominski, C., Schumann, H., Andrienko, G., Andrienko, N.: Stacking-based visualization of trajectory attribute data. IEEE Trans. Vis. Comput. Graph. **18**(12), 2565–2574 (2012)
53. Vajakas, T., Vajakas, J., Lillemets, R.: Trajectory reconstruction from mobile positioning data using cell-to-cell travel time information. Int. J. Geogr. Inf. Sci. **29**(11), 1941–1954 (2015)
54. Von Landesberger, T., Brodkorb, F., Roskosch, P., Andrienko, N., Andrienko, G., Kerren, A.: MobilityGraphs: visual analysis of mass mobility dynamics via spatio-temporal graphs and clustering. IEEE Trans. Vis. Comput. Graph. **22**(1), 11–20 (2015)
55. Wang, H., Calabrese, F., Di Lorenzo, G., Ratti, C.: Transportation mode inference from anonymized and aggregated mobile phone call detail records. In: 13th International IEEE Conference on Intelligent Transportation Systems, pp. 318–323. IEEE (2010)
56. Ware, C., Arsenault, R., Plumlee, M., Wiley, D.: Visualizing the underwater behavior of humpback whales. IEEE Comput. Graph. Appl. **26**(4), 14–18 (2006)
57. Widhalm, P., Yang, Y., Ulm, M., Athavale, S., González, M.C.: Discovering urban activity patterns in cell phone data. Transportation **42**(4), 597–623 (2015)
58. Wood, J., Dykes, J., Slingsby, A.: Visualisation of origins, destinations and flows with OD maps. Cartogr. J. **47**(2), 117–129 (2010)
59. Wood, J., Slingsby, A., Dykes, J.: Visualizing the dynamics of London's bicycle-hire scheme. Cartographica Int. J. Geogr. Inf. Geovis. **46**(4), 239–251 (2011)

60. Zeng, W., Fu, C.W., Müller Arisona, S., Erath, A., Qu, H.: Visualizing waypoints-constrained origin-destination patterns for massive transportation data. Comput. Graph. Forum **35**, 95–107 (2016)
61. Zheng, Y., Zhang, L., Xie, X., Ma, W.Y.: Mining interesting locations and travel sequences from GPS trajectories. In: Proceedings of the 18th International Conference on World Wide Web, pp. 791–800 (2009)

Influence of Errors on the Evaluation of Text Classification Systems

Vanessa Bracamonte[✉], Seira Hidano, and Shinsaku Kiyomoto

KDDI Research, Inc., Saitama, Japan
{va-bracamonte,se-hidano,kiyomoto}@kddi-research.jp

Abstract. Accuracy metrics and explanation of outputs can provide users with useful information about the performance of machine learning-based systems. However, the availability of this information can result in users' overlooking potential problems in the system. This paper investigates whether making errors obvious to the user can influence trust towards a system that has high accuracy but has flaws. In order to test this hypothesis, a series of experiments with different settings were conducted. Participants were shown examples of the predictions of text classification systems, the explanation of those predictions and the overall accuracy of the systems. The participants were then asked to evaluate the systems based on those pieces of information and to indicate the reason for their evaluation decision. The results show that participants who were shown examples where there was a pattern of errors in the explanation were less willing to recommend or choose a system even if the system's accuracy metric was higher. In addition, fewer participants reported that the accuracy metric was the reason for their choice, and more participants mentioned the prediction explanation.

Keywords: Error perception · System evaluation · Machine learning · Model explanation · User study

1 Introduction

The behavior of machine learning models is sometimes not well understood even by developers themselves and their logic can be very complex [2]. This complexity of machine learning models, most of which are black boxes, can result in further complications when it comes to testing them. For example, when a model for assigning a toxicity score to comments (where a toxic comment is defined as "a rude, disrespectful, or unreasonable comment that is likely to make you leave a discussion" [18]) was released to the general public, independent testing [37] found that the API assigned high toxicity score to neutral text when it included words such as "black", "woman" or "gay" [11]. Although accuracy and other performance metrics can be used as indicators of the behavior of a model, these metrics are not always useful for finding issues such as bias.

Users do not necessarily know how machine learning algorithms work or fail [13, 21]. Although there is research to try to make these models more interpretable to

ⓒ The Author(s), under exclusive license to Springer Nature Switzerland AG 2023
A. A. de Sousa et al. (Eds.): VISIGRAPP 2022, CCIS 1815, pp. 161–181, 2023.
https://doi.org/10.1007/978-3-031-45725-8_8

humans, deep learning models are still considered black boxes [7]. In addition to performance metrics, one way of obtaining information about a model is through explanations, and researchers have proposed a multitude of techniques and approaches to explain models [1, 15, 28]. For understanding the behavior of machine learning models, explanation methods have been developed [15, 26, 32]. These explanations can be useful in making the prediction of machine learning models understandable to users [9]. These explanations methods are also used in tools that have been developed specifically to help users, experts and non-experts, evaluate models in detail (e.g. The Language Interpretability Tool [36]). These types of tools can provide performance metrics, explore the prediction output of models and make use of explanation methods to help understand the reason for a particular prediction.

Explanations can be helpful in gaining some understanding of model predictions [9]. On the other hand, viewing explanation does not always result in improved model evaluation [19]. In addition, even for experts such as data scientists explanations can lead to over-trust [19]. As a consequence of over-trust, evaluators might not suspect that the output of a highly-accurate machine learning model could be erroneous. The presence of errors can have an effect on trust and reliance in the context of use of automated systems [10, 12, 17, 30, 34, 35]. However, in an evaluation context it is of course desirable that evaluators should detect errors. Error suspicion can be one way to overcome complacency when evaluating automated systems [22].

The first process for handling errors is detecting the error itself [22]. However, complacency and lack of understanding of system limitations can become barriers that suppress the vigilance needed to undertake the process of error detection [22]. In this way, perception of the system's user experience characteristics [14] or the level of trust [5, 25] might influence the evaluation of automated systems. Non-expert users do not normally seek negative information [29], but when interacting with machine learning systems this can change according to the circumstances of that interaction. Research on machine learning systems for medical decision-making [6] reports that medical domain experts who ran across unexpected results in an automated system began to question whether there are errors. These domain experts also began to test the results under different conditions, regardless of the original task they were assigned to do. This behavior suggests that the unexpected results created suspicion about errors and made the medical domain experts curious about the performance of the system.

Experts can also exhibit the behavior of failing to look for information that contradicts expectations, in the context of using machine learning model explanation tools [19]. Expert evaluators may be over-trusting the tool and the visualization of the explanations, with the consequence that they evaluate the results without suspecting errors in the model [19]. Conversely, when detected, errors in explanations can help users evaluate the performance of machine learning models. Training a model with errors. For example, to evaluate a machine learning model interpretability method [32], a model was trained in such a way that it made predictions based on the background of the image rather than the subject of the image. Therefore, when users viewed the explanations, they saw results that repeatedly showed that the model had made a prediction based on the wrong part of the image. The users specifically reported that this pattern of error was the reason for lack of trust in the model [32].

In this paper, a series of experiments are conducted which test whether presenting errors to evaluators can induce suspicion when they evaluate the output of a machine learning model with high accuracy. Two types of errors are tested: incorrect model predictions (which are explicitly described to evaluators as errors) and errors that appear in explanations (which are not explicitly described as errors to evaluators). In the experiments, participants were shown examples of predictions of movie classification systems, explanation of those predictions and the overall accuracy of the system, and then were asked to evaluate those systems and explain the reason for their opinion. The effect on willingness to recommend and choose between systems, and on the participants' stated reasons, was measured. The results show that error patterns in explanations negatively affected the perception of a system, and more participants that viewed this type of errors reported that the reason for their decision was the explanation itself.

This paper is an extended version of the paper "Effect of Errors on the Evaluation of Machine Learning Systems" [4] presented at the 6th International Conference on Human Computer Interaction Theory and Applications (HUCAPP2022). It includes the analysis and results of a new experiment, and an updated general discussion of the findings.

2 Setup

A series of experiments, with different tasks and error patterns, were conducted to evaluate the effect of errors. Two error presentation approaches were considered: (1) showing incorrect predictions to the evaluator to clearly indicate errors in the system, and (2) showing errors in the explanation of the prediction results (correct or incorrect) of the system, in which the evaluator is not told that there may be a problem in the system.

2.1 Models and Dataset

Two models for movie review sentiment classification, an LSTM [16] and a CNN [23] model, were developed for this study. Because the participants were mostly non-experts, a movie review classification task was considered appropriate. In general, these models can have high accuracy but still show problems (e.g. biased results) [3, 11]. Therefore, these type of models were considered appropriate for the purpose of these experiments.

The models were developed using the Keras deep learning API [20], and the Large Movie Review dataset [27] was used to train and test them. The CNN model had an accuracy of 89% and the LSTM model had an accuracy of 87%. The models were not trained to produce specific error patterns, although the models were not sophisticated and therefore were expected to present flaws.

2.2 Explanation Methods

For the experiments, post hoc explainability techniques which assigns a value to words in a text indicating the influence of that word (feature) on the outcome of the model were used. The explanation values were calculated using the C-Shapley [8] and LIME [32] methods. These are post hoc interpretability method [15] that identify the most important features to the model prediction.

2.3   Evaluation of the Models

The models were evaluated and a number of problems were identified in both of them. Both models had other problems that showed in explanation such as indicating a word as positive, when a human evaluation would consider it negative. In this study, two error patterns of the CNN model were used: the list of words that most strongly contributed to a negative sentiment often contained the words "recommend" and "women" at the top, regardless of the context of the sentence. The LSTM model predictions showed different problems, such as including neutral words such as "and", "the" as words that strongly contributed to the sentiment. The explanations of the LSTM model showed a tendency to indicate words such as "and", "the", and other conjunctions as important words.

In the experiments, the LSTM model is referred to as System A and the CNN model as System B.

2.4   System Output and Explanation Visualization

Explanations can be used to select a word or highlight an area of an image to indicate where the model is "looking", although they do not provide a reason why that feature was selected or if it may have a contradicting value [33]. A type of visualization which highlights the most important words in the text that contribute to the prediction result and shows a bar chart of the top was used to present the explanation results. The visualization of the explanation was adapted from [32]. The class that the word contributes to is indicated by the highlight color. Green was used for words identified as influencing a positive review classification and pink for words identified as influencing a negative review classification. Figure 1 shows examples of the system output and explanation visualization that was shown to participants. The models were used to generate predictions for Movie reviews that were between 50 and 400 words long were used. The models were used to generate their predicted sentiment. The explanation corresponding to those predictions were also generated. The example reviews that would be used in the experiments were manually selected.

3   Experiment 1: Effect on the Evaluation of One System

3.1   Experiment Design

The experiment was designed to evaluate the effect of errors on the recommendation of a single text classification system. For the experiment, two factors with two levels each were defined. The *Error* factor was based on the type of error in the explanation of predictions. In the *Pattern* error level, the word "recommend" was explained as a top negative word in all predictions. As mentioned before, it was hypothesized that patterns would be detected by participants and induce suspicion better than random errors. In the *Random* error level, the explanations did not have any error pattern; instead different words were erroneously explained as positive or negative. The *Example* factor was based on outcome of the system's prediction examples that the participants viewed. In the *Correct* level, all prediction examples were correct; in the *Incorrect* level, all

First of all, I really can't understand how some people "enjoyed" this movie. It's the worst thing I have ever seen. Even the actors seem to be bored...and I think that says it all! However, I have to give my applause to the opening credits creators - that team seems to have a really good future. That's why I recommend the big studios to watch ONLY the opening credits, and one or two special effects sequences (if they're watched outside this movie, it almost looks like a good movie). Better luck (or judgment) next time for the producers of this, this... this "thing!".

System classification result: **Negative review**
Result is: **Correct ✔**

This movie was one of the rolling on the floor laughing movies I have ever seen. Danny De Vito plays Owen perfectly. Momma is excellently portrayed, and was one of the highlights of the movie. At the beginning of the movie it starts of differently then what you would expect. Larry is trying to write a book and is having some troubles. Larry teaches a writing class and Owen tagged after Larry trying to get him to read his story. Owen eventually asks Larry to kill his mother, and in return Owen would kill Larry's ex-wife. The whole movie was really hilarious. One of my favorite parts of the movie is at the end when Owen writes "Throw Momma from the Train". Larry gets furious because he just wrote a book of similar plot. It turns out that Owen wrote a children's pop-up book. I would really recommend this movie. I gave it a 10.

System classification result: **Positive review**
Result is: **Correct ✔**

Fig. 1. System output and explanation visualization examples. The examples show correct predictions but with "recommend" highlighted as a negative word (error pattern). Figure from Bracamonte et al. [4].

prediction examples were incorrect; and in the *Mixed* level half of the predictions were correct and half were incorrect. The combination of factors and levels resulted in six conditions, all of which show some type of error. The participants were assigned to one condition only (between-subjects design).

3.2   Task and Questionnaire

Participants were asked to evaluate a system based on its testing accuracy (89%) and on four examples of its prediction and corresponding explanation. Figure 1 shows examples of the prediction and explanation. The task instructions also explained the meaning of the highlights in the text.

The questionnaire asked about willingness to recommend the system (*"I would recommend the use of this system."*), trust in the system (*"I can trust this system"*), as well as about usefulness of the explanations (*"The explanations were useful to form an opinion about the system."*) and understandability of system's decisions (*"I understand how this system makes decisions in general."*), on a 7-point Likert-scale from *Strongly disagree* to *Strongly agree*.

In addition, an open-ended question on the reasons for recommending or not recommending the system was included. The combination of quantitative and qualitative measures would give an indication of whether the errors had been identified and detected by the participants and whether they had a negative effect on evaluation and perception of the system (induced suspicion). An attention question about the testing accuracy of the system was included; the accuracy percentage was stated in the instructions. Questions about the participants gender, age, and a self-reported machine learning knowledge question on a 7-point scale from *No knowledge* to *Expert* were also included.

3.3   Participant Recruitment

Participants were recruited using the Amazon Mechanical Turk platform. Participation was limited to workers from the USA, Canada, Australia, and the UK who had worked at least 1000 HITS, and who had a 98% worker approval rate. For this study, invalid answers where those in which workers with different IDs had identical responses and where answers to the open-ended questions were completely unrelated to the content of the question. Participants were compensated with $1.50 (approx. 9 min, rate of $10/h).

3.4   Results

A total 324 responses from workers was obtained. Of these, 27 were rejected after review of the attention check question. 8 participants self-assessed as machine learning experts, and their responses were not included in the analysis. In total 289 cases were analyzed. The sample consisted of 111 (38%) female, 175 male (61%) and 3 other/NA participants, ages 19 to 69. The age mean was 36. The majority of participants reported at least some knowledge of machine learning, with only 23 participants reporting no knowledge.

The non-parametric analysis method Aligned Rank Transform (ART) ANOVA [38] was used to measure the effect of the factors. The results of the two-way ANOVA (Table 1) show a significant main effect of *Error* ($p < .01$) on the willingness to recommend the system, with the *Pattern* conditions being lower. The results also show a significant main effect of *Example* ($p < .001$), and the Tukey's HSD test was used for post hoc comparisons between the levels. The results show significant differences between all levels (Table 2). Willingness to recommend decreases for conditions with incorrect prediction examples. The *Incorrect* condition has the lowest median in both *Error* conditions, but in general the effect is stronger for the *Pattern* condition groups.

Table 1. Experiment 1: Two-way ART ANOVA results. Significant p values indicated in bold. Table from Bracamonte et al [4].

	Recommend			Trust			Understandable			Useful		
	F	p	eta2	F	p	eta2	F	p	eta2	F	p	eta2
Error	7.81	**.006**	.03	3.21	.074	.01	.03	.872	.00	.21	.65	.00
Example	39.80	**<.001**	.22	54.74	**<.001**	.28	5.01	**.007**	.03	7.86	**<.001**	.05
Inter	1.55	.214	.01	2.56	.079	.02	.81	.448	.01	3.07	**.048**	.02

Table 2. Experiment 1: Tukey's HSD test post hoc comparison results. Significant p values indicated in bold. Table from Bracamonte et al. [4].

	Recommend	Trust	Understandable	Useful
Correct-Incorrect	**<.001**	**<.001**	**.006**	**<.001**
Correct-Mixed	**<.001**	**<.001**	.616	.577
Incorrect-Mixed	**<.001**	**<.001**	.079	**.013**

With regards to trust in the system, the results show a significant main effect for *Example* (p < .001), but not for *Error* (p = .074). The Tukey's HSD post hoc comparison test results show significant differences between the *Example* levels. The median of trust was lower for conditions that include examples of incorrect predictions (*Mixed* and *Incorrect* conditions). On the other hand, the results show a significant main effect of *Example* for understanding of the system decisions (p < .01) and usefulness of the explanations (*Example* p < .001), but not for *Error*. As shown in Table 2, the Tukey's HSD test results showed significant results only between some levels. The results indicate that participants' willingness to recommend and trust in the system are negatively influenced when presented with errors. In addition, understanding of the system decision and usefulness of the explanations are not as strongly influenced, that is, that errors do not have a strongly negative effect on these perceptions.

3.5 Qualitative Results

The open-ended responses to the question *"Please explain your reason for agreeing/disagreeing (with recommending the system)"* were qualitatively analyzed.

For the analysis of the open-ended answers, a closed coding procedure was used, using the following categories:

- **Accuracy.** Refers to participants reporting that the accuracy of the system was the main reason for their choice.
- **Evidence.** Refers to participants' reason includes evidence such as the highlighted words in the explanations. For example, mentions that the explanation highlighted incorrect or irrelevant words, or that a positive word was erroneously highlighted as negative (or vice versa).
- **Not Specified.** When there is no specific reason or the answer is based on subjective perception.

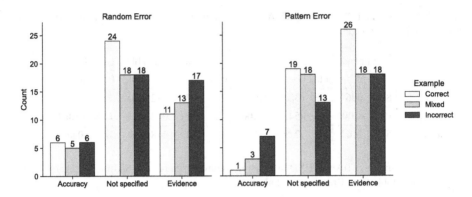

Fig. 2. Experiment 1: Reasons for willingness to recommend the system.

A total of 258 answers to the open-ended question were obtained, with 31 blank responses. Invalid answers (17 answers) were removed from the analysis. The criteria for invalid answers is detailed in Sect. 3.3. One rater coded all answers, and two raters coded 20% of that total. The Cohen's kappa reliability for the two raters was 0.723 (p < .001), indicating good strength of agreement.

The results (Fig. 2) show that in general that more participants in the *Pattern* conditions reported (*Evidence*) in the reason for their recommendation. The content of the *Evidence* answers indicate that participants recognized the pattern in the errors; it may be that the error pattern can be distinguished more clearly when contrasted with a supposedly correct prediction. For example, a participant answered:

> "It's marking of words like recommend as negative is weird. Additionally, it never checked context of the keywords it was scanning, so they seemed to be rated incorrectly for their usage."

Conversely, *Accuracy* answers were the least common in those condition. Answers in this category were straightforward in mentioning accuracy as the reason:

> "because of it has accuracy level 89%"

In both *Pattern* and *Random* error condition groups, *Accuracy* and *Not specified* reasons (e.g. "It doesn't seem completely reliable.") combined made up the majority of answers. However, in the *Pattern* error condition groups their combined number decreased and the number of *Evidence* answers increased. This suggests that errors were more easily recognized when there was a pattern.

4   Experiment 2: Effect on the Comparison of Two Systems

4.1   Experiment Design

The experiment was designed to evaluated the effect of errors on the choice between two text classification systems. The factors of the experiment were the same as the ones described in experiment 1: *Error* (*Random* and *Pattern*) and *Example* (*Correct*, *Mixed* and *Incorrect*). In this case, the error pattern was shown in only one of the systems (System B). This was the same system as the one used for experiment 1. The error pattern was also the same as in experiment 1: "recommend" as a word that contributes to a negative classification. The experiment had a between-subjects design.

4.2 Task and Questionnaire

Participants were asked to compare and evaluate System A and System B, based on their testing accuracy and on four examples of their prediction and explanations. The examples corresponded to the same movie reviews for both systems.

Participants were asked which of the system they would choose (*"Between the two systems, I would choose..."*), with a response scale from *Definitely A* to *Definitely B*. Trust was measured for the each of the systems (*"I can trust system A/B."*), as well as general usefulness of the explanations (*"The explanations were useful to form an opinion about the systems."*), and general understandability of the systems' decisions (*"I understand how the systems make decisions in general."*), on a 7-point Likert-scale from *Strongly disagree* to *Strongly agree*. In addition, an open-ended question on the reasons for the participants' choice between systems was included. Same as in experiment 1, the questionnaire included demographic (age and gender) and machine learning knowledge questions, and an attention question.

4.3 Participant Recruitment

A similar procedure as Experiment 1 was used (Sect. 3.3), with two differences. The worker approval rate was increased to 99% due to finding a large number of invalid answers in the first experiment. In addition, workers were compensated with $2.00 due to the task taking longer to complete than for experiment 1. It took participants approximately 11 min to complete the task, and so were compensated at a rate of $11/h. Although a similar recruitment procedure was used, workers could only participate in one of the experiments.

4.4 Results

A total of 339 worker responses were obtained, 43 of which were rejected after review. Participants that sefl-assessed as machine learning experts were removed as well (17 cases), resulting in 277 valid cases. The sample included 107 (39%) female, 169 male (61%) and 1 other/NA participants, ages 18 to 80. The age mean was 36. Only 14 participants reported no knowledge of machine learning.

The two-way ART ANOVA (Table 3) results show a significant main effect of *Error* ($p < .001$) on the choice between the systems, but the main effect of *Example* was not significant ($p = .954$). Fewer participants chose system B (higher accuracy) in the *Pattern* conditions groups compared to the *Random* groups (Fig. 3). The results show a significant main effect of *Example* on trust in systems A ($p < .001$) and B ($p < .01$), but no significant effect of *Error*. For both trust variables, the results of the Tukey's HSD post hoc comparison (Table 4) show significant differences between the *Correct* and *Incorrect* (Trust in A, p < .001; Trust in B, p < .01), and the *Correct* and *Mixed* (Trust in A, p < .001; Trust in B, p < .05) levels of the *Example* factor, but not between *Incorrect* and *Mixed* (Trust in A, p = .881; Trust in B, p = .897). In general, trust was lower for the *Mixed* and *Incorrect* conditions compared to the *Correct* condition (Fig. 4). On the other hand, the results show no significant main effect of either factor on the perception of usefulness of the explanations or understanding of the systems' decision.

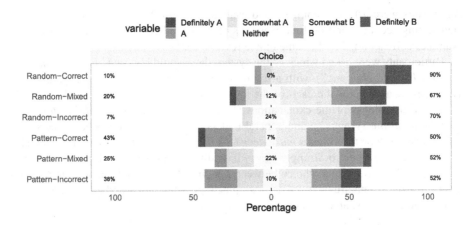

Fig. 3. Experiment 2: Distribution of responses to choice of system.

Table 3. Experiment 2: Two-way ART ANOVA results. Significant p values indicated in bold. Table from Bracamonte et al [4].

	Choice			Trust in A			Trust in B			Understand			Useful		
	F	p	eta2	F	p	eta2	F	p	eta2	F	p	eta2	F	p	eta2
Error	16.09	<.001	.06	3.65	.057	.01	3.37	.067	.01	0.08	.777	.00	.05	.826	.00
Example	0.05	.954	.00	11.74	<.001	.08	6.10	.003	.04	1.38	.254	.01	.54	.585	.00
Inter	0.57	.565	.00	0.21	.812	.00	0.11	.899	.00	2.81	.062	.02	.10	.908	.00

The results indicate that participants that viewed the errors preferred the system with slightly lower accuracy but no error pattern (system A) to the system with higher accuracy but with an error pattern (system B). Other variables were not as strongly affected, although it could be observed that trust was reduced for both systems when participants were shown incorrect prediction examples.

The answers to the open-ended question *"Please explain the reasons for your choice (of system)"* were qualitatively analyzed, using the same coding procedure and categories described in experiment 1. Invalid answers (4 cases) were removed from the analysis. The criteria for invalid answers is described in Sect. 3.3. In total 255 answers and 22 blank responses were obtained. The Cohen's kappa reliability for the two raters

Table 4. Experiment 2: Tukey's HSD test post hoc comparison results. Significant p values indicated in bold. Table from Bracamonte et al. [4].

	Trust in A	Trust in B
Correct-Incorrect	**<.001**	**.004**
Correct-Mixed	**<.001**	**.018**
Incorrrect-Mixed	.881	.897

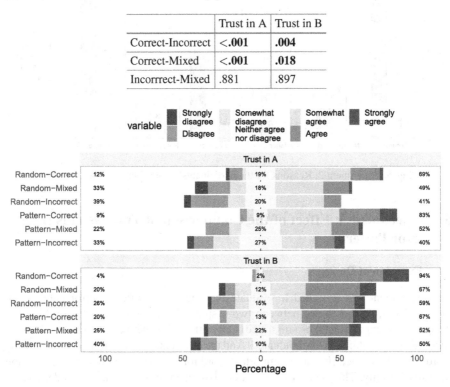

Fig. 4. Experiment 2: Distribution of responses on trust towards the systems.

on 20% of the answers was 0.655 (p < .001), indicating a substantial level of agreement [24]. As Fig. 5 shows, participants in the *Pattern-Correct* and *Pattern-Incorrect* condition groups mentioned *Evidence* in their reasons more frequently than *Accuracy*. The opposite happens in the *Random* condition groups, although the difference between the categories is smaller than in the other conditions. On the other hand, the number of participants' answers in the *Mixed*conditions was more equally distributed between the *Evidence* and *Accuracy* categories. *Not specified* answers were the least frequent in all conditions (e.g. "it seemed better.").

The results indicate that in the *Pattern* condition, participants noticed the error pattern and mentioned it in their reason for choosing system A (lower accuracy but no error patterns) instead of system B. For example, a participant mentioned:

"I can't wrap my head around why 'recommend' would be classified as negative as it is in system B. that's the main reason why I lean somewhat towards A."

In the *Random* condition, more participants mentioned the system accuracy in their reason for choosing system B. For example:

"System B has a more accurate result overall even if only by a small margin."

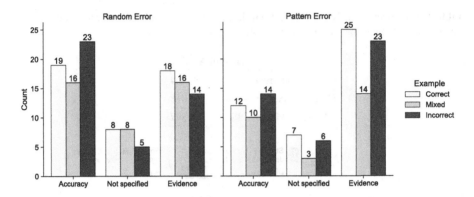

Fig. 5. Experiment 2: Reasons for the participants' choice between the systems.

5 Experiment 3: Effect of the Comparison of Two Systems (Bias Error Pattern)

5.1 Experiment Design

The experiment was designed to evaluate the effect of a different error pattern that indicates bias, on the choice between two systems. Because of the focus on bias, the design of the experiment was simplified. Only differences between *Correct* and *Incorrect* example conditions were evaluated. And the error pattern chosen was one where the word *women* was identified as an important word for a negative sentiment classification in system B only. This type of error pattern is related to a problem of gender-related bias [11]. The task instructions, questionnaire and participant recruitment procedure were the same as for Experiment 2 (Sect. 4).

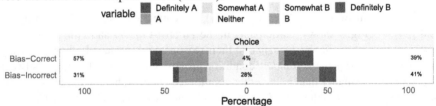

Fig. 6. Experiment 3: Distribution of responses to choice of system.

5.2 Results

In total 60 responses were obtained, with 1 rejected after review. In addition, 2 participants were excluded from analysis due to self-assessing as machine learning experts. This resulted in 57 valid cases. The sample included 14 (25%) female, 43 male (75%) participants, ages 18 to 72. The age mean was 37. Only 2 participants reported no knowledge of machine learning.

The results of a one-way ART ANOVA show a significant effect on trust in system A ($p < .001$) and on understanding of the systems' decision ($p < .05$) (Table 5). This indicates that viewing the *Incorrect* examples had a negative effect on both of these variables. The effect on the other variables was not significant. In particular, the non-significant effect on trust in system B represents a difference from the results of experiment 2 (Figs. 6 and 7).

Table 5. Experiment 3: One-way ART ANOVA results. Significant p values indicated in bold. Table from Bracamonte et al [4].

	Choice			Trust in A			Trust in B			Understand			Useful		
	F	p	eta2	F	p	eta2	F	p	eta2	F	p	eta2	F	p	eta2
Example	0.94	.336	.02	16.25	**<.001**	.23	3.18	.08	.05	6.16	**.016**	.10	2.32	.133	.04

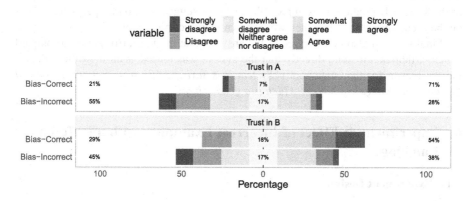

Fig. 7. Experiment 3: Distribution of responses on trust towards the systems.

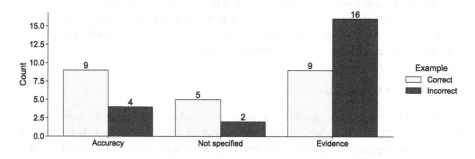

Fig. 8. Experiment 3: Reasons for the participants' choice between the systems.

The open-ended question *"Please explain the reasons for your choice (of system)"* was asked and its responses were coded using the same procedure as for experiment 2. In total 47 answers and 10 blank responses were obtained. The Cohen's kappa reliability was 0.75 (p < 0.01), indicating good agreement. The results show that more participants answered with *Evidence* than *Accuracy* as a reason for their choice when they viewed only incorrect predictions (Fig. 8). As a participant mentioned:

> "System B seems to be categorizing the word Women as a negative word and it does it multiple times."

In the *Correct* condition, the results show that there were the same number of *Accuracy* and *Evidence* answers.

> "It has a slightly higher accuracy rate than does "A.""

Not specified answers were the least frequent in both conditions.

> "in my opinion i can choose a is the best one."

Considering that both conditions (*Correct* and *Incorrect*) showed the bias error pattern in the system B prediction examples, the answers suggest that participants relied less on the accuracy metric when they were shown incorrect predictions.

Finally, it can also be observed in the answers that the bias error pattern prompted some participants to state directly that the system was biased, with or without detailing the reason for that statement (*"System B is sexist"*, *"Because System B labelled "women" as a negative review. Which is a gender bias."*).

6   Experiment 4: Effect of Incorrect Examples (with a Different Language)

6.1   Experiment Design

The experiment was designed to evaluate the effect of errors in Japanese users. In this experiment, random errors were used and the *Example* factor, which is based on outcome of the system's prediction examples that the participants viewed, was simplified to two levels: in the *Incorrect* level, all prediction examples were incorrect; and in the *Mixed* some predictions were correct and some were incorrect. Each participant viewed only one of the conditions (between-subjects design).

6.2   Task and Questionnaire

Similar to the other experiments, participants were asked to evaluate the responses of two systems, A and B. After viewing the output of the systems and their explanations, the participants were asked to answer questions about their content. After viewing the reviews, the questionnaire asked participants to indicate which model they would choose, on a four point response scale. An open-ended question about the reason why the participants had made that choice was included. Questions about perception of trust, understandability and usefulness of each system were also included, and used a six point Likert scale for the answers: ranging from Completely agree to Completely disagree. Attention check questions were also included.

6.3   Participant Recruitment

For this experiment, the services of an online survey company were used. The online survey company distributed the survey to their subscribers and compensated the participants who completed the survey. Participants who were 18 years old or older were recruited.

6.4   Translation

The survey and experiment were conducted in Japan and all our participants were Japanese. The materials used in the survey and experiment were first developed in English, and then translated them to Japanese with the following procedure. The initial English text was translated by a native Japanese speaker and reviewed by a second native Japanese speaker, both fluent in English. After the initial translation, the materials were reviewed in language and content by the authors and final adjustments were conducted.

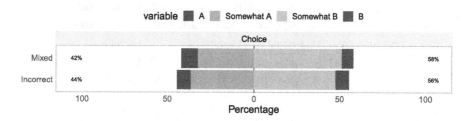

Fig. 9. Experiment 4: Distribution of responses to choice of system.

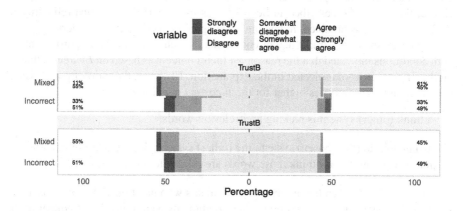

Fig. 10. Experiment 4: Reasons for Japanese participant's choice between the systems.

6.5   Results

The experiment evaluation returned 137 responses, after removing participants who failed the attention check. The gender distribution of the participants was 43% female and 57% male. Their ages ranged from 18 to 77, with an age mean of 46 years-old.

The results of a one-way ART ANOVA (Table 6) show that there was no significant difference in the choice of system between the *Mixed* and *Incorrect* conditions. There was a significant effect on system A's trust (p < .001), understanding of system decision (p < .001) and perception of usefulness (p < .001). In all of these variables, viewing the *Incorrect* examples had a negative effect. Figure 9 and Fig. 10 show the distribution of responses. On the other hand, the effect on trust, understanding and perceived usefulness of system B was not significant.

Table 6. Experiment 4: One-way ART ANOVA results. Significant p values indicated in bold. Table from Bracamonte et al. [4].

Choice			Trust in A			Trust in B		
F	p	eta2	F	p	eta2	F	p	eta2
.01	.92	.00	13.83	**<.001**	.09	.04	.85	0.00

Understand A			Understand B			Useful A			Useful B		
F	p	eta2	F	p	eta2	F	p	eta2	F	p	eta2
5.87	**.017**	.04	.82	.366	.01	15.71	**<.001**	.10	.04	.85	.00

6.6   Qualitative Results

For the analysis of the open-ended answers, to understand the reasons for participant's choice, the procedure described in Sect. 3.5 was used. A Cohen's kappa reliability of 0.73 (p < 0.01) was obtained, indicating good agreement between the coders.

Figure 11 shows the frequency of comments in each category. More participants in both conditions indicated that the reason for their choice was based on *Evidence*, that is, on the important words selected in the explanation. However, the ratio of participants' responses in this category is higher for the *Incorrect* condition.

"I think (other) system is picking up irrelevant words."

"Compared to (the chosen) system, the (other) system picks up a lot of conjunction words, and I don't think those words are related to a judgement criteria."

Conversely, although the number of participants who mentioned *Accuracy* as a reason was the lowest in both conditions, these comments were much less frequent in the *Incorrect* condition compared to *Evidence* comments.

"(Other option) is 2% less accurate."

"It is difficult to choose, but (I chose it) because the percentage is slightly higher."

In the *Mixed* condition, more participants reported their reasons on ambiguous terms or terms that referred to feelings (*Not specified* category).

"Because it fits my intuition."

"I feel that the overall understanding of the text is higher."

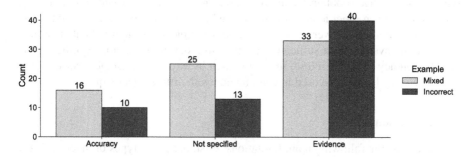

Fig. 11. Experiment 4: Reasons for Japanese participant's choice between the systems.

7   Discussion

The results indicate that showing incorrect predictions and error patterns in the result of a machine learning system can reduce willingness to recommend that system. However, incorrect predictions had different effects compared to error patterns.

Error patterns had an effect on the decision whether to recommend a machine learning system, in the evaluation of one system, although not on perception such as trust. Participants reported that error patterns as the reason for choosing one system over another. Although the participants could see in the description that the system B had higher overall accuracy, they were less willing to choose it when they were in the error pattern condition. In addition, more participants that viewed error patterns explained that they made the choice because of those errors, and did not mention the level of accuracy. In general, the results of the analysis suggest that error patterns in the system with higher accuracy were detected by the participants, and that those patterns made them suspicious of whether its performance regardless of the reported accuracy. In the comparison task, this effect seems stronger, which may be due to participants having the other model as a frame of reference for their decision. When evaluating only one system, the lack of reference to decide against might increase uncertainty in participants' evaluation. This could also explain the high number of participants who did not provide a reason for their evaluation in the first experiment. In the case of where the error pattern is related to bias, some participants also specifically mentioned it in their responses. In comparison to error patterns, incorrect predictions negatively affected perception overall. When comparing two systems, user trust was influenced by incorrect prediction. On the other hand, incorrect predictions did not have influence over whether the participants would choose one system over another. Finally, although the differences in experiment design and sample characteristics does not allow for a direct comparison, still the experiment in a different language and population shows similar results.

Overall, the results indicate that under some conditions participants can more easily detect errors. For the evaluation of machine learning systems, some techniques could be used to make this task easier. Methods for detecting specific text errors with the use of word meaning have been proposed in the context of machine translation [31,39]. Proposals for using bias metrics [3] and failure prediction approaches [3] also exist. While it is true that to obtain a comprehensive view of the performance of automated systems a focus on specific errors is not enough, still some errors may be considered critical enough to affect overall evaluation. For example, errors that indicate that there is bias in the system are a sufficient incentive to redesign a system, regardless of its overall accuracy [11]. Therefore, future research in ways to encourage error detection should be considered, to be used in combination with different techniques.

7.1 Limitations

This study has the following main limitations. First, particular types of machine learning models for text classification, dataset and explanation method were used for the experiments. In addition, only some error patterns were chosen. The results may not generalize to other experiment settings. Second, only a few examples of the system output were included, which were manually selected. This was done to prevent the task from being too long for participants. In real scenarios, users would likely need more information in order to detect patterns of error. Third, the Amazon Mechanical Turk platform was used to recruit participants online, who were from different countries. The majority were also male. The characteristics of this sample means a limitation on the generalization of the results for different populations.

8 Conclusion

In this paper, a series of experiments were conducted to investigate the effect of errors when evaluating the text classification machine learning systems. Two types of approaches were tested: incorrect predictions and errors in the explanation. The results showed participants were less willing to recommend a system when they were shown error patterns than when they were shown random errors. The error patterns also affected choice of system: participants were less willing to choose a higher-accuracy system when it had a pattern of errors. However, when the same system only had errors at random, the participants relied on the reported accuracy level. The participants' reasons for their evaluation also showed that they noticed the errors when these errors formed a pattern, and fewer participants mentioned accuracy as the only reason for their choice. In future research, different conditions should be evaluated to validate these findings.

References

1. Adadi, A., Berrada, M.: Peeking inside the black-box: a survey on explainable artificial intelligence (XAI). IEEE Access **6**, 52138–52160 (2018). https://doi.org/10.1109/ACCESS.2018.2870052
2. Amershi, S., et al.: Software engineering for machine learning: a case study. In: Proceedings of the 41st International Conference on Software Engineering: Software Engineering in Practice, ICSE-SEIP 2010, pp. 291–300. IEEE Press, Piscataway, NJ, USA (2019). https://doi.org/10.1109/ICSE-SEIP.2019.00042
3. Borkan, D., Dixon, L., Sorensen, J., Thain, N., Vasserman, L.: Nuanced metrics for measuring unintended bias with real data for text classification. In: Companion Proceedings of the 2019 World Wide Web Conference, WWW 2019, pp. 491–500. ACM, New York, NY, USA (2019). https://doi.org/10.1145/3308560.3317593
4. Bracamonte, V., Hidano, S., Kiyomoto, S.: Effect of errors on the evaluation of machine learning systems. In: VISIGRAPP (2: HUCAPP), pp. 48–57 (2022)
5. Bussone, A., Stumpf, S., O'Sullivan, D.: The role of explanations on trust and reliance in clinical decision support systems. In: 2015 International Conference on Healthcare Informatics, October 2015, pp. 160–169 (2015). https://doi.org/10.1109/ICHI.2015.26
6. Cai, C.J., et al.: Human-centered tools for coping with imperfect algorithms during medical decision-making. In: Proceedings of the 2019 CHI Conference on Human Factors in Computing Systems, May 2019, pp. 1–14. Association for Computing Machinery, New York, NY, USA (2019). https://doi.org/10.1145/3290605.3300234
7. Chakraborty, S., et al.: Interpretability of deep learning models: a survey of results. In: 2017 IEEE Smartworld, Ubiquitous Intelligence & Computing, Advanced & Trusted Computed, Scalable Computing & Communications, Cloud & Big Data Computing, Internet of People and Smart City innovation (smartworld/SCALCOM/UIC/ATC/CBDcom/IOP/SCI), pp. 1–6. IEEE (2017)
8. Chen, J., Song, L., Wainwright, M.J., Jordan, M.I.: L-Shapley and C-Shapley: efficient model interpretation for structured data. arXiv preprint arXiv:1808.02610 (2018)
9. Cheng, H.F., et al.: Explaining decision-making algorithms through UI: strategies to help non-expert stakeholders. In: Proceedings of the 2019 CHI Conference on Human Factors in Computing Systems, May 2019, pp. 1–12. Association for Computing Machinery, New York, NY, USA (2019). https://doi.org/10.1145/3290605.3300789
10. de Vries, P., Midden, C., Bouwhuis, D.: The effects of errors on system trust, self-confidence, and the allocation of control in route planning. Int. J. Hum Comput Stud. **58**(6), 719–735 (2003). https://doi.org/10.1016/S1071-5819(03)00039-9
11. Dixon, L., Li, J., Sorensen, J., Thain, N., Vasserman, L.: Measuring and mitigating unintended bias in text classification. In: Proceedings of the 2018 AAAI/ACM Conference on AI, Ethics, and Society, December 2018, pp. 67–73. ACM (2018). https://doi.org/10.1145/3278721.3278729
12. Dzindolet, M.T., Peterson, S.A., Pomranky, R.A., Pierce, L.G., Beck, H.P.: The role of trust in automation reliance. Int. J. Hum Comput Stud. **58**(6), 697–718 (2003). https://doi.org/10.1016/S1071-5819(03)00038-7
13. Eslami, M., Vaccaro, K., Lee, M.K., Elazari Bar On, A., Gilbert, E., Karahalios, K.: User attitudes towards algorithmic opacity and transparency in online reviewing platforms. In: Proceedings of the 2019 CHI Conference on Human Factors in Computing Systems, May 2019, pp. 1–14. Association for Computing Machinery, New York, NY, USA (2019). https://doi.org/10.1145/3290605.3300724
14. Frison, A.K., et al.: In UX we trust: investigation of aesthetics and usability of driver-vehicle interfaces and their impact on the perception of automated driving. In: Proceedings of the

2019 CHI Conference on Human Factors in Computing Systems, May 2019, pp. 1–13. Association for Computing Machinery, New York, NY, USA (2019). https://doi.org/10.1145/3290605.3300374

15. Guidotti, R., Monreale, A., Ruggieri, S., Turini, F., Giannotti, F., Pedreschi, D.: A survey of methods for explaining black box models. ACM Comput. Surv. **51**(5), 93:1-93:42 (2018). https://doi.org/10.1145/3236009

16. Hochreiter, S., Schmidhuber, J.: Long short-term memory. Neural Comput. **9**(8), 1735–1780 (1997). https://doi.org/10.1162/neco.1997.9.8.1735

17. Hoff, K.A., Bashir, M.: Trust in automation: integrating empirical evidence on factors that influence trust. Hum. Factors **57**(3), 407–434 (2015)

18. Jigsaw: Unintended bias and names of frequently targeted groups (2018). https://medium.com/the-false-positive/unintended-bias-and-names-of-frequently-targeted-groups-8e0b81f80a23

19. Kaur, H., Nori, H., Jenkins, S., Caruana, R., Wallach, H., Wortman Vaughan, J.: Interpreting interpretability: understanding data scientists' use of interpretability tools for machine learning. In: Proceedings of the 2020 CHI Conference on Human Factors in Computing Systems, CHI 2020, April 2020, pp. 1–14. Association for Computing Machinery, Honolulu, HI, USA (2020). https://doi.org/10.1145/3313831.3376219

20. Keras: Keras documentation: about Keras (2021). https://keras.io/about/

21. Kizilcec, R.F.: How much information? Effects of transparency on trust in an algorithmic interface. In: Proceedings of the 2016 CHI Conference on Human Factors in Computing Systems, CHI 2016, May 2016, pp. 2390–2395. Association for Computing Machinery, New York, NY, USA (2016). https://doi.org/10.1145/2858036.2858402

22. Kontogiannis, T.: User strategies in recovering from errors in man–machine systems. Saf. Sci. **32**(1), 49–68 (1999)

23. Lai, S., Xu, L., Liu, K., Zhao, J.: Recurrent convolutional neural networks for text classification. In: Proceedings of the Twenty-Ninth AAAI Conference on Artificial Intelligence, AAAI 2015, January 2015, pp. 2267–2273. AAAI Press, Austin, Texas (2015)

24. Landis, J.R., Koch, G.G.: The measurement of observer agreement for categorical data. Biometrics **33**, 159–174 (1977)

25. Lee, J.D., See, K.A.: Trust in automation: designing for appropriate reliance. Hum. Factors **46**(1), 50–80 (2004). https://doi.org/10.1518/hfes.46.1.50_30392

26. Lundberg, S.M., Lee, S.I.: A unified approach to interpreting model predictions. In: Guyon, I., et al. (eds.) Advances in Neural Information Processing Systems, vol. 30, pp. 4765–4774. Curran Associates, Inc. (2017). http://papers.nips.cc/paper/7062-a-unified-approach-to-interpreting-model-predictions.pdf

27. Maas, A.L., Daly, R.E., Pham, P.T., Huang, D., Ng, A.Y., Potts, C.: Learning word vectors for sentiment analysis. In: Proceedings of the 49th Annual Meeting of the Association for Computational Linguistics: Human Language Technologies, June 2011, pp. 142–150. Association for Computational Linguistics (2011). http://www.aclweb.org/anthology/P11-1015

28. Mittelstadt, B., Russell, C., Wachter, S.: Explaining explanations in AI. In: Proceedings of the Conference on Fairness, Accountability, and Transparency, FAT* 2019, January 2019, pp. 279–288. Association for Computing Machinery, New York, NY, USA (2019). https://doi.org/10.1145/3287560.3287574

29. Nickerson, R.S.: Confirmation bias: a ubiquitous phenomenon in many guises. Rev. Gen. Psychol. **2**(2), 175–220 (1998). https://doi.org/10.1037/1089-2680.2.2.175

30. Nourani, M., King, J., Ragan, E.: The role of domain expertise in user trust and the impact of first impressions with intelligent systems. In: Proceedings of the AAAI Conference on Human Computation and Crowdsourcing, October 2020, vol. 8, pp. 112–121 (2020). https://ojs.aaai.org/index.php/HCOMP/article/view/7469

31. Raybaud, S., Langlois, D., Smaïli, K.: "This sentence is wrong." Detecting errors in machine-translated sentences. Mach. Transl. **25**(1), 1 (2011). https://doi.org/10.1007/s10590-011-9094-9

32. Ribeiro, M.T., Singh, S., Guestrin, C.: "Why should i trust you?": explaining the predictions of any classifier. In: Proceedings of the 22nd ACM SIGKDD International Conference on Knowledge Discovery and Data Mining, KDD 2016, pp. 1135–1144. ACM, New York, NY, USA (2016). https://doi.org/10.1145/2939672.2939778

33. Rudin, C.: Stop explaining black box machine learning models for high stakes decisions and use interpretable models instead. Nat. Mach. Intel. **1**(5), 206–215 (2019)

34. Sanchez, J., Rogers, W.A., Fisk, A.D., Rovira, E.: Understanding reliance on automation: effects of error type, error distribution, age and experience. Theor. Issues Ergon. Sci. **15**(2), 134–160 (2014). https://doi.org/10.1080/1463922X.2011.611269

35. Sauer, J., Chavaillaz, A., Wastell, D.: Experience of automation failures in training: effects on trust, automation bias, complacency and performance. Ergonomics **59**(6), 767–780 (2016). https://doi.org/10.1080/00140139.2015.1094577

36. Tenney, I., et al.: The language interpretability tool: extensible, interactive visualizations and analysis for NLP models, August 2020. arXiv:2008.05122 [cs]

37. West, J.: Jessamyn West on Twitter: "I tested 14 sentences for "perceived toxicity" using Perspectives. Least toxic: I am a man. Most toxic: I am a gay black woman. Come on https://t.co/M4TF9uYtzE"/Twitter (2017)

38. Wobbrock, J.O., Findlater, L., Gergle, D., Higgins, J.J.: The aligned rank transform for non-parametric factorial analyses using only Anova procedures. In: Proceedings of the SIGCHI Conference on Human Factors in Computing Systems, CHI 2011, May 2011, pp. 143–146. Association for Computing Machinery, New York, NY, USA (2011). https://doi.org/10.1145/1978942.1978963

39. Xiong, D., Zhang, M., Li, H.: Error detection for statistical machine translation using linguistic features. In: Proceedings of the 48th Annual Meeting of the Association for Computational Linguistics, ACL 2010, July 2010, pp. 604–611. Association for Computational Linguistics, USA (2010)

Autonomous Navigation Method Considering Passenger Comfort Recognition for Personal Mobility Vehicles in Crowded Pedestrian Spaces

Yosuke Isono, Hiroshi Yoshitake[(✉)] [iD], and Motoki Shino

The University of Tokyo, Chiba, Japan
isonoyosuke@g.ecc.u-tokyo.ac.jp, hyoshitake@edu.k.u-tokyo.ac.jp,
motoki@k.u-tokyo.ac.jp

Abstract. Autonomous navigation systems for personal mobility vehicles are being developed to support mobility in large-scale facilities such as airports and shopping malls where pedestrians coexist. Passenger comfort, such as not causing anxiety to the passengers, is one of the required functions of autonomous navigation. This study aims to achieve the following two goals. The first goal is to clarify the characteristics of passenger comfort recognition, that is, how the passenger feels comfortable depending on the behavior of the surrounding pedestrians and the vehicle when the personal mobility vehicle moves autonomously in a crowded environment. The second goal is to propose a novel autonomous navigation method based on the clarified characteristics of passenger comfort recognition. To achieve the goals, first, an experiment was conducted to obtain a subjective assessment of passenger comfort using a VR simulator. By focusing on situation awareness as a process affecting passenger comfort recognition, the influence of situation awareness on passenger comfort recognition was analyzed, and the characteristics of passenger comfort recognition were discussed. Based on the characteristics, requirements for comfortable autonomous navigation were set, and a novel autonomous navigation method was proposed. Numerical simulation results showed that the proposed method satisfies the requirements and is a valid method to realize comfortable autonomous navigation in crowded pedestrian spaces.

Keywords: Comfort Recognition · Situation Awareness · Autonomous Navigation · Personal Mobility Vehicle

1 Introduction

This paper is based on the previous work originally presented in [1]. This paper extends the work by proposing and validating a novel autonomous navigation method considering passenger comfort recognition in Sect. 4.

The population of older adults in Japan is increasing yearly, and the number of people with physical disabilities and dementia is also increasing. Thus, there is a growing need for outdoor mobility support using public transportation, shared-ride services, and indoor

© The Author(s), under exclusive license to Springer Nature Switzerland AG 2023
A. A. de Sousa et al. (Eds.): VISIGRAPP 2022, CCIS 1815, pp. 182–202, 2023.
https://doi.org/10.1007/978-3-031-45725-8_9

mobility support after arriving at a destination. In terms of indoor mobility support, the need for this is growing due to the increasing scale of facilities. Currently, most mobility support services at airports and other largescale facilities rely on human labor (e.g., a facility staff pushing a wheelchair). However, the development of autonomous navigation systems for personal mobility vehicles (PMVs), such as electric wheelchairs, is in progress, and it is expected to reduce labor shortages and labor costs [2].

A PMV travels inside the pedestrian space, a mixed space with pedestrians and PMVs. The autonomous navigation systems of PMVs are required to carry the passengers to a designated destination, be safe and free from collisions with static objects and pedestrians, and be comfortable without causing anxiety to the passengers. In this study, we aim to realize an autonomous navigation system of PMVs that is comfortable for passengers and can be used in large-scale facilities (e.g., airports and shopping malls).

Research on passenger comfort in autonomous navigation of PMVs can be roughly divided into two types: research focusing on ride comfort and a sense of security. As for the former type, International Organization for Standardization has established evaluation criteria for acceleration applied to seated human beings [3], and there is research on methods generating smooth paths considering vehicle acceleration and jerk as indicators [4, 5]. For the latter type, the concept of personal space (PS), the space in which people feel uncomfortable with the presence of others, has been studied [6]. PS is perceived as an elliptical area with a long axis in front of oneself. Pham et al. [7] investigated the discomfort of PMV passengers by focusing on the degree of invasion of others into their PS. As methods for generating comfortable paths, researchers focus on static environments where there are no pedestrians [8, 9] and dynamic environments when pedestrians pass by [10]. In this study, PMV's acceleration and jerk are kept below a certain level that does not impair the ride comfort of passengers, and the sense of security is focused on as passenger comfort.

The comfortable autonomous navigation methods avoiding obstacles and passing by pedestrians proposed in previous research assume situations where the PMV can take enough distance from the obstacles and pedestrians. However, many pedestrians exist simultaneously in large-scale facilities such as airports and shopping malls. When the environment is crowded (i.e., with pedestrians above a certain density), pedestrians will inevitably invade the PS of a PMV passenger. It is known that passengers feel uncomfortable when pedestrians invade their PS. However, the characteristics of comfort recognition in a crowded environment where the surroundings changes from time to time and PS are inevitably invaded have not been discussed. Investigating these characteristics of passenger comfort recognition is expected to lead to a novel autonomous navigation method that can reduce discomfort while allowing pedestrians to invade their PS in a crowded environment. Therefore, this study aims to achieve the following two goals. The first goal is to clarify the characteristics of passenger comfort recognition, that is, how the passengers feel comfortable depending on the behavior of the surrounding pedestrians and the PMV when the PMV moves autonomously inside a crowded environment. The second goal is to propose a novel autonomous navigation method considering the characteristics of passenger comfort recognition. Although older people use PMVs more than young people, the participant experiment in this study was conducted on young participants following previous research [11] to obtain fundamental data as an exploratory study aimed at finding factors that constitute passenger comfort recognition. Moreover, this study deals with a mobility scooter as a form of PMV.

The remainder of this paper is organized as follows. Section 2 describes the process of passenger comfort recognition that we set based on previous work. Section 3 describes methods, results, and discussions regarding the investigation of passenger comfort recognition based on a simulator experiment conducted to obtain passenger subjective assessment of comfort when the PMV moves autonomously in the target crowded environment. Section 4 describes the design of a novel autonomous navigation method considering passenger comfort recognition and provides validation results of the proposed novel method based on numerical simulation. Finally, Sect. 5 summarizes the findings of this study.

2   Process of Passenger Comfort Recognition

The driving behavior process of a PMV driver in a crowded environment was focused on considering the passenger comfort recognition process during autonomous navigation in a similar environment. In a crowded environment, drivers understand the state of pedestrians from the observed behavior and posture and select their actions according to their observation. In this way, the driver can select less uncomfortable behavior even in situations where pedestrians inevitably invade their PS. This process of recognition and judgment in driver behavior matches the situation awareness model of Endsley [12]. In Endsley's situation awareness model, information processing consists of "situation awareness," "decision," and "performance of actions." Moreover, the process of "situation awareness" consists of the following three stages:

- Level 1: Perception of the elements in the Current Situation
- Level 2: Comprehension of the Current Situation
- Level 3: Projection of the Future Status

These stages indicate that it is necessary to perceive the objects' shapes and positions (Level 1) and understand what their positional relationships and movements mean to oneself (Level 2). Moreover, it is necessary to predict what the Future Status may be from the Current Situation (Level 3) to recognize the environment. Recognition is affected by task- and system-side factors such as the vehicle's or system's characteristics and personal factors such as memory, goals, and expectations that depend on personal ability and experience.

When focusing on autonomous navigation, the "performance of actions" stage in manual driving is no longer present. However, the passenger can be considered to perceive the surrounding environment and recognize comfort (i.e., feel comfortable or uncomfortable) as a result of the "situation awareness" stage in place of the "decision" stage. Therefore, the passenger comfort recognition process in this study is expressed with the "situation awareness" stage, as shown in Fig. 1. In other words, the passenger recognizes comfort based on the results of situation awareness using elements of the surrounding environment, such as pedestrians, obstacles, and the autonomous PMV as input information.

The relationships between situation awareness and passenger comfort were examined in this study to understand the characteristics of comfort recognition. First, an experiment was conducted to obtain passenger's subjective assessment of comfort when the PMV moves autonomously in the target crowded environment. The effect of Current Situation and Future Status in situation awareness on comfort recognition was analyzed using the obtained data. Finally, the characteristics of passenger comfort recognition were discussed based on the analysis results.

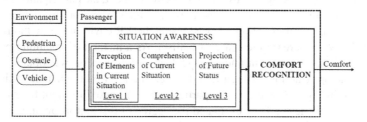

Fig. 1. Process of passenger comfort recognition based on situation awareness [1].

3   Investigation of Passenger Comfort Recognition

3.1   Passenger Comfort Evaluation Experiment

This experiment evaluates how passengers recognize comfort during autonomous navigation of PMVs in the target crowded environment. The experiment requires a quantitative evaluation of passenger comfort to analyze the relationship between passenger comfort and situation awareness.

The experiment was done with a virtual reality (VR) simulator. Scenes with different autonomous movements of a PMV and pedestrians' behavior in a crowded environment were simulated in a VR environment and presented to the participants using a head-mounted display (HMD). In addition, the passenger's degree of discomfort was obtained along the time axis. A VR simulator was adopted in this experiment for two reasons. First, VR simulators can control the behavior of the PMV and pedestrians easily and repeatedly, which is difficult in the real world. Second, VR simulators are free from actual collisions, which is not the case in the real world, where the possibility of collisions remains between the autonomous PMV and pedestrians.

Scene Conditions. The behavior of the autonomous PMV and pedestrians in a crowded environment was simulated numerically to present scenes with different behavior of the autonomous PMV and pedestrians to participants in a VR environment. The environment was set as a 6-m-wide aisle in a shopping mall. Thirty pedestrians approached the PMV, and the pedestrian density of the environment was approximately 0.125 /m². The pedestrians followed the Social Force Model [13], and the initial position, target speed, and destination were set individually. The autonomous navigation method of the PMV in this simulation was based on the Dynamic Window Approach (DWA) [14], a widely used method in robotics. The method also considered the movement of surrounding pedestrians to perform avoidance actions [15]. The numerical simulation was conducted assuming that pedestrians within the measurement range could be recognized accurately and that there was no skidding of the PMV. Under these conditions, 16 scenes with different behaviors of pedestrians and the autonomous PMV were simulated.

Equipment and Methods. The created scenes were simulated in a VR environment using Unity (Unity Technologies) and presented to the participants using VIVE Pro Eye (HTC Corporation). A sample view of the VR environment created based on the simulation is shown in Fig. 2. As for the experimental environment, the participants sat in a real mobility scooter and wore an HMD, as shown in Fig. 3. The mobility scooter's motor was rotated according to the PMV's speed inside the VR environment without moving the actual PMV to increase the sense of realism. As a method of obtaining passenger comfort quantitatively and continuously, the degree of discomfort was obtained in real-time as an analog scale instead of a Likert scale. The lever on the handle indicated by the red circle in Fig. 3 was used. The participants were asked to input their degree of discomfort with the lever. They evaluated the degree of discomfort on an analog scale from 0 to 1, where 1 is the most uncomfortable moment.

The participants first experienced all 16 scenes without evaluating their discomfort. This process was set to familiarize the participants with the equipment, the pedestrian's behavior, and autonomous PMV's behavior. In addition, this process lets the participants define their standard of discomfort during autonomous navigation. The discomfort was then obtained using the method described above. Each of the 16 scenes was played in a random order to remove the order effects.

Fig. 2. Sample image inside the head-mounted display [1].

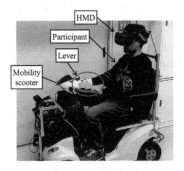

Fig. 3. Experiment setup with a real mobility scooter. (Color figure online)

Participants. The experiment was conducted on healthy young participants to ensure fundamental data as an exploratory study. Ten males in their 20s (23.0 ± 0.77 years old) participated in this experiment. The experimental procedures and details of the experiment were explained to the participants beforehand, and informed consent was obtained. The experiment was conducted with the approval of the Ethics Committee of the University of Tokyo.

3.2 Effects of Current Situation on Comfort Recognition

In this section, the effect of the Current Situation, which corresponds to Levels 1 and 2 of situation awareness in Endsley's model, on the passenger comfort recognition was analyzed. It is known that people feel uncomfortable when others invade their PS [6]. This phenomenon corresponds to the Current Situation. Therefore, the invasion of surrounding pedestrians into the passenger's PS was used as a cue for the analysis. First, the relationship between the sections where the passengers felt uncomfortable and the sections where the PS was invaded was investigated. Second, the relationship between the degree of discomfort and the degree of invasion was investigated.

Analysis of Uncomfortable Sections

Method. The more participants feel uncomfortable at a certain section of the scenes, the more uncomfortable that section will be. Therefore, the number of participants who input discomfort were counted along the time axis for each scene. The sections where two or more participants input discomfort was defined as the "uncomfortable section."

The size of the PMV and the PS is shown in Table 1. The size of the PS was set by considering the difference in the vehicle's size in the previous study [7]. The PS has an oval shape, as shown in Fig. 4, with the passenger's head at the center, an ellipse with the major axis l_f in the front and the minor axis l_s in the side, and a circle with a radius of l_s in the rear.

Table 1. Parameter values of the PMV and PS.

Parameter	Value
Vehicle length	1.19 m
Vehicle width	0.65 m
Front PS (l_f)	5.62 m
Side PS (l_s)	0.80 m

Result. Figure 5 shows the number of participants inputting discomfort in a certain scene, along with the vehicle speed and steering angle. In Fig. 5, the section where pedestrians invade the passenger's PS is filled in black. From Fig. 5, it can be seen that the pedestrian's invasion into the PS of PMV passengers greatly influences the timing

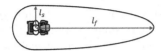

Fig. 4. Definition of PS [1].

of the participant's discomfort input. The uncomfortable section is the area filled in blue in Fig. 5. Among the 16 scenes, there were 46 uncomfortable sections, and 41 of these overlapped with sections where pedestrians invaded the PS. As for the remaining five sections, no pedestrians were invading the PS. However, there were pedestrians near the PS. From the results, it was found that the pedestrians invading PS have a significant impact on passenger discomfort. This result is in line with the results of previous studies.

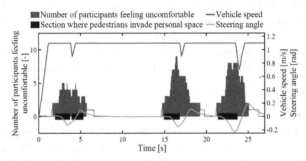

Fig. 5. Changes in the number of participants feeling uncomfortable (Scene No. 3) [1]. (Color figure online)

Analysis of Degree of Discomfort

Method. The results of the previous section indicated that pedestrians invading PS impact passenger discomfort significantly. This section analyzes the quantitative relationship between pedestrian's invasion into the PS and passenger discomfort.

As a quantitative index for pedestrian's invasion into the PS of a PMV passenger, the invasion ratio, which has been used in the previous study [7], was adopted. The invasion ratio is a physical index that expresses the extent to which the PS of a pedestrian is invaded, as shown in Fig. 6. The invasion ratio I is expressed as (1).

$$I = \frac{I_b}{I_a} \tag{1}$$

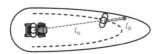

Fig. 6. Definition of invasion ratio into PS [1].

Next, passenger discomfort is quantified. As mentioned in the previous section, it is considered that it is more uncomfortable when more participants input discomfort at the same time. In addition, the larger the input value of discomfort is, the more the participants feel uncomfortable. Figure 7 shows the frequency distribution of discomfort input values on an analog scale among all 16 scenes for two different participants. As seen from the figures, there was a large difference in the input characteristics of discomfort among the participants. Thus, it is inappropriate to directly use the input values of discomfort on the analog scale as a quantification index of discomfort. Therefore, the input value of discomfort was corrected as follows according to the input characteristics of each individual:

$$q' = \begin{cases} 0 & (q = 0), \\ 0.5 & (0 < q \leq q_{median}), \\ 1 & (q_{median} < q \leq 1), \end{cases} \tag{2}$$

where q is the input discomfort value, q' is the corrected discomfort value, and q_{median} is the median of all input values for each individual. The value $\overline{q'}$, which is the average value of all the participants, was used as a quantitative index of passenger discomfort along the time axis. The quantitative time trends of pedestrian invasion ratio and passenger discomfort are shown in Fig. 8 using the above indices.

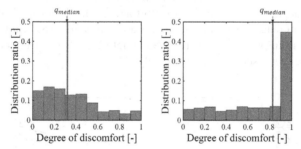

Fig. 7. Examples of input characteristics of the degree of discomfort (left: participant ID 1, right: participant ID 2) [1].

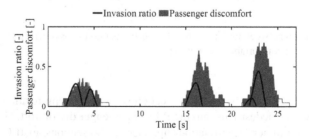

Fig. 8. Trends in invasion ratio and passenger discomfort (Scene No. 3) [1].

The relationship between passenger discomfort in response to pedestrian's invasion ratio was investigated by focusing on the uncomfortable sections. As a measure of pedestrian invasion into the PS during a certain section, the time integral of invasion ratio for all pedestrians who invaded the PS was adopted. I_{ir} represents the time integral of the invasion ratio for a certain section which is expressed as

$$I_{ir} = \sum_{j \in S} \int_{I_j(t)0} I_j(t)dt, \tag{3}$$

where S is the set of pedestrians who invaded the PS in the section of interest, and $I_j(t)$ is the instantaneous value of the invasion ratio of pedestrian j.

As an index of passenger discomfort during a certain section, the time integral of passenger discomfort $\overline{q'}$ was adopted. The time integral was adopted because this discomfort is considered stronger when the input value is larger and the input time is longer. I_{pd} represents the time integral of passenger discomfort for a certain section which is expressed as

$$I_{pd} = \int_{t_1}^{t_2} \overline{q'}(t)dt, \tag{4}$$

where t_1 and t_2 are the start and end timestamps of the uncomfortable section.

Results. Figure 9 shows the relationship between the time integral of the invasion ratio and the time integral of passenger discomfort among the 41 uncomfortable sections. The coefficient of determination for the linear approximation was near 0.6. This result indicates that the invasion ratio of pedestrians into the PS is an important factor in evaluating passenger discomfort quantitatively.

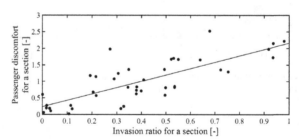

Fig. 9. Relationship between invasion ratio of pedestrians into the passenger's PS and passenger discomfort among uncomfortable sections [1].

Discussion. The results in the previous section showed a strong relationship between the invasion ratio of pedestrians into the PS and passenger discomfort. However, some sections showed a rather weak relationship, such as the sections apart from the linear approximation line. These sections were further analyzed, and two factors affecting passenger discomfort were identified. The first factor was that the vehicle was approaching the wall. There were two sections where the PMV was approaching the wall, and these sections were relatively uncomfortable, as shown in Fig. 10 with red plots. This result was consistent with the previous study [8], where people felt uncomfortable when the distance from the walls was close. The second factor was that the pedestrians invaded the PS of passengers immediately after the scene started. Fourteen sections near the start of the scene were relatively comfortable situations, as shown in Fig. 10 with blue plots. Immediately after the scene starts, the vehicle and the pedestrian accelerate from a stopping state. It is assumed that the sensitivity of passenger discomfort against pedestrian's invasion was low before reaching a steady state, leading to the evaluation of a relatively comfortable section.

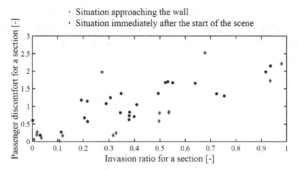

Fig. 10. Sections that showed a relatively weak relationship between the invasion ratio of pedestrians into the PS and passenger discomfort [1]. (Color figure online)

3.3 Effects of Future Status on Comfort Recognition

In this section, the effect of Future Status, which corresponds to Level 3 of situation awareness in Endsley's model, on the passenger comfort recognition is analyzed. The results of the previous chapter showed that pedestrian's invasion into the PS greatly impacts comfort recognition as a factor of the Current Situation. The status before the pedestrian's invasion into the PS (pre-invasion status) is focused on as the Future Status, and the effect on the passenger comfort recognition was analyzed. First, pre-invasion statuses that affect comfort recognition were extracted by comparing the pre-invasion statuses among the relatively comfortable and uncomfortable sections. Second, the effect of the extracted pre-invasion status was examined quantitively.

Comparison of Pre-invasion Statuses

Method. To extract the pre-invasion status that affects passenger comfort recognition, the relationship between the invasion ratio and passenger discomfort, as discussed in the previous section, was analyzed by focusing on the scenes that became relatively uncomfortable and comfortable in response to the invasion ratio. As a method of classifying relatively uncomfortable and comfortable sections, the 25 uncomfortable sections, which were not influenced by the wall or the start of the scene, were linearly approximated, and the sections that fall outside of the 50% prediction intervals were defined as relatively uncomfortable or relatively comfortable sections. The characteristics of the pre-invasion status of these sections were analyzed.

Result. Figure 11 shows the relationship between the invasion ratio and the passenger discomfort for the 25 sections, excluding 16 sections where factors other than pedestrians were involved. It also shows the linear approximation line and the 50% prediction intervals. A comparison of two classified section groups showed that for the sections classified as relatively uncomfortable, the autonomous PMVs did not avoid the pedestrians even though there was enough space to avoid them. Figure 12(a) shows an example where the vehicle could have avoided the pedestrian but did not. In contrast, Fig. 12(b) shows an example where the vehicle could not avoid the pedestrian in the first place. From this, the pre-invasion status that a vehicle did not avoid pedestrians although it could was extracted as a status that leads to passenger discomfort. The difference between the current status of the vehicle, which is not taking any avoidance action, and the passenger's expectation, which is that the vehicle would take an avoidance action, is considered to affect comfort recognition.

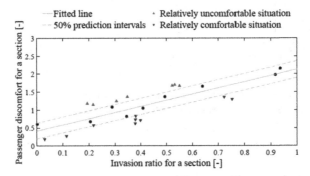

Fig. 11. Classification of relatively uncomfortable and comfortable situations. [1]

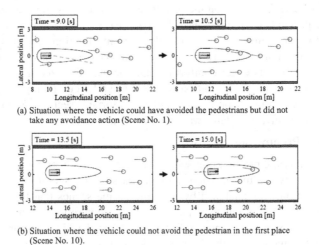

(a) Situation where the vehicle could have avoided the pedestrians but did not take any avoidance action (Scene No. 1).

(b) Situation where the vehicle could not avoid the pedestrian in the first place (Scene No. 10).

Fig. 12. Comparison of the ability to avoid pedestrians [1].

Examination of Effects of Pre-invasion Status on Comfort Recognition

Method. Two factors were quantified to examine the effect of the pre-invasion status extracted in the previous section: whether the vehicle is taking an avoidance action and whether the vehicle can avoid pedestrians.

First, whether the vehicle is taking avoidance actions or not was quantified. A vehicle is considered to be taking an avoidance action if it is decelerating or turning. Thus, the criteria for deceleration action were set as follows:

$$v \leq 0.9 v_{max} \wedge \frac{\Delta v}{\Delta t} \leq 0, \tag{5}$$

where v [m/s] is the vehicle speed and v_{max} is the maximum vehicle speed. The criteria for turning action are set as follows:

$$|\alpha| \geq 2 \vee \left| \frac{\Delta \alpha}{\Delta t} \right| \geq 2.5, \tag{6}$$

where α [degree] is the steering angle. A vehicle is considered to be taking avoidance action when it satisfies (5) or (6).

Next, whether the vehicle can avoid pedestrians or not was quantified. A vehicle can avoid pedestrians if it can travel for a longer time without approaching pedestrians or walls by steering the vehicle. Therefore, the focus is on the duration the vehicle can continue traveling without approaching pedestrians or walls, both when the vehicle continues traveling at the current steering angle and when the steering angle is changed from that angle. Whether or not the vehicle can continue to travel for several seconds is a future phenomenon and thus requires a prediction process. The following describes the method of quantification based on the prediction process. As a prediction process in this study, the vehicle motion is assumed to follow the vehicle model, and the pedestrian position is assumed to have a probabilistic distribution. The probability distribution of the pedestrians is a bivariate normal distribution centered on the position of constant velocity linear motion. The variance is calculated from the actual position error in the scenes. First, the probability p_n of any pedestrian invading the PS after n steps are determined using the method of previous research [16]. Here, pedestrians are limited to a range of 15 m from the vehicle, and the time per step Δt is 0.5 s. In this case, the probability q_n that the vehicle can continue traveling in n steps without approaching pedestrians is expressed as

$$q_n = \left(\prod_{i=1}^{n} (1 - p_i) \right) p_{n+1}. \tag{7}$$

At this time, the expected value T of the time that the vehicle can continue driving without approaching pedestrians is expressed as

$$T = \Delta t \sum_i i q_i. \tag{8}$$

The above process is applied to the case where the vehicle continues to travel at the current steering angle and a steering angle changing from the current angle. The steering angle varies in increments of 0.5° within ±3°. Figure 13 shows an example of the difference in the length of the path the vehicle can continue to travel without approaching pedestrians or walls. If the vehicle continues to move at the current steering angle, a pedestrian will invade the PS a few seconds ahead. However, if the steering angle is turned to the right, a longer path can be drawn without the pedestrian invading the PS.

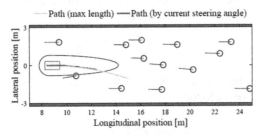

Fig. 13. Difference in path length that the vehicle can continue to travel without approaching pedestrians or walls by different steering angles (Scene No. 1) [1].

Using the above indices, Fig. 14 shows the sections where the vehicle is not taking any avoidance action and the sections where the vehicle is not taking any avoidance action despite being able to avoid the pedestrian, respectively. Here, the criterion for being able to avoid pedestrians is defined as the case where changing the steering angle from the current value increases the travel time T by 1.3 s or more. In Fig. 14, the sections surrounded by the blue dotted line indicate the sections before the pedestrians invade the PS in the uncomfortable sections.

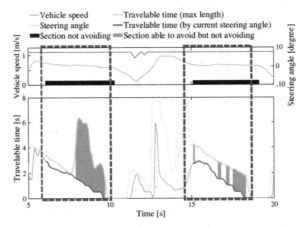

Fig. 14. Sections where the vehicle is not avoiding and the sections where the vehicle can avoid but not avoiding (Scene No. 1) [1]. (Color figure online)

Result. Based on the above process, Fig. 15 shows the length of time the vehicle is not avoiding on the horizontal axis and the length of time that the vehicle can avoid but not avoiding on the vertical axis for the 25 uncomfortable sections. In Fig. 15, if the horizontal axis is greater than 3.35 s and the vertical axis is greater than 0.7 s, six sections can be classified correctly (recall = 0.85) among the relatively uncomfortable sections. Conversely, one section is misclassified (precision = 0.85). Therefore, it is possible to explain the scenes that became relatively uncomfortable for the invasion ratio by focusing on whether the vehicle is taking avoidance actions and whether the vehicle can avoid the pedestrians before invading the PS. On the other hand, in response to the pre-invasion status that a vehicle did not avoid pedestrians although it could and it leads to passenger discomfort, it was found that there is a condition that the status continues for a certain amount of time.

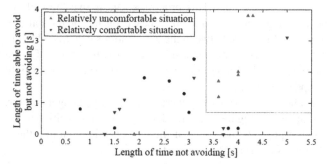

Fig. 15. Classification of situations based on the length of time the vehicle is not avoiding and the length of time the vehicle can avoid but not avoiding [1].

Discussion. The first condition on the horizontal axis (the length of time that the vehicle is not avoiding is more than 3.35 s) suggests that the passenger's awareness toward the pedestrian will become stronger when there is a pedestrian who may invade the PS in the future and if the vehicle does not take any avoidance action and the status continues for a certain period. As a result, the sensitivity of discomfort against the invasion into the PS is expected to increase. The second condition on the vertical axis (the length of time able to avoid but not avoiding is more than 0.7 s) suggests that not taking appropriate avoidance actions when avoidance is possible will lead to stronger discomfort when a threat of invasion into the PS exists for a long time. On the other hand, when it is known that avoidance is not possible, the discomfort can be suppressed to a reasonable level.

3.4   Characteristics of Passenger Comfort Recognition

The characteristics of passenger comfort recognition are summarized based on the previous discussions. As described in Sect. 2, situation awareness was focused on as a process affecting passenger comfort recognition in this study. As a result of analyzing the effect of the Current Situation in situation awareness on comfort recognition (Sect. 3.2), the invasion ratio of pedestrians into the PS had a significant impact on passenger discomfort, similar to previous research results. This result suggests that recognition of the current state of the surrounding environment is included and that one of the outputs of the current state recognition, the invasion ratio into the PS, is an input for comfort recognition.

Next, as a result of analyzing the effect of the Future Status in situation awareness on comfort recognition (Sect. 3.3), the discomfort becomes stronger when a PMV does not take any actions even though it can avoid approaching pedestrians that may invade the PS in the near future, and when this status continues for a certain period. This result suggests that passengers have some expectations of the PMV's behavior and that when the actual behavior differs from these expectations, it leads to stronger discomfort. Moreover, the difference between actual and expected behavior does not immediately strengthen discomfort but does after a certain time. The expected behavior of an autonomous PMV in a crowded environment is to take appropriate action after determining where it can travel to avoid approaching pedestrians. This process suggests that the pedestrian behavior prediction and the judgment of avoidability based on the prediction are included as model elements. The difference between the expectations generated by this process and the actual behavior appears as an increase in the weighting factor of discomfort based on the invasion ratio into the PS described earlier. Furthermore, this weighting factor is assumed to be updated over time.

Based on the above discussions, the characteristics of passenger comfort recognition are summarized in Fig. 16. Figure 16 is a model of comfort recognition based on situation awareness, which represents the effect of the Current Situation and the Future Status in situation awareness on passenger comfort recognition.

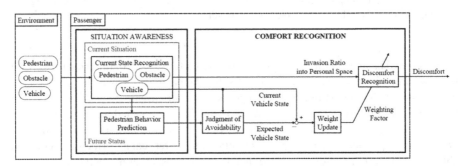

Fig. 16. Characteristics of passenger comfort recognition [1].

4   Proposal of an Autonomous Navigation Method Considering Passenger Comfort Recognition

4.1   Design

Based on the characteristics of passenger comfort recognition identified in the previous chapter, the following were set as requirements for a comfortable autonomous navigation method for PMVs traveling inside a crowded pedestrian space. Each requirement corresponds to the characteristics of comfort recognition identified.

- Low invasion ratio into PS
- Short time able to avoid but not avoiding

As a method to satisfy the first requirement, an item that specifies the invasion ratio into the passenger's PS is used in the evaluation function of DWA, which selects paths that maximizes the evaluation function among candidate paths. The second requirement is satisfied by using the Middle Path Planner, executed between the Global Path Planner and the Local Path Planner, in the path planning of autonomous navigation. Figure 17 shows an overview of the three-layer path planning, including the Middle Path Planner. The Middle Path Planner makes it possible to predict and consider future interactions with pedestrians in advance. The autonomous vehicle can select appropriate avoidance actions and reduce situations where the PMV can avoid pedestrians but not avoiding them.

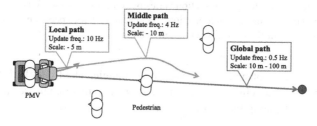

Fig. 17. Overview of the three-layer path planning.

In the Middle Path Planner, candidate paths are three-sectioned paths where the PMV travels for a total of $3T_{middle}$ [seconds], as shown in Fig. 18. The path of each section is a path that advances for T_{middle} [seconds] with a constant speed and steering angle. The Middle Path Planner outputs a middle path that maximizes the evaluation function G_{middle} (9) among the candidate paths.

$$G_{middle} = \beta_{goal}L_{goal} + \beta_{inv}L_{inv} \tag{9}$$

L_{goal} is the distance to the target point x_{goal} that is an output from the Global Path Planner, L_{inv} is the invasion ratio of pedestrians and walls into the passenger's PS, and β_{goal} and β_{inv} are weighting parameters. L_{inv} is expressed by the following Eq. (10).

$$L_{inv} = -\int_0^{3T_{middle}} \gamma^t \left(I_{ped}(t) + I_{wall}(t) \right) dt \tag{10}$$

γ is the discount rate, a constant that adjusts the degree to which future events are considered. $I_{ped}(t)$ represents the invasion ratio of pedestrians into the PS, and $I_{wall}(t)$ represents the invasion ratio of walls into the PS. L_{inv} serves to suppress the invasion of pedestrians and walls into the PS.

The Local Path Planner outputs the vehicle control parameters, i.e., speed and steering angle, considering the mid-range target point x'_{goal} which is a part of the middle path output by the Middle Path Planner. Candidate paths are paths where the PMV proceeds

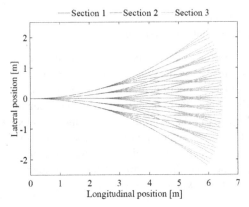

Fig. 18. Example of candidate paths of a middle path. In the example, the speed is set constant at 1.1 m/s. The steering angle of each section varies between $\{-6, -3, 0, 3, 6\}$ degrees from the steering angle of the previous section in Sections 1 and 2, and it varies between $\{-3, 0, 3\}$ degrees from the steering angle of the previous section in Section 3.

T_{local}[seconds] with a constant speed and steering angle. The Local Path Planner outputs the combination of vehicle speed and steering angle that maximizes the evaluation function G_{local} (11) among the candidate paths.

$$G_{local} = \beta'_{goal}L'_{goal} + \beta'_{inv}L'_{inv} \tag{11}$$

L'_{goal} is the distance to the target point x'_{goal}, L'_{inv} is the invasion ratio of pedestrians and walls into the PS, and β'_{goal} and β'_{inv} are weighting parameters. L'_{inv} is expressed by the following Eq. (12).

$$L'_{inv} = -\int_0^{T_{local}} \left(I_{ped}(t) + I_{wall}(t)\right)dt \tag{12}$$

4.2 Validation

The validity of the proposed method was evaluated by comparing evaluation metrics between the proposed method and an existing method, which was used in Sect. 3.1 for scene generation. A numerical simulation was conducted to evaluate the proposed and existing methods.

Method

Scene Conditions. The conditions of the numerical simulation were similar to that in Sect. 3.1. The environment was set as a 6-m-wide aisle. In the aisle, 30 pedestrians approached the PMV, and the pedestrian density was approximately 0.125 /m². The pedestrians followed the Social Force Model [13], and the initial position, target speed, and destination were set individually. Under these conditions, the behavior of PMVs following the proposed and existing methods was simulated in 100 scenes with different conditions for pedestrians, respectively. As shown in Fig. 19, the PMV started from (x,

$y) = (0, 0)$ and headed towards $(x, y) = (40, -1)$. The goal line was set at $x = 32.5$ m, and the autonomous PMV was judged as "finished driving" if the PMV could reach the goal line within 60 s after starting.

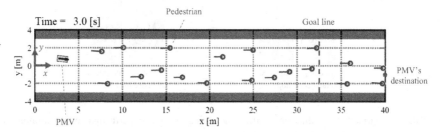

Fig. 19. Overview of the numerical simulation environment.

Evaluation Metrics.   Metrics to evaluate the basic performance of the autonomous navigation method and metrics to evaluate the performance related to passenger comfort were set. "Number of stops" and "time to goal" were adopted as basic performance metrics because reaching the destination in a limited amount of time is one of the requirements of autonomous navigation. Stops were defined as the number of times the PMV's speed reached 0 m/s from the start of the simulation until the PMV reached the goal. Based on the requirements of comfortable autonomous navigation, "time integral of invasion ratio into the PS" and "length of time able to avoid but not avoiding" were set as metrics to evaluate the performance related to passenger comfort. The definition of each metric is the same as in Sect. 3.

Result

Basic Performance.   The results of the evaluation metrics of basic performance for each method are shown in Fig. 20. Each graph shows the mean value and standard deviation of the evaluation metric among 100 scenes with different initial conditions of pedestrians. In addition, the results of the Wilcoxon signed rank test are also shown in each graph. No significant differences were found between the two methods in terms of the "number of stops" (Fig. 20(a)) and "time to goal" (Fig. 20(b)). In other words, the proposed method showed no degradation in the basic performance of autonomous navigation compared to the existing method, even though taking into account the characteristics of passenger comfort recognition.

Performance Related to Passenger Comfort.   The results of the evaluation metrics of performance related to passenger comfort for each method are shown in Fig. 21, showing the same content as Fig. 20. Both metrics, the "time integral of invasion ratio into PS" (Fig. 21(a)) and the "length of time able to avoid but not avoiding" (Fig. 21(b)), were significantly smaller ($p < 0.05$) for the proposed method than for the existing method. This result indicates that the proposed method satisfies the requirements. Therefore, the proposed method is valid for realizing comfortable autonomous navigation for passengers in a crowded pedestrian space.

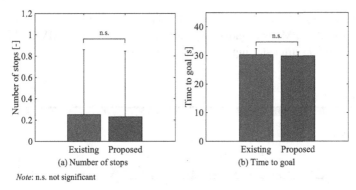

(a) Number of stops

(b) Time to goal

Note: n.s. not significant

Fig. 20. Comparison of evaluation metrics indicating the basic performance of autonomous navigation between existing and proposed methods.

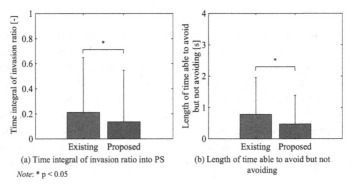

(a) Time integral of invasion ratio into PS

(b) Length of time able to avoid but not avoiding

Note: * p < 0.05

Fig. 21. Comparison of evaluation metrics indicating performance related to passenger comfort of autonomous navigation between existing and proposed methods.

5   Conclusions

This study aimed to achieve the following two goals. The first was to clarify the characteristics of passenger comfort recognition, that is, how the passenger feels comfortable depending on the behavior of the surrounding pedestrians and the vehicle when the personal mobility vehicle moves autonomously in a crowded environment. And the second was to propose a novel autonomous navigation method considering the characteristics of passenger comfort recognition. An experiment was conducted to obtain a subjective assessment of passenger comfort using a VR simulator. By focusing on situation awareness as a process affecting passenger comfort recognition, the influence of situation awareness on passenger comfort recognition was analyzed, and the characteristics of passenger comfort recognition were discussed. Requirements of autonomous navigation methods were set based on the characteristics, and a novel method was proposed and validated by numerical simulation. The followings are the findings obtained in this study:

- The invasion ratio of pedestrians into the passenger's personal space significantly impacts passenger discomfort.
- Discomfort becomes stronger when a personal mobility vehicle does not take any actions to avoid approaching pedestrians, which will invade the personal space in the near future, even though it can, and when this status continues for a certain period.
- Passenger comfort recognition can be expressed using the Current Situation and the Future Status of the situation awareness as inputs.
- An autonomous navigation method that consists of the following is a valid method to realize comfortable autonomous navigation in crowded pedestrian spaces.

    - An evaluation function of the Dynamic Window Approach with an item considering the invasion ratio of pedestrians into the passenger's personal space
    - A path planner that considers the middle path which enables prediction and consideration of future interactions with surrounding pedestrians in advance

This study has the following limitations. Since the experiment described in Sect. 3.1 was conducted in a VR environment using a head-mounted display, the difference in the perceived distance from the surrounding pedestrians and the narrow field of view may have affected the comfort recognition. Moreover, the biased participants, the limited number of participants, and the limited scenes are other limitations of this study. Further studies on the participants with a balance of gender and age, including older people, expanded samples and scenes, and real vehicles, should be conducted as future works to overcome these limitations. Furthermore, we plan to improve the autonomous navigation method following the update of the characteristics of passenger comfort recognition due to the increased samples in the simulator experiment and evaluate the passenger comfort of the proposed method in the VR simulator and real-world experiments in the future.

Acknowledgements. This paper is based on results from a project (JPNP18010) commissioned by the New Energy and Industrial Technology Development Organization.

References

1. Isono, Y., Yoshitake, H., Shino, M.: Passenger comfort recognition during autonomous navigation of personal mobility vehicles in crowded pedestrian spaces. In: Proceedings of the 17th International Joint Conference on Computer Vision, Imaging and Computer Graphics Theory and Applications, vol. 2: HUCAPP. pp. 58–67. INSTICC, SciTePress (2022). https://doi.org/10.5220/0010849700003124
2. Leaman, J., La, H.M.: A comprehensive review of smart wheelchairs: past, present, and future. IEEE Trans. Hum.-Mach. Syst. **47**(4), 486–499 (2017)
3. International Organization for Standardization: Mechanical vibration and shock–evaluation of human exposure to whole-body vibration–part 1: General requirements (ISO Standard No. 2631-1) (1997)
4. Bevilacqua, P., Frego, M., Bertolazzi, E., Fontanelli, D., Palopoli, L., Biral, F.: Path planning maximizing human comfort for assistive robots. In: Proceedings of 2016 IEEE Conference on Control Applications, pp. 1421–1427. IEEE, Buenos Aires (2016)

5. Yoshitake, H., Nishi, K., Shino, M.: Autonomous motion planning in pedestrian space considering passenger comfort. J. Rob. Mechatron. **32**(3), 580–587 (2020)
6. Hall., E.T.: The Hidden Dimension, 2nd. edn. Anchor Books, New York (1982)
7. Pham, T.Q., Nakagawa, C., Shintani, A., Ito, T.: Evaluation of the effects of a personal mobility vehicle on multiple pedestrians using PS. IEEE Trans. Intell. Transp. Syst. **16**(4), 2028–2037 (2015)
8. Morales, Y., Kallakuri, N., Shinozawa, K., Miyashita, T., Hagita, N.: Human-comfortable navigation for an autonomous robotic wheelchair. In 2013 IEEE/RSJ International Conference on Intelligent Robots and Systems, pp. 2737–2743. IEEE, Tokyo (2013)
9. Morales, Y., Watanabe, A., Ferreri, F., Even, J., Shinozawa, K., Hagita, N.: Passenger discomfort map for autonomous navigation in a robotic wheelchair. Robot. Auton. Syst. **103**, 13–26 (2018)
10. Morales, Y., Miyashita, T., Hagita, N.: Social robotic wheelchair centered on passenger and pedestrian comfort. Robot. Auton. Syst. **87**, 355–362 (2017)
11. Gwak, J., Yoshitake, H., Shino, M.: Effects of visual factors during automated driving of mobility scooters on user comfort: an exploratory simulator study. Transport. Res. F: Traffic Psychol. Behav. **81**, 608–621 (2021)
12. Endsley, M.R.: Toward a theory of situation awareness in dynamic systems. Hum. Factors **37**(1), 32–64 (1995)
13. Zanlungo, F., Ikeda, T., Kanda, T.: Social force model with explicit collision prediction. EPL (Europhysics Letters) **93**(6), 68005 (2011)
14. Fox, D., Burgard, W., Thrun, S.: The dynamic window approach to collision avoidance. IEEE Robot. Autom. Mag. **4**(1), 23–33 (1997)
15. Guan, M., Wen, C., Wei, Z., Ng, C.-L., Zou, Y.: A dynamic window approach with collision suppression cone for avoidance of moving obstacles. In 2018 IEEE 16th International Conference on Industrial Informatics, pp. 337–342. IEEE, Porto (2018)
16. Lambert, A., Gruyer, D., Pierre, G.S., Ndjeng, A.N.: Collision probability assessment for speed control. In 2008 11th International IEEE Conference on Intelligent Transportation Systems, pp. 1043–1048. IEEE, Beijing (2008)

The Electrodermal Activity of Player Experience in Virtual Reality Games: An Extended Evaluation of the Phasic Component

Diego Navarro[(✉)] [iD], Valeria Garro [iD], and Veronica Sundstedt [iD]

Blekinge Institute of Technology, 37179 Karlskrona, Sweden
{dna,vgr,vsu}@bth.se
https://www.bth.se/

Abstract. Thanks to its effectiveness, electrodermal activity (EDA) has been previously included as an evaluation metric, within analyses of user experience. In this study, the phasic component of participants' EDA data is examined in relation to their reported experiences when playing a set of virtual reality games, that featured the HTC Vive and Leap Motion controllers for input. Two models are used in the analysis of the phasic component: a deconvolution model and a convex optimization model. Despite having significant differences in their player experiences, results indicate that there are not many significant differences in the phasic component data. Even if some weak correlations were found, the majority of results show no linear correlations between the phasic component data and the reported experience variables. This shows that the phasic component of EDA data should be further investigated in conjunction with other psychophysiological signals because it has only recently demonstrated a weak link with player experience.

Keywords: Electrodermography · Phasic component · Virtual reality · Game experience · Convex optimization · cvxEDA · Deconvolution · Leap motion · HTC vive

1 Introduction

Electrodermal activity (EDA) is recognized as an effective method for identifying and assessing changes in the arousal levels of players when playing video games [21]. Because of this, EDA measurements have been utilized in multiple game research studies, evaluating variables such as emotional responses [3,17]; or cognitive loads [5].

Despite this, the evaluation of game experience has been a predominant topic for EDA data analysis in earlier works. Specially, in the quantification and statistical analysis of experience variables [1,6,15]. The majority of those research works, however,

---

This work has been funded partly by the Knowledge Foundation, Sweden, through the ViaTecH-Synergy project (contract 20170056), and the Human-Centered Intelligent Realities (HINTS) Profile project (contract 20220068).

A. A. de Sousa et al. (Eds.): VISIGRAPP 2022, CCIS 1815, pp. 203–221, 2023.
https://doi.org/10.1007/978-3-031-45725-8_10

have been on video games played on conventional 2D screens. New interaction techniques have emerged with the entry of virtual reality (VR) technologies onto the consumer market, modifying how players engage with video games. The investigation of the effects that these novel VR interaction techniques may have over the game experience, and the respective EDA responses from players, is still in an early stage since few works have been published in this area [7]. This situation provides an opportunity to further explore the potential relationship that may exist between these variables.

Based on the above, the following research question is presented for this study: *How may the differences in game experience correlate with the variations of the respective EDA data from players in VR games?*. Changes in the arousal levels of players during gameplay, and consequently significant differences over the *phasic component* (see Sect. 2) of EDA data, may be an indicator of significant differences in the reported game experience, according to our hypothesis, which holds that there is a strong correlation between the EDA data from players and their respective game experiences.

This work is an extension of previously published preliminary results [19]. It presents a more comprehensive analysis of the phasic component from the participants' EDA data, acquired in a prior experiment [20]. The computation of the phasic component data has been performed applying two different models, a *deconvolution model* and a *convex optimization model* (See Sect. 3); in which peaks over the phasic signal, and their respective amplitude, are analyzed.

2   Background

Electrodermal activity is defined as the measurement of the variations in the electrical conductivity on the skin, caused by Eccrine sweat glands acting as variable resistors [4, 26, 27]. EDA has also been referred to with different terms, such as psychogalvanic reflex and galvanic skin response (GSR) [26]. EDA measurements consist in applying a small and unnoticeable amount of electric voltage on the skin and estimating the variation of the speed in which this voltage travels through it [8]. When the subjects experience strong emotional reactions (i.e. a boost in their arousal levels), the body increases its electrical conductivity caused by higher levels of perspiration on the skin. Therefore, increases in the EDA signal are often associated with increases in the arousal level of people [4].

EDA signals have two main components called tonic and phasic. The *tonic component* describes the slow and gradual changes in the EDA signal over time, establishing a baseline for the EDA signal called skin conductance level (SCL). On the other hand, the *phasic component* characterizes fast varying activity, i.e. quick and abrupt changes in the EDA signal, also referred to as a skin conductance responses (SCR) [4,21].

2.1   Related Work

Previous studies have explored the possible links between EDA data and player experience from different perspectives. For example, the work by Ravaja et al. [23], explored the variations of the phasic component during gameplay. Their analysis combined data from electromyography, heart rate, and EDA. Their results show a strong positive relationship between increases in the phasic component and rewards in the game. Additional work presented by Drachen et al. [6] has also looked at a correlation between EDA and heart rate data to better quantitatively understand the player experience. Here, the genre of first-person shooting games was used. The study showed significant correlations between EDA data and the reported player experience, even with low covariance in the physiological metrics. Nacke et al. [18] also used a first-person shooting game to study the arousal level of players when the music and sound effects were on or off. As a result, the sonic stimuli changes did not have much impact on the EDA data from the players. However, the participants did report significant effects on the player experience. Klarkowski et al. [12,13] presented a couple of publications where the game challenge was researched regarding its correlation with EDA data. Here, the results showed a directly proportional relation between game challenge and EDA data, despite minor discrepancies with other literature [6]. Only a few works have been conducted in the specific area of VR games and EDA data. One example is a study by Egan et al. [7] that analyzed the effect of VR and non-VR environments on player heart rate and EDA data. The study found significant differences between the evaluated physiological metrics.

This paper presents an analysis that extends earlier work on further evaluating EDA data from players manipulating objects in two VR games (a pentomino puzzle and a ball-throwing task). In the previous experiment [20], both player performance and experience were explored when the player was interacting with two different devices: the HTC Vive controller and the Leap Motion controller. For additional details on the experiment design, procedure, and initial EDA data gathering, the reader is referred to [20]. For example, the number of piece grabs to complete the pentomino puzzle or the number of throws to hit all targets were used to measure performance in the game tasks. The overall completion time was also recorded. The player experience was also evaluated by using two different questionnaires. One was filled in after using each interaction technique, and the other was used to compare the interaction techniques after using both technologies in the experiment.

As shown in the previous work, the HTC Vive was perceived to have an improved player experience. The Leap Motion controller hand gestures were not reported to have as high performance as the HTC Vive as a control for input. This was due to the hands not being perceived as reliable for the interaction as the control input with the HTC Vive. However, the previous work also showed potential for both controllers, particularly regarding enjoyment [20]. The EDA data was decided to be analyzed in further detail due to the previously reported significant difference in player performance.

3 Methodology

To analyze the potential correlation that may exist between the recorded EDA data and the reported game experience from players, a statistical analysis of the phasic component was established as the main methodology for this study. The analysis focused on evaluating the amount of SCR peaks abstracted from each calculated phasic component, and the respective amplitude of each of those peaks, in relation to a set of game experience variables.

3.1   EDA Data Capture and Phasic Component Calculation

The raw EDA data was gathered using a Shimmer GSR+ sensor (128 Hz), and recorded using the iMotions biometric platform. The phasic components were then calculated by applying two different models upon the raw EDA measurements: a deconvolution model, and a convex optimization model.

Both models started by cleaning the raw data using a low-pass Butterworth filter [24]. For the deconvolution model, the phasic components were calculated using Benedek and Kaernbach's deconvolution method, which specializes in the separation of superposed signal features, such as SCR peaks [2]. The deconvolution model was carried out automatically by the iMotions biometric platform. For the convex optimization model, the phasic components were calculated using the cvxEDA algorithm presented by Greco et al. [9]. This algorithm was selected for its capabilities to compensate for noise in the EDA measurements, and to customize the smoothness of the outcome for the phasic component calculations [22]. In this way, cvxEDA could be adapted to better describe SCR peaks over the calculated phasic component. All the signal processing routines featured in the convex optimization model were implemented using the Neurokit2 Python framework [14].

3.2   Phasic Component Analysis

For the phasic component analysis, two different metrics were defined: *peaks per minute*, and *average peak amplitude*.

The peaks per minute highlighted the ratio in which SCR peaks occurred within the time required by players to complete each game. The peaks per minute (P_{min}) were calculated using Eq. 1, where SCR_{peak} represents the total number of peaks between the initial exposure time (t_o in ms) and the completion time (t_f in ms), over the completion time divided by $6 * 10^4$ ms.

$$P_{min} = \frac{\sum_{t_o}^{t_f} SCR_{peak}}{\frac{t_f}{6*10^4}} \tag{1}$$

The average peak amplitude, as its name implies, calculated the average amplitude (in μS) of all SCR peaks detected over a single phasic component signal.

Both, peaks per minute and average peak amplitude, aimed to compare how the different input devices might have affected the arousal levels of players (in quantity and intensity respectively) and, consequently, the outcomes of their individual perceived experiences. These metrics were calculated for each game (pentomino and ball-throwing), and for each input device (HTC Vive controller and Leap Motion controller).

3.3   Game Experience Analysis

Two different questionnaires, based on the Game Experience Questionnaire by IJsselsteijn et al. [11], were used to evaluate a set of game experience variables from the players. The first questionnaire was used to assess perceived *competence, level of challenge, tension, positive affect,* and *negative affect* when using a specific input device; and was presented to players upon completion of each pentomino and ball-throwing game. The second questionnaire examined the overall *enjoyment, ease of use, sense of control,* and *preference* when using a specific input device; and was given to players only when they completed both games with it. The questionnaires used a Likert scale, ranging from one to five, to provide a score for the game experience variables.

3.4 Statistical Analyses

A set of statistical tests were conducted to evaluate the differences, and potential correlation, between the peaks per minute, the average peak amplitudes, and the game experience results for the reported player experience of each game, and each input device.

First, to analyze the differences between the calculated phasic component metrics, the Shapiro-Wilk test for normality and the Levene's test for homoscedasticity were used to assess the ANOVA assumptions. A paired t-test was used only for those results that satisfied the ANOVA assumptions, whereas a Wilcoxon signed-rank test was used for all others. Lastly and to evaluate the potential correlation between the phasic component metrics and the player experience variables, a Pearson correlation coefficient analysis was used.

3.5 Implementation Tools

In addition to the tools already mentioned in this section (the iMotions biometric platform and the Neurokit2 framework), a custom Python script (version 3.9) was developed for carrying out all statistical analyses. This script featured three different libraries: Pandas [16] was used to read data sets; and to create, store, and manipulate data frames. ScyPy [28] was used to carry out the different statistical significance tests. Lastly, Maptplotlib [10] was used for generating figures and visualizing results.

3.6 Ethical Considerations

EDA data could be considered sensitive since it allows to assess changes in the arousal state of an individual. Therefore, this study was subjected to ethical vetting and granted approval (dnr: 2018/624) by a regional ethics board in Sweden. Additionally, the identities of participants were confidential and no direct link between participants and their data was established.

4 Results

A total of 20 participants took part in the experimentation from the earlier work that this analysis is based upon [20]. However, only the data from 18 participants were used in this study. The recordings from two participants featured incomplete data sets, due to a poor connection with the Shimmer GSR+ sensor, which was attributed to the range of movements required for the interaction with the Leap Motion controller in the ball-throwing game. An example of the calculated phasic components can be seen in Fig. 1.

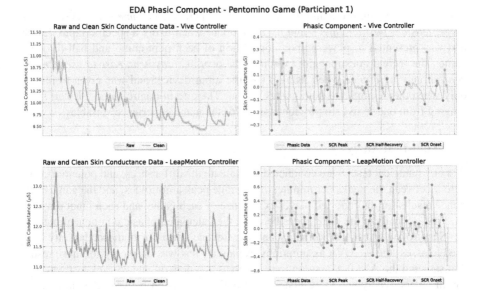

Fig. 1. An example of the calculated phasic component from a single participant. Figures on the left show the raw and the cleaned signals from the EDA data, while figures on the right show the phasic component data (convex optimization model) with their respective peaks, recoveries, and onsets.

4.1 Peaks per Minute

Eight different data sets were generated for the analysis of the peaks per minute: two data sets per game (one per input device), for each phasic component calculation model. Overall, only the peaks per minute in the pentomino game, from convex optimization model, showed statistically significant differences.

Deconvolution Model

An overview of the results for the peaks per minute calculated from the deconvolution model data can be seen in Fig. 2. The ANOVA assumptions were only satisfied by the peaks per minute calculated for the pentomino game. Therefore, a paired t-test was used to evaluate these data sets, which showed no statically significant differences. A Wilcoxon signed-rank test was used for the peaks per minute from the ball-throwing game, showing no statically significant differences between the HTC Vive and the Leap Motion controllers:

- Pentomino game: $t - test_{(1,n=18)} = 0.84, p > 0.05$
- Ball-throwing game: $WSR_{(1,n=18)} = 53, p > 0.05$

Peaks per Minute - Deconvolution Model

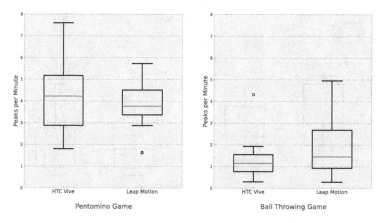

Fig. 2. Overview of the calculated peaks per minute from the deconvolution model results.

Convex Optimization Model

An overview of the results for the peaks per minute calculated from the convex optimization model data can be seen in Fig. 3. None of the calculated results satisfied the ANOVA assumptions and were evaluated with the Wilcoxon singed-rank test. The test showed statistically significant differences for the peaks per minute from the pentomino game. However, no statistically significant differences were found for the peaks per minute from the ball-throwing game:

- Pentomino game: $WSR_{(1,n=18)} = 29, p < 0.05$
- Ball-throwing game: $WSR_{(1,n=18)} = 67, p > 0.05$

4.2   Average Peak Amplitude

Eight different data sets were generated to analyze the average peak amplitudes calculated with both phasic component calculation models. No statistically significant differences were found with this metric.

Deconvolution Model

An overview of the average peak amplitudes obtained with the deconvolution model is shown in Fig. 4. None of these results satisfied the ANOVA assumptions and were analyzed with the Wilcoxon signed-rank test. The results for the pentomino and ball-throwing game showed no statistically significant differences:

Peaks per Minute - Convex Optimization Model

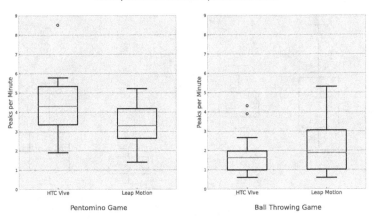

Fig. 3. Overview of the calculated peaks per minute from the convex optimization model results.

- Pentomino game: $WSR_{(1,n=18)} = 99, p > 0.05$
- Ball-throwing game: $WSR_{(1,n=18)} = 98, p > 0.05$

Average Peak Amplitudes - Deconvolution Model

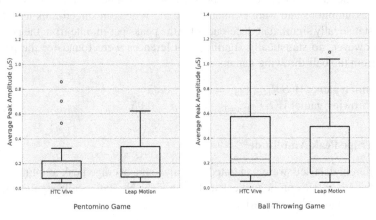

Fig. 4. Overview of the peak amplitude averages from the deconvolution model results.

Convex Optimization Model

An overview of the calculated peak amplitude averages with the convex optimization model is shown in Fig. 5. The ANOVA assumptions were not satisfied by any of the calculated averages, hence a Wilcoxon signed-rank test was applied. Results from the tests showed no statistically significant differences between the average peak amplitudes for the pentomino and the ball-throwing games:

- Pentomino game: $WSR_{(1,n=18)} = 82, p > 0.05$
- Ball-throwing game: $WSR_{(1,n=18)} = 67, p > 0.05$

Average Peak Amplitudes - Convex Optimization Model

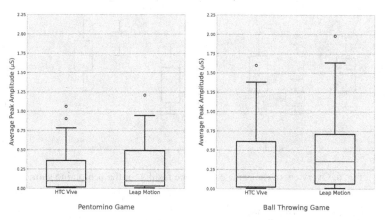

Fig. 5. Overview of the peak amplitude averages from the convex optimization model results.

4.3 Game Experience

For the game experience analysis, six different data sets were generated from the scores gathered through the questionnaires: two for each game, and one for each input device. Overall, most experience variables showed statistically significant differences between the input devices.

Pentomino Game

An overview of the game experience results for the pentomino game can be seen in Fig. 6. None of the scores from the experience variables in the pentomino game satisfied the ANOVA assumptions. Therefore, a Wilcoxon signed-rank test was used to evaluate these data. Results showed that all variables, with the exception of negative affect, showed statistically significant differences between the input devices:

- Competence: $WSR_{(1,n=18)} = 1, p < 0.05$
- Level of challenge: $WSR_{(1,n=18)} = 3.5, p < 0.05$
- Tension: $WSR_{(1,n=18)} = 8, p < 0.05$
- Positive affect: $WSR_{(1,n=18)} = 13.5, p < 0.05$
- Negative affect: $WSR_{(1,n=18)} = 8, p > 0.05$

Ball-Throwing Game

An overview of the game experience results obtained for the ball-throwing game is shown in Fig. 7. None of the scores from the experience variables in the ball-throwing game satisfied the ANOVA assumptions, with the exception of competence. Based on this, a paired t-test was used to analyze the competence data, while all other experience variables were evaluated with the Wilcoxon signed-rank test. Results show that all experience variables had statistically significant differences between the input devices:

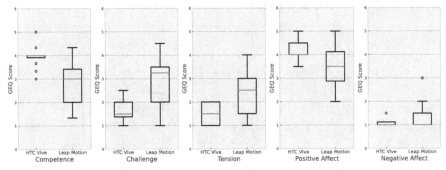

Fig. 6. Overview of the game experience results for the pentomino game.

- Competence: $t - test_{(1,n=18)} = 3.45, p < 0.05$
- Level of challenge: $WSR_{(1,n=18)} = 11, p < 0.05$
- Tension: $WSR_{(1,n=18)} = 24.5, p < 0.05$
- Positive affect: $WSR_{(1,n=18)} = 14, p < 0.05$
- Negative affect: $WSR_{(1,n=18)} = 15, p < 0.05$

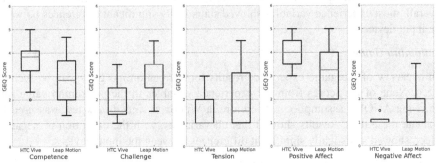

Fig. 7. Overview of the game experience results for the ball-throwing game.

Input Device Experience

An overview of the results obtained for the overall experience between the input devices is shown in Fig. 8. None of the scores for this analysis satisfied the ANOVA assumptions and were examined with the Wilcoxon signed-rank test. Results showed that all experience variables had statically significant differences between the input devices:

- Enjoyment: $WSR_{(1,n=18)} = 18, p < 0.05$
- Ease of use: $WSR_{(1,n=18)} = 4, p < 0.05$
- Sense of control: $WSR_{(1,n=18)} = 5, p < 0.05$
- Preference: $WSR_{(1,n=18)} = 21.5, p < 0.05$

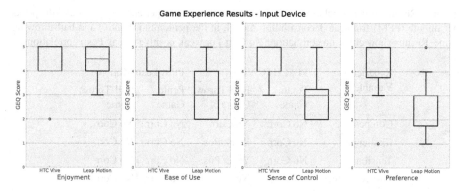

Fig. 8. Overview of the game experience results between the HTC Vive controller and the Leap Motion controller.

4.4 Correlation Analysis

Results from the correlation analysis were classified into five different categories, according to the calculated value for the Pearson coefficient(ρ) for linear correlation [25]:

1. A *strong positive* correlation when ρ was greater than 0.8.
2. A *weak positive* correlation when ρ was greater than 0.4 but lesser than 0.8.
3. *No correlation* when ρ was between the values of 0.4 and -0.4.
4. A *weak negative* correlation when ρ was lesser than -0.4 but greater than -0.8.
5. A *strong negative* correlation when ρ was lesser than -0.8.

Peaks per Minute vs. Game Experience - Deconvolution Model

An overview of the correlation results between the peaks per minute from the deconvolution model, and the game experience variables, can be seen in Table 1.

For the HTC Vive controller in the pentomino game, only negative affect showed a weak positive correlation with the calculated peaks per minute. All other experience variables showed no correlation:

– Competence: $\rho_{(1,n=18)} = 0.014, p > 0.05$
– Challenge: $\rho_{(1,n=18)} = -0.058, p > 0.05$
– Tension: $\rho_{(1,n=18)} = 0.042, p > 0.05$
– Positive affect: $\rho_{(1,n=18)} = -0.209, p > 0.05$
– Negative affect: $\rho_{(1,n=18)} = 0.490, p < 0.05$

In the ball-throwing game, the challenge, tension, and negative affect had a weak positive correlation with the peaks per minute. All other experience variables showed no correlation:

– Competence: $\rho_{(1,n=18)} = -0.257, p > 0.05$
– Challenge: $\rho_{(1,n=18)} = 0.469, p < 0.05$

Table 1. Results of the correlation analysis between the game experience variables and the peaks per minute (PPM) from the deconvolution model, in the pentomino (Pento.) and ball-throwing game. Results show either no correlation (No Corr.) or weak positive (Weak Pos.) correlations.

Experience Variable	PPM HTC Vive		PPM Leap Motion	
	Pento. Game	Ball-Throw. Game	Pento. Game	Ball-Throw. Game
Competence	No Corr.	No Corr.	No Corr.	No Corr.
Challenge	No Corr.	Weak Pos.	No Corr.	No Corr.
Tension	No Corr.	Weak Pos.	No Corr.	No Corr.
Positive Affect	No Corr.	No Corr.	No Corr.	No Corr.
Negative Affect	Weak Pos.	Weak Pos.	No Corr.	No Corr.

- Tension: $\rho_{(1,n=18)} = 0.554, p < 0.05$
- Positive affect: $\rho_{(1,n=18)} = 0.063, p > 0.05$
- Negative affect: $\rho_{(1,n=18)} = 0.669, p < 0.05$

For the Leap Motion controller in the pentomino game, none of the game experience variables showed a correlation with the calculated peaks per minute:

- Competence: $\rho_{(1,n=18)} = -0.048, p > 0.05$
- Challenge: $\rho_{(1,n=18)} = -0.168, p > 0.05$
- Tension: $\rho_{(1,n=18)} = -0.228, p > 0.05$
- Positive affect: $\rho_{(1,n=18)} = -0.221, p > 0.05$
- Negative affect: $\rho_{(1,n=18)} = -0.072, p > 0.05$

Similarly, in the ball-throwing game, no correlation was found between the peaks per minute and the game experience variables:

- Competence: $\rho_{(1,n=18)} = -0.372, p > 0.05$
- Challenge: $\rho_{(1,n=18)} = 0.321, p > 0.05$
- Tension: $\rho_{(1,n=18)} = -0.115, p > 0.05$
- Positive affect: $\rho_{(1,n=18)} = -0.212, p > 0.05$
- Negative affect: $\rho_{(1,n=18)} = 0.173, p > 0.05$

Peaks per Minute vs. Game Experience - Convex Optimization Model

An overview of the results from the correlation analysis between the peaks per minute from the convex optimization model, and the game experience variables, is shown in Table 2.

For the HTC Vive controller, only competence showed a weak positive correlation with the peaks per minute in the pentomino game. All other game experience variables showed no correlation:

- Competence: $\rho_{(1,n=18)} = 0.540, p < 0.05$
- Challenge: $\rho_{(1,n=18)} = -0.117, p > 0.05$

Table 2. Results of the correlation analysis between the game experience variables and the peaks per minute (PPM) from the convex optimization model, in the pentomino (Pento.) and ball-throwing game. Results show either no correlation (No Corr.), weak positive (Weak Pos.), or weak negative (Weak Neg.) correlations.

Experience Variable	PPM HTC Vive		PPM Leap Motion	
	Pento. Game	Ball-Throw. Game	Pento. Game	Ball-Throw. Game
Competence	Weak Pos.	No Corr.	No Corr.	Weak Neg.
Challenge	No Corr.	No Corr.	No Corr.	Weak Pos.
Tension	No Corr.	No Corr.	Weak Neg.	No Corr.
Positive Affect	No Corr.	No Corr.	No Corr.	No Corr.
Negative Affect	No Corr.	Weak Pos.	No Corr.	No Corr.

- Tension: $\rho_{(1,n=18)} = -0.289, p > 0.05$
- Positive affect: $\rho_{(1,n=18)} = 0.309, p > 0.05$
- Negative affect: $\rho_{(1,n=18)} = 0.020, p > 0.05$

In the ball-throwing game, only negative affects showed a weak positive correlation with the peaks per minute. All other game experience variables showed no correlation:

- Competence: $\rho_{(1,n=18)} = -0.031, p < 0.05$
- Challenge: $\rho_{(1,n=18)} = 0.169, p > 0.05$
- Tension: $\rho_{(1,n=18)} = -0.215, p > 0.05$
- Positive affect: $\rho_{(1,n=18)} = -0.146, p > 0.05$
- Negative affect: $\rho_{(1,n=18)} = 0.426, p > 0.05$

For the Leap Motion controller, all game experience variables showed no correlation with the peaks per minute in the pentomino game, with the exception of tension which showed a weak negative correlation:

- Competence: $\rho_{(1,n=18)} = 0.174, p > 0.05$
- Challenge: $\rho_{(1,n=18)} = -0.392, p > 0.05$
- Tension: $\rho_{(1,n=18)} = -0.428, p > 0.05$
- Positive affect: $\rho_{(1,n=18)} = -0.091, p > 0.05$
- Negative affect: $\rho_{(1,n=18)} = -0.185, p > 0.05$

In the ball-throwing game, competence showed a weak negative correlation and challenge showed a weak positive one. All other experience variables showed no correlation with the peaks per minute:

- Competence: $\rho_{(1,n=18)} = -0.410, p > 0.05$
- Challenge: $\rho_{(1,n=18)} = 0.447, p < 0.05$
- Tension: $\rho_{(1,n=18)} = 0.162, p > 0.05$
- Positive affect: $\rho_{(1,n=18)} = -0.345, p > 0.05$
- Negative affect: $\rho_{(1,n=18)} = 0.264, p > 0.05$

Average Peak Amplitude vs. Game Experience - Deconvolution Model

An overview of the results from the correlation analysis between the game experience variables and the average peak amplitudes from the deconvolution model data, is shown in Table 3.

Table 3. Results of the correlation analysis between the game experience variables and the average peak amplitudes (APA) from the deconvolution model, in the pentomino (Pento.) and ball-throwing game. Results show either no correlation (No Corr.), weak positive (Weak Pos.), or weak negative (Weak Neg.) correlations.

Experience Variable	APA HTC Vive		APA Leap Motion	
	Pento. Game	Ball-Throw. Game	Pento. Game	Ball-Throw. Game
Competence	No Corr.	No Corr.	No Corr.	No Corr.
Challenge	No Corr.	Weak Pos.	No Corr.	No Corr.
Tension	No Corr.	Weak Pos.	No Corr.	No Corr.
Positive Affect	No Corr.	No Corr.	Weak Neg.	No Corr.
Negative Affect	No Corr.	No Corr.	No Corr.	No Corr.

For the HTC Vive controller, the game experience variables showed no correlation with the average peak amplitudes in the pentomino game:

- Competence: $\rho_{(1,n=18)} = -0.043, p > 0.05$
- Challenge: $\rho_{(1,n=18)} = 0.367, p > 0.05$
- Tension: $\rho_{(1,n=18)} = 0.224, p > 0.05$
- Positive affect: $\rho_{(1,n=18)} = -0.280, p > 0.05$
- Negative affect: $\rho_{(1,n=18)} = 0.148, p > 0.05$

In the ball-throwing game, challenge and tension had a weak positive correlation with the average peak amplitudes. All other game experience variables showed no correlation:

- Competence: $\rho_{(1,n=18)} = -0.285, p > 0.05$
- Challenge: $\rho_{(1,n=18)} = 0.500, p < 0.05$
- Tension: $\rho_{(1,n=18)} = 0.462, p < 0.05$
- Positive affect: $\rho_{(1,n=18)} = -0.045, p > 0.05$
- Negative affect: $\rho_{(1,n=18)} = 0.188, p > 0.05$

For the Leap Motion controller, only positive affect had a weak negative correlation in the pentomino game. All other game experience variables showed no correlation with the average peak amplitudes:

- Competence: $\rho_{(1,n=18)} = -0.217, p > 0.05$
- Challenge: $\rho_{(1,n=18)} = 0.097, p > 0.05$
- Tension: $\rho_{(1,n=18)} = 0.152, p > 0.05$

- Positive affect: $\rho_{(1,n=18)} = -0.474, p < 0.05$
- Negative affect: $\rho_{(1,n=18)} = 0.190, p > 0.05$

For the ball-throwing game, none of the game experience variables showed a correlation with the average peak amplitudes:

- Competence: $\rho_{(1,n=18)} = -0.112, p > 0.05$
- Challenge: $\rho_{(1,n=18)} = 0.310, p > 0.05$
- Tension: $\rho_{(1,n=18)} = 0.049, p > 0.05$
- Positive affect: $\rho_{(1,n=18)} = -0.098, p > 0.05$
- Negative affect: $\rho_{(1,n=18)} = 0.141, p > 0.05$

Average Peak Amplitude vs Game Experience - Convex Optimization Model

An overview of the results from the correlation analysis between the game experience variables and the average peak amplitude from the convex optimization model data, is shown in Table 4.

Table 4. Results of the correlation analysis between the game experience variables and the average peak amplitudes (APA) from the convex optimization model, in the pentomino (Pento.) and ball-throwing game. Results show either no correlation (No Corr.), weak positive (Weak Pos.), or weak negative (Weak Neg.) correlations.

Experience Variable	APA HTC Vive		APA Leap Motion	
	Pento. Game	Ball-Throw. Game	Pento. Game	Ball-Throw. Game
Competence	No Corr.	No Corr.	No Corr.	No Corr.
Challenge	No Corr.	Weak Pos.	No Corr.	No Corr.
Tension	No Corr.	Weak Pos.	No Corr.	No Corr.
Positive Affect	No Corr.	No Corr.	Weak Neg.	No Corr.
Negative Affect	No Corr.	No Corr.	No Corr.	No Corr.

For the HTC Vive controller, no correlation was found between the experience variables and the average peak amplitude in the pentomino game:

- Competence: $\rho_{(1,n=18)} = -0.088, p > 0.05$
- Challenge: $\rho_{(1,n=18)} = 0.299, p > 0.05$
- Tension: $\rho_{(1,n=18)} = 0.169, p > 0.05$
- Positive affect: $\rho_{(1,n=18)} = -0.279, p > 0.05$
- Negative affect: $\rho_{(1,n=18)} = 0.271, p > 0.05$

Challenge and tension had a weak positive correlation in the ball-throwing game. All other game experience variables showed no correlation with the average peak amplitudes:

- Competence: $\rho_{(1,n=18)} = -0.328, p > 0.05$
- Challenge: $\rho_{(1,n=18)} = 0.545, p < 0.05$
- Tension: $\rho_{(1,n=18)} = 0.510, p < 0.05$
- Positive affect: $\rho_{(1,n=18)} = -0.002, p > 0.05$
- Negative affect: $\rho_{(1,n=18)} = 0.235, p > 0.05$

For the Leap Motion controller, only positive affect showed a weak negative correlation with the peak amplitude averages in the pentomino game. All other game experience variables showed no correlation:

- Competence: $\rho_{(1,n=18)} = -0.257, p > 0.05$
- Challenge: $\rho_{(1,n=18)} = 0.174, p < 0.05$
- Tension: $\rho_{(1,n=18)} = 0.182, p > 0.05$
- Positive affect: $\rho_{(1,n=18)} = -0.487, p < 0.05$
- Negative affect: $\rho_{(1,n=18)} = 0.227, p > 0.05$

No correlation between the game experience variables and the average peak amplitude were found in the ball-throwing game:

- Competence: $\rho_{(1,n=18)} = -0.024, p > 0.05$
- Challenge: $\rho_{(1,n=18)} = 0.288, p > 0.05$
- Tension: $\rho_{(1,n=18)} = -0.077, p > 0.05$
- Positive affect: $\rho_{(1,n=18)} = -0.048, p > 0.05$
- Negative affect: $\rho_{(1,n=18)} = 0.162, p > 0.05$

5 Discussion

The gathered results showed that there were statistically significant differences in all the evaluated game experience variables, with the exception of the negative affect in the pentomino game. In contrast, all the phasic component analysis metrics, with the exception of the peaks per minute from the deconvolution model in the pentomino game, showed no statistically significant differences. Additionally, the correlation analysis showed that, in the majority of cases, there was no linear correlation between the experience variables and the phasic component metrics.

These results may be inconsistent with our proposed hypothesis. Nevertheless, these findings do not yet provide sufficient evidence to reject it with certainty. Previous contributions have shown a correlation between the game experience and the tonic component from players' EDA data [6]. This may suggest that the SCL, the most relevant feature in the tonic component analysis, may establish a stronger relationship with the game experience than the peaks per minute or the average peak amplitude did.

Despite this, the phasic component analysis and the correlation analysis showed rather interesting results. For the pentomino game, the convex optimization model showed significant differences in the peak per minute between the input devices. In fact, Figs. 2 and 3 display noticeable differences in the ranges from the calculated peaks per minute between the models. A similar situation can be also seen over Figs. 4 and 5 for the average peak amplitude. This may be due to the smoothness customization options featured in the cvxEDA algorithm, which may have better described the SCR from the

EDA signal. Furthermore, both phasic component metrics seem to also be affected by the game genre, based on the results illustrated in the previously mentioned figures.

Most of the correlation tests showed no linear correlation between the phasic component metrics and the game experience variables. For the peaks per minute, there was only one similarity between the results obtained with each model: the negative affect in the ball-throwing game showed a weak positive correlation in both models. This result is consistent with previous publications that featured similar methodologies, reporting that positive correlations have only been found between EDA data and negative affects of player experience [6]. For the average peak amplitude, however, the correlation results were identical between the deconvolution and the convex optimization models. This may indicate that, unlike the peaks per minute, the peak amplitude is a metric that remains consistent within the correlation analysis, despite the model used for its calculation. Nevertheless, a more substantial evaluation is required to confirm this assumption.

6   Conclusion and Future Work

This study has presented a comprehensive analysis of the phasic component of EDA data from players, evaluating its potential correlation with their respective game experience, and expanding upon the results documented in previous works. The phasic components were calculated using both, a deconvolution and a convex optimization model; and focused on the analysis of two different metrics: peaks per minute and average peak amplitude. Results show that, despite having statistically significant differences in their game experience, there were no statistically significant differences in the majority of the metrics used to analyze the phasic component. Furthermore, a rather limited correlation between the phasic component and the game experience was established, since the majority of results showed no linear correlation between the evaluated variables.

Future work should focus on expanding the evaluation of EDA data, to include the analysis of the SCL from the tonic component as well. Due to the limited correlation seen from the phasic component alone, future work could also explore the study of phasic component data in combination with other physiological inputs, such as heart rate. Finally, thanks to the consistency in the correlation results from the average peak amplitudes, a deeper analysis of the behavior of this variable among different phasic component calculation models is encouraged.

References

1. Ang, D.: Difficulty in video games: understanding the effects of dynamic difficulty adjustment in video games on player experience. In: Proceedings of the 2017 ACM SIGCHI Conference on Creativity and Cognition - C&C 2017, Singapore, Singapore, pp. 544–550. ACM Press (2017). https://doi.org/10.1145/3059454.3078706. http://dl.acm.org/citation.cfm?doid=3059454.3078706
2. Benedek, M., Kaernbach, C.: A continuous measure of phasic electrodermal activity. J. Neurosci. Methods **190**(1), 80–91 (2010). https://doi.org/10.1016/j.jneumeth.2010.04.028. https://linkinghub.elsevier.com/retrieve/pii/S0165027010002335

3. Bontchev, B.: Adaptation in affective video games: a literature review. Cybern. Inf. Technol. **16**(3) (2016). https://doi.org/10.1515/cait-2016-0032. https://www.degruyter.com/view/j/cait.2016.16.issue-3/cait-2016-0032/cait-2016-0032.xml

4. Boucsein, W.: Electrodermal Activity. Springer, Boston (2012). https://doi.org/10.1007/978-1-4614-1126-0

5. Buchwald, M., Kupinski, S., Bykowski, A., Marcinkowska, J., Ratajczyk, D., Jukiewicz, M.: Electrodermal activity as a measure of cognitive load: a methodological approach. In: 2019 Signal Processing: Algorithms, Architectures, Arrangements, and Applications (SPA), Poznan, Poland, pp. 175–179. IEEE (2019). https://doi.org/10.23919/SPA.2019.8936745. https://ieeexplore.ieee.org/document/8936745/

6. Drachen, A., Nacke, L.E., Yannakakis, G., Pedersen, A.L.: Correlation between heart rate, electrodermal activity and player experience in first-person shooter games. In: Proceedings of the 5th ACM SIGGRAPH Symposium on Video Games - Sandbox 2010, Los Angeles, California, pp. 49–54. ACM Press (2010). https://doi.org/10.1145/1836135.1836143. http://portal.acm.org/citation.cfm?doid=1836135.1836143

7. Egan, D., Brennan, S., Barrett, J., Qiao, Y., Timmerer, C., Murray, N.: An evaluation of heart rate and ElectroDermal activity as an objective QoE evaluation method for immersive virtual reality environments. In: 2016 Eighth International Conference on Quality of Multimedia Experience (QoMEX), Lisbon, Portugal, pp. 1–6. IEEE (2016). https://doi.org/10.1109/QoMEX.2016.7498964. http://ieeexplore.ieee.org/document/7498964/

8. Fowles, D.C., Christie, M.J., Edelberg, R., GRINGS, W.W., Lykken, D.T., Venables, P.H.: Publication recommendations for electrodermal measurements. Psychophysiology **18**(3), 232–239 (1981). https://doi.org/10.1111/j.1469-8986.1981.tb03024.x. https://onlinelibrary.wiley.com/doi/abs/10.1111/j.1469-8986.1981.tb03024.x

9. Greco, A., Valenza, G., Lanata, A., Scilingo, E.P., Citi, L.: cvxEDA: a convex optimization approach to electrodermal activity processing. IEEE Trans. Biomed. Eng. **63**(4), 797–804 (2016). https://doi.org/10.1109/TBME.2015.2474131

10. Hunter, J.D.: Matplotlib: a 2D graphics environment. Comput. Sci. Eng. **9**(3), 90–95 (2007). https://doi.org/10.1109/MCSE.2007.55

11. IJsselsteijn, W., de Kort, Y., Poels, K.: The Game Experience Questionnaire. Technische Universiteit Eindhoven (2013)

12. Klarkowski, M., Johnson, D., Wyeth, P., Phillips, C., Smith, S.: Psychophysiology of challenge in play: EDA and self-reported arousal. In: Proceedings of the 2016 CHI Conference Extended Abstracts on Human Factors in Computing Systems, San Jose, California, USA, pp. 1930–1936. ACM (2016). https://doi.org/10.1145/2851581.2892485. https://dl.acm.org/doi/10.1145/2851581.2892485

13. Klarkowski, M., Johnson, D., Wyeth, P., Phillips, C., Smith, S.: Don't sweat the small stuff: the effect of challenge-skill manipulation on electrodermal activity. In: Proceedings of the 2018 Annual Symposium on Computer-Human Interaction in Play, Melbourne, VIC, Australia, pp. 231–242. ACM (2018). https://doi.org/10.1145/3242671.3242714. https://dl.acm.org/doi/10.1145/3242671.3242714

14. Makowski, D., et al.: Neurokit2: a python toolbox for neurophysiological signal processing. Behav. Res. Methods (2021). https://doi.org/10.3758/s13428-020-01516-y

15. Martey, R.M., et al.: Measuring game engagement: multiple methods and construct complexity. Simul. Gaming **45**(4–5), 528–547 (2014). https://doi.org/10.1177/1046878114553575. http://journals.sagepub.com/doi/10.1177/1046878114553575

16. McKinney, W.: Data structures for statistical computing in python. In: Stéfan van der Walt, Jarrod Millman (eds.) Proceedings of the 9th Python in Science Conference, pp. 56–61 (2010). https://doi.org/10.25080/Majora-92bf1922-00a

17. Moghimi, M., Stone, R., Rotshtein, P.: Affective recognition in dynamic and interactive virtual environments. IEEE Trans. Affect. Comput. **11**(1), 45–62 (2017). https://doi.org/10. 1109/TAFFC.2017.2764896. http://ieeexplore.ieee.org/document/8078217/

18. Nacke, L.E., Grimshaw, M.N., Lindley, C.A.: More than a feeling: measurement of sonic user experience and psychophysiology in a first-person shooter game. Interact. Comput. **22**(5), 336–343 (2010). https://doi.org/10.1016/j.intcom.2010.04.005. https://academic.oup. com/iwc/article-lookup/doi/10.1016/j.intcom.2010.04.005

19. Navarro, D., Garro, V., Sundstedt, V.: Electrodermal activity evaluation of player experience in virtual reality games: a phasic component analysis. In: Proceedings of the 17th International Joint Conference on Computer Vision, Imaging and Computer Graphics Theory and Applications, pp. 108–116. SCITEPRESS - Science and Technology Publications (2022). https://doi.org/10.5220/0011006100003124. https://www.scitepress.org/ DigitalLibrary/Link.aspx?doi=10.5220/00110061000-03124

20. Navarro, D., Sundstedt, V.: Evaluating player performance and experience in virtual reality game interactions using the HTC Vive controller and leap motion sensor. In: Proceedings of the 14th International Joint Conference on Computer Vision, Imaging and Computer Graphics Theory and Applications - HUCAPP, pp. 103–110. INSTICC, SciTePress (2019). https:// doi.org/10.5220/0007362401030110

21. Navarro, D., Sundstedt, V., Garro, V.: Biofeedback methods in entertainment video games: a review of physiological interaction techniques. Proc. ACM Hum.-Comput. Interact. **5**(CHI PLAY), 1–32 (2021). https://doi.org/10.1145/3474695. https://dl.acm.org/doi/10. 1145/3474695

22. Posada-Quintero, H.F., Chon, K.H.: Innovations in electrodermal activity data collection and signal processing: a systematic review. Sensors **20**(2) (2020). https://doi.org/10.3390/ s20020479. https://www.mdpi.com/1424-8220/20/2/479

23. Ravaja, N., Saari, T., Salminen, M., Laarni, J., Kallinen, K.: Phasic emotional reactions to video game events: a psychophysiological investigation. Media Psychol. **8**(4), 343–367 (2006). https://doi.org/10.1207/s1532785xmep0804_2. http://www.tandfonline.com/doi/abs/ 10.1207/s1532785xmep0804_2

24. Selesnick, I., Burrus, C.: Generalized digital butterworth filter design. IEEE Trans. Signal Process. **46**(6), 1688–1694 (1998). https://doi.org/10.1109/78.678493

25. Shevlyakov, G.L., Oja, H.: Robust Correlation: Theory and Applications. Wiley Series in Probability and Statistics. Wiley, Chichester (2016)

26. Stern, R.M., Ray, W.J., Quigley, K.S.: Psychophysiological Recording. Oxford University Press, Oxford (2000). https://doi.org/10.1093/acprof:oso/9780195113594.001.0001

27. Tasooji, R., Buckingham, N., Gračanin, D., Knapp, R.B.: An approach to analysis of physiological responses to stimulus. In: Marcus, A., Wang, W. (eds.) HCII 2019. LNCS, vol. 11583, pp. 492–509. Springer, Cham (2019). https://doi.org/10.1007/978-3-030-23570-3_37

28. Virtanen, P., et al.: SciPy 1.0: fundamental algorithms for scientific computing in python. Nat. Methods **17**, 261–272 (2020). https://doi.org/10.1038/s41592-019-0686-2

MinMax-CAM: Increasing Precision of Explaining Maps by Contrasting Gradient Signals and Regularizing Kernel Usage

Lucas David$^{(\boxtimes)}$ ⓘ, Helio Pedrini ⓘ, and Zanoni Dias ⓘ

University of Campinas, Campinas, SP, Brazil
{lucas.david,helio,zanoni}@ic.unicamp.br

Abstract. While various AI explaining methods has been developed in the last decade, the Class Activation Map (CAM) technique (and derivations thereof) has remains a popular alternative today. Highly versatile, and sufficiently simple, CAM-based techniques have been consistently used to explain the predictions of Convolutional Neural Networks over classification problems. However, many studies conducted to assert the precision of the produced explaining maps have done so on single-label multi-class classification problems, where the task is simplified by focusing and framing the objects of interest in the foreground. In this work, we test and evaluate the efficacy of CAM-based techniques over distinct multi-label sets. We find that techniques that were created with single-label classification in mind (such as Grad-CAM, Grad-CAM++ and Score-CAM) will often produce diffuse visualization maps in multi-label scenarios, overstepping the boundaries of their explaining objects of interest onto objects of different classes. We propose a generalization of the Grad-CAM technique for the multi-label scenario that produces more focused explaining maps by maximizing the activation of a class of interest while minimizing the activation of the remaining classes present in the sample. Our results indicate that MinMax-CAM produces more focused explaining maps over different network architectures and datasets. Finally, we present a regularization strategy that encourages sparse positive weights in the last classifying, while penalizing the association between the classification of a class and the occurrence of correlated patterns, resulting in cleaner activation maps.

Keywords: Computer vision · Multi-label · Explainable artificial intelligence

1 Introduction

The adoption of Convolutional Neural Networks (CNNs) in the solution of a broad set of modern Machine Learning problems is unquestionable [12]. Today, we can easily find such models being employed to image classification [18], object

Supported by CNPq (grants 140929/2021-5 and 309330/2018-1) and LNCC/MCTI.

detection [7] and localization, image segmentation [14], pose estimation [33] and even non-imagery domains, such as audio processing [16], text classification [35] and text-to-speech [27]. As CNNs gradually permeate into many real-world systems, impacting different demographics, the necessity for explaining and accountability becomes urgent. Scientists and engineers working with Machine Learning have since pushed towards the creation of explaining methods that could shed light into their inner workings [1,4,11,17,32,37,40].

Explaining the reasoning behind of an autonomous systems is a challenging task, and yet paramount in increasing reliability and truth of Machine Learning agents in both scientific and industrial scenarios. While the construction of interpretable models is desirable as a general rule, as it facilitates the identification of failure modes while hinting strategies to fix them [19], it is also an essential component in building trust from the general public towards this technology [9].

In this work, we build upon our previous findings around the effectiveness of existing CAM-based explaining methods [5], when evaluated specifically over the more challenging scenario of multi-label problems [3,28]. We reproduce the experimental quantitative results, while also expanding them to a more realistic dataset containing massive class unbalance and unclear semantic boundaries between the objects expressed in samples [15]. We provide better qualitative interpretation and visualization of the obtained solution candidates and expand towards a clear intuition and definition of the methodology. Finally, we propose a simple modification to handle the weight vanishing observed when *kernel usage regularization* [5] is applied to a CNNs over datasets containing large numbers of classes. Similarly to our previous work, our main contributions are:

1. We propose a thoroughly analysis of popular visualization techniques in the literature over a distinct set of multi-label problems, evaluating their results according to the offered coverage over objects belonging to the label of interest, as well as the containment within objects of said label.
2. We propose a modification to CAM-based methods that combines gradient information from multiple labels within a single input image. We demonstrate that our approach presents better scores and cleaner visualization maps than other methods over distinct datasets and architectures.
3. We present a regularization strategy that encourages networks to associate each learned label with a distinct set of patterns, resulting in better separation of concepts and producing cleaner CAM visualizations, with better scores.

The remaining of this work is organized as follows. Section 2 summarizes the explaining methods currently used in literature. Section 3 describes our approach in detail, while Sect. 5 presents the experimental setup used to evaluate our strategy, the datasets and network architectures employed. We discuss our main results in Sect. 6 and present a regularization strategy to improve them in Sect. 4. Finally, we conclude the paper in Sect. 7 by remarking our results and proposing future work.

2   Related Work

In the domain of Computer Vision, visual explanation techniques are frequently employed to describe or indicate, with a certain degree of certainty, salient cues that might have contributed to the decision process of CNNs [34]. These techniques often times produce visual explaining maps: a signal with the same spatial format as the input sample, highlighting regions that most contribute to the answer provided by the model [30].

Gradient-based saliency methods [21] are early examples of this line of work. They produce saliency maps that highlight pixels with most overall contribution towards the score estimated during the decision process of a model, which is accomplished by back-propagating the gradient information from the units of interest, contained in the last layer, onto the input signal. Instances of these methods are Guided Backpropagation [23], which filters out the negative back-propagated gradients; SmoothGrad [22], which averages gradient maps obtained from multiple noisy copies of a single input image; and FullGrad [24], which combines the bias unit partial contributions with the saliency information in order to create a "full gradient" visualization.

Notwithstanding their precision on locating salient regions and objects, gradient-based methods will ultimately fail to identify objects in an image that relate to a specific class of interest. In fact, "sanity checks" have been proposed to test the resulting explaining maps from these methods when class-specific patterns are erased from the model. As examples, we remark the experiments *Model Parameter Randomization* and *Data Randomization* [1] proposed by Adebayo et al. In the former, weights from layers would be progressively (or individually) randomized, from top to bottom, and the effect over the saliency map produced by each method would be observed. In the latter, labels would be permuted in the training set, forcing the network to memorize the noisy annotation. Some techniques, such as the Guided Backpropagation and Guided-CAM methods, were unaffected by the randomization of labels and weights of the top layers, which indicated that they were invariant to class information and highly dependent on low-level features and, thus, lead the authors to conclude that those methods approximated the behavior of edge detectors.

Differently from gradient-based saliency methods, Class Activation Mapping (CAM) can be used to circumvent the lack of sensibility to class [40]. This technique consists in feed-forwarding an input image x over all convolutional layers of a CNN f and obtaining the positional activation signal $A^k = [a_{ij}^k]_{H \times W}$ for the k-th kernel in the last convolutional layer. If $W = [w_k^c]$ is the weight matrix of the last dense layer in f, then the importance of each positional unit a_{ij} for the classification of label c is summarized as:

$$L_{\mathrm{CAM}}^c(f, x) = \mathrm{ReLU}(\sum_k w_k^c A^k) \tag{1}$$

Naturally, CAMs are not without shortcomings. Significant challenges ensue with the employment of CAMs: Firstly, only simple convolutional architectures can be explained through CAM, as it assumes a direct association between the activation convolutional signal and the classification signal. Additionally, when considering the later convolutional layers in the model, CAM will produce activation maps of considerably smaller size when compared to the input images. They must therefore be interpolated to match their original counterparts, which entails explaining maps with fairly imprecise object boundaries localization and highlighting. Furthermore, as the model focus on a few discriminative regions to predict a class for a given sample, the highlighted regions in the visualization map might not completely cover the salient objects associated with that specific class, being strongly affected by the data visual patterns, the explaining method employed [4] and even the model's architecture [19]. In the context of visual explaining maps, this property is often times referred to as *completeness* [29].

Recently, a broad spectrum of CAM-based methods have been developed in an attempt to address the aforementioned problems and improve the quality of the explanations. Gradient signals were leveraged to extend CAM to Grad-CAM [19], in order to explain more complex network architectures, not limited to convolutional networks ending in simple layers such as Softmax classifiers and linear regression models. Let $S_c = f(x)_c$ be the score attributed by the network for class c with respect to the input image x, and $\frac{\partial S_c}{\partial A_{ij}^k}$ be the partial derivative of the score S_c with respect to the pixel (i, j) in the activation map A^k, then:

$$L_{\text{Grad-CAM}}^c(f, x) = \text{ReLU}\left(\sum_k \sum_{ij} \frac{\partial S_c}{\partial A_{ij}^k} A^k\right) \tag{2}$$

Grad-CAM++ was then proposed as an extension of Grad-CAM, in which each positional unit in A^k was weighted by leveling factors to produce maps that evenly highlighted different parts of the image that positively contributed to the classification of class c, providing higher completeness for large objects and multiple instances of the same object in the image [4]. Similarly to Grad-CAM, Grad-CAM++ is defined as:

$$L_{\text{Grad-CAM++}}^c(f, x) = \text{ReLU}\left(\sum_k \sum_{ij} \alpha_{ij}^{kc} \text{ReLU}\left(\frac{\partial S_c}{\partial A_{ij}^k}\right) A^k\right) \tag{3}$$

where

$$\alpha_{ij}^{kc} = \frac{\frac{\partial^2 S_c}{(\partial A_{ij}^k)^2}}{2\frac{\partial^2 S_c}{(\partial A_{ij}^k)^2} + \sum_{ab} A_{ab}^k \frac{\partial^3 S_c}{(\partial A_{ij}^k)^3}}$$

Additionally, two metrics were proposed by Chattopadhay et al. [4]: Increase of Confidence (%IC) and Average Drop (%AD), which have since been constantly employed in the evaluation of visualization techniques.

Another visualization technique worth remarking is Score-CAM [32]. In it, visualization maps are defined as the sum of the activation signals A^k, weighted by factors C^k, that are directly proportional to the classification score obtained when the image pixels are masked by the normalized signal A^k. Formally, Score-CAM is defined as:

$$L_{\text{Score-CAM}}^c(f, x) = \text{ReLU}\left(\sum_k f(x \circ \frac{A^k}{\max A^k})_c A^k\right) \tag{4}$$

More recently, an ever-growing interest in developing even more accurate visualization methods is noticeable. Among many, we remark SS-CAM [31],

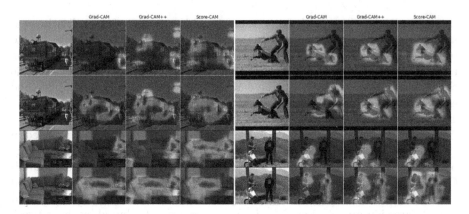

Fig. 1. Explaining maps resulted from the application of various CAM-based visualization techniques over samples in the VOC07 dataset [8].

Ablation-CAM [17], Relevance-CAM [11], LayerCAM [10] and F-CAM [2]. Similarly to Score-CAM, Ablation-CAM is defined as the sum of feature maps A^k, where each map is weighted by the proportional drop in classification score when A^k is set to zero. Relevance-CAM combines the ideas of Grad-CAM with Contrastive Layer-wise Relevance Propagation (CLRP) to obtain a high resolution explaining map that is sensitive to the target class, while LayerCAM incorporates the signals advent from intermediate convolutional layers to increase the quality of explaining maps. Finally, F-CAM replaces the upscaling operational of the CAM by a parameterized reconstruction operation based on local statistics with respect to the objects of interest.

Notwithstanding the consistent progression towards the improvement of visualization results, the aforementioned methods entail significant computing footprint. We further note that much of the work conducted thus far have focused on evaluations over single-label multi-class datasets, such as localization task over ImageNet [19], and little investigation has been conducted over the effectiveness of these visualization techniques in multi-label scenarios. Additionally, studies that used multi-label datasets [4] often focus on single-label explanation (usually considering the highest scoring class as unit of interest).

We set forth the goal of studying visualization techniques proposed so far in the multi-label setting, as well as developing a visualization technique which takes into account the expanded information available in multi-label problems. This study is important, from a scientific and engineering perspective, as it provides a comparison benchmark over more realistic scenarios, in which the capturing conditions are less controlled and more heterogeneous. Additionally, we remark the constantly increasing interest in weakly supervised segmentation [3] and localization [38] problems, in which CAM-based visualization maps are frequently employed as localization cues and class-specific precision is paramount.

As motivation, we start by presenting the visualization maps of classes of interest over a few samples from the Pascal VOC 2007 (VOC07) dataset [8] in Fig. 1. In it, we observe CAM-based methods (specially the most recent versions which attempt to expand the map to cover all parts of the classified object) tend to overflow the boundaries of the object of interest, even expanding over other objects associated with different classes.

3   Contrasting Class Gradient Information

In this section, we describe our CAM-based technique, namely MinMax-CAM, which generates visualization maps by contrasting region contributions for different classes, and thus better incorporating multi-label information into the resulting map. Firstly, we motivate the reader by giving an intuition behind the technique. We then formally define MinMax-Grad-CAM and present its simplification (MinMax-CAM) for "simple" CNNs, comprising only convolutional layers, GAP layers and a last densely connected *sigmoid* classifier. Finally, we describe a MinMax-CAM variant that produces visualization maps with fewer artifacts over the background and co-occurring objects by factoring *positive*, *negative* and *background* contributions.

3.1   Intuition

Containing multiple co-occurring salient objects interacting in different contexts and obtained from various capturing conditions and settings, Multi-label problems are intrinsically more complex than the ones represented in single-label, multi-class datasets. The visual patterns associated with a given class are not necessarily the most prominent visual cue contained in their samples, while statistical artifacts, such as label co-occurrence and context, have great impact on the training and, therefore, the generalization capacity of the model. An example of such problem is remarked by Chan et al.: In the extreme case in which two classes always appear together, no visual cue that effectively distinguishes them can be learned, implying in the internalization of contextual information or correlated patterns, in opposite of the expected visual evidence for individual classes [3]. While one can argue that the occurrence correlation of 100% between two or more classes is not a realistic scenario, fitting a classifier over frequently co-occurring classes (e.g., *dining table* and *chair* in Pascal VOC 2012 dataset [8]) might result in a significant decrease of generalization efficacy and confusing CAMs, as correlating patterns are inadvertently internalized as evidence of occurrence, thus forming false association rules.

We propose a visualization method that attempts to identify the kernel contributing regions for each label c in the input image x by averaging the signals in A^k, weighted by a combination of their direct contributions to the score of c and negative contributions to the remaining labels present in x, that is, finding regions that *maximize* the score of the label c and *minimize* the score of the remaining adjacent labels. To achieve this, we modify the gain function used by Grad-CAM to accommodate both maximizing and minimizing label groups, redefining it as the gradient of an optimization function J_c with respect to the activating signal A_{ij}^k, where J_c is the subtraction between the positive score for label c and the scores of the remaining labels represented within sample x.

3.2   Definition

Let x be a sample from a dataset associated with the set of classes C_x, $c \in C_x$ a class of interest and $N_x = C_x \setminus \{c\}$. At the same time, let f be a trained convolutional network such that $A^k = [a_{ij}^k]_{H \times W}$ is the activation map for the k-th kernel in the last convolutional layer, $W = [w_k^c]$ is the weight matrix of the *sigmoid* classifying layer, containing synaptic values that linearly associate the positional signal A^k to the classification signal for class c. In these conditions, the classification score for c is given by:

$$S_c = f(x)_c = \sum_k w_k^c \frac{1}{hw}(A^k) \tag{5}$$

We consider the focused score for label c as the subtraction between the score S_c and the average score of the remaining classes present in N_x:

$$J_c = S_c - \frac{1}{|N_x|} \sum_{n \in N_x} S_n \tag{6}$$

Finally, MinMax-Grad-CAM is defined as the combination of activation signals A^k, weighted by their respective contributions towards the optimization the objective function J_c:

$$L_{\text{MinMax-Grad-CAM}}^c(f,x) = \text{ReLU}\Big(\sum_k \sum_i \frac{\partial J_c}{\partial A_{ij}^k} A^k\Big) \tag{7}$$

On the other hand, we remark that J_c is a linear function with respect to $S_k, \forall k \in C_x$:

$$\frac{\partial J_c}{\partial A_{ij}^k} = \frac{\partial S_c}{\partial A_{ij}^k} - \frac{1}{|N_x|} \sum_{n \in N_x} \frac{\partial S_n}{\partial A_{ij}^k} \tag{8}$$

Hence, MinMax-Grad-CAM can be rewritten in its more efficient and direct "CAM form" (as demonstrated by Selvaraju et al. [19]), for convolutional networks where the last layer is a linear classifier. In this form, Eq. (7) simplifies to:

$$L_{\text{MinMax-CAM}}^c = \text{ReLU}\Big(\sum_k \big[w_k^c - \frac{1}{|N_x|} \sum_{n \in N_x} w_k^n\big] A^k\Big) \tag{9}$$

In conformity with the literature, we employ the ReLU activation function in both forms (CAM and Grad-CAM) to only retain regions that positively contribute to the maximization of function J_c.

3.3   Reducing Noise by Removing Negative Contributions

Let $g^k = \text{GAP}(A_{ij}^k)$ be a positional-invariant signal describing the evidence of occurrence for a given data pattern k. If the ReLU activation function (or any other non-negative function) is used in the last convolutional layer, then g^k is positive, and $w_k^c > 0$ invariably associate the classification of class c to

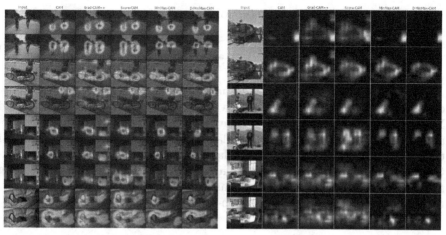

(a) Explaining labels are, from top to bottom: *bicycle, person, motorbike, person, dining table, chair, tv, person* and *sofa*.

(b) Explaining labels are, from top to bottom: *person, train, motorbike, person, chair,* and *dining table.*

Fig. 2. Heatmaps and attention maps produced by CAM-based visualization techniques over the Pascal VOC12 and VOC07 datasets, respectively. Source: David et al [5].

kernels that positively contribute to it. Conversely, $w_k^c < 0$ indicate kernels that negatively contribute to the classification of c.

When the contributions for classes $n \in N_x$ are naively subtracted in Eqs. (6) and (9), negative weights (or gradients) become positive, producing inadvertently a residual highlighting over regions that negatively contribute for the classification of n. We can mitigate this noise by decomposing the contribution factors a_k^c into (a) *positive*, that positively contribute for the classification of c, (b) *negative*, that positively contribute for the classification of $n \in N_x$, and (c) *overall negative*, that negatively contribute for the classification of all classes, frequently overlapping *background* regions in our experiments.

An alternative form (which we denote as D-MinMax-Grad-CAM, for the remaining of this work) can then be formally defined as:

$$L_{\text{D-MinMax-Grad-CAM}}^c = \text{ReLU}\left(\sum_k \alpha_k^c A^k\right) \tag{10}$$

where

$$
\begin{aligned}
\alpha_k^c = \sum_{ij} \Bigg[&\text{ReLU}\left(\frac{\partial S_c}{\partial A_{ij}^k}\right) \\
&- \frac{1}{|N_x|}\text{ReLU}\left(\sum_{n \in N_x}\frac{\partial S_n}{\partial A_{ij}^k}\right) \\
&+ \frac{1}{|C_x|}\min\left(0, \sum_{n \in C_x}\frac{\partial S_n}{\partial A_{ij}^k}\right)\Bigg]
\end{aligned} \tag{11}
$$

Finally, a CAM derivation is also possible:

$$\alpha_k^c = \Big[\mathrm{ReLU}(w_k^c) - \frac{1}{|N_x|}\mathrm{ReLU}(\sum_{n \in N_x} w_k^n) + \frac{1}{|C_x|}\min(0, \sum_{n \in C_x} w_k^n)\Big] \qquad (12)$$

Figure 2a and Fig. 2b exemplify visualization maps obtained from the application of various techniques over a few samples in the Pascal VOC 2012 and VOC 2007 datasets, respectively. While Grad-CAM++ and Score-CAM generated confusing maps, in which the explaining signal overflow the boundaries of the object of interest and even cover large portions of the scenario, MinMax-CAM produced more focused activation maps, where class-specific highlighting avoided objects of different classes. Meanwhile, D-MinMax-CAM has effectively reduced the residual activation over non-salient objects and background regions.

4   Reducing Shared Information Between Classifiers

MinMax-CAM works under the assumption that two distinct labels are not associated with the same set of visual cues present in a single region in the input image. Hence, the contributions being subtracted are associated with different parts of the spatial signal A^k, and the resulting map is more focused than its counterpart generated by CAM. This assumption does not hold when a network has not learned sufficiently discriminative patterns for both labels, which can be caused by an unbalanced set or a subset of frequently co-occurring labels [3]. For instance, *tv monitors* frequently appear together with *chairs* in Pascal VOC 2007, which might teach the network to correlate the occurrence of the latter with the classification of a former. In such scenarios, MinMax-CAM could degenerate the explanation map (Fig. 3a).

Although class co-occurrence and contextual information might present useful information towards the improvement of the classification efficacy of a model, these artifacts tend to cause unexpected highlighting in regions that do not contain the objects associated with classes of interest. Hence, they may also imply in the diminishing the precision of localization cues provided by CAMs, increasing the number of false positive pixels found in them [3].

Poor precision results in CAMs are mitigated in solutions with clear separation between the internalized patterns that discriminate between the existing classes, while penalizing the internalization of contextual patterns, which describe more than a single class at the same time. Examples of early work in this vein are the various augmentation strategies based on sample combination, such as MixUp [39] and CutMix [36]); the context decoupling strategy proposed by Su et al. [25], in which objects are pasted outside their usual context; and the experiments conducted by Chan et al. [3], which evaluated the effect of "balancing" the class distribution — by removing samples containing highly correlating labels — over the DeepGlobe segmentation task [6].

Conversely to the aforementioned data-based strategies, we propose an architectural change that reinforces positive and sparse values in the weight matrix

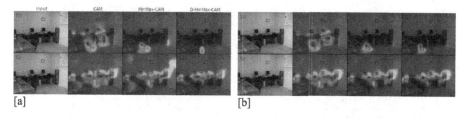

Fig. 3. (a) Example of degenerated CAM in VOC07, in which contributing regions for the detection of class *chair* collide with the ones for class *tv monitor*. (b) Activation maps after the network is trained with regularized weights. Source: David et al. [5].

W, while striving for mutually exclusive usage of the visual signals g^k. These properties are simple and intuitive: The occurrence of visual evidence associated with classes in $C_x \setminus \{c\}$ should not affect the classification score of a given class c. At the same time, invariance between classification score and the absence of evidence of other classes can be reinforced by discouraging the formation of negative associations (weights).

Let K be the number of kernels in the last convolutional layer, C be the number of classes in the dataset, $g = [g^k]_K$ be the feature vector obtained from the pooling of last convolutional layer, $W = [w_k^c]_{K \times C}$ and $b = [b_c]_C$ the weights from the last dense layer and σ the *sigmoid* function. We define the regularization of the weights of the *sigmoid* classifier, namely kernel usage regularization (KUR), as follows:

$$W^r = W \circ \mathrm{softmax}(W)$$
$$y = \sigma(g \cdot W^r + b) \tag{13}$$

When the *softmax* function is applied over each vector W_k, high values w_k^c — implying a strong association between g^k and S_c — will induce $\mathrm{softmax}(w_k)^c \approx 1$, and thus $w_k^{c^r} \approx w_k^c$. As the *softmax* function quickly saturates over a few large values, the remaining associations quickly tend to 0, erasing the influence of the activation signals A^k over $S_n, \forall n \in [0, C] \setminus c)$. Finally, negative values w_k^c should have low $\mathrm{softmax}(w_k)^c$, hence $w_i^{c^r} \approx 0$.

Figure 3b illustrates the activation maps for the network trained with regularized weights. As the simultaneous usage of same kernels for distinct classification units have been regularized, subtracting contributions no longer distort the maps for any of the labels. Activations for the class *chair*, in special, are no longer shifted onto the floor when the contributions for *monitor* are subtracted.

Finally, Fig. 4 illustrate the correlation between the weight classifying vectors, for both *vanilla* and KUR models. Classifying vectors are much less correlated for the model trained with KUR, indicating they are now effectively using distinct activation signals in their decision process.

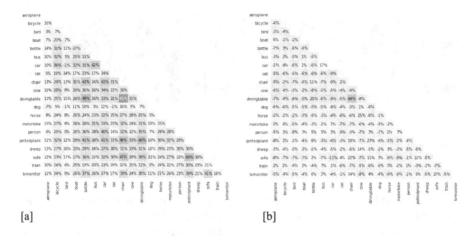

[a]   [b]

Fig. 4. Correlation between the weights vectors in the *sigmoid* classifying layer of (a) a vanilla model trained over VOC07, and (b) a model whose training was regularized with KUR.

4.1 Counterbalancing Activation Vanishing

In spite of the observed effectiveness in separating the available kernels between the classifying units for the VOC 2007, VOC 2012 and P:AfS datasets, its decrease in F1 score over the COCO 2017 dataset is troublesome. Upon closer inspection of this particular model, we observed that *kernel usage reg.* inadvertently causes the weights to vanish when the number of classifying units is high. This is due to the *softmax* function being initially evenly-distributed, with $\mathrm{softmax}_c(x) \approx \frac{1}{c}$. Hence, for a large number of classes c, the initial weights are aggressively pushed towards zero, which obstructs the training process and severely compromises the solution candidate found.

However, we can counter-balancing the effect of the initial configuration of the *softmax* function over the signal distribution by simply multiplying the regularized weights by a scaling factor α, resulting in the restoration of signal's variance. For $\alpha = C$ (the number of classes), we expect the weights to sustain their original variance, as $c \times \mathrm{softmax}_c(w) \approx c\frac{1}{c} = 1$. Figure 5 illustrates the weight distribution for the baseline, KUR and KUR-α, for $\alpha = C$.

5   Experimental Setup

In this section, we detail the experimental procedures employed to evaluate the proposed explaining techniques with respect to the most popular alternatives found in current literature, considering multiple architectures and datasets.

5.1 Evaluations over Architectures and Problem Domains

In conformity with literature, we evaluate the effect of architectural change over the explanations produced by the various visualization techniques by employing

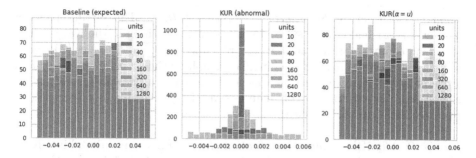

Fig. 5. Weight distribution for vanilla and (kernel usage) regularized weights, for multiple output units.

multiple popular alternatives of Convolutional Neural Network architectures. More specifically, we train and evaluate three architectures over Pascal VOC 2007: VGG16-GAP (VGG16), ResNet101 (RN101) and EfficientNet-B6 (EN6). We approximate the evaluation conditions of previous works [4, 19, 32] by warm-starting from weights pre-trained over the ILSVRC 2012 dataset, and fine tuning the networks over the Pascal VOC 2007 dataset [8].

Similarly to the test battery described above, we further evaluate the different visualization techniques considering five image-related problem sets, resulting in measurements and insights about the behavior and efficacy of these techniques over various scenarios. In these, it is expected that data patterns, class co-occurring groups and semantic contexts greatly differ, providing a more comprehensive understanding of these techniques. A brief summary of the employed datasets, representing the different problem sets, is provided below.

Pascal VOC 2007 (VOC07). The Pascal VOC 2007 dataset [8] is a well established dataset in Computer Vision and Machine Learning literature, being frequently employed in the evaluation of AI explaining methods and techniques. Comprising of 2,501 training samples, 2,510 validation samples and 4,952 test samples, this set contains images with multiple objects belonging to 20 distinct classes.

Pascal VOC 2012 (VOC12). This dataset extends the Pascal VOC 2007 dataset to 5,717 training samples, 5,823 validation samples and 10,991 unlabeled test samples, while sharing the same classes with its previous version [8].

Microsoft Common Objects in Context 2017 (COCO17). The COCO 2017 dataset [13] contains 118,287 training samples, 5,000 validation samples and 40,670 unlabeled test samples. Images in this set are richly annotated with respect to various objects belonging to 80 distinct classes (classification, detection and segmentation annotations are available). Furthermore, this set respects contextual information of classes, by presenting objects in the usual environments and scenarios.

Planet: Understanding the Amazon from Space (P:UAS). This satellite imagery dataset was originally provided by Planet for a competition in the Kaggle platform, and comprises 40,479 training samples and 61,191 test samples [20]. Samples correspond to "chips" of satellite photographs of the Amazon rainforest, and are annotated with respect to their natural features (e.g., *primary forest, water, cloudy, haze*) one the observed human intervention in the area (e.g., *agriculture, road, selective logging, mining*).

Human Protein Atlas Image Classification (HPA). Firstly introduced in a Kaggle competition of same name, this set comprises 31,072 training samples and 11,702 test samples [15]. Each sample is represented by a microscopic image framing cellular bodies and proteins of interest, as well as a label set from the set of 28 available classes (e.g., Nucleoplasm, Cytosol, Plasma membrane, Nucleoli). This dataset represent many computational challenges, and it is used to measure the behavior of explaining techniques over ill-distributed datasets, recurrently found in real-case scenarios. Besides the natural difficulty of learning core visual patterns of intrinsically associated and frequently co-occurring cellular components, we observe an overwhelming class imbalanced in the training set, as well a class distribution shift in the test set, resulting in relative low scores for all competitors in the original Kaggle challenge[1].

5.2   Training Procedure

Firstly, images in all datasets and experiments are resized with the preservation of their original aspect ratio, in which their shortest dimension (height or width) is matched the expected size of the visual receptive field. They are then centrally cropped along their largest dimension to the exact size of the aforementioned field (224×224 for VGG-GAP and 512×512 for ResNet101 and EfficientNetB6). In conformity with literature, we report the visualization results over the validation subset of each dataset.

Before the training procedure, weights of the convolutional pipeline are initialized with the set of weights pre-trained over ImageNet. A Global Average Pooling (GAP) layer and a *sigmoid* dense layer (with the number of units equal to the number of labels in the dataset) are then appended to the pipeline, forming the entire multi-label classification model.

Training is split in two stages. In the first, all layers but the last are frozen (i.e., the gradient of their weights is set to zero), and the model is trained for 30 epochs with a learning rate = 0.1. Approximately 60% of the layers (on the top) are then unfrozen and the model is once again trained for 80 epochs using Stochastic Gradient Descent with learning rate = 0.01 and Nesterov momentum [26] equals to 0.9. Furthermore, we reduce learning rate by a factor of 0.5 and restore the best weights found so far when validation loss does not decrease

---

[1] Human Protein Atlas. Human Protein Atlas Image Classification. In: Kaggle. kaggle.com/competitions/human-protein-atlas-image-classification (Jan 2019). Accessed on Aug 2022.

for 3 epochs. Finally, we interrupt the training procedure if validation loss does not decrease for 20 epochs.

5.3   Evaluation Metrics

In order to evaluate and compare our explaining techniques to current litera-ture in a multi-label setting, we employ slightly modified versions of the met-rics defined by Chattopadhay et al. [4]. Specifically, the *Increase in Confidence* (Eq. (14)) and *Average Drop* (Eq. (15)) metrics are extended to take into con-sideration the classification units associated with each classes present in each sample, in opposite of only considering the most intensively activating unit. Notwithstanding, it is worth remarking that the equations considered in this work will reduce to their conventional form, as commonly employed in liter-ature, in single-label classification problems. Concomitantly, three new metrics were designed to better evaluate the inadvertent activation of the produced class-specific explanation maps over objects associated with co-occurring classes.

We describe below the aforementioned metrics in detail, providing their for-mal definition, as well as the intuition behind them. We remark that while the *micro-average* form was used in their respective equations for simplicity, it does not capture well the unbalanced nature of multi-label problems [28]. Hence, we report metrics in their *macro-averaged* form (or *class-frequency balanced*) in Sect. 6, in which metric results are computed separately for each class and averaged, removing the impact of label frequency in the overall result.

Increase in Confidence (%IC). The rate in which masking the input image x_i by the visualization mask M_i^c has produced a higher classification score $O_{ic}^c = f(M_i^c \circ x_i)^c$ than the baseline $Y_i^c = f(x_i)^c$:

$$\frac{1}{\sum_i |C_i|} \sum_i^N \sum_{c \in C_i} [Y_i^c < O_{ic}^c] \tag{14}$$

This metric measures scenarios where removing background noise must improve classification confidence. We report results for this metric in compli-ance with literature, but raise the following question regarding the consistency of this metric: the classifying units of a *sigmoid* classifier are not in direct com-petition with each other for total activation energy, as it happens with units in *softmax* classifiers. For an ideal classifier, in which concepts are perfectly sep-arated and no false correlation exist, one could argue that the removal of an object from an image should not affect the classification score of another object.

Average Drop (%AD). The rate of drop in the confidence of a model for a particular image x_i and label c, when only the highlighted region $M_i^c \circ x_i$ is fed to the network:

$$\frac{1}{\sum_i |C_i|} \sum_i^N \sum_{c \in C_i} \frac{\max(0, Y_i^c - O_{ic}^c)}{Y_i^c} \tag{15}$$

Average Drop expresses the idea that masking the image with an accurate mask should not decrease confidence in the label of interest, that is, it measures if your mask is correctly positioned on top of the important regions that determine the label of interest.

Average Drop of Others (%ADO). The rate of drop in the confidence of a model for a particular image x_i and labels $n \in N_i = C_i \setminus \{c\}$, when only the highlighted region $M_i^c \circ x_i$ is fed to the network:

$$\frac{1}{\sum_i |C_i|} \sum_i^N \sum_{c \in C_i} \frac{1}{|N_i|} \sum_{n \in N_i} \frac{\max(0, Y_i^n - O_{ic}^n)}{Y_i^n} \tag{16}$$

This metric captures the effect of a mask M_i^c over objects of other labels N_i present in x_i, in which the masking of the input x_i for a given class c should cause the confidence in other labels to drop. One expects an ideal mask to not retain any objects of other classes, that is, $f(M_i^c \circ x_i)^n \approx 0, \forall n \in N_i$.

Average Retention (%AR). The rate of retention of confidence of a model for a particular image x_i and label c, when the region highlighted by the visualization map for label c is occluded:

$$\frac{1}{\sum_i |C_i|} \sum_i^N \sum_{c \in C_i} \frac{\max(0, Y_i^c - \bar{O}_{ic}^c)}{Y_i^c} \tag{17}$$

where $\bar{O}_{ic}^c = f((1 - M_i^c) \circ x_i)^c$.

While *Average Drop* measures if the map M_i^c is correctly positioned over an object of label c, *Average Retention* attempts to capture if M_i^c covers all regions occupied by objects of label c, that is, masking the input with an accurate complement mask $(1 - M_i^c)$ should decrease confidence in class c.

Average Retention of Others (%ARO). The rate of retention of confidence of a model for a particular image x_i and labels $n \in N_i$, when the region highlighted by the visualization map for label c is occluded:

$$\frac{1}{\sum_i |C_i|} \sum_i^N \sum_{c \in C_i} \frac{1}{|N_i|} \sum_{n \in N_i} \frac{\max(0, Y_i^n - \bar{O}_{ic}^n)}{Y_i^n} \tag{18}$$

This metric evaluates if the masking of input x_i for all labels but c retains the confidence of the model in detecting these same labels. An ideal mask complement for class c should cover all objects of the other classes, that is, $f((1 - M_i^c) \circ x_i)^n \approx f(x_i)^n, \forall n \in N_i$.

F_1- **and** F_1+ **Scores.** Although the aforementioned metrics cover the various facets of the evaluation of AI explaining methods over multi-label scenarios, it may create difficulties in the analysis or interpretation of the results, requiring a high degree of attention and memorization from readers. Hence, the summarizing of results presents itself as an interesting strategy in this regard, providing the reader a simpler form to evaluate the overall behavior of said methods.

We opted to combine similar measurements using a harmonic mean (F_1 score). More specifically, we consider (a) F_1- as the harmonic mean between *Average Drop* and *Average Retention of Others*, both error measures; and (b) F_1+: the harmonic mean between *Average Retention* and *Average Drop of Others*, both score functions (higher is better).

6 Results

In this section, we report the evaluation results for well-established CAM-based techniques (CAM, Grad-CAM++, Score-CAM), commonly employed in literature, while comparing them to the two forms described in Sect. 3 (MinMax-CAM and D-MinMax-CAM). We then discuss the properties and limitations of our technique. We further illustrate their differences by presenting and discussing qualitative examples.

Table 1. Report of metric scores per method, considering multiple architectures over the Pascal VOC07 dataset. Source: David et al. [5].

Metric	Model	CAM	Grad-CAM++	Score-CAM	MinMax-CAM	D-MinMax-CAM
	Eb6	**39.67%**	25.13%	30.50%	34.23%	39.49%
%IC	RN101	27.68%	31.03%	**40.76%**	26.61%	23.83%
	VGG16	5.65%	8.27%	**12.78%**	4.18%	3.76%
	Eb6	22.94%	36.87%	**22.10%**	28.09%	23.71%
%AD	RN101	25.24%	17.90%	**10.79%**	32.58%	39.25%
	VGG16	39.34%	29.22%	**19.27%**	46.78%	50.34%
	Eb6	29.43%	19.35%	20.17%	**39.82%**	31.99%
%ADO	RN101	32.73%	12.48%	14.72%	44.03%	**46.49%**
	VGG16	29.61%	18.52%	15.74%	39.33%	**39.50%**
	Eb6	**11.74%**	8.40%	9.92%	10.50%	9.10%
%AR	RN101	**16.54%**	14.04%	14.94%	14.27%	12.00%
	VGG16	40.38%	39.04%	**42.70%**	33.82%	31.00%
	Eb6	1.61%	2.53%	2.28%	**0.99%**	1.47%
%ARO	RN101	2.44%	3.94%	3.43%	1.28%	**1.16%**
	VGG16	8.84%	12.10%	12.96%	3.47%	**3.34%**
	Eb6	2.82%	4.54%	1.91%	**1.86%**	2.64%
F_1-	RN101	4.05%	5.62%	**2.20%**	2.38%	2.21%
	VGG16	13.52%	15.39%	13.42%	6.23%	**6.00%**
	Eb6	**15.79%**	10.14%	5.96%	15.40%	12.96%
F_1+	RN101	**20.84%**	11.97%	6.89%	19.85%	17.13%
	VGG16	31.70%	23.50%	22.19%	**32.16%**	29.94%

6.1 Comparison Between Architectures

For completeness purposes, we reproduce here the results over distinct architectures presented by David et al. [5]. Table 1 enumerate these results over VOC07 validation set, considering the EfficientNet-B6 (Eb6), ResNet-101 (RN101) and VGG16-GAP (VGG16) architectures. We observe that Grad-CAM++ and Score-CAM are associated with the highest *Increase in Confidence* (%IC) for most architectures (two out of three). For EfficientNet-B6, CAM obtained the highest value for this metric (39.67%), closely followed by D-MinMax-CAM (39.49%). For the remaining architectures, MinMax-CAM and D-MinMax-CAM present slightly lower %IC than CAM, while always loosing to Grad-CAM++ and Score-CAM.

CAM, Grad-CAM++ and Score-CAM obtain the best *Average Drop* (%AR) and *Average Retention* (%AD) scores, as these metrics favor methods producing diffuse activation maps. Grad-CAM++ and Score-CAM obtained a significantly lower %AD compared to the remaining techniques, while CAM obtained marginally higher %AR scores than both MinMax alternatives, indicating that Grad-CAM++ and Score-CAM are better at covering the characteristic sections of objects, while CAM and MinMax produce smaller activation maps.

Conversely, MinMax consistently achieves better results for %ADO and %ARO, as these metrics favor methods that produce more focused class-specific maps. When considering the F_1- metric, MinMax result in the best scores for two out of the three architecture, scoring significantly higher than CAM and Grad-CAM++, which further indicates that they are quite successful at removing regions containing objects associated to the classes N_x, while still focusing on determinant regions for the classification of c. Finally, while Score-CAM presents the best F_1- score for the RN101 architecture (2.2%), MinMax and D-MinMax-CAM closely approximate this result (2.38% and 2.21%, respectively).

When considering the F_1+ score metric, CAM and MinMax-CAM present the highest results, and are closely followed by D-MinMax-CAM. Meanwhile, the Grad-CAM++ and Score-CAM techniques present noticeably lower scores for this metric, indicating that CAM, MinMax-CAM and D-MinMax-CAM are more successful in covering large portions of objects associated with class c without spreading over objects of adjacent classes.

6.2 Evaluation over Distinct Problem Domains

Table 3 reports the results for the various explaining techniques, considering multiple datasets. Once again, CAM, Grad-CAM++ and Score-CAM produce the best %IC, %AD and %AR values. We attribute this to the proclivity of these techniques to retain large portions of the image, maintaining contextual information of the sample. Conversely, D-MinMax-CAM wins against the literature techniques by a large margin when considering %ADO, %ARO and F_1- score. Finally, CAM and MinMax-CAM present similar results for F_1+ score, consistently ahead of Grad-CAM++ and Score-CAM.

When considering evaluation performance, no significant difference was observed in time execution between CAM, Grad-CAM++, MinMax-CAM and D-MinMax-CAM. Score-CAM, on the other hand, entailed a considerable higher execution time, considering is high computational footprint, taking approximately 16 h and 29 h to complete over VOC07 and P:UAS, respectively, and over 59 h to complete over COCO17 and HPA.

6.3   Kernel Usage Regularization

Table 2 reports the F_1 and F_2 scores over validation and test sets (when available) for both baseline and regularized models. We see a slight increase in F_1 and F_2 score in most cases, indicating that this regularization has positive impact on overall score of the classifier. Conversely, a noticeable decrease in score can be observed for the COCO17 dataset, which is associated with the high number of classes present in this set, implying an aggressively regularized training. By retraining the RN101 architecture over the COCO17 dataset, regularized with KUR-α s.t. $\alpha = 80$, we obtain a F_1 score of 75.55%. Finally, a decrease in F_1 score when evaluated the vanilla and KUR models over the HPA private and public test subsets is also noticeable, although small. We hypothesize that better results can be achieved with a careful finetune of hyperparameters (such as *learning rate* and α).

Examples of Class-specific Activation Maps extracted from COCO17 dataset by various visualization techniques are illustrated in Fig. 6. Once again, we observe more focused visualization maps for MinMax-CAM and D-MinMax-CAM: the *persons* next to the *buses* (first two rows) and the *tennis racket* (third and forth rows), as well as the multiple objects in the street scenario (last four rows). On the other hand, examples of visualization maps are presented in Fig. 7. We observe Grad-CAM++, Score-CAM, and CAM, but to a lower extent, producing similar explaining maps for many of the examples of this set, which is also supported by their close score results reported in Table 3. Maps for different classes in the same sample seem to frequently highlight the same salient

Table 2. Multi-label classification score over multiple datasets, considering the baseline and regularized (KUR) models. Results expanded from David et al. [5].

Metric	Dataset	Baseline	KUR
F_1	VOC07 Test	84.26%	**85.85%**
F_1	VOC12 Val	85.05%	**85.90%**
F_2	P:UAS Val	87.80%	**88.24%**
F_2	P:UAS Private Test	89.22%	**89.81%**
F_2	P:UAS Public Test	89.62%	**90.10%**
F_1	COCO17 Val	**75.64%**	74.23%
F_1	HPA Private Test	**36.05%**	35.54%
F_1	HPA Public Test	**39.72%**	39.46%

Table 3. Report of metric scores per visualization technique, over multiple datasets. Results expanded from David et al. [5].

Metric	Dataset	CAM	Grad-CAM++	Score-CAM	MinMax-CAM	D-MinMax-CAM
%IC	P:UAS	6.09%	7.05%	**11.59%**	6.22%	6.27%
	COCO17	30.21%	32.98%	**44.69%**	23.12%	19.20%
	VOC07	27.68%	31.03%	**40.76%**	26.61%	23.83%
	VOC12	27.75%	25.40%	**35.10%**	24.70%	21.66%
	HPA	8.64%	9.29%	**11.27%**	7.63%	5.89%
%AD	P:UAS	55.25%	49.00%	**43.37%**	64.24%	66.88%
	COCO17	27.42%	17.56%	**9.62%**	40.22%	47.43%
	VOC07	25.24%	17.90%	**10.79%**	32.58%	39.25%
	VOC12	24.47%	18.69%	**10.60%**	29.17%	34.22%
	HPA	49.78%	47.02%	**41.50%**	54.16%	64.21%
%ADO	P:UAS	43.61%	33.67%	34.06%	60.04%	**60.62%**
	COCO17	51.49%	20.59%	24.45%	68.04%	**71.90%**
	VOC07	32.73%	12.48%	14.72%	44.03%	**46.49%**
	VOC12	36.44%	14.92%	18.46%	43.65%	**45.02%**
	HPA	24.01%	18.95%	17.07%	29.46%	**39.50%**
%AR	P:UAS	46.42%	**49.45%**	48.01%	37.16%	32.74%
	COCO17	**27.70%**	25.60%	26.64%	24.44%	22.79%
	VOC07	**16.54%**	14.04%	14.94%	14.27%	12.00%
	VOC12	**16.23%**	14.71%	16.22%	14.60%	13.06%
	HPA	29.15%	28.49%	**30.59%**	25.60%	15.44%
%ARO	P:UAS	25.48%	29.46%	28.13%	20.84%	**18.55%**
	COCO17	5.26%	7.92%	7.71%	3.31%	**3.13%**
	VOC07	2.44%	3.94%	3.43%	1.28%	**1.16%**
	VOC12	2.29%	3.76%	3.32%	1.21%	**1.14%**
	HPA	6.69%	9.32%	10.56%	3.60%	**1.32%**
F_1-	P:UAS	30.68%	32.07%	28.46%	28.35%	**26.42%**
	COCO17	8.23%	9.94%	7.39%	5.82%	**5.64%**
	VOC07	4.05%	5.62%	**2.20%**	2.38%	2.21%
	VOC12	3.89%	5.70%	4.30%	2.26%	**2.17%**
	HPA	10.89%	14.26%	15.10%	6.45%	**2.54%**
F_1+	P:UAS	39.54%	35.11%	35.41%	**41.00%**	37.01%
	COCO17	34.05%	21.45%	23.82%	**34.07%**	32.44%
	VOC07	**20.84%**	11.97%	6.89%	19.85%	17.13%
	VOC12	**21.25%**	13.87%	16.39%	20.25%	18.60%
	HPA	**22.85%**	18.30%	18.29%	22.71%	18.79%

regions, indicating these are, indeed, not class-specific. At the same time, both MinMax strategies present distinct visualization maps for multiple classes in a same sample, for most examples.

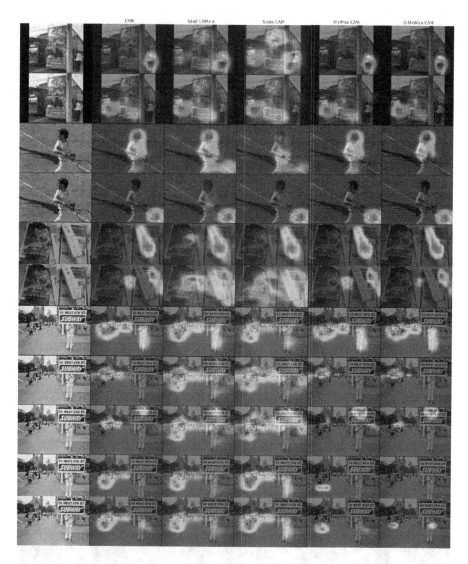

Fig. 6. Class Activation Maps produced by various visualization techniques over COCO17, considering the vanilla RN101 model.

Table 4 displays the results of various visualization techniques over multiple datasets, employing a RN101 network trained with KUR. Score-CAM score the highest for %IC on all but one set, while Grad-CAM++ obtains the second place among most evaluations. Moreover, CAM closely follows the two best-placed techniques, while achieving the best score over the P:UAS dataset. D-MinMax-CAM shows the best F_1- scores in all datasets but one, staying in third place with a difference of 0.53 percent points from the winner (Score-CAM). Finally,

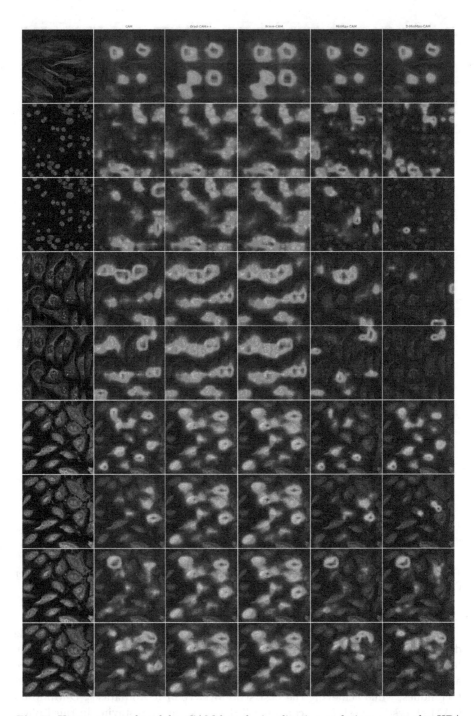

Fig. 7. Heatmaps produced by CAM-based visualization techniques over the HPA dataset.

Table 4. Report of metric scores per visualization technique, over multiple datasets. Classification models were regularized with KUR during training. Results expanded from David et al. [5].

Metric	Dataset	CAM	Grad-CAM++	Score-CAM	MinMax-CAM	D-MinMax-CAM
%IC	P:UAS	**15.60%**	14.39%	14.13%	11.43%	11.54%
	COCO17	34.43%	36.81%	**37.87%**	21.47%	21.49%
	VOC07	28.71%	28.07%	**34.93%**	23.90%	24.99%
	VOC12	33.32%	34.90%	**37.30%**	29.54%	29.36%
	HPA	11.19%	15.73%	**17.55%**	10.31%	5.79%
%AD	P:UAS	42.51%	42.67%	**39.50%**	51.96%	52.53%
	COCO17	22.52%	19.86%	**13.91%**	41.29%	41.39%
	VOC07	22.89%	18.65%	**11.69%**	29.80%	34.19%
	VOC12	16.09%	15.32%	**10.46%**	22.22%	22.85%
	HPA	46.41%	42.61%	**39.81%**	49.92%	59.99%
%ADO	P:UAS	38.34%	35.46%	35.21%	**49.58%**	49.51%
	COCO17	46.97%	37.63%	25.57%	69.17%	**69.28%**
	VOC07	37.30%	20.06%	17.27%	47.16%	**48.60%**
	VOC12	29.66%	21.89%	15.95%	42.07%	**42.46%**
	HPA	27.23%	21.51%	20.76%	32.38%	**33.43%**
%AR	P:UAS	**47.28%**	46.50%	43.61%	43.17%	43.01%
	COCO17	**34.40%**	34.21%	28.13%	30.05%	30.04%
	VOC07	**18.64%**	17.35%	16.91%	16.02%	14.72%
	VOC12	**18.66%**	18.37%	17.72%	17.10%	16.99%
	HPA	26.49%	**26.52%**	25.73%	23.91%	13.57%
%ARO	P:UAS	25.43%	26.35%	26.80%	20.79%	**20.72%**
	COCO17	7.14%	7.85%	11.36%	4.24%	**4.23%**
	VOC07	2.44%	3.45%	3.95%	1.35%	**1.22%**
	VOC12	2.59%	2.89%	4.00%	1.22%	**1.20%**
	HPA	7.62%	10.12%	10.24%	5.00%	**1.53%**
F_1-	P:UAS	27.02%	27.68%	**26.62%**	26.86%	27.15%
	COCO17	10.08%	10.38%	11.15%	**7.33%**	7.33%
	VOC07	4.12%	5.41%	2.69%	2.47%	**2.28%**
	VOC12	3.97%	4.30%	4.96%	2.24%	**2.21%**
	HPA	11.86%	14.03%	13.48%	8.49%	**2.92%**
F_1+	P:UAS	36.53%	35.05%	34.46%	**39.15%**	39.03%
	COCO17	38.08%	34.42%	25.19%	40.64%	**40.65%**
	VOC07	**23.89%**	17.87%	8.10%	22.38%	20.97%
	VOC12	21.99%	19.28%	16.24%	**22.84%**	22.78%
	HPA	**23.52%**	20.56%	19.96%	23.38%	15.65%

MinMax-CAM and D-MinMax-CAM showed the best results in 3 out of 5 tests for the F_1+ score, while achieving a similar score to the winner (CAM) over VOC07, and the worst results when evaluated over HPA.

When comparing the results from regularized models to the ones obtained from their unregularized counterparts, we observe an overall increase in both %IC and F_1+ score for most CAM techniques and datasets. Notwithstanding, F_1- score results improved for 9 out of 25 tests, while staying relatively similar over VOC07 and VOC12. Finally, it is noticeable the decrease in difference between the results from MinMax-CAM and D-MinMax-CAM, across all metrics and datasets. This can be attributed to the regularization factor, which penalizes the existence of negative weights, approximating $\max(0, w_k^c)$ to w_k^c and, thus, D-MinMax-CAM to MinMax-CAM.

7   Conclusions

In this work, we conducted an empirical evaluation of existing visualization techniques over the multi-label setting, considering distinct datasets and problem domains. We proposed generalizations of the well-known *Increase in Confidence* and *Average Drop* metrics, accounting for the objects associated with the various available classes within each sample, and presented three new metrics that capture the effectiveness of visualization maps in images containing objects of distinct labels. We concluded that existing techniques, designed solely over the optimization of *Increase in Confidence* and *Average Drop*, tend to produce diffuse maps, highlighting inaccurate regions with respect to the class of interest.

We presented a visualization technique that produces Class Activation Maps considering both the activation maximization for a class of interest and the activation minimization for adjacent co-occurring classes. We further refined this technique by decomposing it into *positive*, *negative* and *background* contributions in order to produce cleaner visualization maps with minimal contextual residue. We evaluated our technique over different datasets and architectures, obtaining encouraging results from the multiple metrics while maintaining processing footprint in the same order as CAM, Grad-CAM and Grad-CAM++, obtaining similar performance and execution time requirements.

Finally, we proposed Kernel Usage Regularization, which penalizes the usage of class co-occurrence information in the training process by reinforcing positive and sparse weights in the classification layer. Our quantitative results suggest that this strategy is effective in creating cleaner visualization maps while promoting better classification scores in most datasets.

As future work, we propose to apply and evaluate our techniques over weakly supervised localization and weakly supervised segmentation problems, by integrating them to existing regularization strategies that reinforce *completeness* — a current weakness in our approach —, resulting in activation maps that are complete, boundary-aware and class-specific. Furthermore, we intent to study new ways to decouple label contextual information by distilling label-specific knowledge.

References

1. Adebayo, J., Gilmer, J., Muelly, M., Goodfellow, I., Hardt, M., Kim, B.: Sanity checks for saliency maps. In: 32nd International Conference on Neural Information Processing Systems (NIPS), pp. 9525–9536. Curran Associates Inc., Red Hook, NY, USA (2018)
2. Belharbi, S., Sarraf, A., Pedersoli, M., Ben Ayed, I., McCaffrey, L., Granger, E.: F-CAM: full resolution class activation maps via guided parametric upscaling. In: IEEE/CVF Winter Conference on Applications of Computer Vision (WACV), pp. 3490–3499 (2022)
3. Chan, L., Hosseini, M.S., Plataniotis, K.N.: A comprehensive analysis of weakly-supervised semantic segmentation in different image domains. Int. J. Comput. Vision (IJCV) **129**(2), 361–384 (2021)
4. Chattopadhay, A., Sarkar, A., Howlader, P., Balasubramanian, V.N.: Grad-CAM++: generalized gradient-based visual explanations for deep convolutional networks. In: IEEE Winter Conference on Applications of Computer Vision (WACV), pp. 839–847. IEEE (2018)
5. David., L., Pedrini., H., Dias., Z.: MinMax-CAM: improving focus of cam-based visualization techniques in multi-label problems. In: 17th International Joint Conference on Computer Vision, Imaging and Computer Graphics Theory and Applications - Volume 4: VISAPP, pp. 106–117. INSTICC, SciTePress (2022). https://doi.org/10.5220/0010807800003124
6. Demir, I., et al.: Deepglobe 2018: a challenge to parse the earth through satellite images. In: IEEE Conference on Computer Vision and Pattern Recognition Workshops, pp. 172–181 (2018)
7. Dhillon, A., Verma, G.K.: Convolutional neural network: a review of models, methodologies and applications to object detection. Progr. Artif. Intell. **9**(2), 85–112 (2020)
8. Everingham, M., Van Gool, L., Williams, C.K., Winn, J., Zisserman, A.: The pascal visual object classes (VOC) challenge. Int. J. Comput. Vision (IJCV) **88**(2), 303–338 (2010)
9. Huff, D.T., Weisman, A.J., Jeraj, R.: Interpretation and visualization techniques for deep learning models in medical imaging. Phys. Med. Biol. **66**(4), 04TR01 (2021)
10. Jiang, P.T., Zhang, C.B., Hou, Q., Cheng, M.M., Wei, Y.: Layercam: exploring hierarchical class activation maps for localization. IEEE Trans. Image Process. **30**, 5875–5888 (2021). https://doi.org/10.1109/TIP.2021.3089943
11. Lee, J.R., Kim, S., Park, I., Eo, T., Hwang, D.: Relevance-CAM: your model already knows where to look. In: IEEE/CVF Conference on Computer Vision and Pattern Recognition (CVPR), pp. 14944–14953 (2021)
12. Li, Z., Liu, F., Yang, W., Peng, S., Zhou, J.: A survey of convolutional neural networks: analysis, applications, and prospects. IEEE Trans. Neural Netw. Learn. Syst. (TNNLS) (2021)
13. Lin, T.Y., et al.: Microsoft COCO: common objects in context. In: Fleet, D., Pajdla, T., Schiele, B., Tuytelaars, T. (eds.) European Conference on Computer Vision (ECCV), pp. 740–755. Springer International Publishing, Cham (2014)
14. Minaee, S., Boykov, Y.Y., Porikli, F., Plaza, A.J., Kehtarnavaz, N., Terzopoulos, D.: Image segmentation using deep learning: a survey. IEEE Trans. Pattern Anal. Mach. Intell. (PAMI), p. 1 (2021). https://doi.org/10.1109/TPAMI.2021.3059968

15. Ouyang, W., et al.: Analysis of the human protein atlas image classification competition. Nat. Methods **16**(12), 1254–1261 (2019). https://doi.org/10.1038/s41592-019-0658-6

16. Pons, J., Slizovskaia, O., Gong, R., Gómez, E., Serra, X.: Timbre analysis of music audio signals with convolutional neural networks. In: 25th European Signal Processing Conference (EUSIPCO), pp. 2744–2748. IEEE (2017)

17. Ramaswamy, H.G., et al.: Ablation-CAM: visual explanations for deep convolutional network via gradient-free localization. In: IEEE/CVF Winter Conference on Applications of Computer Vision (WACV), pp. 983–991 (2020)

18. Rawat, W., Wang, Z.: Deep convolutional neural networks for image classification: a comprehensive review. Neural Comput. **29**(9), 2352–2449 (2017)

19. Selvaraju, R.R., Cogswell, M., Das, A., Vedantam, R., Parikh, D., Batra, D.: Grad-CAM: Visual explanations from deep networks via gradient-based localization. In: IEEE International Conference on Computer Vision (ICCV), pp. 618–626 (2017)

20. Shendryk, I., Rist, Y., Lucas, R., Thorburn, P., Ticehurst, C.: Deep learning - a new approach for multi-label scene classification in PlanetScope and sentinel-2 imagery. In: IEEE International Geoscience and Remote Sensing Symposium (IGARSS), pp. 1116–1119 (2018)

21. Simonyan, K., Vedaldi, A., Zisserman, A.: Deep inside convolutional networks: visualising image classification models and saliency maps. CoRR abs/1312.6034 (2014)

22. Smilkov, D., Thorat, N., Kim, B., Viégas, F.B., Wattenberg, M.: SmoothGrad: removing noise by adding noise. arXiv:1706.03825 (2017)

23. Springenberg, J., Dosovitskiy, A., Brox, T., Riedmiller, M.: Striving for simplicity: the all convolutional net. In: International Conference on Learning Representations (ICLR) - Workshop Track (2015)

24. Srinivas, S., Fleuret, F.: Full-gradient representation for neural network visualization. arXiv preprint arXiv:1905.00780 (2019)

25. Su, Y., Sun, R., Lin, G., Wu, Q.: Context decoupling augmentation for weakly supervised semantic segmentation. arXiv:2103.01795 (2021)

26. Sutskever, I., Martens, J., Dahl, G., Hinton, G.: On the importance of initialization and momentum in deep learning. In: International Conference on Machine Learning (ICML), pp. 1139–1147. PMLR (2013)

27. Tachibana, H., Uenoyama, K., Aihara, S.: Efficiently trainable text-to-speech system based on deep convolutional networks with guided attention. In: IEEE International Conference on Acoustics, Speech and Signal Processing (ICASSP), pp. 4784–4788 (2018). https://doi.org/10.1109/ICASSP.2018.8461829

28. Tarekegn, A.N., Giacobini, M., Michalak, K.: A review of methods for imbalanced multi-label classification. Pattern Recogn. **118**, 107965 (2021). https://doi.org/10.1016/j.patcog.2021.107965, https://www.sciencedirect.com/science/article/pii/S0031320321001527

29. Vilone, G., Longo, L.: Explainable artificial intelligence: a systematic review. arXiv preprint arXiv:2006.00093 (2020)

30. Vilone, G., Longo, L.: Notions of explainability and evaluation approaches for explainable artificial intelligence. Inf. Fusion **76**, 89–106 (2021). https://doi.org/10.1016/j.inffus.2021.05.009

31. Wang, H., Naidu, R., Michael, J., Kundu, S.S.: SS-CAM: smoothed score-cam for sharper visual feature localization. arXiv preprint arXiv:2006.14255 (2020)

32. Wang, H., et al.: Score-CAM: score-weighted visual explanations for convolutional neural networks. In: IEEE/CVF Conference on Computer Vision and Pattern Recognition Workshops (CVPRW), pp. 111–119 (2020)

33. Wei, S.E., Ramakrishna, V., Kanade, T., Sheikh, Y.: Convolutional pose machines. In: IEEE conference on Computer Vision and Pattern Recognition (CVPR), pp. 4724–4732 (2016)
34. Xu, F., et al.: Explainable AI: a brief survey on history, research areas, approaches and challenges. In: Tang, J., Kan, M.Y., Zhao, D., Li, S., Zan, H. (eds.) Natural Language Processing and Chinese Computing, pp. 563–574. Springer International Publishing, Cham (2019)
35. Yao, L., Mao, C., Luo, Y.: Graph convolutional networks for text classification. In: AAAI Conference on Artificial Intelligence, vol. 33, pp. 7370–7377 (2019)
36. Yun, S., Han, D., Oh, S.J., Chun, S., Choe, J., Yoo, Y.: CutMix: regularization strategy to train strong classifiers with localizable features. In: IEEE/CVF International Conference on Computer Vision (CVPR), pp. 6023–6032 (2019)
37. Zeiler, M.D., Fergus, R.: Visualizing and understanding convolutional networks. In: Fleet, D., Pajdla, T., Schiele, B., Tuytelaars, T. (eds.) ECCV 2014. LNCS, vol. 8689, pp. 818–833. Springer, Cham (2014). https://doi.org/10.1007/978-3-319-10590-1_53
38. Zhang, D., Han, J., Cheng, G., Yang, M.H.: Weakly supervised object localization and detection: a survey. IEEE Transactions on Pattern Analysis and Machine Intelligence, p. 1 (2021). https://doi.org/10.1109/TPAMI.2021.3074313
39. Zhang, H., Cisse, M., Dauphin, Y.N., Lopez-Paz, D.: MixUp: beyond empirical risk minimization. arXiv preprint arXiv:1710.09412 (2017)
40. Zhou, B., Khosla, A., Lapedriza, A., Oliva, A., Torralba, A.: Learning deep features for discriminative localization. In: IEEE Conference on Computer Vision and Pattern Recognition (CVPR), pp. 2921–2929 (2016)

DIAR: Deep Image Alignment and Reconstruction Using Swin Transformers

Monika Kwiatkowski[(✉)] ⓘ, Simon Matern ⓘ, and Olaf Hellwich ⓘ

Computer Vision and Remote Sensing, Technische Universität Berlin, Marchstr. 23, Berlin, Germany
m.kwiatkowski@tu-berlin.de

Abstract. When taking images of some occluded content, one is often faced with the problem that every individual image frame contains unwanted artifacts, but a collection of images contains all relevant information if properly aligned and aggregated. In this paper, we attempt to build a deep learning pipeline that simultaneously aligns a sequence of distorted images and reconstructs them. We create a dataset that contains images with image distortions, such as lighting, specularities, shadows, and occlusion. We create perspective distortions with corresponding ground-truth homographies as labels. We use our dataset to train Swin transformer models to analyze sequential image data. The attention maps enable the model to detect relevant image content and differentiate it from outliers and artifacts. We further explore using neural feature maps as alternatives to classical key point detectors. The feature maps of trained convolutional layers provide dense image descriptors that can be used to find point correspondences between images. We utilize this to compute coarse image alignments and explore its limitations.

Keywords: Swin transformer · Image alignment · Image reconstruction · Deep homography estimation · Vision transformer

1 Introduction

This paper attempts to solve the problem of image reconstruction and alignment simultaneously. Specifically, we deal with image sets that contain distortions and are related by a 2D homography. When taking photos of panoramas or planar objects, such as magazines, paintings, facades, or documents, the resulting images often contain unwanted artifacts. The images may contain varying lighting conditions, shadows, and occlusions. Each artifact corrupts the original content. In order to combine information from all images, the images have to be aligned, and the information has to be aggregated. In this work, we utilize deep image features for image alignment. Furthermore, we use Video Swin Transformers for spatio-temporal analysis of the aligned image sequences and aggregation. This paper is a continuation of the work by Kwiatkowski and Hellwich (2022) [9].

© The Author(s), under exclusive license to Springer Nature Switzerland AG 2023
A. A. de Sousa et al. (Eds.): VISIGRAPP 2022, CCIS 1815, pp. 248–267, 2023.
https://doi.org/10.1007/978-3-031-45725-8_12

We provide the following improvements to the initial paper:

1. We developed a new synthetic dataset. We improve the original data generation by using a ray-tracing pipeline. The dataset contains more realistic lighting and shadows. Furthermore, we take images from different perspectives and provide ground-truth homographies. The library can further be used for image alignment tasks.
2. In addition to solving an image reconstruction task, we also align the images using their neural feature maps. We use feature maps as dense key point descriptors and compute matches between images using a cosine similarity score.
3. Following the success of Vision Transformers (ViT) [7,12] and their extensions to video [1,13] we explore their use for image reconstruction. (Video) Vision transformers compute spatio-temporal attention maps. They have been shown to be able to compute spatial features that are on par with Convolutional neural networks. Furthermore, transformers are the state of the art deep learning models for sequential data. Both of these properties are essential for image reconstruction. A local image feature can only be determined as an artifact by analyzing the context within the image and across the image sequence.
4. We explore various forms of aggregating feature maps. We show that computing attention maps over the sequence allows for a better aggregation compared to the original concept of Deep Sets.

2   Related Work

Deep Image Alignment. The classical approach to estimating homographies uses sparse image descriptors to compute matches between image points [8]. A homography can then be estimated from the matches using random sample consensus (RANSAC). A variety of methods have been developed to improve on the classical approach with neural networks. Some methods aim at replacing image descriptors, such as SIFT [14], with trainable feature maps [2,11,17]. The advantage of these methods is that they can learn robust image features that are distinctive in their corresponding dataset. Additionally, they can be easily integrated into many classical computer vision pipelines.

Neural networks have also been trained on matching image patches directly [16,18]. Graph neural networks or transformers enable a model to analyze points not only individually but in relation to each other. A computed match should therefore be consistent with neighboring matches; otherwise, it is likely an outlier.

One can also describe the estimation of a homography as a regression problem [5]. The model takes two images as input and outputs eight values that can be interpreted as the parameters of a homography.

Deep Image Stitching combines information from multiple images. The images are simultaneously aligned and stitched along overlapping regions. This way, image alignment and image reconstruction can be combined into a single differentiable end-to-end pipeline [15]. There have also been attempts to use neural representations of images for image alignment and stitching. BARF [10] uses neural radiance fields to store 2D or 3D scenes inside a neural network. During the training of the network, both the content of the scene and the relative orientation of cameras are estimated. BARF uses a form of Bundle Adjustment that produces very accurate results. However, none of these methods can deal with outliers and artifacts. Furthermore, BARF does not learn any prior that is transferable to other image sequences.

(Vision) Transformers have become the state-of-the-art model for sequential data [6,19]. Transformers compute attention maps over the whole input sequence. Each token in a sequence is compared with every other token, which enables embeddings with a global context. It has been shown that Transformers can also be applied to image tasks [7,12]. Images can be treated as a sequence of image patches. The same idea has also been also extended to video [1,13]. Videos can be split into spatio-temporal patches and processed as a sequence. In this work, we want to train video transformers to aggregate image sequences. Using spatial and temporal information, it should be possible to determine whether a patch contains a defect or an outlier. The reconstruction should then reconstruct the underlying content by combining partial information from the larger context of the sequence.

3 Dataset

Figure 1 illustrates the data generation process. We use paintings from the Wiki Art dataset [4] as our ground-truth labels for reconstruction. Any other image dataset could also be used, but Wiki Art contains a large variety of artworks from various periods and art styles. We believe the diversity of paintings makes the reconstruction more challenging and reduces biases towards a specific type of image. We take an image from the dataset and use it as a texture on a plane in 3D. We randomize the generation of cameras by sampling from a range of 3D positions. The field of view of the camera is also randomly sampled to create varying zoom effects. This also creates a variety of intrinsic camera parameters. We randomly generate light sources. The type of light source is randomly sampled, e.g., spotlight, point light, or area light, their position, and corresponding parameters, such as intensity or size.

Furthermore, we generate geometric objects and put them approximately in between the plane and the camera's positions. We utilize Blender's ability to apply different materials to textures. We apply randomized materials to the image texture and occluding objects. The appearance of occluding object can be diffuse, shiny, reflective, and transparent. The material properties also change the effect lighting has on the plane. It changes the appearance of specularities, shadows, and overall brightness.

Finally, we iterate over the cameras and render the images. Blender's physically-based path tracer, Cycles, is used for rendering the final image. Path-tracing enables more realistic effects compared to rasterization. It allows the simulation of effects, such as reflections, retractions, and soft shadows, which are not possible in the original dataset generation pipeline [9].

Using this data generation, we create two datasets. One contains misaligned images; the other contains aligned images.

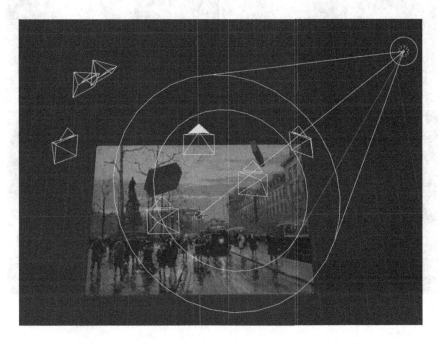

Fig. 1. Illustration of a randomly generated scene using Blender. The plane shows a painting. The white pyramids describe randomly generated cameras; the yellow cone describes a spotlight. Geometric objects serve as occlusions and cast shadows onto the plane. (Color figure online)

3.1 Aligned Dataset

We create one dataset that only consists of aligned image sequences. To enforce the alignment, we use a single static camera that perfectly fits the image plane. The camera's viewing direction is set to be perpendicular to the image plane and centered on the image plane. We adjust the vertical and horizontal field of view such that only the image can be seen. Furthermore, we generate a ground truth label by removing all light sources and occluding objects. We only use ambient illumination for rendering the picture.

Figure 2 shows a sequence of distorted images that are also aligned. Figure 3 shows the corresponding ground-truth label. We generate $\sim$ 15000 image sequences, each containing ten distorted images as our dataset. This dataset is used for training the image reconstruction task. We create another test set with 100 sequences, each containing 50 distorted images. We use the test set to analyze how well our models perform on varying sequence sizes.

Fig. 2. Four randomly generated images that are aligned.

Fig. 3. The image shows the output of our rendering pipeline when only ambient lighting is used. The image is free of any artifacts.

3.2 Misaligned Dataset

In addition to the aligned dataset, we generate images with perspective distortions. For each randomly generated camera, we render an image. In order to evaluate the image alignment with reconstruction, we also generate a single ground truth image as described in Sect. 3.1 under ambient lighting conditions. We need a common reference frame that is aligned with the ground-truth label in order to measure alignment and reconstruction simultaneously. Using the label directly as input creates an unwanted bias for the model. Therefore, another aligned image is created that contains distortions.

Figure 4 shows a sequence of distorted images. The first image contains various artifacts, but it is free of perspective distortions.

Homography. Since we take images of planar objects, all our images are related by 2D homographies. A point with pixel coordinates (x, y) in image i is projected onto the coordinates (x', y') in image j with the homography H_{ij}:

$$\lambda \begin{pmatrix} x' \\ y' \\ 1 \end{pmatrix} = \underbrace{\begin{bmatrix} h_{11} & h_{12} & h_{13} \\ h_{11} & h_{22} & h_{23} \\ h_{31} & h_{32} & h_{33} \end{bmatrix}}_{H_{ij}} \begin{pmatrix} x \\ y \\ 1 \end{pmatrix} \tag{1}$$

H_{ij} can be exactly computed from four point-correspondences. Since we know the camera's positions in space and their intrinsic parameters, we can calculate the projection points explicitly. We project each of the four corners X_k $k = 1, .., 4$ of the paintings into the i-th camera image plane $x_k^{(i)}$ using their projection matrices:

$$x_k^{(i)} = PX_k \tag{2}$$

$$= K_i[I|0] \begin{bmatrix} R_i & t_i \\ 0 & 1 \end{bmatrix} X_k \quad k = 1, .., 4 \tag{3}$$

(R_i, t_i) describes the global rotation and translation of the camera, K_i describes the intrinsic camera parameters. Using the four-point pairs $x_k^{(i)} \leftrightarrow x_k^{(j)}$ $k = 1, .., 4$, we can compute the homography using the Direct Linear Transform (DLT) [8].

Fig. 4. Four images containing perspective distortions. The first image is aligned with the camera's view, but it also contains image distortions.

4   Deep Image Alignment

In order to align the images, we chose to use convolutional feature maps as image descriptors. It has been shown by methods, such as Ransac-Flow [17] or Pixel-Perfect SfM [11], that it is possible to use convolutional layers as dense keypoint descriptors. Figure 5 shows two images and their corresponding feature maps.

Let $I \in \mathbb{R}^{H \times W}$ be an image and $I' = f_\theta(I) \in \mathbb{R}^{H \times W \times C}$ a feature map from a convolutional neural network. We can treat each individual pixel in I' as a key point with a descriptor of dimension C Using this approach any image of resolution $(H \times W)$ can be described as a collection of points described by a data matrix $X_I = (x_1, \cdots, x_{WH})^T \in \mathbb{R}^{HW \times C}$. Given two collection of keypoints X_1 and X_2 we can compute similarity scores S_{ij} between any point $x_i \in X_1$ and $x_j \in X_2$. We use the cosine similarity:

$$S(x_i, x_j) = \frac{<x_i, x_j>}{|x_i| \cdot |x_j|} \tag{4}$$

$$S = \text{norm}(X_2 X_1^T) \tag{5}$$

The score matrix S can be computed and does not require the images to have the same resolution. Every pixel in one image is compared with every pixel in another image. We can compute matches by filtering pairs with a maximal

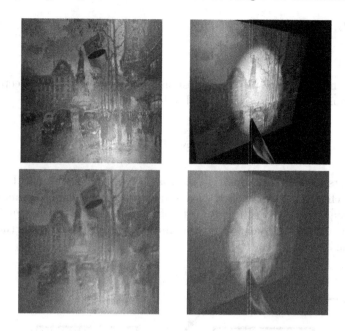

Fig. 5. A pair of images and their corresponding feature maps.

similarity score. Each point pair should be each other's best match; otherwise, there is ambiguity between descriptors. If $x_i = \arg\max_k S(x_k, x_j)$ and $x_j = \arg\max_k S(x_i, x_k)$, then (x_i, x_j) are a match.

The score matrix S and their matches can be computed efficiently. We additionally follow the implementation of Ransac-Flow by using image pyramids to make the descriptors and matching more scale invariant. For any image at scale $I_s \in \mathbb{R}^{sH \times sW}$, we can again compute keypoints $X_{I_s} \in \mathbb{R}^{k^2 HW \times C}$. We can concatenate the descriptors into a single matrix $X \in \mathbb{R}^{N \times C}$, where $N = \sum_k k^2 HW$. We can compute matches as before.

We can use the matches to estimate our homographies as described in 3.2. Using RANSAC, we can further filter out matches and estimate a homography. Given a homography described as a function $H_{ij} : (x, y) \mapsto (x', y')$, we can warp image $I_i(x, y)$ into $I_j(x, y)$ using $I_i(H_{ij}(x, y))$.

This is a general approach that can be integrated into any differentiable pipeline. For our implementation, we use the first three layers of a ResNet that was pre-trained on ImageNet1K.

5   Architecture

5.1   Deep Residual Sets

For our architecture, we use Deep Residual Sets as our baseline. Deep sets can be decomposed into an encoder ϕ and a decoder ρ as follows [21]:

$$f(x_1, x_2, \cdots, x_N) = \rho \left(\sum_{i=1}^{N} \phi(x_i) \right) \tag{6}$$

Deep sets have useful properties, such as permutation invariance. In the original approach, Deep Residual Sets have shown promising results for image reconstruction [9]. The architecture consists of residual blocks, downsampling, and upsampling layers. Further average pooling was used to aggregate the embeddings along the sequence (Fig. 6).

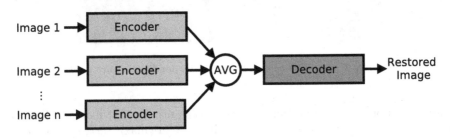

Fig. 6. Initial architecture (figure taken from [9]).

The main disadvantage of deep sets is that they struggle to remove outliers along the sequence. If an image contains an occlusion, the corresponding embedding of the outlier is pooled into the final embedding. The decoder often struggles to remove them and can only attenuate these artifacts.

In order to remove outliers, they must first be identified within the sequence using contextual information. Deep sets analyze each element independently and, therefore, can't solve this problem. Transformer models, on the other hand, provide a better solution for this problem since they compute attention maps over the whole sequence.

5.2   Video Swin Transformer

Transformers have been shown to be powerful sequential models [6,19]. Transformers compute attention over a sequence by computing pairwise embeddings between tokens. This principle allows for very general sequence processing. However, their main disadvantage is their quadratic memory consumption with regard to the sequence length. Applying them to high-dimensional images is not a trivial task. Transformers have been successfully applied to vision tasks by using special partitioning schemes on images [7]. Images aren't processed pixel by pixel but rather over larger patches. The original Vision Transformer (ViT) has a low inductive bias, which allows them to learn more general feature extraction, but also increases training time. Several architectures have been proposed to improve the efficiency of vision transformer models.

Swin transformers provide an efficient way to process images and videos as sequences [12]. Figure 7 illustrates how a Swin transformer operates. Given is an image consisting of 8×8 pixels. Using a predefined window size, here 4×4, the k-th layer splits the input into 2×2 patches. The patches are passed to a transformer layer, and self-attention maps are computed. In the next layer, the windows are shifted by half the window size using a cyclic shift. The new patches are also passed to a self-attention layer. The combination of both layers allows efficient computation of attention across non-overlapping

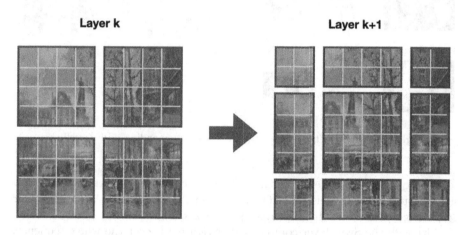

Fig. 7. An illustration of the partitioning scheme of two consecutive Swin layers. The input of layer k consists of $W \times W$ pixels. Using a window size of $M \times M$ creates $\frac{W}{M} \times \frac{W}{M}$ patches. In layer $k + 1$ the windows are shifted by $\frac{M}{2} \times \frac{M}{2}$.

The same concept has been extended to video with Video Swin Transformers [13]. The window size is extended with a time dimension. Given a video with size $T \times H \times W$ and a window size $P \times M \times M$ the video is divided into spatio-temporal patches of size $\frac{T}{P} \times \frac{H}{M} \times \frac{W}{M}$.

5.3 Image Reconstruction Using Swin Transformers

Although Deep Residual Sets provide a good baseline for image reconstruction, their main disadvantage is their lack of contextual information between images. We would like to alleviate this disadvantage by replacing the pooling layer with a transformer model. Specifically, we apply a Video Swin Transformer on the concatenated embeddings of the individual images. Figure 8 illustrates our architecture. We use residual blocks for the encoding of each individual image and for the final decoding. The feature maps are concatenated, processed as a sequence, and given into the Swin layers. The Swin transformer is primarily used for aggregating information across the sequence. We use the downsampling and upsampling layers within our residual blocks. We do not use any downsampling or merging layers from the original Swin transformer.

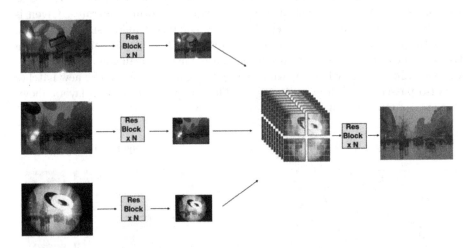

Fig. 8. The architecture uses residual blocks for encoding and decoding.

We explore three different Swin modules by changing the temporal window size. We use three models DIAR(1, 7, 7), DIAR(2, 7, 7) and DIAR(3, 7, 7). Our graphics card could not handle larger patch sizes.

Although the Swin layer computes attention maps over the whole sequence, it does not aggregate information into a single element as a pooling layer does. Let $[x_1, \cdots, x_T] \in \mathbb{R}^{(T,H,W,C)}$ be the stacked feature maps with dimensionality (H, W, C). Let $[e_1, \cdots, e_T] = Swin(x) \in \mathbb{R}^{(T,H,W,C)}$ be the computed embedding from the Swin layer. We explore various methods of aggregating the stacked embeddings into a single feature map for reconstruction.

– Average pooling without embedding (Deep sets): $y = \sum_i x_i$
– Average pooling with embedding: $y = \sum_i e_i$
– Weighted sum: $y = \sum x_i \sigma(e)_i$, where $\sigma()$ describes the softmax function.

5.4   Training

All models are trained on the synthetic dataset of aligned sequences. The dataset contains 15000 image sequences. We use 10% as a validation set. We train our models on an NVIDIA RTX 3090 with 24 GB memory. We train with a batch size of 20 for 100 epochs. We use the Adam optimizer with a learning rate of $\lambda = 0.001$.

6   Evaluation

6.1   Aggregation

As mentioned in Sect. 5.3 we evaluate different aggregation methods. We compare the original Deep Sets with Swin-based methods. Figure 9 shows the progression of the models on the validation set performance.

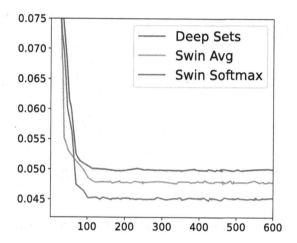

Fig. 9. Deep sets clearly fall behind attention-based models. Aggregating the embeddings using a weighted sum provides the best reconstruction.

The graphic clearly shows that transformers improve aggregation. The figure also indicates that computing a softmax and aggregating the individual feature maps with a weighted sum is superior to average pooling over the Swin embedding. Based on these results, all further Swin models use softmax.

6.2   Image Reconstruction

We use a test set containing 100 sequences, each with 50 distorted images. To evaluate our models, we use the metrics root-mean-squared error (RMSE), peak signal-to-noise ratio (PSNR), and structural similarity index measure (SSIM). In addition to our deep learning methods, we compare them with non-deep learning methods that provide a reasonable baseline for methods that deal with outlier removal. The following methods are also evaluated:

- Median of images
- Average of images
- Robust PCA (RPCA) [3],
- Intrinsic image decomposition (MLE) [20]

The Figs. 10,11 and 12 illustrate the average performance of each model given different sequence lengths. The deep learning models have a by far lower RMSE and higher PSNR. All deep learning methods have low SSIM (Figs. 13 and 14).

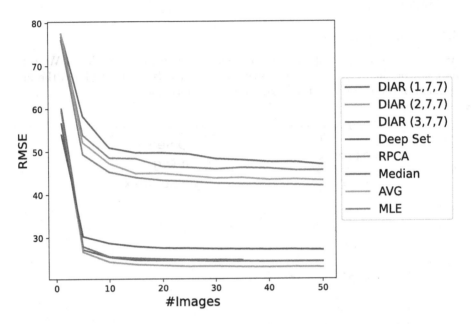

Fig. 10. The graph shows the average RMSE for different input lengths.

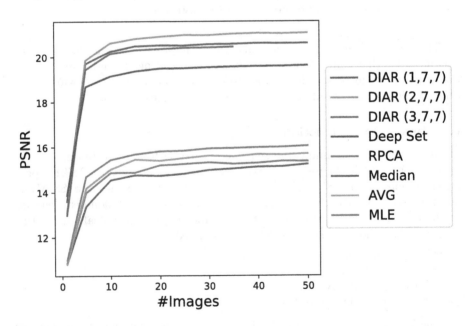

Fig. 11. The graph shows the average PSNR for different input lengths.

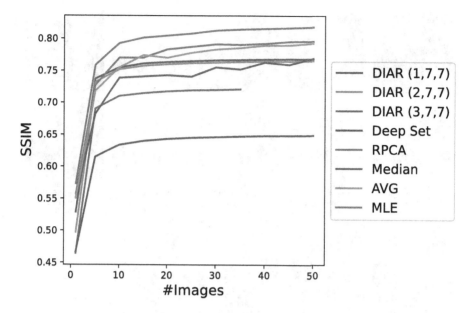

Fig. 12. The graph shows the average SSIM for different input lengths.

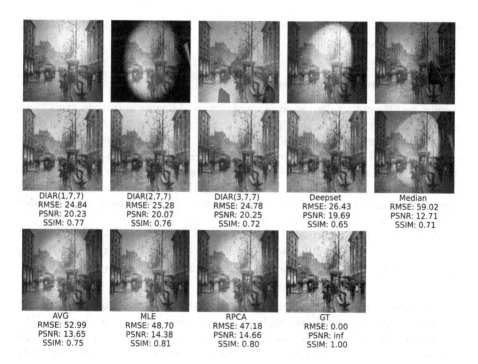

Fig. 13. The first row shows a distorted sequence. The results below show the reconstruction of various methods.

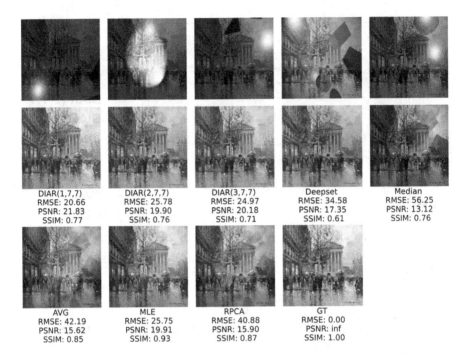

Fig. 14. The first row shows a distorted sequence. The results below show the reconstruction of various methods.

6.3 Alignment and Reconstruction:

Finally, we attempt to align a sequence of distorted images and reconstruct them using an image processing pipeline that consists of differentiable and trainable components. First, we use a pre-trained ResNet to compute dense feature maps for each image. Then we compute pairwise matches using cosine similarity. With the computed matches, we can estimate a homography between each image and a reference frame. We align each image with the reference frame. Finally, we apply our trained neural networks for reconstruction. We also apply our other methods to have a comparison.

We measure the quality of the alignment by using our image metrics on the reconstructions. Additionally, we can compare the quality of the homography directly. We use two error metrics to evaluate the alignment error.

1. Given the ground-truth matrix H and an estimate H', we can't directly take the norm between them. Homographies are equivalent under scale , however $|H - H'| \neq |\lambda H - H'|$. We normalize both homographies, such that their determinants are equal to 1: $det(\hat{H}) = det(\hat{H}') = 1$. Figure 19 visualizes the distribution of the error over all images.

2 Given the ground-truth matrix H and an estimate H', we calculate the projection error. We define four fixed point $x_1 = (-1, -1), x_2 = (1, -1), x_3 = (-1, 1), x_4 = (1, 1)$. We measure the average projection error $|Hx_i - H'x_i|$

The boxplots Figs. 15, 16 and 17 show how each reconstruction method deals with the aligned/misaligned images. The transformer seems to be able to handle the perspective distortions better. This might be due to the fact that the Swin transformers learn to understand outliers. They might be better at dealing with complete misalignment or gross distortions.

$$\hat{H} = \frac{1}{\sqrt[3]{det(H)}} H \tag{7}$$

We then compute the norm between them.

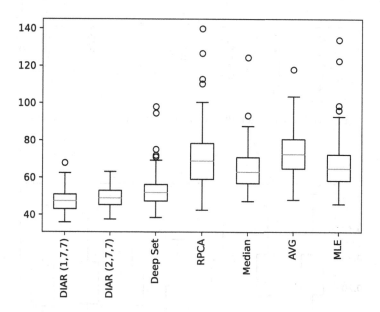

Fig. 15. Box plot for RMSE for each reconstruction method.

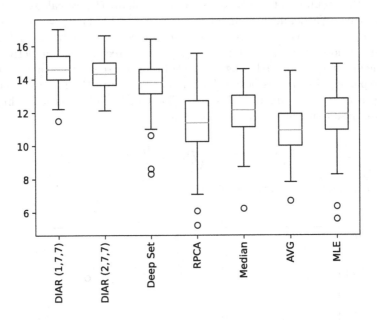

Fig. 16. Box plot for PSNR for each reconstruction method.

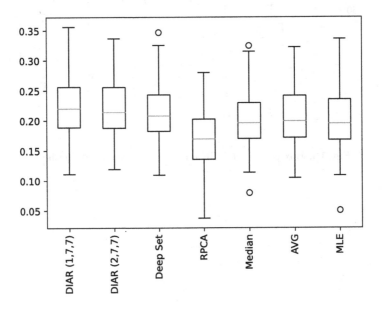

Fig. 17. Box plot for SSIM for each reconstruction method.

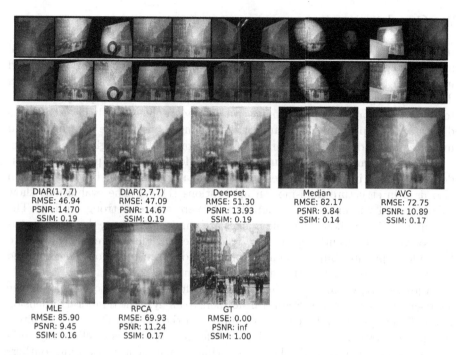

Fig. 18. The first row shows a sequence of distorted images. The second row shows the estimated alignment. The results of each reconstruction method are also shown.

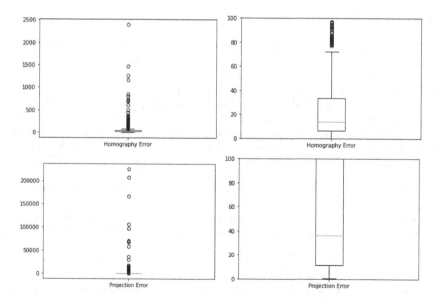

Fig. 19. The box plots illustrate the distribution of projection errors and homography errors. The box plots on the right are zoomed in order to see the median. The box plot indicates that the data is skewed and contains large outliers.

7   Conclusion

In this paper, we attempted to solve two problems simultaneously: alignment of images using deep image features and reconstructing the content from distorted images. For this, we created a synthetic dataset that contains various distortions due to lighting, shadows, and occlusion. Furthermore, we added perspective distortions with corresponding ground-truth homographies. We believe that this dataset can be particularly useful for developing robust image descriptors and matching methods due to the variety of distortions and challenging illumination.

We implement a general-purpose method for computing point correspondences between images using neural feature maps. Similar methods have been also used in structure-from-motion applications [11,17]. The evaluations show that many of the images are aligned, but there also are strong outliers. The example in Fig. 18 shows that the images are aligned. However, the alignment is too coarse for an accurate pixel-wise reconstruction. Further refinement has to be made. A possible improvement is to use bundle adjustment on the computed image matches to improve the initial estimation.

Additionally, we discussed the use of transformers and attention for image aggregation tasks. We used Swin transformers to analyze the temporal dimension more efficiently. This allowed us to improve on the original Deep Set architecture [9]. The evaluations showed that transformers enable us to efficiently combine information from multiple images while simultaneously avoiding outliers and artifacts.

References

1. Arnab, A., Dehghani, M., Heigold, G., Sun, C., Lučić, M., Schmid, C.: Vivit: a video vision transformer. In: Proceedings of the IEEE/CVF International Conference on Computer Vision, pp. 6836–6846 (2021)
2. Balntas, V., Lenc, K., Vedaldi, A., Mikolajczyk, K.: Hpatches: a benchmark and evaluation of handcrafted and learned local descriptors. In: CVPR (2017)
3. Bouwmans, T., Javed, S., Zhang, H., Lin, Z., Otazo, R.: On the applications of robust PCA in image and video processing. Proc. IEEE **106**(8), 1427–1457 (2018)
4. Danielczuk, M., et al.: Segmenting unknown 3d objects from real depth images using mask R-CNN trained on synthetic data. In: Proceedings of IEEE International Conference on Robotics and Automation (ICRA) (2019)
5. DeTone, D., Malisiewicz, T., Rabinovich, A.: Deep image homography estimation. arXiv preprint arXiv:1606.03798 (2016)
6. Devlin, J., Chang, M.W., Lee, K., Toutanova, K.: Bert: Pre-training of deep bidirectional transformers for language understanding. arXiv preprint arXiv:1810.04805 (2018)
7. Dosovitskiy, A., et al.: An image is worth 16 × 16 words: Transformers for image recognition at scale. arXiv preprint arXiv:2010.11929 (2020)
8. Hartley, R., Zisserman, A.: Multiple View Geometry in Computer Vision. Cambridge University Press, Cambridge (2003)
9. Kwiatkowski, M., Hellwich, O.: Specularity, shadow, and occlusion removal from image sequences using deep residual sets. In: VISIGRAPP (4: VISAPP), pp. 118–125 (2022)

10. Lin, C.H., Ma, W.C., Torralba, A., Lucey, S.: Barf: Bundle-adjusting neural radiance fields. In: Proceedings of the IEEE/CVF International Conference on Computer Vision, pp. 5741–5751 (2021)

11. Lindenberger, P., Sarlin, P.E., Larsson, V., Pollefeys, M.: Pixel-perfect structure-from-motion with featuremetric refinement. In: Proceedings of the IEEE/CVF International Conference on Computer Vision, pp. 5987–5997 (2021)

12. Liu, Z., et al.: Swin transformer: hierarchical vision transformer using shifted windows. In: Proceedings of the IEEE/CVF International Conference on Computer Vision. pp. 10012–10022 (2021)

13. Liu, Z., et al.: Video Swin transformer. In: Proceedings of the IEEE/CVF Conference on Computer Vision and Pattern Recognition, pp. 3202–3211 (2022)

14. Lowe, D.G.: Distinctive image features from scale-invariant keypoints. Int. J. Comput. Vision $60(2)$, 91–110 (2004)

15. Nie, L., Lin, C., Liao, K., Liu, S., Zhao, Y.: Unsupervised deep image stitching: Reconstructing stitched features to images. IEEE Trans. Image Process. 30, 6184–6197 (2021)

16. Sarlin, P.E., DeTone, D., Malisiewicz, T., Rabinovich, A.: Superglue: learning feature matching with graph neural networks. In: Proceedings of the IEEE/CVF Conference on Computer Vision Ana Pattern Recognition, pp. 4938–4947 (2020)

17. Zeiler, M.D., Fergus, R.: Visualizing and understanding convolutional networks. In: Fleet, D., Pajdla, T., Schiele, B., Tuytelaars, T. (eds.) ECCV 2014. LNCS, vol. 8689, pp. 818–833. Springer, Cham (2014). https://doi.org/10.1007/978-3-319-10590-1_53

18. Sun, J., Shen, Z., Wang, Y., Bao, H., Zhou, X.: LOFTR: detectoR-free local feature matching with transformers. In: Proceedings of the IEEE/CVF Conference on Computer Vision and Pattern Recognition (CVPR), pp. 8922–8931, June 2021)

19. Vaswani, A., et al.: Attention is all you need. In:Advances in Neural Information Processing Systems, vol. 30 (2017)

20. Weiss, Y.: Deriving intrinsic images from image sequences. In: Proceedings Eighth IEEE International Conference on Computer Vision. ICCV 2001, vol. 2, pp. 68–75. IEEE (2001)

21. Zaheer, M., Kottur, S., Ravanbakhsh, S., Poczos, B., Salakhutdinov, R.R., Smola, A.J.: Deep sets. In: Advances in Neural Information Processing Systems, vol. 30 (2017)

Active Learning with Data Augmentation Under Small vs Large Dataset Regimes for Semantic-KITTI Dataset

Ngoc Phuong Anh Duong, Alexandre Almin, Léo Lemarié,
and B. Ravi Kiran(✉) ⓘ

Navya, Machine Learning, Paris, France
{anh.duong,alexandre.almin,leo.lemarie,ravi.kiran}@navya.tech
https://navya.tech/en/

Abstract. Active Learning (AL) has remained relatively unexplored for LiDAR perception tasks in autonomous driving datasets. In this study we evaluate Bayesian active learning methods applied to the task of dataset distillation or core subset selection (subset with near equivalent performance as full dataset). We also study the effect of application of data augmentation (DA) within Bayesian AL based dataset distillation. We perform these experiments on the full Semantic-KITTI dataset. We extend our study over our existing work [14] only on 1/4th of the same dataset. Addition of DA and BALD have a negative impact over the labeling efficiency and thus the capacity to distill datasets. We demonstrate key issues in designing a functional AL framework and finally conclude with a review of challenges in real world active learning.

Keywords: Active learning · Point clouds · Semantic segmentation · Data augmentation · Label efficiency · Dataset distillation

1 Introduction

Autonomous driving perception datasets in the point cloud domain including Semantic-KITTI [8] and Nuscenes [10] provide a large variety of driving scenarios & lighting conditions, along with variation in the poses of on-road obstacles. Large scale datasets are created across different sensor sets, vehicles and sites. There are multiple challenges in creating a functional industrial grade autonomous driving dataset [28]. During the phase of creating a dataset, these following key steps are generally followed:

- Defining the operation design domain of operation of the perception models. This involves parameters (but are not limited to) such as minimum & maximum distance, speed & illumination, classes to be recognized in the scene, relative configurations of objects or classes w.r.t ego-vehicle.
- Defining sensor set (camera, LiDAR, RADAR, ...), number of sensors, their extrinsics & intrinsic parameters, the blind spots, the intersection in field of views.
- Choosing target vehicles and locations over which logs should be collected,

A. A. de Sousa et al. (Eds.): VISIGRAPP 2022, CCIS 1815, pp. 268–280, 2023.
https://doi.org/10.1007/978-3-031-45725-8_13

- Collecting logs given the Operational Domain Design (ODD) parameters [13], vehicles and various geographical locations,
- Sampling key frames from perception data and selecting samples to annotate,
- Creating a curated labeled dataset by using human experts annotators
- Incrementally improving the dataset for a given model by using active learning strategies.

As we observe the active learning strategies appear after an initial rich dataset has been created. We shall study how active learning strategies work in a large dataset regime in this paper. Large-scale point clouds datasets have high redundancy that makes training of Deep Neural Network (DNN) architectures costlier for very little gain in performance. This redundancy is mainly due to the temporal correlation between point clouds scans, the similar urban environments and the symmetries in the driving environment (driving in opposite directions at the same location). Hence, data redundancy can be seen as the similarity between any pair of point clouds resulting from geometric transformations as a consequence of ego-vehicle movement along with changes in the environment. Data augmentations (DA) are transformations on the input samples that enable DNNs to learn invariances and/or equivariances to said transformations [3]. DA provides a natural way to model the geometric transformations to point clouds in large-scale datasets due to ego-motion of the vehicle.

This extended study following our paper [14] demonstrates results on full dataset distillation on the Semantic-KITTI dataset. In the original study we evaluated the effect of data augmentation on the quality of heuristic function to select informative samples in the active learning loop. We experimented on a 6000 samples train subset and 2000 samples test subset of Semantic-KITTI. The results showed an increase in performance of label efficiency that data augmentation methods achieved. In this study we extend the same experiments to the full dataset and note several negative results in label efficiency. We provide possible explanations and demonstrate key challenges in active learning pipeline in real the world.

In the current study we have extended our previous work and performed the dataset distillation over the complete Semantic-KITTI dataset. Contributions include:

1. An evaluation of Bayesian AL methods on the complete Semantic-KITTI dataset using data augmentation as well as heuristics from BAAL libraries [5,6].
2. We compare the AL study from [14] that is performed on a smaller subset (1/4th) of same dataset with the full study, and demonstrate that the data augmentation schemes as well as BALD Bayesian heuristic have negligible gains over a random sampler. We point out the key issues underlying this poor performance.
3. A qualitative analysis on labelling efficiency with increasing dataset size.
4. An ablation study comparing 2 different models: SqueezeSegv2 and SalsaNext within an AL framework.
5. A summary of key real-world challenges in active learning.

Like many previous studies on AL, we do not explicitly quantify the amount of redundancy in the datasets and purely determine the trade-off of model performance with smaller subsets w.r.t the original dataset.

1.1 State of the Art

Autonomous vehicles require large amounts of perception data. Their data pipelines frequently include active learning methods to amortize the cost of new incoming informative data for existing models. We summarize in this section a quick survey of AL pipelines for deep learning models used in AV perception tasks. Active learning pipelines have changed with the introduction of deep learning methods, readers can find a state of the art review by authors [26].

Authors [16] evaluate AL pipeline for 3D object detection in point clouds which generate 2D region proposals to locate frustums containing object in LiDAR 3D space for annotation. For point clouds semantic segmentation, LESS [22] divides LiDAR sequence into a set of connected components for both human and pseudo labeling. LiDAL [20] exploits the inter-frame uncertainty and diversity among LiDAR frames.

One of the key challenges in uncertainty-based methods (later demonstrated in Sect. 3.2) in AV datasets is the temporal correlation among samples due to local point cloud density and limited ego-vehicle movement, which leads to a selection of similar or redundant samples having high uncertainty scores. Authors [18] proposed a scalable production system for object detection that makes use of uncertainty score and feature vector embeddings of each image in diversity-based methods to encourage both uncertainty and diversity in the selection. ReDAL [30] employs Similar Region Penalization, a greedy algorithm considering both informative and diverse regions for label acquisition for point clouds semantic segmentation. Our later work [2] proposed a distance-based sampling method for point clouds sequential datasets as an approximation sampling before uncertainty computation which not only ensures the diversity in selection, but also reduces the expensive uncertainty computation for point clouds samples.

Besides AL heuristics and approximate sampling, there are several other strategies can be integrated into typical AL pipeline to improve labeling efficiency. Authors [17] take advantages of unlabeled data using semi-supervised learning (SSL) to distill information from unlabeled data in training. In the real-world, self-training can also boost model performance along with AL with the least human labeling effort.

2 Methodology

Following our previous study [14] on Semantic-KITTI dataset [8] we now use the full dataset. We evaluate the same models SqueezeSegV2 [29], SalsaNext [12] with MontreCarlo Dropout layer. We use the range image representation of pointclouds required by the Rangenet++ architectures by authors [24].

We shall use the same terminology as [14] and redirect users to definitions of *Labeled dataset*, *Labeled pool* $L \subset D$ and a unlabeled pool $U \subset D$ s.t $L \cup U = D$. The Query size B, also called a *budget*, defines how many samples we add to in each step of AL loop. Acquisition function, known as heuristic, provides uncertainty score for each pixel. T refers to the number of MC iterations. *Subset model* f_L refers to model trained L, *Aggregation function* $a : \mathbb{R}^{W \times H \times C \times T} \rightarrow \mathbb{R}^+$ that aggregates scores over pixels.

Table 1. Active learning (AL) parameter setup (first line for [14] result).

Data related parameters			AL Hyper parameters				
Range image resolution	Total pool size	Test pool size	Init set size	Budget	MC Dropout	AL steps	Aggregation
1024x64	6000	2000	240	240	0.2	25	sum
Range image resolution	Total pool size	Test pool size	Init set size	Budget	MC Dropout	AL steps	Aggregation
1024x64	16241	6960	1041	800	0.2	20	sum
Hyper parameters for each AL step							
Max train iterations	Learning rate (LR)	LR decay	Weight decay	Batch size	Early stopping		
					Evaluation period	Metric	Patience
100000	0.01	0.99	0.0001	16	500	train mIoU	15

In our previous study [14] we have identified BALD [19], which uses MC Iterations to select samples maximizing information gain between the predictions from model parameters, to be a robust heuristic function. We apply DA (same as in our previous study [14]) on the range image projection. Performance of the AL pipeline for coreset selection is still performed using *Labeling efficiency*, while the model's performance is evaluated using mIoU for the segmentation task.

In this study, we evaluated the performance of BALD and the effect of data augmentation (DA) on the full Semantic-KITTI, as an extension our existing work [14] which is only on 1/4th of the same dataset. As in [14], we follow a Bayesian AL loop using MC Dropout with *sum* as an aggregation function to obtain the final score per range image. Top $B(budget)$ samples of the unlabeled pool ranked based on these scores are selected for each AL step. The total number of AL steps can be deduced from budget size, $n_{AL} = |D|/B$. The difference in experimental setup is in table 1. We use 16000 randomly chosen samples from Semantic-KITTI over the 23201 samples available. The rest is used as test set. At each training step, we train from scratch, as suggested by [7].

We evaluate LE mIoU as our metric on the test set of 6960 samples. For quicker training, we use early stopping based on the stability of training mIoU over *patience * evaluation_period* iterations.

3   Validation and Results

The Fig. 1, demonstrates all the trainings performed on the full Semantic-KITTI dataset. The models SalsaNext (SN) and SqueezeSegv2 (SSV2) were chosen to be evaluated. The models both use rangenet based representations as mentioned earlier. The SSV2 model was trained with and without data augmentation, using a baseline random sampler, the model was also evaluated with BALD heuristic function. SN model was mainly evaluated in the AL framework using data augmentation and with BALD.

The goals here have been to compare the effect of:

- Data augmentation on the label efficiency over a large dataset.
- Difference in model capacity (SN with 6.7M parameters vs SSV2 with 1M parameters).
- Difference in performance of random sampler vs the BALD heuristic (Fig. 1).

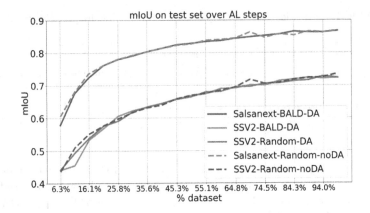

Fig. 1. Mean IoU vs dataset size (in percentage) using random and BALD heuristic based samplers under the effect of data augmentation.

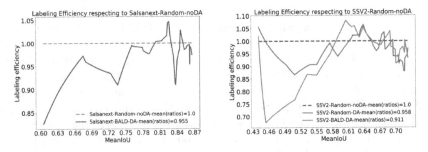

Fig. 2. SalsaNext & SSV2 models evaluated w.r.t the Random sampling baseline. The plots demonstrate the label efficiency.

3.1   Class Based Learning Efficiency

In this section we study the variation of ClassIoU for all classes in the Semantic-KITTI dataset. Along with this we also study the variation from mIoU of the fully supervised (FS) model, expressed by:

$$\Delta cIOU[i] = cIoU[i] - mIoU_{\text{FS}} \tag{1}$$

where i is the index of the active learning loop (or the perception of dataset). This score basically subtracts the mean performance away from the class IoU scores to demon-strate deviations from the mean. The objective of such as measure is to demonstrate the rate at which each class IoU reaches its maximum contribution.

The $\Delta cIOU[i]$ score represents the deviation of the class IoU from the models full supervised mean performance. When this deviation is positive and large, these represent classes that have been learnt efficiently at the AL-Step i, while negative scores represent classes that have been learnt poorly. This score enables us to determine visually when each class reaches its maximum performance and

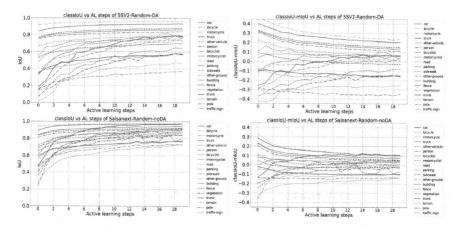

Fig. 3. Top Left: Class IoU for SSV2 model Top Right: Deviation from mean IoU from Eq. 1. Bottom, the same for the SalsaNext model.

decide when any incremental addition of samples would have little impact on the final CioU.

Class-frequency and ClassIoU: In Fig. 3 we observe that several majority classes like ROAD, TERRAIN, BUILDING, VEGETATION do not demonstrate any large change in their IoUs after the 6th AL step, while classes such as BICYCLE, POLE, PERSON, OTHER VEHICLE are the slowest to learn their maximum performance. The majority classes produce a positive deviation from mIoU while the least frequent classes produce a negative deviation from mIoU.

DA Effect on ClassIoU: In Fig. 4 we plot the $\Delta cIOU[i]$ scores to demonstrate how fast different classes are learnt over the AL loop (different subset sizes of the full dataset). With this plot we would like to observe the change in sample complexity for each class with and without data augmentations using baseline random sampling.

Model Complexity on ClassIoU: We evaluate two models on the Semantic-KITTI dataset: SSV2 model vs SalsaNext model. We compare the performances of these models in terms of how fast they learn different classes, see Fig. 5. We observe that majority of classes have had a large jump within the first 3–4 AL steps for the SalsaNext model, demonstrate how model capacity plays an important role in the sample complexity of learning certain classes.

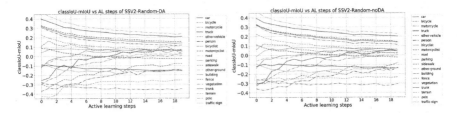

Fig. 4. Deviation of Class IoU from mIoU for the SSV2 model: with and without data augmentation applied.

3.2 Dataset Size Growth: 1/4 Semantic-KITTI vs Full Semantic-KITTI

In our previous study on Semantic-KITTI [14] we have evaluated the performance of AL methods while applying data augmentation on 1/4th subset of the Semantic-KITTI dataset. As expected, DA sampled harder samples by eliminating similar samples learnt by invariance. That is to say, models trained with DA are prone to select samples different from the trained samples and their transformations, thus reducing redundancy in the selection.

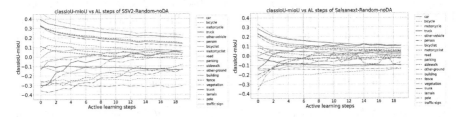

Fig. 5. Deviation of ClassIoU from mIoU comparision: Between SSV2 and SN models.

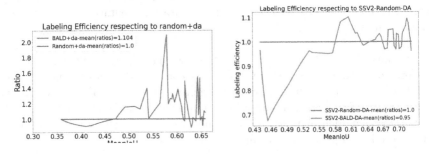

Fig. 6. Comparison of the BALD performance. Left: AL training on Semantic-KITTI subset 1/4 from [14], Right: AL training on Semantic-KITTI full dataset from this study. We observe that the two LE are poor in the initial steps, with subsequent increases in the future AL steps.

On the other hand, although DA significantly reduce redundancy in 1/4 Semantic-KITTI experiments, there is almost no increment in the gain by DA in full Semantic-KITTI experiments. This can be seen in Fig. 6 and could be mainly attributed to the following reasons (we hypothesize):

1. Larger dataset includes larger amount of near similar or redundant samples, but all standalone uncertainty-based methods still encounter the problem of high-score similar samples. Semantic-KITTI is a sequential dataset and thus contain similar scans due to temporal correlation. Thus random sampling breaks this redundancy, while methods like BALD are unable to due to above said reasons. Potential solutions for this problem are mentioned in future work and challenges section below.
2. The gain by DA is getting smaller as dataset size increases because some augmented samples can be found in larger dataset (when dataset is getting larger) or test domain.
3. From the hypothesis, uncorrelated-to-real-world DA can increase uncertainty in predictions of unnecessary sample points, leading wrong prediction and impractical sampling selection.

3.3   t-SNE Problem Analysis

t-SNE [23] is a technique used to visualize high-dimensional data in low-dimensional spaces such as 2D or 3D by minimizing Kullback-Leibler divergence between the low-dimensional distribution and the high-dimensional distribution.

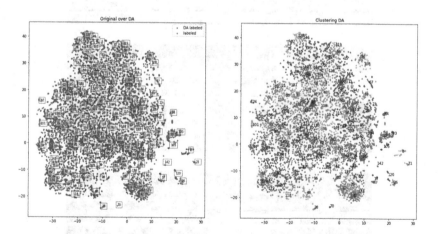

Fig. 7. Left image is a t-SNE visualization of labeled and DA(labeled) at step 0. Right image is t-SNE visualization of DA(labeled) clustering region by K-means.

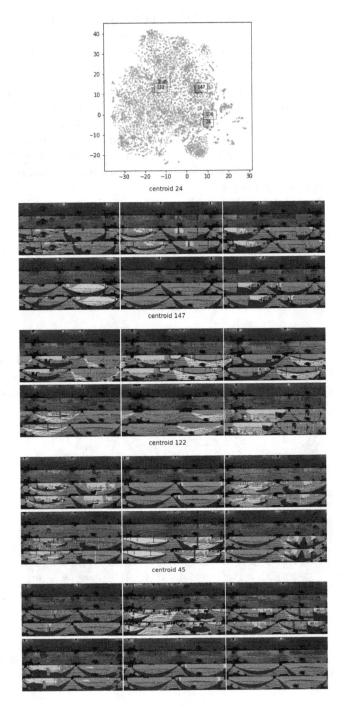

Fig. 8. Visualization of samples deviating from dataset distribution.

To visualize whether DA is relevant for Semantic-KITTI, we use t-SNE to reduce score images of labeled and DA(labeled) at AL step 0 of Semantic-KITTI/4's to 2D vector and plot on 2D axes (Fig. 7). The samples located in regions with dense red color are out-of-training-set-distribution candidates at AL step 0. Visualization of the candidates is in Fig. 8.

In the Fig. 9, deep red spots show that there are a lot of selected high-score samples concentrated in the same location.

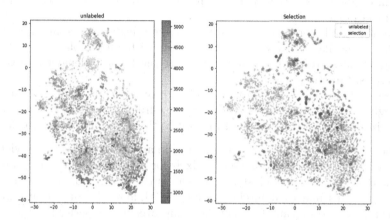

Fig. 9. Left image is a t-SNE visualization of unlabeled pool at step 0, whose colors are corresponding to heuristic scores. Right image is the t-SNE visualization of selected samples and unlabeled pool.

4   Conclusion

Core subset extraction/dataset distillation experiments were carried out on Semantic-KITTI dataset using SalsaNext and SSV2 models. The results of data augmentation and BALD heuristic were limited and did not perform any better than a random sampling method, the first baseline in active learning methods. These limited improvements are an important observation for active learning benchmarks, even though they constitute in marginal gains, and aids further studies to focus on other ways to improve labeling efficiency.

4.1   Challenges and Future Scope

Active learning strategies struggle with large-scale datasets such as point clouds in the real-world scenario. Data augmentation's have a strong effect on the quality of the heuristic function. It is thus key to evaluate data augmentation schemes that are dataset dependant, especially when unlabeled pool is just a small subset of target domain. Inappropriate or overwhelming augmentation can cause out-of-distribution, reducing model bias to target domain. [15] propose a adaptive data augmentation algorithm for image classification, which looks for a small transform maximizing the loss on that transformed sample.

The final aggregation score in an active learning framework is a cruicial choice. Aggregation is required when working on detection or segmentation tasks, while most AL study has been focused on classification. Here are a few choices of aggregation functions and how they affect the final ranking of images from which to sample:

- Sum of all scores: select a sample having a balance of high score and high number of elements.
- Average of all scores: select a sample having a high score comparable to the others regardless of the number of elements within a sample.
- Max of all scores: select a sample having the highest element scores of all samples, targeting noises.
- Weighted average of all scores: similar to average but focus on the given weights. The class weights can be inverse-frequency class weights or customized based on the use case to prioritize the selection for certain classes.

It is noted that for our proposed method, sum and average eventually yield the same rankings because the number of pixels for range images are constant.

Another key issue in industrial datasets is the filtering or exclusion of corrupted or outlier images/pointclouds from the AL loop. [11] show that removing top highest uncertain samples as outliers improves model performances.

To avoid selection of similar high-score samples and to reduce the sensitivity and bias of the model when training on a small dataset, a potential strategy can be an integration of diversity. Some hybrid methods, such as [4,21,27,31], are shown to have more competitive results comparing to standalone uncertainty-based methods for datasets containing high rate of redundancy, but their computations are often costly for large scale point clouds datasets. Another strategy is using temporal information to sample [1] before or after uncertainty computation. Although it has low computation cost, it cannot ensure the dissimilarity among different samples.

Dropout Issues: According to authors [11,25], MC Dropout is observed to lack of diversity for uncertainty estimation. To address this problem, [9,11] use multiple checkpoints during training epochs from different random seeds.

Finally, Pool-based AL might not be a proper AL strategy in real-world scenario for large scale datasets because of unlimited instances streamed sequentially, but limited at any given time. Due to memory limitation, it is impossible to store or re-process all past instances. In this case, stream-based methods are more pertinent by querying annotator for each sample coming from the stream. Although this type of query is often computationally inexpensive, the selected samples are not as informative as the ones selected by pool-based AL due to the lack of exploitation underlying distribution of datasets.

Active learning at large dataset regimes are computationally difficult to optimize and furthermore leads to various design issues in heuristics function definition, subsampling policies to handle large unlabeled pools, and finally storage of large scale logged data.

Acknowledgements. This work was granted access to HPC resources of [TGCC/CINES/IDRIS] under the allocation 2021- [AD011012836] made by GENCI (Grand Equipment National de Calcul Intensif). It is also part of the Deep Learning Segmentation (DLS) project financed by ADEME.

References

1. Aghdam, H.H., Gonzalez-Garcia, A., van de Weijer, J., López, A.M.: Active learning for deep detection neural networks (2019). https://doi.org/10.48550/ARXIV.1911.09168, https://arxiv.org/abs/1911.09168
2. Almin, A., Lemarié, L., Duong, A., Kiran, B.R.: Navya3dseg - Navya 3d semantic segmentation dataset; split generation for autonomous vehicles (2023). https://doi.org/10.48550/ARXIV.2302.08292, https://arxiv.org/abs/2302.08292
3. Anselmi, F., Rosasco, L., Poggio, T.: On invariance and selectivity in representation learning. Inf. Inference J. IMA **5**(2), 134–158 (2016)
4. Ash, J.T., Zhang, C., Krishnamurthy, A., Langford, J., Agarwal, A.: Deep batch active learning by diverse, uncertain gradient lower bounds (2020)
5. Atighehchian, P., Branchaud-Charron, F., Freyberg, J., Pardinas, R., Schell, L.: Baal, a Bayesian active learning library (2019). https://github.com/ElementAI/baal/
6. Atighehchian, P., Branchaud-Charron, F., Lacoste, A.: Bayesian active learning for production, a systematic study and a reusable library (2020)
7. Beck, N., Sivasubramanian, D., Dani, A., Ramakrishnan, G., Iyer, R.: Effective evaluation of deep active learning on image classification tasks (2021)
8. Behley, J., et al.: Semantickitti: a dataset for semantic scene understanding of lidar sequences (2019)
9. Bengar, J.Z., et al.: Temporal coherence for active learning in videos (2019). https://doi.org/10.48550/ARXIV.1908.11757, https://arxiv.org/abs/1908.11757
10. Caesar, H., et al.: nuscenes: A multimodal dataset for autonomous driving (2020)
11. Chitta, K., Alvarez, J.M., Haussmann, E., Farabet, C.: Training data subset search with ensemble active learning. arXiv preprint arXiv:1905.12737 (2019)
12. Cortinhal, T., Tzelepis, G., Aksoy, E.E.: Salsanext: fast, uncertainty-aware semantic segmentation of lidar point clouds for autonomous driving (2020). https://doi.org/10.48550/ARXIV.2003.03653, https://arxiv.org/abs/2003.03653
13. Czarnecki, K.: Operational design domain for automated driving systems. Waterloo Intelligent Systems Engineering (WISE) Lab, University of Waterloo, Canada, Taxonomy of Basic Terms (2018)
14. Duong., A., Almin., A., Lemarié., L., Kiran., B.: Lidar dataset distillation within bayesian active learning framework understanding the effect of data augmentation. In: Proceedings of the 17th International Joint Conference on Computer Vision, Imaging and Computer Graphics Theory and Applications - Volume 4: VISAPP, pp. 159–167. INSTICC, SciTePress (2022). https://doi.org/10.5220/0010860800003124
15. Fawzi, A., Samulowitz, H., Turaga, D., Frossard, P.: Adaptive data augmentation for image classification. In: 2016 IEEE International Conference on Image Processing (ICIP), pp. 3688–3692 (2016). https://doi.org/10.1109/ICIP.2016.7533048
16. Feng, D., Wei, X., Rosenbaum, L., Maki, A., Dietmayer, K.: Deep active learning for efficient training of a lidar 3d object detector. In: 2019 IEEE Intelligent Vehicles Symposium (IV), pp. 667–674. IEEE (2019)

17. Gao, M., Zhang, Z., Yu, G., Arık, S.Ö., Davis, L.S., Pfister, T.: Consistency-based semi-supervised active learning: towards minimizing labeling cost. In: Vedaldi, A., Bischof, H., Brox, T., Frahm, J.-M. (eds.) ECCV 2020. LNCS, vol. 12355, pp. 510–526. Springer, Cham (2020). https://doi.org/10.1007/978-3-030-58607-2_30

18. Haussmann, E., et al.: Scalable active learning for object detection. In: 2020 IEEE Intelligent Vehicles Symposium (IV), pp. 1430–1435. IEEE (2020)

19. Houlsby, N., Huszár, F., Ghahramani, Z., Lengyel, M.: Bayesian active learning for classification and preference learning (2011)

20. Hu, Z., et al.: LiDAL: inter-frame uncertainty based active learning for 3D LiDAR semantic segmentation. In: Avidan, S., Brostow, G., Cissé, M., Farinella, G.M., Hassner, T. (eds.) Computer Vision. ECCV 2022. LNCS, vol. 13687, pp. 248–265. Springer, Cham (2022). https://doi.org/10.1007/978-3-031-19812-0_15

21. Kirsch, A., van Amersfoort, J., Gal, Y.: BatchBald: efficient and diverse batch acquisition for deep Bayesian active learning (2019)

22. Liu, M., Zhou, Y., Qi, C.R., Gong, B., Su, H., Anguelov, D.: Less: label-efficient semantic segmentation for lidar point clouds. In: Avidan, S., Brostow, G., Cissé, M., Farinella, G.M., Hassner, T. (eds.) Computer Vision. ECCV 2022. LNCS, vol. 13699, pp. 70–89. Springer, Cham (2022). https://doi.org/10.1007/978-3-031-19842-7_5

23. van der Maaten, L., Hinton, G.: Visualizing data using T-SNE. J. Mach. Learn. Res. **9**, 2579–2605 (2008)

24. Milioto, A., Vizzo, I., Behley, J., Stachniss, C.: Rangenet++: fast and accurate lidar semantic segmentation. In: 2019 IEEE/RSJ International Conference on Intelligent Robots and Systems (IROS), pp. 4213–4220. IEEE (2019)

25. Pop, R., Fulop, P.: Deep ensemble Bayesian active learning: addressing the mode collapse issue in Monte Carlo dropout via ensembles (2018). https://doi.org/10.48550/ARXIV.1811.03897, https://arxiv.org/abs/1811.03897

26. Ren, P., et al.: A survey of deep active learning. ACM Comput. Surv. (CSUR) **54**(9), 1–40 (2021)

27. Sener, O., Savarese, S.: Active learning for convolutional neural networks: a core-set approach (2018)

28. Uricár, M., Hurych, D., Krizek, P., Yogamani, S.: Challenges in designing datasets and validation for autonomous driving. arXiv preprint arXiv:1901.09270 (2019)

29. Wu, B., Zhou, X., Zhao, S., Yue, X., Keutzer, K.: SqueezeSegV2: improved model structure and unsupervised domain adaptation for road-object segmentation from a lidar point cloud (2018)

30. Wu, T.H., et al.: ReDAL: region-based and diversity-aware active learning for point cloud semantic segmentation (2021). 10.48550/ARXIV.2107.11769, https://arxiv.org/abs/2107.11769

31. Yuan, S., Sun, X., Kim, H., Yu, S., Tomasi, C.: Optical flow training under limited label budget via active learning (2022). https://doi.org/10.48550/ARXIV.2203.05053, https://arxiv.org/abs/2203.05053

Transformers in Unsupervised Structure-from-Motion

Hemang Chawla[1,2(✉)] , Arnav Varma[1] , Elahe Arani[1,2] , and Bahram Zonooz[1,2]

[1] Advanced Research Lab, NavInfo Europe, Eindhoven, The Netherlands
{hemang.chawla,arnav.varma,elahe.arani}@navinfo.eu
[2] Department of Mathematics and Computer Science, Eindhoven University of Technology, Eindhoven, The Netherlands
https://www.navinfo.eu/expertise/artificial-intelligence/

Abstract. Transformers have revolutionized deep learning based computer vision with improved performance as well as robustness to natural corruptions and adversarial attacks. Transformers are used predominantly for 2D vision tasks, including image classification, semantic segmentation, and object detection. However, robots and advanced driver assistance systems also require 3D scene understanding for decision making by extracting structure-from-motion (SfM). We propose a robust transformer-based monocular SfM method that learns to predict monocular pixel-wise depth, ego vehicle's translation and rotation, as well as camera's focal length and principal point, simultaneously. With experiments on KITTI and DDAD datasets, we demonstrate how to adapt different vision transformers and compare them against contemporary CNN-based methods. Our study shows that transformer-based architecture, though lower in run-time efficiency, achieves comparable performance while being more robust against natural corruptions, as well as untargeted and targeted attacks. (Code: https://github.com/NeurAI-Lab/MT-SfMLearner).

Keywords: Structure-from-motion · Monocular depth estimation · Monocular pose estimation · Camera calibration · Natural corruptions · Adversarial attacks

1 Introduction

Scene understanding tasks have benefited immensely from advances in deep learning over the years [58]. Several existing methods in computer vision for robotics [33], augmented reality [25], and autonomous driving [43] have been using convolutional neural networks (CNNs) with its properties of spatial locality and translation invariance [31] resulting in excellent performance. With the advent of vision transformers [11,54], models with the ability to learn from the global context have even outperformed CNNs for some tasks such as object detection [5] and semantic segmentation [59]. Nevertheless, despite performance improvements in curated test sets, safe deployment of models requires further consideration of robustness and generalizability.

H. Chawla and A. Varma—Equal contribution.

A. A. de Sousa et al. (Eds.): VISIGRAPP 2022, CCIS 1815, pp. 281–303, 2023.
https://doi.org/10.1007/978-3-031-45725-8_14

Different neural network architectures have been shown to have different effects on model performance, robustness, and generalizability on different tasks [9,21]. CNNs have localized linear operations and lose feature resolution during downsampling to increase their limited receptive field [57]. Transformers, with their different layers that simultaneously attend more to global features with no inductive bias in favor of locality lead to more globally coherent predictions [52]. Among these architectures, transformers have been found to be more robust for tasks such as classification [2,45], object detection, and semantic segmentation [22] despite requiring more training data and being more computationally expensive [6]. Although several studies have compared their performance on 2D vision tasks [22], studies that evaluate their performance on 3D scene understanding tasks such as monocular Structure-from-Motion (SfM) are lacking.

SfM is a prominent problem in 3D computer vision in which the 3D structure is reconstructed by simultaneously estimating scene depth, camera poses, and intrinsic parameters. Traditional methods for SfM rely on correspondence search followed by incremental reconstruction of the environment, and are able to handle a diverse set of scenes [50]. Instead, most deep learning based methods for SfM primarily focus on depth estimation with pose and intrinsics estimation as auxiliary tasks [18,37]. Deep learning methods have increasingly been employed, either in replacement or together with traditional methods, to deal with issues of low-texture, thin structures, misregistration, failed image registration, etc. [60]. While most of the existing works for depth estimation were based on CNNs [16,18,37,40], transformer-based approaches to supervised depth estimation have also been proposed [47]. However, unsupervised methods that do not require ground truth collected from costly LiDARs or RGB-D setups are often favored, as they can potentially be applied to innumerable data. Methods that utilize transformer ingredients [24] such as attention have been proposed to improve depth estimation, but transformer encoders have scarcely been adopted for depth and pose estimation.

In this work, we perform a comparative analysis between CNN- and transformer-based architectures for unsupervised depth estimation. We show how vision transformers can be adapted for *unsupervised* depth estimation with our method Monocular Transformer SfMLearner (MT-SfMLearner). We evaluate how the architecture choices for individual depth and pose estimation networks impact the depth estimation performance, as well as robustness to natural corruptions and adversarial attacks. Since SfM depends upon the knowledge of camera intrinsics, we also introduce a modular approach to predict the camera focal lengths and principal point from the input images, which can be utilized within both CNN- and transformer-based architectures. We also study the accuracy of intrinsics and pose estimation, including the impact of learning camera intrinsics on depth and pose estimation. Finally, we compare the computational and energy efficiency of the architectures for depth, pose, and intrinsics estimation.

This work is an extended version of our study comparing transformers and CNNs for unsupervised depth estimation [53]. While the previous work demonstrated how vision transformers that were built for classification-like tasks can be also used for unsupervised depth estimation, here we demonstrate that our method also extends to other transformer architectures. We also perform an additional evaluation on a more challenging dataset to further substantiate the generalizability of our study. Additionally, we also compare the impact of architectures on the performance of the auxiliary pose prediction task, including when the camera instrincs are learned simultaneously. With a more general purpose method, additional experiments, quantitative results, and visualizations, this work presents a way to compare the trade-off between the performance, robustness, and efficiency of transformer- and CNN-based architectures for monocular unsupervised depth estimation.

2 Related Works

The simultaneous estimation of Structure-from-Motion (SfM) is a well-studied problem with an established toolchain of techniques [50]. Although the traditional toolchain is effective and efficient in many cases, its reliance on accurate image correspondence can cause problems in areas of low texture, complex geometry/photometry, thin structures, and occlusions [60]. To address these issues, several of the pipeline stages have recently been tackled using deep learning, e.g., feature matching [23], pose estimation [3], and stereo and monocular depth estimation [16]. Of these, unsupervised monocular depth estimation in particular has been extensively explored with CNN-based depth and pose networks, with pose estimation as an auxiliary task [1,16,18,37,60]. These learning-based techniques are attractive because they can utilize external supervision during training and may circumvent the aforementioned issues when applied to test data. However, learned systems might not be robust to shifts in distribution during test time.

Recently, transformer-based architectures [11,52], which outperform CNN-based architectures in image classification, have been proven to be more robust in image classification [2,42], as well as dense prediction tasks such as object detection and semantic segmentation [22]. Motivated by their success, researchers have replaced CNN encoders with transformers in scene understanding tasks such as object detection [5,35], semantic segmentation [51,59], and supervised monocular depth estimation [47,57]. Our previous work [53] and MonoFormer [1] further extend transformer-based architectures to unsupervised monocular unsupervised depth estimation. However, ours is the only work that comprehensively demonstrates the robustness of transformer-based architectures for unsupervised SfM. We now provide analyses to establish generalizability of our approach across multiple datasets, transformer-based architectures, and auxiliary SfM tasks such as pose estimation and intrinsics estimation.

3 Method

We study the impact of using vision transformer based architectures for unsupervised monocular Structure-from-Motion (SfM) in contrast to contemporary methods that utilize CNN-based architectures.

3.1 Monocular Unsupervised SfM

For training unsupervised SfM networks, we utilize videos captured from monocular cameras. Given a video sequence with n images, both the depth and pose estimation networks are trained simultaneously. This is unlike supervised networks, where depth

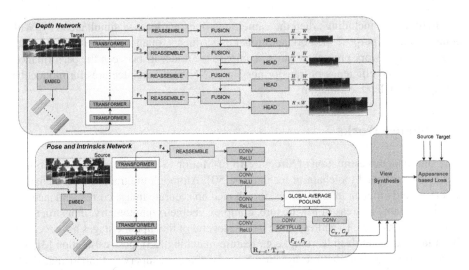

Fig. 1. An overview of Monocular Transformer Structure from Motion Learner (MT-SfMLearner) with learned intrinsics. We readapt modules from Dense Prediction Transformer (DPT) and Monodepth2 to be trained with appearance-based losses for unsupervised monocular depth, pose, and intrinsics estimation. * refers to optional modules that may not be present in all transformer-based architectures. Figure modified from [53].

or pose estimation may be trained independently. The input to the depth estimation network $f_D : \mathbb{R}^{H \times W \times 3}$ is a single image, for which it outputs pixel-wise depth in $\mathbb{R}^{H \times W}$. The input to the pose estimation network $f_E : \mathbb{R}^{H \times W \times 6}$ is a pair of images, for which it outputs the relative translation (t_x, t_y, t_z) and rotation $(r_x, r_y, r_z) \in \mathbb{R}^6$, which is used to form the affine transformation $\begin{bmatrix} \hat{R} & \hat{T} \\ 0 & 1 \end{bmatrix} \in SE(3)$. To train both networks simultaneously, a batch consists of triplets of temporally consecutive RGB images $\{I_{-1}, I_0, I_1\} \in \mathbb{R}^{H \times W \times 3}$. While I_0 is input into the depth estimation network, $\{I_{-1}, I_0\}$ and $\{I_0, I_1\}$ are input into the pose estimation network to predict the next and previous relative pose. The perspective projection model links together the predicted depth $\hat{D}$ and pose $\hat{T}$ such that,

$$p_s \sim K\hat{R}_{s \leftarrow t} \hat{D}_t(p_t) K^{-1} p_t + K\hat{T}_{s \leftarrow t}. \tag{1}$$

This is used to warp the source images $I_s \in \{I_{-1}, I_1\}$ to the target image $I_t \in \{I_0\}$ as part of the view synthesis (see Fig. 1), where K represents the camera intrinsics. For each triplet, two target images $\hat{I}_0$ are synthesized, which are compared with the real target image, to compute the appearance-based *photometric* loss. Additionally, we utilize a smoothness loss [18] on the predicted depth for regularization.

3.2 Architecture

Depth Network. For the depth network, we use a transformer-based architecture in the encoder, and readapt the decoder from the DPT [46]. There are five components of the depth network:

Table 1. Architecture details of the *Reassemble* modules. DN and PN refer to depth and pose networks, respectively. The subscripts of DN refer to the transformer stage from which the respective *Reassemble* module takes its input (see Fig. 1). The input image size is $H \times W$, p refers to the patch size, $N_p = H \cdot W/p^2$ refers to the number of patches in the image, s refers to the stride of the *Embed* module and d refers to the feature dimension of the transformer features. Table modified from [53].

Encoder	Operation	Input size	Output size	Function	Parameters (DN_1, DN_2, DN_3, DN_4, PN_4)
DeiT	Read	$(N_p + 1) \times d$	$N_p \times d$	Drop readout token	–
	Concatenate	$N_p \times d$	$d \times \frac{H}{p} \times \frac{W}{p}$	Transpose & Unflatten	–
	Pointwise Convolution	$d \times \frac{H}{p} \times \frac{W}{p}$	$N_c \times \frac{H}{p} \times \frac{W}{p}$	Change to N_c channels	$N_c =$ $[96, 768, 1536, 3072, 2048]$
	Strided Convolution	$N_c \times \frac{H}{p} \times \frac{W}{p}$	$N_c \times \frac{H}{2p} \times \frac{W}{2p}$	$k \times k$ convolution, stride= 2, N_c channels, padding= 1	$k = [-, -, -, 3, -]$
	Transpose Convolution	$N_c \times \frac{H}{p} \times \frac{W}{p}$	$N_c \times \frac{H}{\alpha} \times \frac{W}{\alpha}$	$\frac{p}{\alpha} \times \frac{p}{\alpha}$ deconvolution, stride= $\frac{p}{\alpha}$, N_c channels	$\alpha = [4, 8, -, -, -]$
PVT	Reshape	$\frac{HW}{64s^2} \times N_b$	$N_b \times \frac{H}{8s} \times \frac{W}{8s}$	Reshape token to image-like 2D representations	$N_b = [-, -, -, 512, 512]$

- ***Embed*** module, which is part of the encoder, takes an image $I \in \mathbb{R}^{H \times W \times 3}$ and converts image patches of size $p \times p$ to $N_p = H \cdot W/p^2$ tokens $t_i \in \mathbb{R}^d$ $\forall i \in [1, 2, ...N_p]$. This is implemented as a $p \times p$ convolution with stride $s \leq p$. The output of this module may be concatenated with a *readout* token $\in \mathbb{R}^d$, depending on the transformer based architecture.
- ***Transformer*** block, which is also part of the encoder, consists of multiple transformer stages that process these tokens with self-attention modules [54]. Self-attention processes inputs at constant resolution and can simultaneously attend to global and local features.
- ***Reassemble*** modules in the decoder are responsible for extracting image-like 2D representations from the features of the transformer block. At least one reassemble module is used, and additional modules may be used depending on the transformer-based architecture. The exact details of the *Reassemble* modules can be found in Table 1.
- ***Fusion*** modules in the decoder, based on RefineNet [34], are responsible for progressively fusing the features of the encoder or the *Reassemble* modules with the features of the decoder. The module is also responsible for upsampling the features by 2 at each stage. Unlike DPT, we enable batch normalization in the decoder, as it was found to be helpful for unsupervised depth prediction. We also reduce the number of channels in the *Fusion* block to 96 from 256 in DPT.

Table 2. Architecture details of *Head* modules in Fig. 1. Source: [53].

Layers
32 3 × 3 *Convolutions*, stride=1, padding= 1
ReLU
Bilinear Interpolation to upsample by 2
32 *Pointwise Convolutions*
Sigmoid

- **Head** modules after each *Fusion* module predict depth on four scales, according to previous unsupervised methods [17]. Unlike DPT, *Head* modules use 2 convolutions instead of 3 as we did not find any difference in performance. For the exact architecture of the *Head* modules, see Table 2.

Pose Network. For the pose network, we adopt an architecture similar to that of the depth network, with a transformer-based architecture in the encoder, but the decoder from Monodepth2 [17]. Since the input to the transformer for the pose network consists of two images concatenated along the channel dimension, we repeat the *Embed* module accordingly. Unlike the depth network, we only use a single *Reassemble* module to pass transformer tokens to the decoder, independently of the transformer-based architecture used. For details of the structure of this Reassemble module, refer to Table 1.

When both depth and pose networks use transformers as described above, we refer to the resulting architecture as Monocular Transformer Structure-from-Motion Learner (*MT-SfMLearner*).

3.3 Intrinsics

As seen in Eq. 1, unsupervised monocular SfM requires knowledge of the ground truth camera intrinsics. Intrinsics are given by

$$K = \begin{bmatrix} f_x & 0 & c_x \\ 0 & f_y & c_y \\ 0 & 0 & 1 \end{bmatrix}, \tag{2}$$

where f_x and f_y refer to the focal lengths of the camera along the x-axis and y-axis, respectively. c_x and c_y refer to x and y coordinates of the principal point in the pinhole camera model. Most unsupervised SfM methods are trained with intrinsics known a priori. However, the intrinsics may vary within a dataset with videos collected from different camera setups or over a long period of time. These parameters can also be unknown for crowdsourced datasets.

Therefore, we introduce an intrinsics estimation module. We modify the pose network to additionally estimate the focal lengths and principal point along with the translation and rotation. Concretely, we add a convolutional path in the pose decoder to learn the intrinsics. The features before activation from the penultimate decoder layer are passed through a global average pooling layer. This is followed by two branches of pointwise convolutions that reduce the number of channels from 256 to 2. One branch uses softplus activation to estimate focal lengths along the x and y axes, as the focal length is always positive. The other branch estimates the principal point without employing any activation, as the principal point does not have such a constraint. Note that the pose decoder is the same for both CNN- and transformer-based architectures. Consequently, the intrinsics estimation method can be modularly utilized with both architectures. Figure 1 demonstrates MT-SfMLearner with learned intrinsics.

3.4 Appearance-Based Losses

Following contemporary unsupervised monocular SfM methods, we adopt the *appearance-based losses* and an *auto-masking* procedure from CNN-based Monodepth2 [17] for the transformer-based architecture described above. We employ a photometric per-pixel minimum reprojection loss composed of the pixel-wise ℓ_1 distance as well as the Structural Similarity (SSIM) between the real and synthesized target images, along with a multiscale edge-aware *smoothness* loss on the depth predictions. We also use auto-masking to disregard the temporally stationary pixels in the image triplets. Finally, to reduce texture-copy artifacts, we calculate the total loss after upsampling the depth maps, predicted at 4 scales by the decoder, to the input resolution.

4 Experiments

We compare the CNN and transformer architectures for their impact on unsupervised monocular depth and pose estimation, including when the camera intrinsics are unknown and when they are estimated simultaneously.

4.1 Datasets

KITTI. For depth estimation, we report results on the Eigen Split [12] of KITTI [13] dataset after removing the static frames as per [60], unless stated otherwise. This split contains $39,810$ training images, 4424 validation images, and 697 test images, respectively. This dataset captures scenes from rural, city and highway areas around Karlsruhe, Germany. All results are reported on the per-image scaled dense depth prediction without post-processing [17] for an image size of 640×192, unless otherwise stated.

For pose estimation in Sect. 4.6, we report results on the Odom Split [60] of the KITTI dataset for an image size of 640×192, unless stated otherwise. This split contains 8 training sequences (sequences $00-02, 04-08$) and two test sequences $(09, 10)$.

Dense Depth for Autonomous Driving. For depth estimation, we also report results on the Dense Depth for Autonomous Driving (DDAD) dataset [18], for an image size of 640×384 unless otherwise noted. It contains 12650 training samples from 150 sequences and 3950 test samples from 50 sequences, respectively. This dataset contains samples with long range depth (up to $250\,m$) from a diverse set of urban scenarios in multiple cities of the United States (Ann Arbor, Bay Area, Cambridge, Detroit, San Francisco) and Japan (Odaiba, Tokyo).

4.2 Architecture

For the transformer-based architecture in our depth and pose encoders, we use DeiT-base [52] except in Sect. 4.6, where we use PVT-b4 [55] to demonstrate that our approach generalizes to other transformer-based architectures. The *Embed* module of DeiT-base has a patch size $p = 16$ and stride $s = 16$, while that of PVT-b4 has a patch size $p = 7$ and a stride $s = 4$. DeiT-base employs 12 *Transformer* stages with features F_1, F_2, F_3, and F_4 (see Fig. 1) taken from the 3rd, 6th, 9th, and final stages to be sent to the decoder. PVT-b4, meanwhile, employs 4 transformer stages, each of which contributes to the features sent to the decoder. Finally, DeiT-base uses 4 *Reassemble* modules in the depth encoder, while PVT-b4 uses only one *Reassemble module* in the depth encoder. The exact architecture of the Reassemble modules can be found in Table 1.

4.3 Implementation Details

The networks are implemented in PyTorch [41] and trained on a TeslaV100 GPU for 20 epochs at a resolution of 640×192 with batch sizes 12 for DeiT-base encoder and 8 for PVT-b4 encoder, unless otherwise mentioned. The depth and pose encoders are initialized with ImageNet [10] pre-trained weights. We use the Adam [26] optimizer for CNN-based networks and AdamW [36] optimizer for transformer-based networks with initial learning rates of $1e^{-4}$ and $1e^{-5}$, respectively. The learning rate is decayed after 15 epochs by a factor of 10. Both optimizers use $\beta_1 = 0.9$ and $\beta_2 = 0.999$.

4.4 Evaluation Metrics

Depth Estimation. We measure the error and accuracy of depth estimation using various metrics. For error, we use the absolute relative error (Abs Rel) [49], squared relative error [28] (Sq Rel), linear root mean squared error (RMSE) [32], log scale invariant RMSE [12] (RMSE log). For accuracy, we measure under three thresholds, reported as ratios [30] ($\delta < 1.25$, $\delta < 1.25^2$, $\delta < 1.25^3$).

Pose Estimation. We measure translation and rotational errors for all possible subsequences of length $(100, 200, \ldots, 800)m$, and report the average of the values. The translation error is reported as a percentage and the rotation error as degrees per $100m$ [14].

Intrinsics Estimation. We measure the percentage error from its ground truth value for each camera intrinsic parameter.

Efficiency. We measure computational and energy efficiency using frames per second (fps) and Joules per frame, respectively.

4.5 Impact of Architecture

Since unsupervised monocular depth estimation networks simultaneously train a pose network (see Eq. 1), we investigate the impact of each network's architecture on depth estimation. We consider CNN-based (C) and Transformer-based (T) networks for depth

Table 3. Quantitative results on KITTI Eigen split for all four architecture combinations of depth and pose networks. The best results are displayed in bold, and the second best are underlined. Source: [53].

Architecture	Error↓				Accuracy↑		
	Abs Rel	Sq Rel	RMSE	RMSE log	$\delta < 1.25$	$\delta < 1.25^2$	$\delta < 1.25^3$
C, C	**0.111**	0.897	4.865	0.193	**0.881**	<u>0.959</u>	0.980
C, T	0.113	0.874	4.813	0.192	<u>0.880</u>	**0.960**	<u>0.981</u>
T, C	<u>0.112</u>	<u>0.843</u>	**4.766**	<u>0.189</u>	0.879	**0.960**	**0.982**
T, T	0.112	**0.838**	<u>4.771</u>	**0.188**	0.879	**0.960**	**0.982**

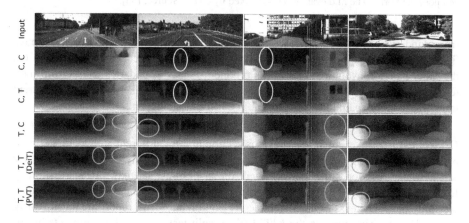

Fig. 2. Disparity maps on KITTI Eigen for qualitative comparison of all four architecture combinations of depth and pose networks. Example regions where the global receptive field of transformers is advantageous are highlighted in green. Example areas where local receptive field of CNNs is advantageous are highlighted in white. Source: [53]. (Color figure online)

and pose estimation. The four resulting combinations of (Depth Network, Pose Network) architectures, in ascending order of impact of transformers on depth estimation, are (C, C), (C, T), (T, C), and (T, T). To compare the transformer-based architecture fairly with CNN-based networks, we utilize Monodepth2 [17] with ResNet-101 [19] in the depth and pose encoders. All four combinations are trained thrice on the KITTI Eigen split using the settings described in Sect. 4.3 and the known ground-truth camera intrinsics.

On Performance. Table 3 shows the best results on depth estimation for each architecture combination of depth and pose networks. We observe that MT-SfMLearner, i.e. the combination of transformer-based depth and pose networks, performs best under two of the *error* metrics and two of the *accuracy* metrics. The remaining combinations show comparable performance on all metrics. Figure 2 also shows more uniform estimates for larger objects, such as vehicles, vegetation, and buildings, when the depth is learned using transformers. Transformers also estimate depth more coherently for reflections

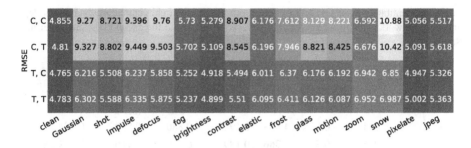

Fig. 3. RMSE for natural corruptions of KITTI Eigen test set for all four combinations of depth and pose networks. The i.i.d evaluation is denoted by *clean*. Source: [53].

from windows of vehicles and buildings. This is likely because of the larger receptive fields of the self-attention layers, which lead to more globally coherent predictions. On the other hand, convolutional networks produce sharper boundaries and perform better on thinner objects such as traffic signs and poles. This is likely due to the inherent inductive bias for spatial locality present in convolutional layers.

On Robustness. We saw in the previous section that the different architecture combinations perform comparably on the independent and identically distributed (i.i.d) test set. However, networks that perform well on an i.i.d test set may still learn shortcut features that reduce robustness on out-of-distribution (o.o.d) datasets [15]. Therefore, we study the robustness of each architecture combination. We report the mean RMSE across three training runs on the KITTI Eigen split test set for all experiments in this section.

Natural Corruptions: Following [20] and [39], we generate 15 corrupted versions of the KITTI i.i.d test set at the highest severity(= 5). These corruptions are changes to images that correspond to variations expected in nature, such as those due to *noise* (Gaussian, shot, impulse), *blur* (defocus, glass, motion, zoom), *weather* (snow, frost, fog, brightness) and *digital* (contrast, elastic, pixelate, JPEG). We observe in Fig. 3 that learning depth with transformer-based architectures instead of CNN-based architecture leads to a significant improvement in the robustness to all natural corruptions.

Untargeted Adversarial Attack: Untargeted adversarial attacks make changes to input images that are imperceptible to humans to generate adversarial examples that can induce general prediction errors in neural networks. We employ Projected Gradient Descent (PGD) [38] to generate untargeted adversarial examples from the test set at attack strength $\epsilon \in \{0.25, 0.5, 1.0, 2.0, 4.0, 8.0, 16.0\}$. The gradients are calculated with respect to the appearance-based training loss. Following [29], the adversarial perturbation is computed over $min(\epsilon + 4, \lceil 1.25 \cdot \epsilon \rceil)$ iterations with a step size of 1. When the test image is from the beginning or end of a sequence, the training loss is only calculated for the feasible pair of images. Figure 4 demonstrates a general improvement in untargeted adversarial robustness when learning depth or pose with a transformer-based architecture instead of a CNN-based architecture.

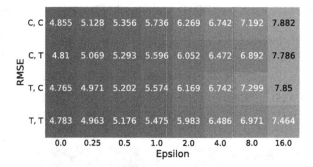

Fig. 4. RMSE for adversarial corruptions of KITTI Eigen test set generated using the PGD attack at all attack strengths (0.0 to 16.0) for the four combinations of depth and pose networks. Attack strength 0.0 refers to i.i.d evaluation. Source: [53].

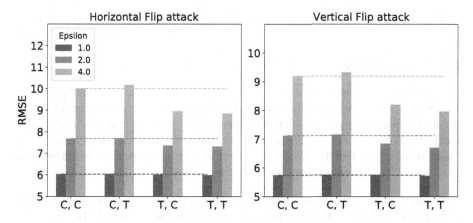

Fig. 5. RMSE for adversarial corruptions of KITTI Eigen test set generated using targeted horizontal and vertical flip attacks for all four combinations of depth and pose networks. Source: [53].

Targeted Adversarial Attack: Finally, targeted adversarial attacks make changes imperceptible for humans to generate adversarial examples that can induce *specific* prediction errors in neural networks. Deriving from [56], we generate targeted adversarial examples to fool the networks into predicting horizontally and vertically flipped estimates. To this end, we use the gradients with respect to the RMSE loss, where the targets are symmetrical horizontal and vertical flips of the predictions on the clean test set images. This evaluation is conducted at attack strength $\epsilon \in \{1.0, 2.0, 4.0\}$. Figure 5 shows an improvement in robustness to targeted adversarial attacks when depth is learned using transformer-based architectures instead of CNN-based architectures. Furthermore, the combination where both depth and pose are learned using transformer-based architectures is the most robust.

Therefore, MT-SfMLearner, where depth and pose are learned with transformer-based architectures, provides the highest robustness against natural corruptions and untargeted and targeted adversarial attacks, according to studies on image classification [2,42]. This can be attributed to their global receptive field, which allows for better adjustment to the localized deviations by accounting for the global context of the scene.

Table 4. Quantitative results on DDAD (complete). The best results are shown in bold.

Architecture	Error↓				Accuracy↑		
	Abs Rel	Sq Rel	RMSE	RMSE log	$\delta < 1.25$	$\delta < 1.25^2$	$\delta < 1.25^3$
Packnet [18]	0.178	7.521	14.605	0.254	0.831	0.928	0.963
C, C	**0.151**	**3.346**	14.229	0.243	0.814	0.929	0.967
T,T	**0.151**	3.821	**14.162**	**0.237**	**0.820**	**0.935**	**0.970**

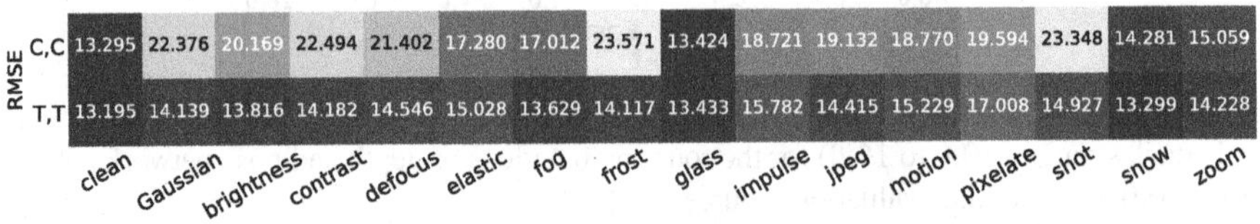

	clean	Gaussian	brightness	contrast	defocus	elastic	fog	frost	glass	impulse	jpeg	motion	pixelate	shot	snow	zoom
C,C	13.295	22.376	20.169	22.494	21.402	17.280	17.012	23.571	13.424	18.721	19.132	18.770	19.594	23.348	14.281	15.059
T,T	13.195	14.139	13.816	14.182	14.546	15.028	13.629	14.117	13.433	15.782	14.415	15.229	17.008	14.927	13.299	14.228

Fig. 6. RMSE for natural corruptions of DDAD. The i.i.d evaluation is denoted by *clean*.

4.6 Generalizability

The previous section showed that the use of transformers in the depth and pose estimation network contributes to the improved performance and robustness of depth estimation compared to their convolutional counterparts. We now examine whether this conclusion holds when examining on a different dataset or with a different transformer-based encoder. Note that the experiments herein directly show the comparison between (C,C) and (T,T). All comparisons assume known ground-truth camera intrinsics.

Different Dataset. We compare on the DDAD dataset, which has scenes from a variety of locations, and has a ground truth depth of a longer range than KITTI. As earlier, we compare both the performance of depth estimation on i.i.d test set as well as the robustness to natural corruptions and adversarial attacks.

Performance: We report the best performance for each architecture on i.i.d in Table 4. Note that (T,T) outperforms (C,C) in almost all metrics. This confirms the generalizability of i.i.d performance of transformers across datasets. Additionally, we note that transformers also outperform the 3D convolutional PackNet architecture designed to handle long-range depth as curated within DDAD, despite a lack of inductive bias for the same in transformers.

Robustness: Next, we compare the robustness of the architectures against natural corruptions and adversarial attacks on the DDAD dataset. Note that this analysis is performed on a subset of the DDAD test set, consisting of a randomly selected subset of 11 of the 50 test sequences. In particular, these sequences are #{151, 154, 156, 167, 174, 177, 179, 184, 192, 194, 195}. For robustness evaluation, we report the mean RMSE across three training runs.

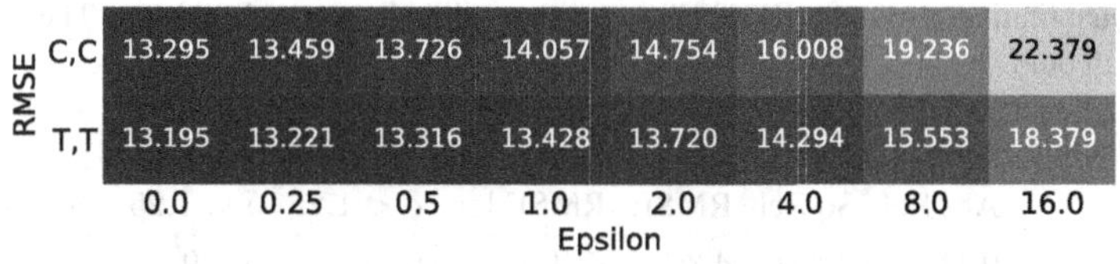

RMSE
C,C
T,T
13.295
13.459
13.726
14.057
14.754
16.008
19.236
22.379
13.195
13.221
13.316
13.428
13.720
14.294
15.553
18.379
0.0
0.25
0.5
1.0
2.0
4.0
8.0
16.0
Epsilon

Fig. 7. RMSE for untargeted attacks on DDAD. The i.i.d evaluation is denoted by *clean*.

Figure 6 compares the robustness of the architectures to natural corruptions. We find that transformers are significantly better at handling across natural corruptions. Figure 7 further compares the robustness of architectures with untargeted adversarial perturbations. We find that transformers are also better against untargeted adversarial attacks, with the difference becoming more pronounced as the attack strength increases. Finally, Fig. 8 compares the robustness of the architectures with the targeted horizontal and vertical flip attacks. Again, we find that transformers are also more robust to targeted attacks.

The above experiments confirm the generalizability of robustness of transformers across datasets.

Different Encoder Backbone. While we utilized the Data Efficient Image Transformer (DeiT) backbone for the encoder in previous experiments, we now evaluate MT-SfMLearner with the Pyramid Vision Transformer (PVT) backbone. As earlier, we compare both the performance of depth estimation on i.i.d test set as well as the robustness to natural corruptions and adversarial attacks for the KITTI Eigen split.

Performance: We report the best performance for each architecture on i.i.d in Table 5. Note that (T,T) with PVT outperforms not only (C,C) but also (T,T) with DeiT in all metrics. This can be attributed to the design of PVT, built particularly for dense prediction tasks, such as depth estimation. Figure 2 further shows continued globally coherent predictions for large objects and reflections for PVT. Furthermore, PVT improves on thin structures over DeiT, likely due to its overlapping patch embedding, which allows

Horizontal Flip attack
Vertical Flip attack
Epsilon
1.0
2.0
4.0
RMSE
22
21
20
19
18
17
16
15
14
C,C
T,T
C,C
T,T

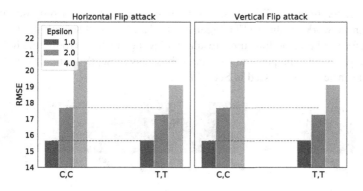

Fig. 8. RMSE for adversarial corruptions of DDAD generated using horizontal and vertical flip attacks. The i.i.d evaluation is denoted by *clean*.

Table 5. Quantitative results on KITTI Eigen with modified encoder backbone. The best results are shown in bold.

Architecture	Error↓				Accuracy↑		
	Abs Rel	Sq Rel	RMSE	RMSE log	$\delta < 1.25$	$\delta < 1.25^2$	$\delta < 1.25^3$
C, C	0.111	0.897	4.865	0.193	0.881	0.959	0.980
T,T (DeiT)	0.112	0.838	4.771	0.188	0.879	0.960	**0.982**
T,T (PVT)	**0.107**	**0.780**	**4.537**	**0.183**	**0.890**	**0.963**	0.982

for better learning of local information. This confirms the generalizability of i.i.d performance of transformers across different encoder backbones.

Robustness: Next, we compare the robustness of the architectures against natural corruptions and adversarial attacks. For robustness evaluation, we report the mean RMSE across three training runs.

Figures 9, 10, and 11 compare the robustness of the architectures to natural corruptions, untargeted adversarial attack, and targeted horizontal and vertical flip attack. We find that both transformer architectures are significantly better at handling natural corruptions as well as untargeted and targeted adversarial attacks. We hypothesize that PVT has much higher robustness than even DeiT due to its spatial feature pyramid and overlapping patch embedding that helps to maintain local continuity in the image.

Therefore, the above experiments also confirm the generalizability of the robustness of transformers across encoder backbones.

4.7   Auxiliary Tasks

Unsupervised monocular SfM requires access to relative pose between image pairs and camera intrinsics corresponding to the input, in addition to depth. As discussed in Sect. 3, a network is simultaneously trained for the pose and (optionally) camera intrinsics estimation along with the depth estimation network. While we have studied depth estimation in detail in the previous subsections, here we examine if the improved performance with transformers comes at the expense of the performance on auxiliary tasks.

Intrinsics Estimation: In Table 6, we examine the accuracy of our proposed intrinsics estimation network on the KITTI Eigen split. We observe that both the CNN-based and transformer-based architectures result in a low percentage error on the focal length and principal point. The performance and robustness of depth estimation with learned camera intrinsics are discussed in Sect. 4.8.

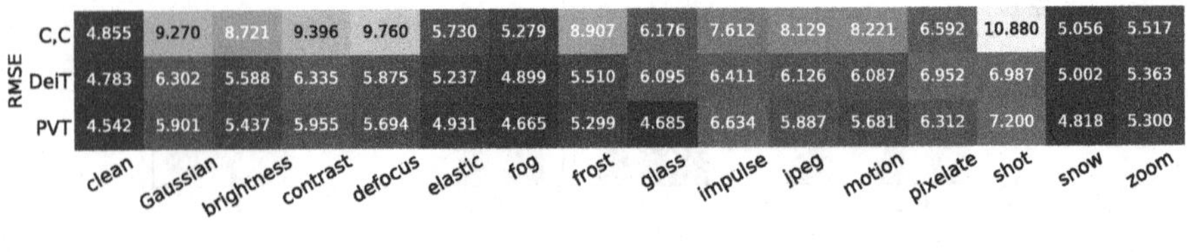

RMSE	clean	Gaussian	brightness	contrast	defocus	elastic	fog	frost	glass	impulse	jpeg	motion	pixelate	shot	snow	zoom
C,C	4.855	9.270	8.721	9.396	9.760	5.730	5.279	8.907	6.176	7.612	8.129	8.221	6.592	10.880	5.056	5.517
DeiT	4.783	6.302	5.588	6.335	5.875	5.237	4.899	5.510	6.095	6.411	6.126	6.087	6.952	6.987	5.002	5.363
PVT	4.542	5.901	5.437	5.955	5.694	4.931	4.665	5.299	4.685	6.634	5.887	5.681	6.312	7.200	4.818	5.300

Fig. 9. RMSE for natural corruptions of KITTI Eigen including PVT. The i.i.d evaluation is denoted by *clean*.

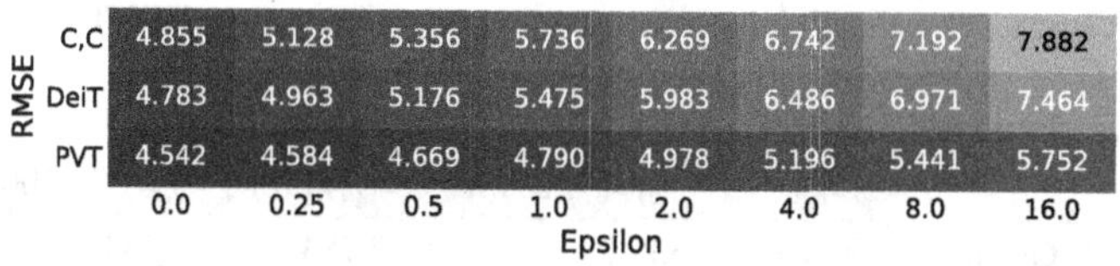

RMSE
C,C 4.855 5.128 5.356 5.736 6.269 6.742 7.192 7.882
DeiT 4.783 4.963 5.176 5.475 5.983 6.486 6.971 7.464
PVT 4.542 4.584 4.669 4.790 4.978 5.196 5.441 5.752
0.0 0.25 0.5 1.0 2.0 4.0 8.0 16.0
Epsilon

Fig. 10. RMSE for untargeted attacks on KITTI Eigen, including T, T (PVT). The i.i.d evaluation is denoted by *clean*.

Horizontal Flip attack
Vertical Flip attack
Epsilon
1.0
2.0
4.0
RMSE
12
11
10
9
8
7
6
5
C,C
DeiT
PVT
C,C
DeiT
PVT

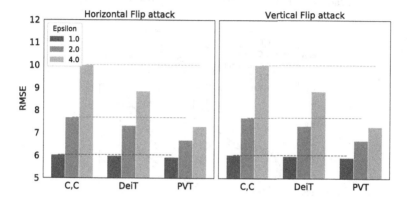

Fig. 11. RMSE for adversarial corruptions of KITTI Eigen including T, T (PVT) generated using horizontal and vertical flip attacks. The i.i.d evaluation is denoted by *clean*.

Pose Estimation: In Table 7, we examine the accuracy of the pose estimation network on the KITTI Odom split, including when the intrinsics are unknown. We observe that both the translation and rotation errors for sequence 09 are lower with (T,T) than with (C,C) when the camera intrinsics are given. However, the opposite is true for Sequence 10. We also observe that the translation and rotation errors for both sequences are similar to when the ground truth intrinsics are known a priori. Figure 12 visualizes the predicted trajectories with both architectures, including when the intrinsics are unknown.

Overall, we conclude that the benefits of using transformers do not come at the expense of its performance on intrinsics or pose estimation. Note that while auxiliary tasks perform well, traditional methods continue to dominate with several methods combining deep learning approaches with the traditional methods [3, 8]

Table 6. Percentage error for intrinsics prediction. Source: [53].

Network	Error(%) ↓			
	f_x	c_x	f_y	c_y
C,C	−1.889	-2.332	2.400	-9.372
T,T	−1.943	-0.444	3.613	-16.204

Table 7. Impact of estimating intrinsics on pose estimation for the KITTI Odom split.

Network	Intrinsics	Seq 09		Seq 10	
		$t_{err}(\%) \downarrow$	$r_{err}(°/100m) \downarrow$	$t_{err}(\%) \downarrow$	$r_{err}(°/100m) \downarrow$
C,C	Given	10.376	3.237	7.784	2.444
	Learned	14.052	4.047	11.780	3.338
T,T	Given	6.998	2.181	8.983	3.666
	Learned	7.624	2.099	9.537	3.962

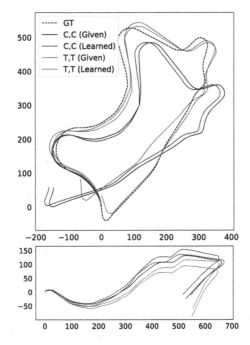

Fig. 12. Origin-aligned trajectories on KITTI Odom split for (C,C) and (T,T) showing the impact of learning intrinsics.

4.8   Depth Estimation with Learned Camera Intrinsics

We analyze the impact on performance and robustness of depth estimation when the camera intrinsics are unknown a priori and the network is trained to estimate it. The experiments are performed on the KITTI Eigen split.

Performance: Table 8 compares the accuracy and error for depth estimation when intrinsics are learned and when they are given a priori. We observe that depth error and accuracy for transformer-based architectures continue to be better than those for CNN-based architectures, even when the intrinsics are learned. Additionally, we observe that the depth error and accuracy metrics are both similar to those when the ground truth intrinsics are known. This is also substantiated in Fig. 13 where learning of the intrinsics does not cause artifacts in depth estimation.

Table 8. Impact of estimating intrinsics on depth estimation for KITTI Eigen split. Source: [53].

Network	Intrinsics	Depth Error↓				Depth Accuracy↑		
		Abs Rel	Sq Rel	RMSE	RMSE log	$\delta < 1.25$	$\delta < 1.25^2$	$\delta < 1.25^3$
C,C	Given	0.111	0.897	4.865	0.193	0.881	0.959	0.980
	Learned	0.113	0.881	4.829	0.193	0.879	0.960	0.981
T,T	Given	0.112	0.838	4.771	0.188	0.879	0.960	0.982
	Learned	0.112	0.809	4.734	0.188	0.878	0.960	0.982

Fig. 13. Disparity maps for qualitative comparison on KITTI, when trained with and without intrinsics (K). The second and fourth rows are same as the second and the fifth rows in Fig. 2. Source: [53].

Robustness: As before, we also evaluate networks trained with learned intrinsics for their robustness against natural corruptions, untargeted attack, and targeted adversarial attacks. We report the mean RMSE (μRMSE) across all corruptions and for all attacks strengths in targeted adversarial attacks in Table 9, the RMSE on the untargeted adversarial attack in Fig. 14 averaged over three runs. We observe that both the architectures maintain similar robustness against natural corruptions and adversarial attacks when the intrinsics are learned simultaneously as opposed to when intrinsics are known a priori. Additionally, similar to the scenario with known ground truth intrinsics, transformers with learned intrinsics is more robust than its convolutional counterpart.

4.9 Efficiency

In order to deploy the architectures for use in robots and autonomous driving systems, it is important to examine their suitability for real-time application. Thus, we evaluate the networks on their computational and energy efficiency.

Table 10 reports the average speed and the average energy consumption during inference for depth, as well as pose and intrinsics networks for both architectures. These metrics are computed over 10,000 forward passes on NVidia GeForce RTX 2080 Ti. We observe that both architectures run in real-time with an inference speed > 30 fps. Nevertheless, the energy consumption and computational costs for transformer-based architecture are higher than those of its CNN-based counterpart.

Table 9. Mean RMSE (μRMSE) for natural corruptions, horizontal (H) and vertical (V) adversarial flips of KITTI, when trained with and without ground truth intrinsics. Source: [53].

Architecture	Intrinsics	Natural corruptions	Adversarial attack	
		μRMSE$\downarrow$	μRMSE$\downarrow$ (H)	μRMSE$\downarrow$ (V)
C, C	Given	7.683	7.909	7.354
	Learned	7.714	7.641	7.196
T, T	Given	5.918	7.386	6.795
	Learned	5.939	7.491	6.929

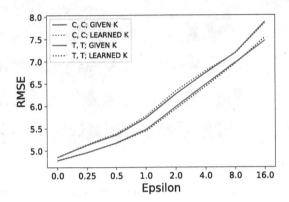

Fig. 14. RMSE for adversarial corruptions of KITTI generated using untargeted PGD attack, when trained with and without ground truth intrinsics (K). Source: [53].

Table 10. Inference Speed and Energy Consumption for depth, pose, and intrinsics estimation using CNN- and transformer-based architectures. Source: [53].

Architecture	Estimate	Speed$\uparrow$	Energy$\downarrow$
C,C	Depth	84.132	3.206
	Intrinsics/ Pose	97.498	2.908
T,T	Depth	40.215	5.999
	Intrinsics/ Pose	60.190	4.021

4.10   Comparing Performance

Having established the benefits of transformers for depth estimation, we now evaluate MT-SfMLearner, where both depth and pose networks are transformer-based, with contemporary neural networks for their error and accuracy on unsupervised monocular depth estimation. Note that we do not compare with methods that use ground-truth depth or semantic labels during training. We also do not compare against methods that use multiple frames for depth estimation. In Table 11, we observe that MT-SfMLearner (DeiT) achieves comparable performance against other methods including those with a heavy encoder such as ResNet-101 [24] and PackNet with 3D convolutions [18].

We also observe that MT-SfMLearner (PVT) outperforms these methods, including contemporary transformer-based methods such as MonoFormer [1].

Table 11. Quantitative results comparing MT-SfMLearner with existing methods on KITTI Eigen split. For each category of image sizes, the best results are displayed in bold, and the second best results are underlined. Table modified from [53].

Methods	Resolution	Error↓				Accuracy↑		
		Abs Rel	Sq Rel	RMSE	RMSE log	$\delta < 1.25$	$\delta < 1.25^2$	$\delta < 1.25^3$
CC [48]	832×256	0.140	1.070	5.326	0.217	0.826	0.941	0.975
SC-SfMLearner [4]	832×256	0.137	1.089	5.439	0.217	0.830	0.942	0.975
Monodepth2 [17]	640×192	0.115	0.903	4.863	0.193	0.877	0.959	0.981
SG Depth [27]	640×192	0.117	0.907	4.844	0.194	0.875	0.958	0.980
PackNet-SfM [18]	640×192	0.111	0.829	4.788	0.199	0.864	0.954	0.980
Poggi et. al [44]	640×192	0.111	0.863	4.756	0.188	0.881	0.961	0.982
Johnston & Carneiro [24]	640×192	**0.106**	0.861	4.699	0.185	0.889	0.962	0.982
HR-Depth [37]	640×192	0.109	0.792	4.632	0.185	0.884	0.962	**0.983**
G2S [7]	640×192	0.112	0.894	4.852	0.192	0.877	0.958	0.981
MonoFormer [1]	640×192	0.108	0.806	4.594	0.184	0.884	**0.963**	**0.983**
MT-SfMLearner (DeiT)	640×192	0.112	0.838	4.771	0.188	0.879	0.960	0.982
MT-SfMLearner (PVT)	640×192	0.107	**0.780**	**4.537**	**0.183**	**0.890**	**0.963**	0.982

5 Conclusion

This work investigates the impact of transformer-based architecture on the unsupervised monocular Structure-from-Motion (SfM). We demonstrate that learning both depth and pose using transformer-based architectures leads to highest performance and robustness in depth estimation across multiple datasets and transformer encoders. We additionally establish that this improvement in depth estimation doesn't come at the expense of auxiliary tasks of pose and intrinsics estimation. We also show that transformer-based architectures predict uniform and coherent depths, especially for larger objects, whereas CNN-based architectures provide local spatial-bias, especially for thinner objects and around boundaries. Moreover, our proposed intrinsics estimation module predicts intrinsics with low prediction error while maintaining performance and robustness on depth estimation. However, transformer-based architectures are more computationally demanding and have lower energy efficiency than their CNN-based counterpart. Thus, we contend that this work assists in evaluating the trade-off between performance, robustness, and efficiency of unsupervised monocular SfM for selecting the suitable architecture.

References

1. Bae, J., Moon, S., Im, S.: Deep digging into the generalization of self-supervised monocular depth estimation. In: Proceedings of the AAAI Conference on Artificial Intelligence, vol. 37, pp. 187–196 (2023)

2. Bhojanapalli, S., Chakrabarti, A., Glasner, D., Li, D., Unterthiner, T., Veit, A.: Understanding robustness of transformers for image classification. In: Proceedings of the IEEE/CVF International Conference on Computer Vision, pp. 10231–10241 (2021)

3. Bian, J.W., et al.: Unsupervised scale-consistent depth learning from video. Int. J. Comput. Vision **129**(9), 2548–2564 (2021)

4. Bian, J., et al.: Unsupervised scale-consistent depth and ego-motion learning from monocular video. Adv. Neural Inf. Process. Syst. **32**, 35–45 (2019)

5. Carion, N., Massa, F., Synnaeve, G., Usunier, N., Kirillov, A., Zagoruyko, S.: End-to-end object detection with transformers. In: Vedaldi, A., Bischof, H., Brox, T., Frahm, J.-M. (eds.) ECCV 2020. LNCS, vol. 12346, pp. 213–229. Springer, Cham (2020). https://doi.org/10.1007/978-3-030-58452-8_13

6. Caron, M., Touvron, H., Misra, I., Jégou, H., Mairal, J., Bojanowski, P., Joulin, A.: Emerging properties in self-supervised vision transformers. In: Proceedings of the International Conference on Computer Vision (ICCV) (2021)

7. Chawla, H., Varma, A., Arani, E., Zonooz, B.: Multimodal scale consistency and awareness for monocular self-supervised depth estimation. In: 2021 IEEE International Conference on Robotics and Automation (ICRA). IEEE (2021)

8. Chawla, H., Jukola, M., Brouns, T., Arani, E., Zonooz, B.: Crowdsourced 3D mapping: a combined multi-view geometry and self-supervised learning approach. In: 2020 IEEE/RSJ International Conference on Intelligent Robots and Systems (IROS), pp. 4750–4757. IEEE (2020)

9. Croce, F., Hein, M.: On the interplay of adversarial robustness and architecture components: patches, convolution and attention. arXiv preprint arXiv:2209.06953 (2022)

10. Deng, J., Dong, W., Socher, R., Li, L.J., Li, K., Fei-Fei, L.: Imagenet: a large-scale hierarchical image database. In: 2009 IEEE Conference on Computer Vision and Pattern Recognition, pp. 248–255. IEEE (2009)

11. Dosovitskiy, A., et al.: An image is worth 16×16 words: transformers for image recognition at scale. In: ICLR (2021)

12. Eigen, D., Puhrsch, C., Fergus, R.: Depth map prediction from a single image using a multi-scale deep network. Adv. Neural Inf. Process. Syst. **27**, 2366–2374 (2014)

13. Geiger, A., Lenz, P., Stiller, C., Urtasun, R.: Vision meets robotics: the kitti dataset. Int. J. Rob. Res. **32**(11), 1231–1237 (2013)

14. Geiger, A., Lenz, P., Urtasun, R.: Are we ready for autonomous driving? the kitti vision benchmark suite. In: Conference on Computer Vision and Pattern Recognition (CVPR) (2012)

15. Geirhos, R., et al.: Shortcut learning in deep neural networks. Nat. Mach. Intell. **2**(11), 665–673 (2020)

16. Godard, C., Mac Aodha, O., Brostow, G.J.: Unsupervised monocular depth estimation with left-right consistency. In: Proceedings of the IEEE Conference on Computer Vision and Pattern Recognition, pp. 270–279 (2017)

17. Godard, C., Mac Aodha, O., Firman, M., Brostow, G.J.: Digging into self-supervised monocular depth estimation. In: Proceedings of the IEEE/CVF International Conference on Computer Vision, pp. 3828–3838 (2019)

18. Guizilini, V., Ambrus, R., Pillai, S., Raventos, A., Gaidon, A.: 3D packing for self-supervised monocular depth estimation. In: Proceedings of the IEEE/CVF Conference on Computer Vision and Pattern Recognition, pp. 2485–2494 (2020)

19. He, K., Zhang, X., Ren, S., Sun, J.: Deep residual learning for image recognition. In: Proceedings of the IEEE Conference on Computer Vision and Pattern Recognition, pp. 770–778 (2016)

20. Hendrycks, D., Dietterich, T.: Benchmarking neural network robustness to common corruptions and perturbations. In: Proceedings of the International Conference on Learning Representations (2019)
21. Huang, H., Wang, Y., Erfani, S., Gu, Q., Bailey, J., Ma, X.: Exploring architectural ingredients of adversarially robust deep neural networks. Adv. Neural. Inf. Process. Syst. **34**, 5545–5559 (2021)
22. Jeeveswaran, K., Kathiresan, S., Varma, A., Magdy, O., Zonooz, B., Arani, E.: A comprehensive study of vision transformers on dense prediction tasks. In: Proceedings of the 17th International Joint Conference on Computer Vision, Imaging and Computer Graphics Theory and Applications - VISAPP, INSTICC, SciTePress (2022)
23. Jiang, B., Sun, P., Luo, B.: Glmnet: graph learning-matching convolutional networks for feature matching. Pattern Recogn. **121**, 108167 (2022)
24. Johnston, A., Carneiro, G.: Self-supervised monocular trained depth estimation using self-attention and discrete disparity volume. In: Proceedings of the IEEE/CVF Conference on Computer Vision and Pattern Recognition, pp. 4756–4765 (2020)
25. Kästner, L., Frasineanu, V.C., Lambrecht, J.: A 3D-deep-learning-based augmented reality calibration method for robotic environments using depth sensor data. In: 2020 IEEE International Conference on Robotics and Automation (ICRA), pp. 1135–1141. IEEE (2020)
26. Kingma, D.P., Ba, J.: Adam: a method for stochastic optimization. arXiv preprint arXiv:1412.6980 (2014)
27. Klingner, M., Termöhlen, J.-A., Mikolajczyk, J., Fingscheidt, T.: Self-supervised monocular depth estimation: solving the dynamic object problem by semantic guidance. In: Vedaldi, A., Bischof, H., Brox, T., Frahm, J.-M. (eds.) ECCV 2020. LNCS, vol. 12365, pp. 582–600. Springer, Cham (2020). https://doi.org/10.1007/978-3-030-58565-5_35
28. Koch, T., Liebel, L., Fraundorfer, F., Korner, M.: Evaluation of cnn-based single-image depth estimation methods. In: Proceedings of the European Conference on Computer Vision (ECCV) Workshops (2018)
29. Kurakin, A., Goodfellow, I., Bengio, S., et al.: Adversarial examples in the physical world (2016)
30. Ladicky, L., Shi, J., Pollefeys, M.: Pulling things out of perspective. In: Proceedings of the IEEE Conference on Computer Vision and Pattern Recognition, pp. 89–96 (2014)
31. LeCun, Y., Bottou, L., Bengio, Y., Haffner, P.: Gradient-based learning applied to document recognition. Proc. IEEE **86**(11), 2278–2324 (1998)
32. Li, C., Kowdle, A., Saxena, A., Chen, T.: Towards holistic scene understanding: Feedback enabled cascaded classification models. Adv. Neural Inf. Process. Syst. **23**, 1–9 (2010)
33. Li, J., Dai, Y., Wang, J., Su, X., Ma, R.: Towards broad learning networks on unmanned mobile robot for semantic segmentation. In: 2022 International Conference on Robotics and Automation (ICRA), pp. 9228–9234. IEEE (2022)
34. Lin, G., Milan, A., Shen, C., Reid, I.: Refinenet: multi-path refinement networks for high-resolution semantic segmentation. In: Proceedings of the IEEE Conference on Computer Vision and Pattern Recognition, pp. 1925–1934 (2017)
35. Liu, Z., et al.: Swin transformer: hierarchical vision transformer using shifted windows. arXiv preprint arXiv:2103.14030 (2021)
36. Loshchilov, I., Hutter, F.: Decoupled weight decay regularization. arXiv preprint arXiv:1711.05101 (2017)
37. Lyu, X., et al.: Hr-depth: high resolution self-supervised monocular depth estimation. CoRR arXiv:2012.07356 (2020)
38. Madry, A., Makelov, A., Schmidt, L., Tsipras, D., Vladu, A.: Towards deep learning models resistant to adversarial attacks. In: 6th International Conference on Learning Representations, ICLR 2018, Vancouver, BC, Canada, 30 April–3 May 2018, Conference Track Proceedings. OpenReview.net (2018). https://openreview.net/forum?id=rJzIBfZAb

39. Michaelis, C., et al.: Benchmarking robustness in object detection: autonomous driving when winter is coming. arXiv preprint arXiv:1907.07484 (2019)

40. Ming, Y., Meng, X., Fan, C., Yu, H.: Deep learning for monocular depth estimation: a review. Neurocomputing **438**, 14–33 (2021)

41. Paszke, A., et al.: Pytorch: an imperative style, high-performance deep learning library. Adv. Neural. Inf. Process. Syst. **32**, 8026–8037 (2019)

42. Paul, S., Chen, P.Y.: Vision transformers are robust learners. arXiv preprint arXiv:2105.07581 (2021)

43. Peng, M., Gong, Z., Sun, C., Chen, L., Cao, D.: Imitative reinforcement learning fusing vision and pure pursuit for self-driving. In: 2020 IEEE International Conference on Robotics and Automation (ICRA), pp. 3298–3304. IEEE (2020)

44. Poggi, M., Aleotti, F., Tosi, F., Mattoccia, S.: On the uncertainty of self-supervised monocular depth estimation. In: Proceedings of the IEEE/CVF Conference on Computer Vision and Pattern Recognition, pp. 3227–3237 (2020)

45. Raghu, M., Unterthiner, T., Kornblith, S., Zhang, C., Dosovitskiy, A.: Do vision transformers see like convolutional neural networks? arXiv preprint arXiv:2108.08810 (2021)

46. Ranftl, R., Bochkovskiy, A., Koltun, V.: Vision transformers for dense prediction. ArXiv preprint (2021)

47. Ranftl, R., Lasinger, K., Hafner, D., Schindler, K., Koltun, V.: Towards robust monocular depth estimation: mixing datasets for zero-shot cross-dataset transfer. IEEE Trans. Pattern Anal. Mach. Intell. (TPAMI) **44**, 1623–1637 (2020)

48. Ranjan, A., et al.: Competitive collaboration: joint unsupervised learning of depth, camera motion, optical flow and motion segmentation. In: Proceedings of the IEEE Conference on Computer Vision and Pattern Recognition, pp. 12240–12249 (2019)

49. Saxena, A., Sun, M., Ng, A.Y.: Make3d: learning 3D scene structure from a single still image. IEEE Trans. Pattern Anal. Mach. Intell. **31**(5), 824–840 (2008)

50. Schonberger, J.L., Frahm, J.M.: Structure-from-motion revisited. In: Proceedings of the IEEE Conference on Computer Vision and Pattern Recognition, pp. 4104–4113 (2016)

51. Strudel, R., Garcia, R., Laptev, I., Schmid, C.: Segmenter: transformer for semantic segmentation. In: Proceedings of the IEEE/CVF International Conference on Computer Vision, pp. 7262–7272 (2021)

52. Touvron, H., Cord, M., Douze, M., Massa, F., Sablayrolles, A., Jégou, H.: Training data-efficient image transformers & distillation through attention. In: International Conference on Machine Learning, pp. 10347–10357. PMLR (2021)

53. Varma., A., Chawla., H., Zonooz., B., Arani., E.: Transformers in self-supervised monocular depth estimation with unknown camera intrinsics. In: Proceedings of the 17th International Joint Conference on Computer Vision, Imaging and Computer Graphics Theory and Applications, vol. 4: VISAPP, pp. 758–769. INSTICC, SciTePress (2022). https://doi.org/10.5220/0010884000003124

54. Vaswani, A., et al.: Attention is all you need. Adv. Neural Inf. Process. Syst. **30**, 5998–6008 (2017)

55. Wang, W., et al.: Pvt v2: improved baselines with pyramid vision transformer. Comput. Visual Media **8**(3), 415–424 (2022)

56. Wong, A., Cicek, S., Soatto, S.: Targeted adversarial perturbations for monocular depth prediction. Adv. Neural Inf. Process. Syst. **33**, 8486–8497 (2020)

57. Yang, G., Tang, H., Ding, M., Sebe, N., Ricci, E.: Transformer-based attention networks for continuous pixel-wise prediction. In: ICCV (2021)

58. Yao, J., Fidler, S., Urtasun, R.: Describing the scene as a whole: joint object detection, scene classification and semantic segmentation. In: 2012 IEEE Conference on Computer Vision and Pattern Recognition, pp. 702–709. IEEE (2012)

59. Zheng, S., et al.: Rethinking semantic segmentation from a sequence-to-sequence perspective with transformers. In: Proceedings of the IEEE/CVF Conference on Computer Vision and Pattern Recognition, pp. 6881–6890 (2021)
60. Zhou, T., Brown, M., Snavely, N., Lowe, D.G.: Unsupervised learning of depth and ego-motion from video. In: Proceedings of the IEEE Conference on Computer Vision and Pattern Recognition, pp. 1851–1858 (2017)

A Study of Aerial Image-Based 3D Reconstructions in a Metropolitan Area

Susana Ruano[(✉)] and Aljosa Smolic

V -SENSE, Trinity College Dublin, Dublin, Ireland
{ruanosas,smolica}@tcd.ie

Abstract. We present a study of image-based 3D reconstruction methods that use aerial images in large-scale metropolitan areas. Specifically, the study analyzes both open-source methods from the state of the art, and some of the most used commercial photogrammetry applications. The performance of these methods is measured against the densest annotated LiDAR point cloud available at a city scale. The study not only analyzes the accuracy and completeness of the reconstruction methods in the metropolitan area as in previous studies, but it also evaluates their performance for different city elements such as trees, windows, roofs, etc. which are present in the annotated ground truth model.

Keywords: Study · 3D Reconstruction · Structure-from-motion · Multi-view stereo

1 Introduction

Urban environments have been extensively studied for many purposes such as path planning, to improve the acquisition of images, to create 3D reconstructions [27], or to perform semantic segmentation of roads in the city using RGB-thermal images [29]. The creation of datasets and benchmarks focused on metropolitan areas is therefore an interesting topic and new classified point clouds of cities and datasets of multimodal aerial sources are being released, both for semantic segmentation [3], and also to perform path planning [21]. These recent publications show that despite the progress in computer vision techniques there is still a need for a common framework to evaluate them under the same conditions in different domains.

It is common knowledge that especially image-based 3D reconstruction techniques have been struggling to find the appropriate ground-truth data to evaluate the algorithms. Numerous research efforts were done to provide a successful solution to this by creating benchmarks: since the earliest works [19] which provide a few samples to evaluate the algorithms, to the more recent and complete benchmarks which cover multiple scenarios [7,18]. However, it is still challenging to have a great extension of the city covered with enough accuracy. Generally, specific equipment such as a LiDAR is needed to collect the ground truth making it unaffordable for most people. In particular, to cover a large extension of an urban environment, not only the equipment but also the planning of a mission (e.g., flight of an helicopter) is a barrier for creating new datasets.

A metropolitan area can accommodate a great variety of elements: buildings, roads, parks, etc. Its diversity can present a challenge for 3D reconstruction techniques and the ground-truth data available does not typically provide detailed information about these elements the city contains. However, in the same way that general purpose 3D reconstruction benchmarks include a great variety of scenarios, a benchmark for the study of an urban environment would benefit from having this type of information. Previous studies [30] remark the importance of including the categorization of the city to support the observations made about the quality of the reconstructions.

The creation of 3D models from a collection of images has been studied for many years [2,4,10,16,17,22,25] and it is a fundamental problem of computer vision [5]. The techniques to create 3D models can be considered specific cases, such as aerial images of a mountainous area [14] which can be later used in augmented reality applications [13], but they are normally general purpose methods. A complete pipeline to obtain an image-based reconstruction includes two different stages: Structure-from-Motion (SfM) and Multi-View Stereo (MVS). The former, to recover a sparse model and the camera poses, and the later, to obtain a detailed dense point cloud. There are very popular open-source techniques which are normally used in the 3D reconstruction studies [23], but there are also some commercial solutions with different licenses that can be used to obtain 3D models from images, which are not included in the studies very often.

In this paper, we present an extension of the previous work [15] with an evaluation for image-based 3D reconstruction pipelines not limited to combination of open-source techniques. We expand the previous work by including commercial applications in the evaluation and thus improving the study of a metropolitan area. We use the annotated point cloud of DublinCity [30] and make use of the initial study done in [15] where the city is analyzed. The analysis not only includes the evaluation at scene level but also per category of urban element, as it was done in the benchmark.

2   Previous Work

Benchmarks have been used to evaluate image-based reconstructions for decades. The first attempts were limited in various aspects [19]: they have a limited number of ground-truth models (only two), they were focused only in a part of the 3D reconstruction pipeline (MVS), and the ground-truth was acquired in a very controlled environment. With time, these type of benchmarks have been enhanced with different sets of images taken under specific lighting conditions and with additional 3D ground-truth models [1]. Nevertheless, the limitation of having all the images acquired in a controlled setting was not tackled until the EPFL benchmark was released [24]. In that work, the ground truth provided was acquired with a terrestrial LiDAR. Since then, outdoor scenarios started to be considered in the evaluations. However, as it is the pioneer for outdoor environments, it has the same drawback as the very first indoor benchmarks: the variety of models captured for the benchmark was small and the coverage of the scene was narrow. Still, it was a significant progress.

The limitation regarding the variety of models and scenarios was overcome with two other benchmarks released at a very similar time: Tanks and Temples [7] and the ETH3D benchmark [18]. The former is used to evaluate the output of the complete image-based 3D reconstruction pipeline (i.e., the dense point cloud) and instead of providing a collection of images they give as input a video. The later is focused on the MVS stage, and therefore, it provides the camera calibration and poses along with the set of images. A terrestial LiDAR was used in these benchmarks to capture the ground-truth, and in some scenes including buildings, some details such as the roofs were not covered.

Other types of LiDAR that can be used to acquire the ground truth are: 3D Mobile Laser Scanning (MLS) and Aerial Laser Scan (ALS). This type of equipment is the one typically used to acquire ground-truth data that covers large metropolitan areas. Among city benchmarks, some of them do not include images alongside such as the the TerraMobilita/iQmulus benchmark [26], Paris-rue-madame dataset [20] and the Oakland 3D Point Cloud dataset [11]. Others, do not use the images to create the 3D reconstructions (like in the Toronto/Vaihingen ISPRS benchmark used in [28]), instead the point cloud is used. Some of the benchmarks that include images such as the Kitti benchmark [8], and the ISPRS Test project on Urban Classification and 3D Building Reconstruction [12] are not focused on the evaluation of the MVS output; instead, they focus on the evaluation of other tasks such as stereo, object detection, or reconstructions made from roofs.

Some of the benchmarks cited above have an annotated point cloud of the city [11,20,26], but as pointed out, they do not provide images, with the exception of the ISPRS Test project on Urban Classification and 3D Building Reconstruction [12] and the Ai3Dr Benchmark [15]. The main difference between these last two regarding the ground-truth model is the density. The former is about six points per m^2 and the later around 350 points per m^2. Also, the later uses the a very rich annotated point cloud [30], and two different types of images, as opposed to a single set as in the former. Our work is an extension of the evaluation presented in the Ai3Dr Benchmark, including an extension of the pipelines evaluated under the same conditions.

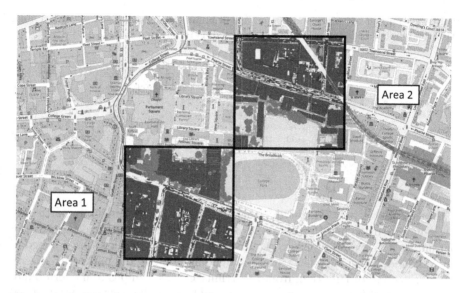

Fig. 1. Areas under evaluation. The areas of the city considered in this study are highlighted in the map with a top view of the ground truth.

3   Urban Environment

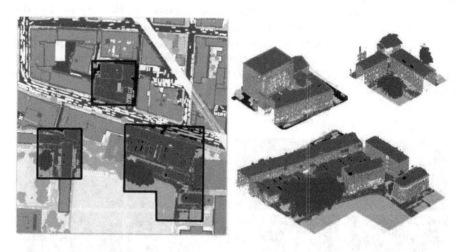

Fig. 2. Hidden areas. On the left, an example of a hidden area (in color) over the whole region (in grey). On the right, the hidden area represented in 3D [15].

Table 1. Number of points and percentage of points per class in each evaluated area. Also the number of points and percentage used as the hidden zone [15].

		undefined	facade	window	door	roof	r. window	r. door	sidewalk	street	grass	tree
Area 1	# points (×10³)	1397	3048	540	40	10727	481	3	2029	3210	1587	3471
	percentage	5.27	11.49	2.04	0.15	40.43	1.81	0.01	7.65	12.10	5.98	13.08
	hidden # p. (×10³)	1015	1816	312	27	2849	247	2	1602	2441	1353	2720
	hidden pct	7.06	12.63	2.17	0.19	19.81	1.72	0.01	11.14	16.97	9.41	18.91
Area 2	# points (×10³)	1615	2776	308	40	7807	112	3	2789	2642	4061	2852
	percentage	6.46	11.10	1.23	0.16	31.22	0.45	0.01	11.15	10.57	16.24	11.41
	hidden # p. (×10³)	1262	1547	220	27	2708	47	1	2010	1993	2226	1897
	hidden pct	9.05	11.105	1.58	0.19	19.43	0.34	0.01	14.42	14.30	15.97	13.61

The metropolitan area evaluated in this paper is the city of Dublin. In particular, the same extension used in the Ai3Dr benchmark [15] is considered for the evaluation. As it is explained there, two different regions of the city were selected to be evaluated, which include a variety of buildings, streets and parks with diverse styles, sizes and distribution, from the Trinity College campus to modern buildings as well as different structures such as trail tracks. These regions are depicted in Fig. 1 and we refer to them as *Area 1* and *Area 2* from now on.

3.1   Ground Truth

A selection of the DublinCity [30] annotated point cloud is used as ground truth for this evaluation, which includes a representative part of the city. The areas were carefully analyzed from the whole extension of the city in [15], discarding the ones with the following characteristics: small extension (less than 250×250 m² of the city), those areas with a low percentage of points in certain categories such as trees or grass, tiles that contain elements which are temporarily in the city and can degrade the performance (e.g., cranes) and those ones which have less that 90% of points classified.

Fig. 3. Oblique and nadir images. A sample of oblique images (left) and nadir ones (right).

Accordingly, the representative areas *Area 1* and *Area 2* correspond to these selected pieces of ground truth. This ensures a balanced distribution of points in each category while avoiding parts which can diminish the evaluation. It also guarantees the content is representative and diverse enough to make an evaluation per urban object category. Lastly, the magnitude of the city to be analyzed is also adequate so the algorithms process them in a reasonable amount of time.

As explained in [15], we are also using *hidden areas* for the evaluation (see and example in Fig. 2). These consist of meaningful sections of a particular area, selected to preserve the meaningfulness of the class distribution for the evaluation. However, the specific sections of the ground truth are not disclosed to the final user to avoid fine tuning to a specific region during the online evaluation.

3.2   Image Sets

We use three different sets of images to build the 3D models of each area: oblique, nadir, and a combination of both. Images in the oblique and nadir sets come from the groups described in [30] (Fig. 3 illustrates a sample of each of these images). As the original dataset contains a significantly large amount of images, both oblique and nadir, we use the selection done in [15]. Therefore, we use only the ones that will have a meaningful contribution to the 3D reconstruction of each of our areas. For the selection, COLMAP's SfM algorithm [16] was used with the complete image datasets, and every image that does not contribute to at least 1500 3D points was discarded. This is was done for both oblique and nadir image sets.

3.3   Urban Categorization

Table 1 illustrates how the 3D points in the ground-truth models are distributed, with respect to their class, both for the complete models and also the hidden areas. The table shows that roof is the class with higher point count, and also its percentage is more balanced in the hidden areas with respect to other classes. The class door is the one with the lowest point count, and the undefined data, which could potentially introduce errors or other inaccuracies, represents a maximum of 9% of the points of all areas. Other relevant metrics are that *Area 1* has almost twice the number of window points than *Area 2* and four times of roof windows; while *Area 2* has three times more grass points.

4   Experimental Setup

The goal of this study is to evaluate the performance of image-based 3D reconstruction techniques in the metropolitan area described in Sect. 3. The inputs of the 3D reconstruction processes are three different set of aerial images (oblique, nadir and combined) and the GPS data captured in the flight. This information is given in the EPSG 29902 reference system in separate files, and, in particular, the nadir set has also geographic information embedded as Exif metadata. All this information is available in the Ai3Dr benchmark. As this study is an extension of [15], we analogously evaluate the final result of the 3D reconstruction process (i.e., the final dense point cloud generated by the methods) and not the intermediate stages (SfM or MVS) separately.

The reasons to choose this approach were essentially two. Firstly, make it adaptable to new approaches that may not follow the typical steps of the pipeline. Secondly, as the measurements of the camera positions available are based on GPS and no additional information (e.g., the orientation of the camera) is given, these measurements are used only as a coarse approximation and are not indicated to be used as ground truth for evaluating intermediate steps.

4.1   3D Reconstruction Techniques

We can divide the 3D reconstruction techniques evaluated in two groups: open-source techniques and commercial applications. On the one hand, the former techniques are freely available, they are usually focused on one specific step of the process but some of them can be mixed to complete the pipeline. Users have access to the details in the code, they are typically used to solve general purpose reconstruction problems, and they have multiples parameters to be configured to adapt the algorithms to specific cases. Commercial applications are in general prepared for a specific type of reconstructions, and they have free trials available but later one needs to pay for the software. The details of the algorithms used are not disclosed, there are intermediate steps of refinement, they have usable interfaces, and default parameters are well adjusted for the tasks. Also, they are fast and are well optimized.

We are combining several open-source SfM and MVS algorithms to create the open-source 3D reconstruction pipelines. Firstly, for SfM, we use COLMAP [16], which includes a geometric verification strategy that helps improving robustness on both initialization and triangulation, and includes an improved bundle adjustment algorithm with outlier filtering. Furthermore, we use two different SfM approaches implemented in OpenMVG: a global one [10] based on the fusion of relative motions between image pairs, and an incremental one [9] that iteratively adds new estimations to the initial reconstruction minimizing the drift with successive steps of non-linear refinement. Secondly, for MVS, we also use COLMAP's approach [17] that jointly estimates depth and normal information and makes a pixel-wise view selection using photometric and geometric priors. Moreover, we also use OpenMVS [17] which does efficient patch-based stereo matching followed by a depth-map refinement process.

There are several commercial applications that are used to create image-based 3D reconstructions in professional environments. We evaluate three of the most popular applications: Agisoft Metashape[1], Pix4D[2] and RealityCapture[3].

---

[1] https://www.agisoft.com/.

[2] https://www.pix4d.com/.

[3] https://www.capturingreality.com/.

Agisoft Metashape is a stand-alone photogrammetry software that generates 3D models from a colletion of images and they can be used for cultural heritage works, for GIS applications, etc. They cover a large range of specific applications in their professional edition. Among their features we can find digital elevation model generation, dense point cloud editing and multispectral imagery processing. They also offer a python scripting binding and their program can be used in Windows, Linux and MacOs. Pix4D offers a photogrammetry suite specialized in mobile and drone mapping. They offer solutions for inspection, agriculture and surveying. We have selected the Pix4Dmapper product to make the reconstructions, because although Pix4Dmatic is expected to perform photogrammetry at large scale, we found that more information (e.g., orientation of the camera) was needed for initiate the standard procedure. Pix4D is not available for Linux. RealityCapture is a photogrammetry software recently acquired by Epic Games. They offer a solution to different task such as 2D-3D mapping, 3D printing, full body scans, assets for games, etc. They claim to have a long trajectory and recognition in the computer vision since they have created CMPMVS [6] and their researchers are also recongnized in the community. Their application is available for Windows only.

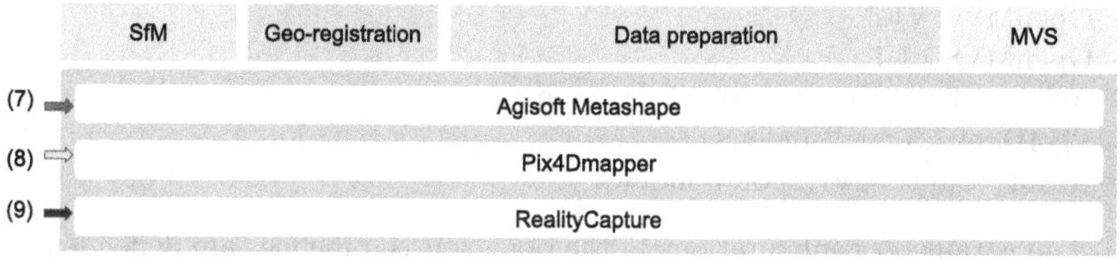

	SfM	Geo-registration	Data preparation	MVS
(7) ➡			Agisoft Metashape	
(8) ⇨			Pix4Dmapper	
(9) ➡			RealityCapture	

Fig. 4. Scheme of 3D reconstruction pipelines tested. (1) to (6) as in [15], (7) Metashape, (8) Pix4D, (9) RealityCapture.

4.2 Pipelines Under Study

Using the aforemention 3D reconstruction techniques, we list here the pipelines that are tested in this study:

1. COLMAP(SfM) + COLMAP(MVS)
2. COLMAP(SfM) + OpenMVS
3. OpenMVG-g + COLMAP(MVS)
4. OpenMVG-g + OpenMVS
5. OpenMVG-i + COLMAP(MVS)
6. OpenMVG-i + OpenMVS
7. Metashape
8. Pix4Dmapper
9. RealityCapture

As it is depicted in Fig. 4, pipelines (7) to (9), which correspond to commercial applications, are treated as a complete solution from the input to the output. For pipelines (1)-(6), we use the same configuration as in [15], which correspond to the pipelines assembled with open-source techniques and four stages are needed: SfM, geo-registration, data preparation and MVS. Feature detection and matching are done in the SfM step. Then, the GPS information is used to coarsely register the sparse cloud to the ground truth. The following step is a preparation for performing the densification, and the final one is the densification itself. A different approach is followed in the pipelines (7)-(9) because they consist of closed solutions for all the stages of the pipeline. The coarse registration is done establishing EPSG:29902 as coordinate system for the output. The nadir images have enough information to be geo-referenced without using additional data but for the oblique set, the geographic information provided in the benchmark is needed. Depending on the method, the registration can be done in different stages. For example, (7) can calculate the reconstruction in a local coordinate system and then change it when exporting the point cloud, however, (8) requires to have the coordinate estimation beforehand to have good results.

The versions of each software used in this study are :

- COLMAP v3.6
- OpenMVG v1.5
- OpenMVS v1.1
- Agisoft Metashape Pro v1.7.5 for Linux
- Pix4D v4.7.5 for Windows
- Reality Capture v1.2 for Windows

The parameter configurations in the open-source pipelines are dependent on the stage of the pipeline and the method, as indicated in [15]. In general terms, COLMAP's parameters are the same as in DublinCity [30] in all the stages of the pipeline. OpenMVG also uses the default parameters and OpenMVS uses the parameters reported in the ETH3D benchmark. We used the default parameters as well in the Metashape, Reality Capture, and Pix4D.

4.3   Alignment

The output of the aforementioned image-based 3D reconstruction pipelines is coarsely registered to the ground truth thanks to the geographical information. This is the same situation as in [15]. There, it is shown that the coarsely registration needs a refinement process in order to be perfectly aligned. The registration refinement process typically consists of a 7DoF ICP algorithm, a strategy as followed in [7], for example. Schops et al. [18] use a more sophisticated approach using the color information of the laser scan, something that is not available in our case. For our approach, we follow the same strategy as in [15], further refined with a 7DoF ICP process with the point cloud and the ground truth.

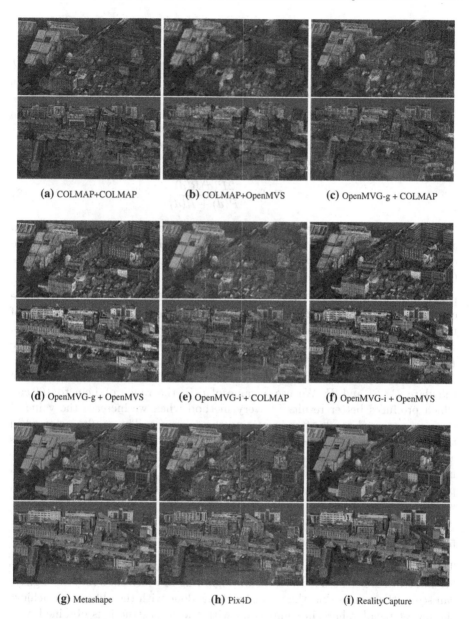

(a) COLMAP+COLMAP   **(b)** COLMAP+OpenMVS   **(c)** OpenMVG-g + COLMAP

(d) OpenMVG-g + OpenMVS   **(e)** OpenMVG-i + COLMAP   **(f)** OpenMVG-i + OpenMVS

(g) Metashape   **(h)** Pix4D   **(i)** RealityCapture

Fig. 5. Qualitative 3D reconstruction results. Point clouds obtained with the oblique and nadir images combined in *Area 1* (top) and *Area 2* (bottom).

5   Experimental Results

Following the work in [7,15,30], we use the following measurements to evaluate performance:

– **Precision**, P: measures the accuracy of the reconstruction.

$$P(d) = \frac{|dist_{I \to G}(d)|}{|I|} 100 \qquad (1)$$

– **Recall**, R: measures the completeness of the reconstruction.

$$R(d) = \frac{|dist_{G \to I}(d)|}{|G|} 100 \qquad (2)$$

– **F score**, F: a combination of both P and R.

$$F(d) = \frac{2P(d)R(d)}{P(d) + R(d)} \qquad (3)$$

Where d is a given threshold distance, I is the point cloud under evaluation and G is the ground-truth point cloud. $|\cdot|$ is the cardinality and $dist_{I \to G}(d)$ are the points in I with a distance to G less than d and $dist_{G \to I}(d)$ is analogous (i.e., $dist_{A \to B}(d) = \{a \in A \mid \min_{b \in B} \|a - b\|_2 < d\}$, A and B being point clouds). To perform the evaluation per class, the point under evaluation is assigned the same class as its nearest neighbor in the ground-truth. Although there are plenty of metrics that can be used to measure the quality of the reconstruction algorithms, such as the mean distance to the ground truth, as used in [23], P, R, and therefore F, are more robust to outliers.

For each pipeline, set of images and area (including the hidden parts), we calculate P, R, and F. We use a value of d in the range of 1 cm to 100 cm, which produces better results in every method when we increase the value of d, as an expected result after increasing the tolerance. The results reported in this evaluation use a value of 25 cm for d, similar to [15,30], which represents a good compromise between the limitations of the image resolution and the meaningfulness of the precision, since selecting a very small distance would mean poorer performances for all the methods and with a larger distance the precision would be less informative.

5.1 Scene Level Evaluation

Table 2 shows the evaluation at scene level. This means that all the points in the ground truth are treated in the same way, ignoring to which class they belong. We can see in the results that the reconstructions done with the oblique set achieve the lowest recall values, in comparison with the reconstructions obtained with the other sets of images, in both areas (also in the hidden parts). Therefore, for this set of images, having a good precision value is determinant to achieve a good F score. Among the pipelines created with open-source methods, COLMAP + COLMAP has the best performance for this type of images in both areas. However, some commercial solutions outperform it. Specifically, the best score in *Area 2* is obtained with Pix4D, whereas in *Area 1* it is with Metashape.

In the nadir set, the recall is usually higher than the precision so the accuracy is not as determinant as in the oblique sets to obtain a good F score. These results suggest that having different camera angles and less coverage of the same parts of the scene (as it is the case in the oblique set but not in the nadir one) makes the recall value decrease while the precision remains similar. As it can be observed, COLMAP + COLMAP is the best pipeline in *Area 1* whereas OpenMVG-i + OpenMVS is the best in *Area 2* (even in the hidden parts), among the open-source methods. Moreover, among the commercial solutions, we also see different winning methods in *Area 1* and *Area2*: Reality Capture and Pix4D, respectively. For the reconstructions obtained with the combined imagery, OpenMVG-g + OpenMVS and OpenMVG-i + OpenMVS are the open-source pipelines with the highest F score: the former in *Area 1* and latter in *Area 2*. This is slightly different for the commercial solutions as they present their best results with the same method for both the nadir and the combined set of images. In fact, the F score of the reconstructions obtained with the nadir and the combined sets of images is much more similar in the commercial applications than in the others. This suggest that the nadir images are very well treated by the commercial solutions. We can also observe that some open-source pipelines have higher recall values in the nadir and combined sets, although this is not enough to beat the commercial ones. However, for the combined set of images, where the open-source techniques have their best results, the difference between this and the worst performing method of the commercial applications is not very significant. 79.36 and 79.5 for OpenMVG-g + OpenMVS and Pix4D, respectively, in *Area 1* and, analogously, 81.13 and 81.53 for OpenMVG-i + OpenMVS and Metashape in *Area 2*.

The qualitative results obtained from the reconstructions with the oblique and nadir images together in Area 1 and Area 2, are shown in Fig. 5. The render was done using the same configuration (e.g., size of the points) to make it comparable. We can observe from these results that the point cloud obtained with COLMAP + COLMAP (Fig. 5 (a)) is sharper than the one obtained with COLMAP + OpenMVS (Fig. 5 (b)) in both areas, in accordance with the precision values (74.89 and 27.93 in Area 1; 76.54 and 24.7 in Area 2). We can also see that the highest precision value in Area 1, 87.87 is obtained with Reality-Capture (Fig. 5 (i)) with a very sharp reconstruction. Moreover, there are also differences in the completeness of the reconstructions: OpenMVG-i + OpenMVS (Fig. 5 (f)) and OpenMVG-g + OpenMVS (Fig. 5 (d)) are denser than the rest, this time among all the methods including the commercial ones in both areas. However, their F score values (79.36 and 76.76 in Area 1; 80.64 and 81.13 in Area 2) confirm that, as it can be appreciated in the images, the commercial software seems to give sharper reconstructions (Fig. 5 (g)-(i)), and therefore the best scores in the open-source pipelines are finally worse than all of their F scores (79.5, 80.68, 80.99 in Area 1 and 81.54, 82.73, 85.06 in Area 2), thanks to the higher values in precision.

5.2   Urban Category Centric Evaluation

Additionally, we present a summary of the same measurements calculated above but this time per urban element category. This summary shows three tables, one

Table 2. Study of urban areas (quantitative). Each row shows the results of a specific 3D reconstruction pipeline giving the precision / recall / F score for d=25cm obtained for the reconstruction in each set of images in each area. The best score for each area and image set is in bold letters and the pipelines are as follows: (1) COLMAP + COLMAP, (2) COLMAP + OpenMVS, (3) OpenMVG-g + COLMAP, (4) OpenMVG-g + OpenMVS, (5) OpenMVG-i + COLMAP, (6) OpenMVG-i + OpenMVS, (7) Metashape, (8) Pix4D, (9) RealityCapture.

Area 1		
oblique	nadir	oblique and nadir
(1) **79.18** / 60.5 / **68.59**	**73.08** / 68.98 / **70.97**	74.89 / 74.15 / 74.52
(2) 22.74 / 28.28 / 25.21	23.96 / 46.23 / 31.57	27.93 / 60.84 / 38.29
(3) 49.42 / 13.09 / 20.69	44.02 / 47.95 / 45.9	48.74 / 58.24 / 53.07
(4) 61.07 / 57.1 / 59.02	56.61 / **73.46** / 63.94	**78.27** / **80.49** / **79.36**
(5) 37.13 / 16.59 / 22.94	36.59 / 43.62 / 39.8	39.48 / 51.36 / 44.64
(6) 55.12 / **64.37** / 59.39	49.14 / 70.75 / 58.0	74.19 / 79.5 / 76.76
(7) 81.6 / **72.5** / **76.78**	84.26 / **76.61** / 80.25	82.91 / **78.56** / 80.68
(8) 77.41 / 49.64 / 60.49	87.23 / 71.41 / 78.53	86.79 / 73.34 / 79.5
(9) **82.54** / 66.95 / 73.93	**87.67** / 75.82 / **81.32**	**86.87** / 75.86 / **80.99**

Area 2		
oblique	nadir	oblique and nadir
(1) **80.48** / 65.51 / **72.23**	74.97 / 72.34 / 73.63	76.54 / 77.98 / 77.25
(2) 26.85 / 41.81 / 32.7	24.45 / 49.96 / 32.83	24.7 / 63.53 / 35.57
(3) 36.92 / 15.7 / 22.03	33.26 / 36.4 / 34.76	41.94 / 50.3 / 45.74
(4) 40.23 / 54.27 / 46.21	**75.2** / 75.92 / **75.56**	79.3 / 82.03 / 80.64
(5) 38.11 / 15.11 / 21.64	43.76 / 52.0 / 47.52	36.62 / 48.53 / 41.74
(6) 58.52 / **70.43** / 63.92	71.44 / **79.0** / 75.03	**79.77** / **82.54** / 81.13
(7) 80.96 / **75.24** / 78.0	87.63 / **78.49** / 82.81	83.36 / **79.79** / 81.53
(8) **94.35** / 67.53 / **78.72**	**94.39** / 76.21 / **84.33**	**93.68** / 77.9 / **85.06**
(9) 83.77 / 73.06 / 78.05	90.37 / 78.32 / 83.92	87.49 / 78.46 / 82.73

hidden Area 1		
oblique	nadir	oblique and nadir
(1) **78.68** / 49.89 / **61.06**	**72.69** / 62.77 / **67.37**	74.54 / 68.34 / 71.3
(2) 23.55 / 18.97 / 21.01	24.42 / 36.88 / 29.39	28.38 / 50.45 / 36.32
(3) 43.12 / 6.61 / 11.46	42.52 / 38.01 / 40.14	48.48 / 48.74 / 48.61
(4) 56.57 / 48.7 / 52.34	56.03 / **69.48** / 62.03	**75.36** / **75.76** / **75.56**
(5) 30.83 / 8.88 / 13.79	36.51 / 35.47 / 35.98	38.79 / 42.08 / 40.37
(6) 52.93 / **59.33** / 55.95	48.47 / 67.81 / 56.53	70.56 / 75.02 / 72.72
(7) 79.11 / 65.14 / **71.45**	82.46 / **70.3** / 75.9	80.76 / **73.08** / **76.73**
(8) 78.87 / 36.21 / 49.64	86.19 / 63.61 / 73.2	84.63 / 65.27 / 73.7
(9) **80.55** / 58.45 / 67.74	**86.25** / 69.37 / **76.89**	**85.39** / 69.53 / 76.65

hidden Area 2		
oblique	nadir	oblique and nadir
(1) **80.06** / 61.48 / **69.55**	73.63 / 68.9 / 71.18	75.5 / 75.27 / 75.39
(2) 27.05 / 37.02 / 31.26	24.24 / 43.98 / 31.25	24.4 / 56.88 / 34.15
(3) 36.47 / 13.19 / 19.37	33.08 / 31.82 / 32.43	40.97 / 43.7 / 42.29
(4) 40.31 / 54.08 / 46.19	**74.93** / 74.31 / **74.62**	77.19 / 79.52 / 78.34
(5) 35.24 / 12.3 / 18.24	43.7 / 47.28 / 45.42	35.35 / 42.39 / 38.55
(6) 56.16 / **67.58** / 61.34	67.99 / **77.08** / 72.25	**78.38** / **80.49** / **79.42**
(7) 78.79 / **71.82** / **75.14**	86.26 / **75.34** / 80.43	81.59 / **77.3** / 79.39
(8) **92.9** / 61.53 / 74.03	**93.55** / 72.04 / 81.4	**92.58** / 73.93 / **82.21**
(9) 81.7 / 69.44 / 75.07	89.22 / 75.25 / **81.64**	85.76 / 75.27 / 80.17

Table 3. Study of F score per urban element. Column P indicates the pipeline that generated the best F score. If the pipeline or F score calculated with the hidden ground-truth differs from those ones calculated with the complete one, they are shown in square brackets. Pipelines are numbered as: (1) COLMAP + COLMAP, (2) COLMAP + OpenMVS, (3) OpenMVG-g + COLMAP, (4) OpenMVG-g + Open-MVS, (5) OpenMVG-i + COLMAP, (6) OpenMVG-i + OpenMVS, (7) Metashape, (8) Pix4D, (9) RealityCapture.

	AREA 1					
	oblique		nadir		combined	
	P	F score	P	F score	P	F score
facade	(7)	73.69 [72.25]	(7)	78.35 [76.69]	(7)	79.34 [77.82]
window	(7)	73.49 [71.72]	(7)	74.71 [73.67]	(7)	75.95 [74.46]
door	(7)	62.81 [62.46]	(7)	65.37 [64.32]	(7)	66.11 [64.42]
roof	(7)	88.66 [85.28]	(9)	91.04 [89.18]	(9) [(7)]	91.32 [89.53]
r. window	(7)	80.4 [79.9]	(9)	85.3 [85.77]	(8)	88.29 [86.8]
r. door	(8) [(4)]	60.84 [65.94]	(8)	72.46 [82.12]	(8)	82.44 [89.4]
sidewalk	(7)	83.55 [83.17]	(8)	90.64 [90.45]	(9)	90.15 [90.12]
street	(7)	85.76 [84.76]	(9)	92.73 [92.58]	(9)	92.46 [92.34]
grass	(9)	88.97 [87.96]	(9)	89.16 [87.92]	(9)	90.84 [89.98]
tree	(6)	31.74 [32.55]	(4)	38.47 [38.37]	(1) [(6)]	40.92 [40.21]
	AREA 2					
	oblique		nadir		combined	
	P	F score	P	F score	P	F score
facade	(7)	73.87 [71.99]	(7)	82.4 [81.67]	(7)	80.54 [79.71]
window	(8)	68.84 [69.89]	(7)	73.98 [74.1]	(7)	73.33 [73.1]
door	(7)	55.52 [57.13]	(7)	64.7 [64.87]	(7)	62.28 [63.26]
roof	(8)	90.08 [87.61]	(8)	93.34 [92.49]	(8)	94.26 [93.84]
r. window	(8)	88.35 [87.65]	(8)	88.55 [88.63]	(8)	89.25 [90.08]
r. door	(8)	72.64 [68.00]	(9) [(7)]	75.11 [67.43]	(9) [(8)]	74.04 [65.84]
sidewalk	(9)	87.59 [88.14]	(9)	91.92 [91.39]	(9)	91.99 [91.77]
street	(7)	86.04 [85.04]	(9)	92.55 [92.15]	(9)	92.83 [92.38]
grass	(9)	95.31 [93.43]	(8)	95.9 [93.79]	(6)	96.36 [94.91]
tree	(1)	25.34 [28.09]	(1)	33.7 [35.08]	(1)	39.45 [41.34]

per measurement. F score in Table 3, Precision in Table 4 and Recall in Table 5. Each row has the results of a specific class (i.e., urban category) and each column corresponds to a unique set of images. The result presented is the maximum score obtained among the nine pipelines tested (see Sect. 4.2) and the pipeline that generated the score is shown in column P. The results for the hidden area are presented in squared brackets if they differ from the ones calculated with the complete area.

Table 4. Study of precision per urban element. Column P indicates the pipeline that generated the best precision. If the pipeline or precision calculated with the hidden ground-truth differs from those ones calculated with the complete one, they are shown in square brackets. Pipelines are numbered as: (1) COLMAP + COLMAP, (2) COLMAP + OpenMVS, (3) OpenMVG-g + COLMAP, (4) OpenMVG-g + OpenMVS, (5) OpenMVG-i + COLMAP, (6) OpenMVG-i + OpenMVS, (7) Metashape, (8) Pix4D, (9) RealityCapture.

	AREA 1					
	oblique		nadir		combined	
	P	precision	P	precision	P	precision
facade	(7)	82.25 [81.35]	(7)	86.7 [85.94]	(7)	84.82 [83.82]
window	(7)	67.51 [67.01]	(9)	70.91 [70.56]	(7)	68.81 [68.24]
door	(8)	73.71 [74.08]	(9) [(8)]	67.02 [65.42]	(9)	66.31 [64.65]
roof	(9)	91.38 [90.61]	(9)	92.85 [92.21]	(9)	93.27 [92.61]
r. window	(8)	83.22 [89.29]	(8)	86.72 [87.92]	(8)	89.93 [89.62]
r. door	(8)	84.91 [85.2]	(9) [(8)]	77.16 [86.11]	(8)	78.24 [85.37]
sidewalk	(8)	97.63 [97.5]	(8)	97.12 [97.45]	(8)	96.13 [95.94]
street	(8)	97.31 [97.11]	(8)	97.37 [97.27]	(8) [(9)]	95.76 [95.62]
grass	(9)	95.21 [94.66]	(8)	98.03 [97.77]	(8)	96.95 [96.64]
tree	(9)	80.27 [79.5]	(8)	87.34 [86.8]	(8)	86.11 [85.44]
	AREA 2					
	oblique		nadir		combined	
	P	precision	P	precision	P	precision
facade	(8)	90.4 [89.8]	(7)	88.98 [88.93]	(8)	86.67 [85.76]
window	(8)	76.11 [74.17]	(9)	74.22 [73.14]	(8)	71.73 [69.62]
door	(8)	78.59 [76.08]	(8)	78.18 [77.27]	(8)	76.79 [75.53]
roof	(8)	97.18 [96.82]	(8)	96.34 [96.31]	(8)	96.38 [96.08]
r. window	(8)	95.51 [95.8]	(8)	93.45 [93.46]	(8)	93.83 [93.63]
r. door	(8)	79.94 [70.23]	(9) [(7)]	82.08 [78.08]	(8)	78.19 [69.25]
sidewalk	(8)	96.34 [96.11]	(8)	96.72 [96.31]	(8)	97.03 [96.74]
street	(8)	97.09 [97.02]	(8)	97.26 [96.98]	(8)	97.72 [97.52]
grass	(8)	99.48 [99.14]	(8)	99.5 [99.25]	(8)	99.43 [99.15]
tree	(8)	94.05 [93.58]	(8)	93.4 [92.97]	(8)	92.63 [92.05]

Analyzing the results that were obtained per class across all the image sets available, we can observe that although in [15] the method that most frequently got the maximum precision was COLMAP + COLMAP, the commercial applications are better in all the categories, and Pix4D is the one that most frequently gets the maximum precision. Roof, sidewalk, street and grass are the categories which obtained the best results. When looking at the recall, the pipeline OpenMVG-i + OpenMVS was the one that more frequently achieved the highest

Table 5. Study of recall per urban element. Column P indicates the pipeline that generated the best recall. If the pipeline or recall calculated with the hidden ground-truth differs from those ones calculated with the complete one, they are shown in square brackets. Pipelines are numbered as: (1) COLMAP + COLMAP, (2) COLMAP + OpenMVS, (3) OpenMVG-g + COLMAP, (4) OpenMVG-g + Open-MVS, (5) OpenMVG-i + COLMAP, (6) OpenMVG-i + OpenMVS, (7) Metashape, (8) Pix4D, (9) RealityCapture.

AREA 1						
	oblique		nadir		combined	
	P	recall	P	recall	P	recall
facade	(7)	66.73 [64.98]	(7)	71.46 [69.23]	(7)	74.52 [72.62]
window	(7)	80.63 [77.14]	(7)	81.98 [78.85]	(7)	84.73 [81.93]
door	(7)	62.75 [63.33]	(4)	65.95 [66.12]	(4)	68.76 [67.99]
roof	(7)	87.53 [83.27]	(7)	90.34 [88.33]	(4)	92.25 [91.65]
r. window	(7) [(6)]	83.34 [84.01]	(7)	86.05 [86.28]	(4)	91.54 [93.07]
r. door	(4)	56.41 [71.34]	(8)	71.6 [78.49]	(8)	87.13 [93.84]
sidewalk	(7)	81.44 [80.82]	(4)	90.37 [91.4]	(4)	92.88 [92.56]
street	(7)	82.34 [81.48]	(4)	92.97 [92.75]	(4)	95.45 [95.68]
grass	(9)	83.49 [82.15]	(9)	83.95 [82.22]	(6)	88.45 [87.43]
tree	(6)	20.94 [21.65]	(4) [(6)]	25.82 [25.8]	(2)	29.44 [28.76]
AREA 2						
	oblique		nadir		combined	
	P	recall	P	recall	P	recall
facade	(7)	70.17 [67.85]	(7)	76.73 [75.5]	(7)	78.1 [77.00]
window	(7)	70.24 [71.28]	(7)	74.93 [75.22]	(6)	77.05 [77.71]
door	(7)	52.32 [55.95]	(7)	62.84 [64.51]	(6)	68.94 [68.34]
roof	(7)	86.48 [84.19]	(8)	90.52 [88.96]	(8)	92.24 [91.71]
r. window	(8)	82.19 [80.78]	(8) [(6)]	84.14 [84.97]	(4) [(6)]	85.78 [87.82]
r. door	(8)	66.56 [65.91]	(9)	69.23 [60.44]	(9) [(8)]	71.81 [62.76]
sidewalk	(6)	84.66 [84.74]	(6)	93.77 [93.31]	(6)	94.71 [94.59]
street	(7)	83.1 [81.74]	(4)	95.47 [95.05]	(6)	96.31 [95.66]
grass	(7)	93.93 [91.61]	(4)	95.08 [92.82]	(6)	96.88 [95.67]
tree	(1)	15.03 [17.01]	(1)	21.62 [22.82]	(2)	26.58 [30.28]

scores among the open-source methods [15]. When we include the commercial software in the analysis, we see that they are not the best in all the image categories and sets of images, as it was the case with the precision. Now, on the results with the reconstruction from the combined set, we can see how the OpenMVG-g + OpenMVS and OpenMVG-i + OpenMVS are still the best in the majority of classes (in *Area 1* and n *Area 2*, respectively), in accordance with the results obtained in the scene level evaluation.

When looking at the F score, the class with lowest F score values is tree and the results are really influenced by the low values of the recall. We can see that for this class the winning methods are the open-source solutions whereas for the rest of the categories the commercial solutions are the best. These results confirm the hypothesis in [30]: trees in the parks of the city can degrade the scores of the reconstructions. We can also analyze the results depending on the image set under study. For example, with the combined set, according to [15] the pipelines with best performance in the majority of classes among the open-source techniques were OpenMVG-g + OpenMVS in *Area 1* and OpenMVG-i + OpenMVS in *Area 2*. These results are in accordance with the ones commented before, which does not consider the class information (Table 2). However, when looking at the nine pipelines, the methods RealityCapture and Pix4D (which were the best in Area 1 and Area 2, respectively, in the scene evaluation) have a different behaviour when looking at the specific urban elements. RealityCapture is the most frequent winner among all the urban categories, whereas Pix4D is only the winner in the roof and r. window (with around 31% of occupancy), suggesting that the main reason why this was the winner method is because it is the best in this specific category.

5.3   General Pipeline Evaluation

We can also observe that, in general, the open-source pipelines that obtained the best results are COLMAP + COLMAP, OpenMVG-g + OpenMVS and OpenMVG-i + OpenMVS. These results are in accordance with previous studies that used the same kind of metric, where COLMAP + COLMAP and OpenMVG-i + OpenMVS obtained the best results [7]. In particular, in that study OpenMVG-g + OpenMVS never has better results than COLMAP + COLMAP, but this situation is plausible in our study given the different camera trajectories (aerial grid configuration vs circle around an object), software versions and parameters used. Pix4D was also compared in that study, obtaining the best results for some categories, in accordance to what we observe in this study.

COLMAP used as MVS is better than OpenMVS only if it is applied after COLMAP SfM, whereas OpenMVS is better using the other SfM methods tested. This leads to the necessity to test not only a particular MVS method but a complete pipeline since it is going to be influenced by: the results obtained in the SfM step, the data conversion and preparation for the MVS step, as well as memory and computing limitations. The commercial applications used in the evaluation give better results than the open-source pipelines in general, and are prepared to handle large amounts of data, as part of their photogrammetry pipelines. Also, some of them provide by default a 3D mesh along with the point cloud. However, some have other disadvantages such as the limitation of supporting only certain operating systems, and all of them are not freely available.

6 Conclusion

We have presented in this paper a study of image-based 3D reconstruction pipelines in a metropolitan area, using exclusively aerial images. This study not only takes under consideration open-source 3D reconstruction techniques but also commercial photogrammetry solutions which are widely used in the industry. The final dense point cloud is evaluated at scene level and per urban category, thus allowing for a finer examination. Thanks to that, we see the influence of urban categories (e.g., roof) in the F scores. We also support the hypothesis done about how parks can degrade the F score values in a scene level evaluation (mainly because of the presence of trees) with facts. We have concluded that the commercial applications have better scores in the majority of the scenarios but the best solution of the open-source techniques is not far from them. When choosing the best 3D reconstruction pipeline other aspects apart from the F score might be important: the budget, the equipment, the possibility of adapting the algorithms for some specific needs, etc. In this study we have created an exhaustive and comprehensive review and we believe that it can be useful for those who want to see how 3D reconstruction methods perform using aerial images from a city.

Acknowledgements. This publication has emanated from research conducted with the financial support of Science Foundation Ireland (SFI) under the Grant Number 15/RP/2776.

References

1. Aanæs, H., Jensen, R.R., Vogiatzis, G., Tola, E., Dahl, A.B.: Large-scale data for multiple-view stereopsis. Int. J. Comput. Vis. **120**(2), 153–168 (2016). https://doi.org/10.1007/s11263-016-0902-9
2. Barnes, C., Shechtman, E., Finkelstein, A., Goldman, D.B.: Patchmatch: a randomized correspondence algorithm for structural image editing. ACM Trans. Graph. (ToG) **28**(3), 24 (2009)
3. Can, G., Mantegazza, D., Abbate, G., Chappuis, S., Giusti, A.: Semantic segmentation on swiss3dcities: a benchmark study on aerial photogrammetric 3d pointcloud dataset. Pattern Recogn. Lett. **150**, 108–114 (2021)
4. Furukawa, Y., Ponce, J.: Accurate, dense, and robust multiview stereopsis. IEEE Trans. Pattern Anal. Mach. Intell. **32**(8), 1362–1376 (2010)
5. Hartley, R., Zisserman, A.: Multiple view Geometry in Computer Vision. Cambridge University Press, Cambridge (2003)
6. Jancosek, M., Pajdla, T.: Multi-view reconstruction preserving weakly-supported surfaces. In: CVPR 2011, IEEE (2011)
7. Knapitsch, A., Park, J., Zhou, Q.Y., Koltun, V.: Tanks and temples: benchmarking large-scale scene reconstruction. ACM Trans. Graph. **36**(4), 1–13 (2017)
8. Menze, M., Geiger, A.: Object scene flow for autonomous vehicles. In: CVPR 2015 (2015)
9. Moulon, P., Monasse, P., Marlet, R.: Adaptive structure from motion with *a contrario* model estimation. In: Lee, K.M., Matsushita, Y., Rehg, J.M., Hu, Z. (eds.) ACCV 2012. LNCS, vol. 7727, pp. 257–270. Springer, Heidelberg (2013). https://doi.org/10.1007/978-3-642-37447-0_20

10. Moulon, P., Monasse, P., Marlet, R.: Global fusion of relative motions for robust, accurate and scalable structure from motion. In: ICCV 2013 (2013)
11. Munoz, D., Bagnell, J.A., Vandapel, N., Hebert, M.: Contextual classification with functional max-margin markov networks. In: CVPR 2009 (2009)
12. Rottensteiner, F., Sohn, G., Gerke, M., Wegner, J.D., Breitkopf, U., Jung, J.: Results of the ISPRS benchmark on urban object detection and 3d building reconstruction. ISPRS J. Photogrammetry Remote Sens. **93**, 256–271 (2014)
13. Ruano, S., Cuevas, C., Gallego, G., García, N.: Augmented reality tool for the situational awareness improvement of UAV operators. Sensors **17**(2), 297 (2017)
14. Ruano, S., Gallego, G., Cuevas, C., García, N.: Aerial video georegistration using terrain models from dense and coherent stereo matching. In: Geospatial InfoFusion and Video Analytics IV; and Motion Imagery for ISR and Situational Awareness II. International Society for Optics and Photonics (2014)
15. Ruano, S., Smolic, A.: A benchmark for 3d reconstruction from aerial imagery in an urban environment. In: VISIGRAPP (5: VISAPP), pp. 732–741 (2021)
16. Schönberger, J.L., Frahm, J.M.: Structure-from-motion revisited. In: CVPR 2016 (2016)
17. Schönberger, J.L., Zheng, E., Frahm, J.-M., Pollefeys, M.: Pixelwise view selection for unstructured multi-view stereo. In: Leibe, B., Matas, J., Sebe, N., Welling, M. (eds.) ECCV 2016. LNCS, vol. 9907, pp. 501–518. Springer, Cham (2016). https://doi.org/10.1007/978-3-319-46487-9_31
18. Schops, T., et al.: A multi-view stereo benchmark with high-resolution images and multi-camera videos. In: CVPR 2017 (2017)
19. Seitz, S.M., Curless, B., Diebel, J., Scharstein, D., Szeliski, R.: A comparison and evaluation of multi-view stereo reconstruction algorithms. In: CVPR 2006 (2006)
20. Serna, A., Marcotegui, B., Goulette, F., Deschaud, J.E.: Paris-rue-madame database: a 3d mobile laser scanner dataset for benchmarking urban detection, segmentation and classification methods (2014)
21. Shahid, M., et al.: Aerial cross-platform path planning dataset. In: Proceedings of the IEEE/CVF International Conference on Computer Vision, pp. 3936–3945 (2021)
22. Snavely, N., Seitz, S.M., Szeliski, R.: Modeling the world from internet photo collections. Int. J. Comput. Vis. **80**, 189–210 (2008)
23. Stathopoulou, E.K., Welponer, M., Remondino, F.: Open-source image-based 3d reconstruction pipelines: review, comparison and evaluation. The International Archives of Photogrammetry, Remote Sensing and Spatial Information Sciences (2019)
24. Strecha, C., Von Hansen, W., Van Gool, L., Fua, P., Thoennessen, U.: On benchmarking camera calibration and multi-view stereo for high resolution imagery. In: CVPR 2008 (2008)
25. Sweeney, C., Hollerer, T., Turk, M.: Theia: A fast and scalable structure-from-motion library. In: Proceedings of the ACM International Conference on Multimedia, pp. 693–696. ACM (2015)
26. Vallet, B., Brédif, M., Serna, A., Marcotegui, B., Paparoditis, N.: Terramobilita/iqmulus urban point cloud analysis benchmark. Comput. Graph. **49**, 126–133 (2015)
27. Yan, F., Xia, E., Li, Z., Zhou, Z.: Sampling-based path planning for high-quality aerial 3d reconstruction of urban scenes. Remote Sens. **13**(5), 989 (2021)
28. Zhang, L., Li, Z., Li, A., Liu, F.: Large-scale urban point cloud labeling and reconstruction. ISPRS J. Photogrammetry Remote Sens. **138**, 86–100 (2018)

29. Zhou, W., Liu, J., Lei, J., Yu, L., Hwang, J.N.: Gmnet: graded-feature multilabel-learning network for RGB-thermal urban scene semantic segmentation. IEEE Trans. Image Process. **30**, 7790–7802 (2021)
30. Zolanvari, S., et al.: DublinCity: annotated lidar point cloud and its applications. In: 30th BMVC (2019)

Author Index

Printed in the United States
by Baker & Taylor Publisher Services